Mindshaping

Mindshaping

A New Framework for Understanding Human Social Cognition

Tadeusz Wiesław Zawidzki

A Bradford Book
The MIT Press
Cambridge, Massachusetts
London, England

MIT Press books may be purchased at special quantity discounts for business or sales promotional use. For information, please email special_sales@mitpress.mit.edu or write to Special Sales Department, The MIT Press, 55 Hayward Street, Cambridge, MA 02142.

This book was set in Stone Sans and Stone Serif by the MIT Press. Printed and bound in the United States of America.

Library of Congress Cataloging-in-Publication Data

Zawidzki, Tadeusz.
Mindshaping : a new framework for understanding human social cognition / Tadeusz Wiesław Zawidzki.
    p.   cm.
Includes bibliographical references and index.
ISBN 978-0-262-01901-9 (hbk. : alk. paper)
1. Social perception. 2. Social psychology. 3. Social cognitive theory. I. Title.
HM1041.Z33   2013
302'.12—dc23
2012038062

10 9 8 7 6 5 4 3 2 1

For Zofia Zyta Zawidzka, Tadeusz Witold Zawidzki, and Elżbieta Aniela Zawidzki: first-rate mindshapers all.

Who can guess what convoluted nonsense may be brewing in the minds of our fellow men, sometimes along with deep intuitions.

—Czesław Miłosz, *A Year of the Hunter* (1994)

The uniformity that unites us in communication and belief is a uniformity of resultant patterns overlying a chaotic subjective diversity of connections between words and experience. Uniformity comes where it matters socially. ... Different persons growing up in the same language are like different bushes trimmed and trained to take the shape of identical elephants. The anatomical details of twigs and branches will fill the elephantine form differently from bush to bush, but the overall outward results are alike.

—Willard Van Orman Quine, *Word and Object* (1960)

The reality of a man's life isn't found only where he is. It's also found in the other lives that shape his—first of all, the lives of those he loves ... but also the lives of unknown others—powerful or downtrodden—fellow citizens, policemen, professors, invisible companions in mines and factories, diplomats and dictators, religious reformers, artists who create myths that govern our behavior—all told, humble representatives of the sovereign accidents that reign over even the most orderly existence.

—Albert Camus, *Discours de Suède* (1958)

Contents

Preface

The central thesis of this book is that mindshaping (Mameli, 2001) is the linchpin of the human sociocognitive syndrome. Much of what follows is devoted to elucidating the notion of mindshaping and discussing its many instantiations in human social experience. The basic idea is that we are distinguished in our social behavior from other species primarily by our sophisticated, complex, diverse, and flexible capacities to shape each other's minds. Examples include sophisticated imitation, pedagogy, irresistible conformism, norm institution, cognition and enforcement, and narrative self- and group constitution. The claim that mindshaping constitutes the linchpin of the human sociocognitive syndrome amounts to the following: without mindshaping, none of the other components of distinctively human social cognition—sophisticated language, sophisticated and pervasive cooperation, and even sophisticated mindreading—would be possible. This distinctively human sociocognitive syndrome would not have evolved without mindshaping, and were mindshaping somehow removed from it now, the other components would disappear as well.

This thesis seeks to displace the reigning metaphor in the sciences of human social cognition: mindreading. According to this metaphor, our distinctive sociocognitive profile can be traced entirely to our mindreading virtuosity: what sets us apart is that we are natural psychologists of unparalleled skill, capable of representing each other's mental states with a reliability, accuracy, and sophistication unmatched by any other species. Mindreading means different things to different people, and a major burden of what follows, especially chapter 1 and chapter 3, is making clear distinctions among the varieties of mindreading and identifying those that are distinctive of human beings. We share many mindreading capacities with nonhuman animals. For this reason, these mindreading capacities cannot be what, in the received view, sets us apart. But we have good evidence that one variety of mindreading—which has been the focus of most philosophical and psychological research into human social cognition—is distinctive of human beings: the accurate attribution of propositional attitudes like belief and desire. Many researchers simply assume that the distinctively human sociocognitive syndrome depends most fundamentally on this capacity. This claim is the specific target of my critical agenda: I argue that the attribution of full-blown propositional attitudes cannot have evolved before sophisticated practices of mindshaping aimed at making us easily interpretable to each other. It is likely that sophisticated mindshaping coevolved in the human lineage with improved versions of sociocognitive capacities that we *share* with nonhuman primates, such as tracking the goals of conspecifics and anticipating the rationally and informationally constrained behavioral means they select to achieve them. However, as I argue, even highly sophisticated versions of such behavior tracking do not amount to the attribution of full-blown propositional attitudes. The capacity to attribute such mental states depends on, and had to await, the evolution of sophisticated mindshaping practices, especially linguistic practices like norm institution and narrative self- and group constitution.

The distinction between the mindreading- and mindshaping-focused understandings of human social cognition cannot be captured in terms of simple empirical tests. No crucial experiment can vindicate one understanding at the expense of the other. In fact, the mindshaping-focused understanding embraces many of the same empirical results as the mindreading-focused understanding, although it interprets them differently and attaches greater importance to some and lesser importance to others. If scientific frameworks were judged only by their ability to explain or predict specific empirical results, then this would jeopardize the interest of the project I pursue in this book. However, as philosophers of science have long appreciated (Kuhn, 1977), there is more to scientific virtue than just empirical adequacy. Theories and paradigms are also evaluated on the basis of nonempirical virtues like simplicity, coherence with the rest of what science tells us about the world, and suggestiveness of new directions for research. Different metaphors afford different interpretations of the same data, and some interpretations are simpler, more consistent with other disciplines, and more suggestive than others. In what follows, I make the case that mindshaping affords interpretations of empirical data that are superior to those afforded by mindreading along these nonempirical dimensions.

Mindreading evokes the following picture of human social cognition. Our epistemic relations to each other are no different from our epistemic relations to the nonhuman world. Other people are mysterious phenomena animated by unobservable causes that are completely independent of our attempts to understand them. Individual human beings must learn to infer these causes to better predict and control other human beings, just as is the case with nonhuman phenomena. They do so by attempting to represent these unobservable causes, and they succeed to the extent that they represent them accurately. Our social accomplishments—pervasive, institutionalized cooperation and coordination, language, and so on—can all be explained in terms of such individualized sociocognitive accomplishments. In short, according to the mindreading metaphor, distinctively human social cognition is conceptualized as an individual accomplishment, involving the accurate representation of independently constituted, unobservable mental causes of behavior.

In contrast, mindshaping, as I formulate it here, treats our epistemic relations to each other as very different from those we hold to the nonhuman world. Our frameworks for interpreting human behavior succeed so well because they are simultaneously frameworks for *regulating* human behavior (McGeer, 2007). The states we attribute to each other in interpretation are not independent of our interpretive frameworks because those frameworks shape the states our minds are likely to enter. We do not first discover independent facts about what causes behavior, and then inform our attempts to control each other with such discoveries. Our social accomplishments are not by-products of individualized cognitive feats, like the discovery of some unobservable causal factor. Rather, through a form of "group selection,"[1] simultaneously interpretive and regulative frameworks that support our social accomplishments, including pervasive, institutionalized cooperation and coordination, language, and so on, have evolved. In the mindshaping metaphor, distinctively human social cognition is conceptualized as a group accomplishment, involving simultaneously interpretive and regulative frameworks that function to shape minds, which these frameworks can then be used to easily and usefully interpret. In what follows, I hope to illustrate, through a detailed reading of a variety of empirical work, that this conceptualization brings greater simplicity and unity to a greater variety of empirical results from the sciences of social cognition than does the mindreading conceptualization. I also hope to give the reader a taste of how suggestive of new research the mindshaping metaphor can be.

Mindshaping inevitably evokes a discredited image of the human mind: that it is entirely the product of shaping by environmental factors—regimes of punishment and reward instituted by society. This behaviorist understanding of the human mind has rightfully been discredited since the cognitivist revolution of the 1960s. The evidence that human minds bring to their learning environments highly complex cognitive mechanisms is overwhelming. However, this in no way contradicts the thesis that mindshaping constitutes the linchpin of the human sociocognitive syndrome. The various kinds of mindshaping all require sophisticated cognitive mechanisms in both "shapees" and shapers. This does not, however, imply that these cognitive mechanisms involve sophisticated mindreading, especially the attribution of full-blown propositional attitudes. What follows departs from common contemporary presuppositions not in the assumption that human social learning presupposes complex cognitive equipment but in the assumption that this cognitive equipment must include a capacity to attribute full-blown propositional attitudes. On the contrary, I argue that the capacity to accurately attribute full-blown propositional attitudes is parasitic, in phylogeny and today, on prior capacities to shape minds.

A related worry: some might balk at the term "mindshaping." To many, "mind" connotes the enduring, underlying mechanisms that implement all intelligent human behavior, including social learning and other forms of mindshaping. Such "core cognition" (Carey, 2009) is not subject to shaping or learning; rather, it makes them possible. Relative to core cognition, the kinds of dispositions that *are* subject to modification—for example, public language lexicons and accents, musical and other aesthetic preferences, skills like tool use or game play, and so on—seem too ephemeral to count as significant parts of the mind. Perhaps "behavior shaping" is a better term.[2] However, our commonsense notion of "mind" surely connotes more than enduring core cognition. For example, no one thinks that quotidian mind*reading* succeeds in discovering and tracking the activity of core cognition; it took decades of careful scientific research to identify such fundamental components of the mind. Similarly, it is no part of my claim, nor need it be, that quotidian mind*shaping* aims to alter core cognition. The varieties of mindshaping that I explore here all aim to alter behavioral dispositions. It is hard to see how altering behavioral dispositions is possible without altering minds in some sense. Hence "mindshaping" is an appropriate term.

A final caveat: the view I defend is entirely neutral on questions of mechanism. I have no strong views on whether or not the competencies I describe are implemented by innate, special-purpose symbolic modules, or by general-purpose, experience-driven neural networks, or by some hybrid of the two, or by some other alternative. Compelling evidence supports all these approaches to understanding the "how?" of human cognition, and it is likely that the brain employs a diversity of mechanisms with varied architectures. I focus here on the "why?" of human social cognition: the functions that sustain our sociocognitive capacities.

My strategy is largely empirical. I think a close reading of contemporary research into human social cognition across a variety of disciplines makes a strong case for the thesis that mindshaping is the key innovation behind the human sociocognitive syndrome. However, this is more than just a survey. I deploy philosophical analysis to make clear the distinctions between varieties of both mindreading and mindshaping and to make explicit precisely what sorts of cognitive capacities each different variety presupposes. For example, many theorists slide easily from the claim that distinctively human social phenomena, like culture, language, and pervasive cooperation, require a form of social cognition more sophisticated than mere behavioral generalization to the claim that they require the capacity to attribute full-blown propositional attitudes like beliefs and desires. But this claim ignores a variety of alternatives that are more sophisticated than mere behavioral generalization yet do not qualify as propositional attitude attribution. Many theorists also make facile assumptions about what beliefs and desires are, and consequently underestimate the cognitive sophistication presupposed by their accurate attribution. This has important consequences for assumptions about the viability of propositional attitude attribution as our primary means of navigating the social world. The definition of mindshaping also calls for some philosophical sophistication, as it is not apparent how one can intelligently shape a mind without first representing it accurately, which would make sophisticated mindshaping parasitic on sophisticated mindreading. So the reader should expect a philosophically responsible close reading of a variety of empirical literature pertaining to human social cognition, marshaled in support of the mindshaping-as-linchpin hypothesis. I turn now to a brief overview of what I intend to accomplish in each of the seven chapters.

Chapter 1 provides an overview of the entire project and, in particular, a detailed unpacking of what I call "the human sociocognitive syndrome."[3] I argue that human social cognition is distinguished from other varieties by four broadly related capacities: sophisticated mindreading, sophisticated mindshaping, extremely diverse and pervasive cooperation, and structurally complex and semantically flexible language. In the received view, sophisticated mindreading forms the linchpin of this sociocognitive syndrome: without our capacity to accurately attribute propositional attitudes, none of the other components are possible. Chapter 1 sets the agenda for the rest of the book, arguing that contrary to the received view, the human sociocognitive syndrome relies on sophisticated mindshaping rather than on sophisticated mindreading.

The goal of chapter 2 is to clarify what mindshaping is. To this end, I defend a philosophical analysis of the notion, grounded in Ruth Millikan's (1984) notion of biological proper function. Basically, any mechanism the proper function of which is getting a target mind to match a model in certain respects counts as a mindshaping mechanism. I then deploy this understanding to taxonomize the varieties of mindshaping observed in both human and nonhuman populations. It turns out that human mindshaping is distinguished from nonhuman varieties in four ways: (1) the sheer variety of the respects in which it can make targets match models; (2) the fact that only humans find matching models intrinsically motivating, rather than merely a means to further ends; (3) the socially distributed nature of much human mindshaping, for example, the involvement of teachers; and (4) the ontological status of models used in some human mindshaping, for example, fictional characters or idealized agents. The main burdens of chapter 2 are to (1) provide a clear definition of mindshaping, (2) survey the empirical literature to illustrate its varieties, and (3) show how human mindshaping can be distinguished from nonhuman varieties without assuming that it presupposes sophisticated mindreading, like propositional attitude attribution.

Chapter 3 motivates the project of the book by means of a critical discussion of the received view of human social cognition, that is, the view that sophisticated mindreading, and especially propositional attitude attribution, forms the basis of most distinctively human sociocognitive accomplishments. I raise a variety of objections to this assumption, all based on the observation that, due to the *holism* of the propositional attitudes, the relations between observable behavior and propositional attitudes are too complex for propositional attitude attribution to help with the accurate and timely prediction of behavior. This explains why propositional attitude attribution does not occur among nonhuman species, even highly social and intelligent ones like contemporary great apes. However, it raises a deep puzzle about the evolution of human mindreading: how and why did our ancestors develop this capacity, given its relative intractability as a tool for behavioral prediction? I end chapter 3 by suggesting that only with prior, sophisticated mindshaping, ensuring cognitive homogeneity in populations of likely interactants, can distinctively human mindreading be reliable and timely enough to evolve.

Chapter 4 defends a detailed phylogenetic account tracing the evolution of distinctively human mindshaping in human prehistory. I begin with Sterelny's (2003, 2007, 2012) proposal that cooperation explains our distinctive evolutionary trajectory. I then argue that, for various reasons, sophisticated mindreading and, in particular, propositional attitude attribution cannot help explain the evolution of cooperation. On the contrary, drawing on a variety of empirical evidence, as well as models proposed by philosophers and evolutionary game theorists, I argue that various mechanisms of mindshaping aimed at homogenizing human populations best explain the roots of human cooperation. In particular, mindshaping dispositions and practices, like irresistible conformism, pedagogy, and norm institution and enforcement, make possible a form of group selection without which distinctively human cooperation would not be possible. Furthermore, such mindshaping dispositions and practices can also explain human virtuosity at forming plural subjects, which is crucial to explaining how we succeed in coordinating on cooperative projects in which we are already motivated to engage.

Chapter 5 addresses one of the central objections to the mindshaping-as-linchpin hypothesis. Many of the distinctively human mindshaping mechanisms and practices taxonomized in chapter 2, and employed to explain human phylogeny in chapter 4, presuppose competence in a structurally complex and semantically flexible public language. However, it is commonly assumed that human language use presupposes sophisticated mindreading and, in particular, the capacity to attribute full-blown propositional attitudes. One reason for this is that utterances of public language typically suggest multiple interpretations, and understanding the communicative intentions of one's interlocutors seems to be the only way of eliminating such indeterminacy (Sperber & Wilson, 1995, 2002). Another reason is that influential theories of the phylogeny of human language presuppose the capacity to attribute propositional attitudes (Bickerton, 1998, 2000, 2002; Origgi & Sperber, 2000). I address the first reason by distinguishing between full-blown propositional attitude attribution and what Dennett (1987) calls adopting the "intentional stance." While full-blown propositional attitude attribution requires mindreading, I argue that (some of Dennett's own characterizations of it notwithstanding) adopting the intentional stance does not.[4] I then argue that adopting the intentional stance, without any kind of mindreading, can better mitigate interpretive indeterminacy in conversation than full-blown propositional attitude attribution. I address the second reason by defending an alternative model of the phylogeny of human language.

Selection for increasingly complex ritualistic signaling systems, aimed at advertising reliability and competence in coordination on cooperative projects, can explain how contemporary human language became structurally complex, without assuming a prior capacity to attribute propositional attitudes.

Chapter 6 extends the defense of the project by addressing influential interpretations of recent evidence concerning the ontogeny of human mindreading. In these interpretations, human children acquire the capacity to attribute propositional attitudes before learning a language (Scott & Baillargeon, 2009; Buttelmann et al., 2009), and they cannot learn a language without first being able to attribute communication-relevant propositional attitudes to adult models (Bloom, 2000, 2002). Extending the strategy of chapter 5, I argue that the data are better interpreted as showing that very young human children adopt versions of the intentional stance without attributing full-blown propositional attitudes. When this capacity is supplemented with infant dispositions to treat stereotyped adult communicative behavior as pedagogical (Csibra & Gergely, 2009), the acquisition of language can be explained without assuming that prelinguistic infants can attribute full-blown propositional attitudes. I end chapter 6 with a brief survey of persuasive evidence that human infants and children are default "mindshapers" and "mindshapees" from a very young age.

An implication of chapters 2 through 6 is that there seems to be very little for full-blown propositional attitude attribution to do. Adopting the intentional stance, when supplemented with pervasive, diverse, and sophisticated mindshaping practices, should be enough to explain most distinctively human sociocognitive feats. How and why, then, did our species develop the capacity to attribute full-blown propositional attitudes? In particular, what use would sensitivity to a distinction between mental reality and behavioral appearance have served if the sophisticated tracking of behavioral patterns made possible by the intentional stance, supplemented by mindshaping, was sufficient for highly reliable behavioral prediction? Chapter 7 argues that full-blown propositional attitude attribution, and the distinction between behavioral appearance and mental reality that it presupposes, first evolved to serve a *social* rather than an *epistemic* function. That is, rather than enabling more accurate representations of others' thoughts, propositional attitude attribution allowed individuals to maintain, rehabilitate, or diminish each other's social status in the wake of counternormative behavior, like reneging on explicit discursive commitments. As Jerome Bruner (1990) argues, narratives appealing to an agent's propositional attitudes often seem to perform an exculpatory or justificatory function, normalizing apparently deviant behavior by identifying reasons for it. Recent work in social psychology (Malle et al., 2007) confirms this idea. In chapter 7, I draw on such evidence to defend the view that propositional attitudes function primarily as components of justificatory and regulative, self-constituting narratives that ensure that likely interactants' expectations are appropriately and mutually adjusted. I conclude the book with a brief survey of the wide swath of psychological and philosophical inquiry that the notion of mindshaping has the potential to integrate.

Acknowledgments

This book has been a long time coming. Along the way, I've profited greatly from the generous help of numerous friends and colleagues. The final product is immeasurably better due to their (often unwitting) input and support. Of course, I'm entirely to blame for any remaining flaws.

I'm most grateful to J. Robert Thompson and Shannon Spaulding for their detailed and copious feedback on earlier drafts of this project. Not only did they patiently read very rough chapter drafts, but their insightful comments and suggestions regarding research of which I was unaware helped move the project in more promising directions. And as if this weren't enough, they helped organize an online reading group of the first complete draft, enlisting an incredibly energetic, generous, and talented group of young philosophers and cognitive scientists whose regular feedback through the spring and summer of 2010 dramatically improved the quality of the final product while helping me sustain the energy I needed to complete it. I am grateful to Olle Blomberg, Ryan DeChant, Mitch Herschbach, Richard Moore, Josh Shepherd, and Michael Wilby for their enthusiastic participation in the reading group and their many extremely helpful suggestions. I feel fortunate to have had this many creative and insightful thinkers devote so much of their energy to helping me with this project.

Another online forum helped germinate the ideas in this book: Pete Mandik generously agreed to host discussion of a draft of the paper from which this project sprang on his *Brain Hammer* blog in the fall of 2006. The project started off on the right foot thanks to comments from participants in the blog discussion.

I must also express my deep gratitude to the Department of Philosophy at George Washington University for the supportive and stimulating environment they provided during the drafting of this book. Most of my colleagues have read all or parts of earlier drafts, providing extremely helpful comments at departmental brown bags, as well as in less formal contexts. I thank David DeGrazia not just for detailed comments on a number of chapters but for being a true mentor when I needed it most. I'm also deeply grateful to Eric Saidel, Jeff Brand, Michele Friend, Gail Weiss, Paul Churchill, and Bill Griffiths for reading and responding to early drafts of bits of the book and challenging me in ways that made it better. I am exceedingly lucky to work in such a supportive and exceptionally collegial department.

I am also fortunate to be at an institution that values and supports interdisciplinary collaboration. This has made possible regular contact with fellow members of the Mind-Brain-Evolution Cluster and the Mind-Brain Institute at George Washington University. I want especially to thank Chet Sherwood and Francys Subiaul for their friendship, support, and constant updates on the latest in comparative psychology and neuroscience.

Others who have provided helpful feedback to earlier versions of the ideas presented here include Robert Lurz, Javier Gomez-Lavin, Amy Kind, Cynthia MacDonald, Whit Schonbein, Marc Slors, and Şerife Tekin. I also thank Rik Hine for drawing my attention to the very apt quotation by Czesław Miłosz employed as one of the epigraphs.

I would also like to acknowledge the support of Dan Dennett. Besides the tremendous intellectual debt that this project owes his groundbreaking work in philosophy of mind, I am grateful for some highly useful feedback Dan found time to give me regarding my interpretation of some of his views, though I'm not sure I take them in a direction that he fully endorses. Dan is truly a giant on whose shoulders I try, perilously, to perch. He has been an invaluable source of support, not just in this project but also throughout my career.

I also owe a huge intellectual debt to Dan Hutto, whose *Folk Psychological Narratives* (2008) crystallized my own growing reservations about orthodox approaches to human social cognition. Besides his important intellectual influence, Dan has been supportive in more practical ways as well and was instrumental in making this project a reality.

I would also like to thank four anonymous reviewers employed by the MIT Press to evaluate the penultimate draft. Their comments were rigorous, detailed, and challenging. I hope I have gone some way toward satisfactorily addressing their worries in the final version. Either way, their efforts undoubtedly improved the final product. The whole MIT Press team deserves kudos for their extreme professionalism and patient support. I'm especially grateful to my former editor, Tom Stone, for believing in me early in the project, to my current editor, Philip Laughlin, for his continuing support and professionalism, to the manuscript editor, Judy Feldmann, for her very prompt and professional management of the production process, and to the copy editor, William G. Henry, for his very thorough read-through and helpful suggestions.

Last but not least, I thank my family—Kate, Sophia, and Anton Zawid-zki—for putting up with my moodiness during this stressful and seemingly interminable endeavor. I can go back to being a full-time husband and father again! Thanks are due to Kate not just for her patience, love, and support but also for taking time out of her own busy schedule to proof and format the references. I don't think I could have finished when I needed to without her help.

1   The Human Sociocognitive Syndrome

1   Our Sociocognitive "Linchpin": Mindreading or Mindshaping?

Despite vigorous debate about a variety of issues, a consensus is growing among cognitive scientists interested in the evolutionary origins of human social cognition. The consensus concerns how to characterize the human sociocognitive syndrome, or the set of sociocognitive capacities that distinguishes our species from our closest primate relatives. This consensus is about *what* has evolved in the human lineage; it is the background to dramatic disagreement about two *how*-questions: how these capacities evolved, and how they are implemented in the brain. Consensus has it that human social cognition is distinguished from nonhuman social cognition by four broadly related capacities: sophisticated mindreading, sophisticated mindshaping,[1] pervasive cooperation, and structurally complex and flexible symbolic communication.

Cognitive scientists have also reached a strong though somewhat less pervasive consensus on the relations of phylogenetic dependency among these four capacities. According to many researchers, sophisticated mindreading is the linchpin holding the human sociocognitive syndrome together. Without sophisticated mindreading, it is claimed, sophisticated mindshaping, pervasive cooperation, and structurally complex and flexible symbolic communication would not be possible (Humphrey, 1980; Tooby & Cosmides, 1995, xvii; Baron-Cohen, 1999; Leslie, 2000, p. 61; Mithen, 2000; Sperber, 2000; Dunbar, 2000, 2003, 2009; Siegal, 2008, p. 22).[2] This largely unquestioned background assumption is often asserted without argument to motivate research into mental state attribution. For example, in a recent paper claiming to show that even seven-month-old infants have some understanding of others' mental states, Kovács et al. (2010) begin as follows:

Humans are guided by internal states such as goals and beliefs. Without an ability to infer others' mental states, society would be hardly imaginable. Social interactions, from collective hunting to playing soccer to criminal justice, critically depend on the ability to infer others' intentions and beliefs. Such abilities are also at the foundation of major evolutionary conundra. For example, the human aptitude at inferring mental states might be one of the crucial preconditions for the evolution of the cooperative social structure in human societies. (1830)

According to this view, the other components of the human sociocognitive syndrome depend on sophisticated mindreading, especially propositional attitude attribution. We are able to shape each other's minds so much more effectively than nonhuman primates, through imitation, pedagogy, and norm enforcement, for example, because our capacity for mindreading is so much more sophisticated than theirs. Just as shaping the physical world, that is, engineering, improves dramatically when guided by more sophisticated and accurate theories of physical domains, so human mindshaping is a dramatic improvement over nonhuman mindshaping because it is guided by a more sophisticated and accurate theory of mind. We succeed in cooperating in a dramatically wider variety of endeavors, of a dramatically greater complexity, involving far greater numbers of interactants than nonhuman primates, because we are far better mindreaders, and hence far better at anticipating each other's behavior. Finally, our capacity for structurally complex and flexible symbolic communication both is made possible by sophisticated mindreading and makes possible even more sophisticated mindreading. Language is the paradigm of human communication, though there are other uniquely and universally human forms, like music and dance used in ritual. And according to the received view, language is made possible by distinctively human mindreading, especially the recognition of communicative intentions, and also makes possible a kind of mindreading unmatched by any other species: we can learn each other's thoughts, to seemingly arbitrary degrees of precision, by communicating them to each other.

The principal goal of this book is to articulate and defend an alternative picture of the relations of phylogenetic dependency between the four capacities that comprise the human sociocognitive syndrome. In this alternative, sophisticated mindreading is not the linchpin that holds the whole syndrome together. Sophisticated mindreading is unlikely to evolve or remain stable in social contexts that have not already been structured by sophisticated forms of mindshaping. On the contrary, sophisticated mindreading is possible only in social contexts comprising minds that have already been shaped to be easily, mutually interpretable. In the alternative I defend, sophisticated mindshaping, presupposing mindreading capacities little more sophisticated than those available to our closest nonhuman cousins,[3] emerged in the hominid lineage leading to modern humans because such mindshaping made possible dramatic improvements in cooperation. Structurally complex and flexible symbolic communication evolved, first and foremost, as a mindshaping, cooperation-enhancing tool. This then made sophisticated mindreading possible, including the attribution of full-blown propositional attitudes, like beliefs and desires with linguistically specifiable contents.[4]

This characterization of the distinction between the received and alternative views is somewhat oversimplified. For example, everyone agrees that we use structurally complex, flexible symbolic communication to shape our social environment in ways that are conducive to cooperation. Proponents of the received view acknowledge that the four components of the human sociocognitive syndrome likely *coevolved*. Improvements in mindreading made possible improvements in mindshaping, cooperation, and communication. These then likely set up social structures that selected for improved mindreading, setting off a coevolutionary spiral (Pinker, 2003). However, in the received view, sophisticated mindreading is the first and most important step in this process. Evolution of mindshaping, cooperation, and communication in more humanlike directions is impossible without prior evolution of more humanlike mindreading.

The received view follows directly from the following assumptions: (1) humanlike mindreading is both possible and biologically advantageous in populations not yet characterized by humanlike mindshaping, cooperation, and communication, and (2) these latter three capacities are impossible without humanlike mindreading. To defend the mindshaping-first alternative, I argue that (1) more humanlike mindreading is *not* possible or biologically advantageous in populations lacking humanlike mindshaping, cooperation, and communication, and (2) these capacities can exist before humanlike mindreading. Making these arguments is the principal task of this book. In the course of making them, I also illustrate the variety, sophistication, pervasiveness, and biological uniqueness of human mindshaping and argue that many everyday interpretive practices widely assumed to serve a primarily mindreading function actually serve a primarily mindshaping function. In the rest of this chapter, I make the various concepts and distinctions central to my arguments clearer by briefly reviewing the latest literature on distinctively human mindreading, mindshaping, cooperation, and communication. First I turn to a brief note on the methodological challenges faced by any account of the evolution of and relations of phylogenetic dependency between the components of the human sociocognitive syndrome.

2   The Nature and Value of Evolutionary Hypotheses about Cognition

The most obvious objection to the project I have outlined concerns the value of engaging in speculations as unconstrained by data as hypotheses about the evolution of cognitive traits. Given that cognitive traits do not fossilize, it seems impossible to avoid the pitfalls of "just-so" storytelling. Despite this, we have seen an explosion of recent speculation concerning the evolution of the four components of the human sociocognitive syndrome. Since this book seeks to contribute to this literature, I will not spend much time defending an endeavor the value of which it takes for granted. However, I will outline a two-part defense against criticism of speculation about the evolutionary origins of cognitive capacities. First, I will review the surprisingly rich variety of indirect evidence that can keep such speculation responsible. Second, I will outline some of the important roles that evolutionary speculation can play in suggesting hypotheses and constraining research in other areas of cognitive science.

Before I turn to these arguments, let me clarify the approach to evolutionary explanation that I assume in this book. The core notion is that of an "evolutionarily stable strategy" (ESS) (Maynard-Smith, 1982; Lessard, 2006). According to this perspective, phylogenetic hypotheses aim to explain why some trait came to invade a population of interbreeding organisms and how it has remained stable against invasion by mutants that lack the trait.[5] Here is how I intend to apply this perspective to the human sociocognitive syndrome. The question of phylogenetic priority and determination between mindreading and mindshaping becomes the following. We begin with the last common ancestor we share with contemporary chimpanzees (henceforth LCA). We then attempt to infer, using all available evidence, what kinds of mindreading and mindshaping were likely possible for that species. Next we take into account other known, relevant features of their ecology and ask the following question: is it more likely that more humanlike mindreading invaded such a population before more humanlike mindshaping, or is the opposite more likely? In addition, we ask whether the presence of one or the other in a population would make invasion by the other more likely. Given this framework, one can phrase the central thesis of this book with more precision. I argue that it is much more likely that humanlike mindshaping invaded populations of the LCA or its descendants than that humanlike mindreading did. I also argue that once such mindshaping was stable, it made more humanlike mindreading more likely to invade. The details of the argument turn on the unviability of humanlike mindreading in populations without mindshaping practices that make individuals more easily interpretable to each other. It also appeals to ecological factors that made pervasive and sophisticated cooperation central to the success of our precursors, and the claim that such cooperation is impossible without the kind of humanlike mindshaping that makes humanlike mindreading viable.

Although we have no direct evidence concerning the cognitive capacities of the LCA and other human precursors, we do have a variety of indirect evidence. Most obviously, we can consult the fossil record. Although neural tissue and cognitive capacities do not fossilize, the skeletal remains that do fossilize often provide decent evidence of cognitive capacity. Most obviously, the size and shape of fossilized hominid skulls give some indication of cognitive capacity. Although brain size is not a perfect index of cognitive capacity, absolute brain size is the best anatomical correlate of humanlike cognition among primates (Sherwood et al., 2008, pp. 444–446). Skull endocasts can also reveal gross patterns of brain organization (p. 442). Skull size and shape can be used to reliably date dramatic expansions in brain size in the hominid lineage. These can be correlated with other evidence to suggest hypotheses about what drove such dramatic expansions. For example, if there is no evidence of dramatic ecological change correlating with such expansions, this is reason to think that they were driven by social factors, for example, expanding group sizes or competition with other groups (Sterelny, 2007). Furthermore, such fossil data can also be correlated with archaeological data, for example, early stone tools and their geographical distribution, to suggest hypotheses about the correlation between neural expansion and extent and quality of tool use, as well as social complexity sufficient to allow for long-range migration.

Another interesting source of evidence concerns interactions between cranial and postcranial changes. For example, there is strong evidence of bipedality in fossilized remains of extinct hominid species going back as far as 4.4 million years (Lovejoy et al., 2009). But radical cranial expansion imposes severe costs on bipedal mammals because bipedality constrains the size of the birth canal through which large-headed neonates must pass (DeSilva & Lesnik, 2008). Such costs must be added to the already considerable metabolic costs of supporting a large brain (Aiello & Wheeler, 1995). We can infer from such facts that the benefits of having a larger brain at a certain point in hominid history must have been considerable indeed. The evidence suggests that brain expansion among our precursors began to accelerate significantly with the rise of *Homo erectus* about 1.8 million years ago (Holloway et al., 2004). This suggests that dramatic, perhaps runaway selection pressures for increased cognitive capacities must have arisen in this time period. Whatever these selection pressures were, they must have overpowered the considerable costs of birthing large-headed neonates and nutritionally meeting their extreme metabolic needs. According to one plausible hypothesis, the birthing problem was partially mitigated because the neonates of large-headed, bipedal hominids were born with incompletely developed brains, in small, partially collapsed skulls, as human neonates are (Aiello, 1996). This suggestion has significant implications for hypotheses about our precursors' socioecology and related cognitive capacities.

The premature-brain-at-birth hypothesis suggests that, as adult brain size expanded, infants were born increasingly helpless. Provisioning such infants with requisite calories would require alloparenting—mothers would have to be helped by other members of a population, including fathers and blood relatives. This would require a degree of cooperation unmatched among extant nonhuman hominids. In addition, prolonged childhood would increase the opportunities for, and importance of, mindshaping practices like guided imitation and pedagogy. That increasing degrees of neural growth would occur postnatally while infants were exposed to contingent environmental stimuli—both physical and social—suggests that hominids in our lineage developed minds that were far more plastic and sensitive to local contingencies than those of other primates. While species whose brains are almost fully wired at birth have neurocognitive profiles almost entirely determined by genes, and therefore by transgenerationally stable aspects of the environment, species like our own, in which much brain wiring occurs postnatally, would have far more locally sensitive neurocognitive profiles. This has potentially profound implications for mindreading. The task of tracking the mental properties of humans and human precursors is bound to be exceptionally difficult if the course of neural development is driven to such a degree by contingent environmental regularities. Such populations are likely to display far less cognitive and behavioral homogeneity than populations in which most neural development is complete prenatally and hence fixed genetically. This inevitably makes mindreading more challenging in human beings and their immediate precursors than in other primates. I will expand on these hypotheses in the rest of the book, especially chapter 4, which examines the evolution of distinctively human mindshaping. The foregoing is merely a taste of how far even indirect fossil evidence can take us in developing responsible hypotheses about the phylogenesis of the human sociocognitive syndrome.

The second most important source of evidence constraining phylogenetic hypotheses is the archaeological record. This is admittedly a very noisy signal. For example, McBrearty and Brooks (2000) argue that Euro-centric prioritization of archaeological exploration, and demographic bias-ing that results from denser populations leaving more artifacts, have led to dramatic misinterpretations of the archaeological record. According to these misinterpretations, distinctively human cognition is a relatively recent phenomenon, emerging suddenly about fifty thousand years ago. McBrearty and Brooks argue that recent excavations in Africa contradict this hypothesis, suggesting a gradual emergence of humanlike cognition and social organization over the last 200,000 to 300,000 years. Despite such controversies, as archaeological evidence accumulates, it supports respon-sible conjecture about the phylogenesis of the human sociocognitive syn-drome. For example, artifacts found in locations at great distances from the materials of which they are made provide good evidence of elaborate, long-distance trade routes, requiring complex social networks (McBrearty & Brooks, 2000). Ornamentation of artifacts and evidence of bodily ornamen-tation, like red ocher, indicate the marking of ethnic groups, an important signal of group selection for cooperative traits (Sterelny, 2003, 2012, pp. 54–55). Finally, the geographic diversity of technology and ornament is an important signal of the human sociocognitive syndrome. Despite their wide geographic range, protohuman hominids, like *Homo erectus*, had an extremely uniform, stereotyped tool kit, suggesting important social and cognitive differences from our own species (Mithen, 1996).

Another major source of evidence constraining phylogenetic hypoth-eses about human cognitive capacities comes from comparative psychol-ogy, neuroanatomy, and genetics. Humans differ in significant ways from their genetically closest living nonhuman relatives. Genetic evidence can support remarkably precise dating of the emergence of cognitive traits. For example, neuropsychological studies have shown the FOXP2 gene to play an important role in human language use (Lai et al., 2001). Important dif-ferences between humans and other extant primates at this gene locus have been identified and dated to the last 200,000 years (Enard et al., 2002). Significant behavioral differences also distinguish human beings from their closest nonhuman relatives. Comparative psychology has shown that all nonhuman primates lack the human capacities for belief attribution, fine-grained and flexible imitation, sophisticated cooperation, and complex language (Tomasello et al., 2005). This makes it likely that the LCA lacked these capacities, too, and gives us a good idea of the basic sociocognitive profile from which ours evolved. Finally, there are also significant neural differences between human beings and their closest nonhuman relatives. The most obvious and well-supported difference is in absolute brain size

(Sherwood et al., 2008). But many have also argued that there are significant differences in the sizes of different brain regions relative to the rest of the brain and to overall body mass. For example, the visual cortex appears to take up a far smaller proportion of the human brain than the brains of nonhuman primates, while the opposite is true of the prefrontal cortex (p. 441). Also, lateralization appears to be more pronounced in the human brain than in the brains of other primates (pp. 432–433).

The final major source of evidence constraining phylogenetic hypotheses about the human sociocognitive syndrome comes from comparative studies of different human populations. Although the universality of a trait is not an infallible marker of its genetic basis, it certainly makes it more likely that the trait is the product of genes selected for in human evolution. There is little doubt that the four components of the human sociocognitive syndrome are present in all nonpathological human populations.

Thus, although responsible speculation about the phylogenesis of the human sociocognitive syndrome is extremely challenging, requiring the integration of information across numerous disciplines, it is not impossible. At least four distinct kinds of evidence provide substantial constraints. Furthermore, formulating responsible hypotheses about the evolutionary roots of human cognition is not only possible; it plays an important role in cognitive science. The foundational metaphor of contemporary cognitive science likens the mind/brain to an information processor or computer. And to explain the behavior of an information processor, one must first specify the task in which it is engaged. This is the point of the three-level methodology that Marr (1982) proposes for computational cognitive science. The top, or computational, level specifies what task a cognitive process is trying to accomplish. The middle, or algorithmic, level specifies, at an abstract level, how the cognitive process accomplishes the task, that is, what kinds of algorithms it uses, and over what kinds of representations these algorithms are defined. The lowest, or implementational, level specifies, in neural terms, how the brain implements these algorithms.

When it comes to biological information processors, like the human brain, there appear to be only two ways of addressing questions at the top, computational level. Like Marr (1982), one can appeal to intuition or introspection to specify in what task some cognitive process is engaged. For example, Marr argues that human vision consists in mapping a two-dimensional retinal image onto a cognitive representation of a three-dimensional scene. This certainly seems like the task that vision accomplishes. However, there are many reasons to think that our introspectively grounded intuitions about the tasks in which our brains are engaged can be systematically misleading (Clark, 1997, epilogue). Indeed, Churchland et al. (1994) criticize Marr's model of vision on precisely these grounds. They argue that a better guide to the tasks in which human and other biological cognitive processes are engaged is evolutionary pedigree.[6] The human visual system evolved primarily to guide locomotion, not to construct detailed representations of three-dimensional scenes. According to Churchland et al., the human visual system is a messy, unprincipled "bag of tricks" for guiding an organism around ecologically plausible terrains. The growing evidence that human vision is implemented in at least two independently functioning pathways—the dorsal pathway devoted to locating objects and the ventral pathway devoted to classifying them (Milner & Goodale, 2006)—supports this view, as well as general skepticism about introspection-guided intuition as a method for determining the tasks in which brains are engaged. There is no intuitive or introspective reason to expect that the brain's capacity to locate objects should be completely dissociable from its capacity to classify them. But from an evolutionary perspective, this makes perfect sense. Even very simple organisms need a quick, automatic capacity to visually locate objects, since this is necessary for effective locomotion through a cluttered environment. More sophisticated capacities for classifying objects according to various properties, like color, are likely more recent evolutionary innovations—new tricks added to the already existing collection.

Thus if one wants to avoid the pitfalls of introspection- and intuition-guided speculation about what tasks the human mind/brain performs, the only alternative appears to be responsible speculation about what it evolved to do. This is one important role that evolutionary hypotheses can play in cognitive science. I think many assumptions about human social cognition have been based on intuition-based hypotheses about what social cognition is for, similar to Marr's hypothesis about what vision is for. It seems intuitively compelling that one cannot accomplish any social tasks—communicating, cooperating, mindshaping—without first constructing accurate models of the minds of one's interactants. Thus the principal task of human social cognition must be accurate mindreading. The analogy to Marr's claim about vision is instructive. It is also intuitive that vision cannot successfully guide navigation through, or manipulation of, the physical environment without first constructing an accurate, detailed model of its three-dimensional structure. However, as Churchland et al. argue, naturally evolved cognitive systems seldom respect our intuitions. There may be far messier and less principled, though far more efficient and robust, solutions discovered by naturally evolved systems. Such possibilities can be uncovered only with the help of responsible speculation about phylogenesis. I argue that when this perspective is applied to the human sociocognitive syndrome, sophisticated mindshaping turns out to be a far more important component of human sociocognitive competence than sophisticated mindreading.

Besides enabling cognitive scientists to frame the question of what cognitive processes are for without relying entirely on introspectively guided intuition, phylogenetic hypotheses also suggest explanations for otherwise puzzling experimental results. For example, it is well established that human beings are much better at reasoning about social norm violation than about nonsocial contingencies, even when these are formally similar (Cosmides, 1989). When asked whether there is a rule that a card with a vowel on one side must have an even number on the other, subjects systematically fail to consider cards they know to have odd numbers on one side, even though turning such cards over could show that the rule does not hold if even one has a vowel on the other side. In contrast, subjects have no trouble engaging in such reasoning when the topic is norm violation. For example, if the rule states that if one is drinking alcohol, one must be twenty-one or older, subjects automatically respond by checking both whether all those drinking alcohol are twenty-one *and* whether all those younger than twenty-one are not drinking alcohol. This is a paradigm-setting result for evolutionary psychology: it is taken to indicate that the human mind includes a cognitive module dedicated to detecting cheaters, something that is highly plausible given widely accepted hypotheses about prevalent social circumstances in human evolution (Cosmides & Tooby, 1992). Counterintuitive empirical results concerning similarities and differences in sexual preference between the genders (Carruthers, 2006, pp. 41–42), amount of care devoted to offspring depending on various contextual factors (pp. 42–43), and even improved memory for arbitrary words in survival-related versus survival-neutral contexts (Nairne & Pandeirada, 2008) are also easily explained from an evolutionary perspective. There is an increasing body of empirical evidence concerning human psychology that makes sense only relative to responsible hypotheses about the evolutionary raisons d'être of human cognitive capacities.

3 Mindreading

"Mindreading" (Nichols & Stich, 2003) has become a term of art in the literature on human social cognition. It refers to a phenomenon also called "mentalizing" (Goldman, 2006) or exercising one's "theory of mind" (Premack & Woodruff, 1978). These terms are used rather loosely, referring to a diverse assortment of phenomena. In its most inclusive sense, "mind-reading" refers to the exercise of a cognitive capacity aimed at anticipating the behavior of other agents, on the basis of *some* appreciation of the mental states responsible for it. But this characterization obscures significant differences among the phenomena that different theorists call "mindreading." Since the goal of this book is to defend a theory of the phylogenesis of distinctively human mindreading (as dependent on distinctively human mindshaping), I need to say something about what is distinctive of human mindreading.

Many theorists of human social cognition have distinguished between high-level and low-level mindreading (Carruthers, 2006, 2009a; Apperly & Butterfill, 2009; Apperly, 2011), and this distinction comes close to the distinction I want to make between human and nonhuman mindreading. High-level mindreading typically involves the capacity to represent mental states *as such*. Most research into human social cognition has focused on the attribution of a specific category of mental states, that is, the propositional attitudes, like belief and desire; for this reason, I restrict my discussion to the propositional attitudes. Philosophers typically understand propositional attitudes and other mental states as concrete, unobservable causes of behavior. In addition, propositional attitudes are mental states with semantic properties: they represent the world as being a certain way, and this representation can be either satisfied or not, for example, in the case of beliefs, true or false, and, in the case of desires, fulfilled or unfulfilled. This is why the capacity to attribute false beliefs has figured so prominently as a test of full-blown human sociocognitive competence (Wellman et al., 2001). Furthermore, consensus has it that propositional attitudes can involve individually variable ways of representing the same facts, often called "modes of presentation." For example, Lois Lane can form beliefs about Superman by representing him not as Superman but as Clark Kent instead. Finally, it is widely held that propositional attitudes have tenuous connections to observable circumstances and behavior because of holism: how one reacts to a certain environmental situation depends not just on one propositional attitude but on indefinitely large networks of them (Morton, 1996, 2003; Bermúdez, 2003b, 2009). For example, the belief that it is raining alone does not trigger umbrella retrieval; it must be joined with a desire to stay dry that is stronger than competing desires, appropriate beliefs about locations of umbrellas, appropriate beliefs about the costs of umbrella retrieval, and so forth. Thus if high-level mindreading requires representing mental states as such, then high-level attribution of propositional attitudes requires representing them as unobservable, concrete causes of behavior, that (mis)represent the world as being a certain way, under individually variable modes of presentation, with complex connections to other propositional attitudes, perceptions, and behavior.

Apperly (2011) calls this characterization of high-level mindreading the "normative account": it specifies the competence attributors of propositional attitudes are *supposed* to have. However, as Apperly (2011) repeatedly illustrates, it is possible to pass behavioral tests of socio-cognitive competence with a less sophisticated understanding of propositional attitudes. For example, he argues that the standard test for whether or not human children can attribute false beliefs can be passed with no understanding that different agents might represent the same facts under different modes of presentation, or that propositional attitudes must combine with indefinitely many other mental states to yield behavior. According to Apperly (2011), infants and non-human animals often pass behavioral tests of propositional attitude understanding without fulfilling the normative account, i.e., without representing propositional attitudes as such. This is what he calls "low-level" mindreading. Apperly assumes that "low-level" mindreading still involves the attribution of unobservable causes that can misrepresent the state of the world or otherwise go unsatisfied. However, it does *not* involve an appreciation that the same situations can be represented under different modes of presentation, or that the link between observable situations and behavior is holistically constrained, i.e., mediated by indefinitely large networks of propositional attitudes.

Evidence suggests that some nonhuman animals, both closely and distantly related to *Homo sapiens*, are sensitive to or can track each other's propositional attitudes without necessarily representing them as such. That is, they can differentiate between behaviors caused by different beliefs and other mental states and respond flexibly and adaptively to these differences without thinking of these behaviors as caused by full-blown propositional attitudes. For example, chimpanzees appear to take into account whether or not a dominant conspecific has seen food being cached: if the dominant sees the caching, subordinates are less likely to access the cache (Hare et al., 2000, 2001). Western scrub jays, members of the amazingly precocious corvid family of birds, seem even more adept at this kind of mindreading than chimpanzees. Experiments have shown that these birds are much more likely to cache food in hard-to-observe locations, like behind barriers, in the shade, or farther away, when other birds observe them (Clayton et al., 2007). Given the intense competition for food among these birds, this is clearly a form of deception and requires some sensitivity to what conspecifics are likely to see. Such an interpretation is bolstered by evidence that western scrub jays keep track of what *different individual* conspecifics have witnessed when *recaching* food, and only individuals who have *themselves* pilfered others' caches engage in such deceptive strategies.

Whether or not such deceptive strategies require concepts of other minds and mental states, like false beliefs, is still the subject of much controversy. Even the most sanguine comparative psychologists restrict chimpanzee theory of mind to *some kind of appreciation* of conspecifics' goals, perceptions, and knowledge, denying that they appreciate false belief (Call & Tomasello, 2008). For example, sensitivity to a dominant conspecific's knowledge or ignorance of the location of recently cached food need not imply sensitivity to false beliefs. To track another's false belief, one must be capable of anticipating specific behaviors guided by the belief. But chimpanzees appear to know only that an ignorant, dominant conspecific is less likely to contest food retrieval, *not* the specific behaviors to which his false belief will lead, for example, searching where he thinks the food is (Hare et al., 2001). The jury, however, is still out. A definitive verdict on whether or not chimpanzees are sensitive to the contents of each other's beliefs must await new experimental approaches (Lurz, 2011). Anecdotal evidence suggests that chimpanzees can be extremely clever at tactical deception, and it is hard to explain such capacities without appeal to some understanding of false belief (Menzel, 1974). Nevertheless, even if a capacity for such *sensitivity* to false beliefs can be established, it would still not constitute high-level propositional attitude attribution in the sense I intend. As Apperly's (2011) thorough review of the comparative and developmental literature shows, an agent can be sensitive to false beliefs and other propositional attitudes without representing them as such.

The distinction between distinctively human and nonhuman mindreading therefore appears to be the following. Though nonhuman mindreaders show a kind of sensitivity to or ability to track at least some propositional attitudes, in their flexible and adaptive responses to the behaviors they cause, we find little evidence that this sensitivity is mediated by representations of propositional attitudes as such. Their sociocognitive feats do not require understanding that others' behavior is the product of unobservable *causes*, which represent situations under individually variable *modes of presentation* and influence behavior only tenuously, via *interaction with indefinitely large networks of other mental states* (Bermúdez, 2009). Although much human social cognition is plausibly similarly low level (Hutto, 2008), we are also capable of representing each other's propositional attitudes as such. The focus of this book is the evolution of the latter capacity: how and why did our species, and apparently *only* our species, evolve the capacity to understand behavior as caused by unobservable mental states, which represent situations under individually variable modes of presentation and influence behavior only tenuously due to holism, that is, constraint by whole networks of other mental states?

To make this question more precise, I contrast this characterization of full-blown, distinctively human mindreading with what Dennett (1987) has called adopting the "intentional stance." Dennett's position is a plausible characterization of a variety of low-level mindreading, of which some nonhuman animals and human infants are capable, and all normal humans employ in their unreflective, quotidian interactions. This is, admittedly, a departure from the letter of Dennett's discussions of the intentional stance; he often characterizes this notion as an analysis of full-blown propositional attitude attribution. However, Dennett's understanding of what propositional attitudes are is somewhat heterodox. He does *not* see them as concrete, unobservable mental states with causal control over behavior.[7] Rather, he sees them as abstract posits, akin to centers of gravity in physics, which help track robust patterns of observable behavior (Dennett, 1991b). In Dennett's view, to attribute propositional attitudes is *not* to speculate about the concrete causes responsible for behavior. Rather, it is to situate behavior in a *rational, normative* framework, to see it as a reasonable response relative to goals and available information (Zawidzki, 2012).

For example, in one of his most famous illustrations of the intentional stance, Dennett considers our interpretation of moves by a chess-playing computer (1978, pp. 4–9). According to Dennett, to interpret such moves from the intentional stance is *precisely not* to speculate about the algorithms that are causally responsible for them. We need know nothing about the design of the computer. Instead, interpretation requires only an understanding of *chess*: the goal of the game (checkmate) and the available information (piece configurations on the board, rules of chess, effective strategies). Applying this to quotidian interpretation of and by biological agents, adopting the intentional stance requires only the interpretation of bouts of behavior as goal directed and rationally constrained by available information, not the attribution of concrete, unobservable causes with content represented via individually variable modes of presentation.[8]

Both developmental (Gergely & Csibra, 2003) and comparative (Wood & Hauser, 2008) psychologists employ a similar framework for explaining low-level mindreading. According to Gergely and Csibra, infants as young as six and one-half months (Csibra, 2008) assume that agents pursue goals by the most efficient means available, given situational constraints. Wood and Hauser (2008) find evidence of similar reasoning in nonhuman primates. Such interpretive competence does not require speculating about concrete, unobservable causes of behavior or appreciating that these causes are full-blown propositional attitudes, that is, states with content represented via individually variable modes of presentation and holistically constrained influence on behavior. It requires only a sensitivity to certain abstract properties of bouts of behavior, namely, that they aim at specific goals and constitute the most rational means to those goals given environmental constraints. Gergely and Csibra (2003) call this the "teleological stance" or "the naive theory of rational action."

This very basic sociocognitive competence can also be supplemented with sensitivity to behavioral indicators of information access, like gaze direction, to yield an even more powerful understanding of rational action, which still falls short of high-level mindreading because it requires no attribution of concrete, unobservable mental states with content represented via individually variable modes of presentation and holistically constrained causal influence on behavior. Adopting this "enhanced teleological stance" (Zawidzki, 2011) allows interpreters to appreciate that different agents might have access to different information, and hence their goal-directed behavior might be rationally constrained by different situational factors. For example, subordinate chimpanzees that notice that dominant competitors have no line of sight on a location in which food is being cached apparently do *not* expect them to select means to the goal of food retrieval that are most efficient *relative to situational constraints of which only the subordinates are informed.* They take into account that different individuals are governed by different situational constraints, depending on the information to which they have access.[9] This "enhanced teleological stance" amounts to Dennett's intentional stance: behavior is predicted based on a rationality assumption governing the relationship between its goals and available information. Agents are assumed to engage in behavior that constitutes the most efficient means to goals relative to information to which they have access. If this is a tacit theory employed by human and nonhuman interpreters, it is a theory of observable behavior, not of the underlying mental causes responsible for it.[10]

One way of appreciating this, which plays an important role in the arguments of chapter 7, is that full-blown propositional attitude attribution supports, while adopting the intentional stance does *not* support, an appearance–reality distinction applied to agent behavior. The holism of the propositional attitudes ensures that any observed behavior is always compatible with mutually inconsistent propositional attitude attributions. Two qualitatively identical, counterfactually robust patterns of observable behavior may be caused by different propositional attitudes. This is not the case for adopting the intentional stance: if a particular attribution of goals and information access successfully rationalizes a pattern of behavior and supports prediction of future behavior, then, according to Dennett (1991b), there is no further fact of the matter about the agent's "true," unobservable beliefs and desires. Even if some pattern of behavior is indeterminate between multiple intentional stance interpretations, Dennett argues that there is no further fact of the matter about what propositional attitudes actually cause it; brute indeterminacy must simply be accepted. For this reason, most philosophers find Dennett's proposals hard to accept: it is difficult to give up the intuition that some determinate mental fact of the matter lies behind the behavioral appearances.

This characterization of low-level mindreading is even more deflationary than Apperly's (2011): not only are apparently sophisticated sociocognitive feats possible without an appreciation of different modes of presentation and the holistic connection between propositional attitudes and behavior, but there is no need to think of behavior as caused by concrete, unobservable mental states that can misrepresent the world. All that is necessary is a capacity to adopt the intentional stance, by which I mean a capacity to parse bouts of behavior into goals and rationally constrained means of achieving them, given information to which interpretive targets have access, where this access is understood entirely in terms of behavioral indicators, like gaze direction, and not in terms of unobservable cognitive states, like beliefs.

Thus I assume the following taxonomy of varieties of mindreading. The social cognition of nonhuman animals, human infants, and human adults engaged in unreflective, quotidian interactions is often guided by tacit knowledge of behavioral patterns, sometimes highly abstract ones, involving categories like "goal," "efficient means," "information access," and "teleological rationality." The most sophisticated examples of such low-level mindreading plausibly involve adopting something like Dennett's intentional stance. As Dennett (1991c) himself makes clear, this is better characterized as an unreflective, tacitly encoded "craft" than an explicit theory. Low-level mindreading can, of course, involve even less sophisticated representations of behavioral patterns. For example, nonhuman animals and human infants use straightforward induction to anticipate future behavior and are sensitive to various nonrational behavioral regularities, such as correlations between facial expressions of emotion and subsequent behavior (Parr, 2001; Andrews, 2007, 2008).

In addition, some adult human social cognition is guided by the representation of propositional attitudes as such. We can predict each other's behavior based on attributions of concrete, unobservable mental causes, which represent situations under individually variable modes of presentation and must combine with indefinitely broad networks of other mental states to yield behavior. This is more than a tacit theory of observable behavior; it is a theory of the underlying mental causes of observable behavior. One of the main goals of the book is to show that the evolution of this latter form of sophisticated, high-level mindreading depended on already extant, sophisticated, and distinctively human mindshaping practices. As will become clear, it is likely that such mindshaping practices both required and selected for more sophisticated versions of the intentional stance than those of which contemporary nonhuman animals are capable. However, these mindshaping practices did not require high-level mindreading in the sense defined here, and such high-level mindreading was not possible without them.

4 Mindshaping

The term "mindshaping" is not commonly used in the literature on human social cognition. I adopt it from Mameli (2001). Mameli argues that through the mechanism of social expectancies, folk assumptions about human psychology can become self-fulfilling prophecies. For example, assumptions about gender lead adults to expect male and female infants to have different psychologies: while boys are supposed to be aggressive and quick to anger, girls are supposed to be passive and easily upset. For this reason, adults tend to interpret the same behavior differently depending on perceived gender. If they think a crying infant is a boy, they interpret him as being angry. If they think the same crying infant is a girl, they interpret her as being upset. These interpretations give rise to social expectancies: adults expect a crying male infant to act in aggressive ways and a crying female infant to act in passive ways, for example, to seek comfort. Such expectancies affect the way adults interact with infants, for example, being more quick to comfort a crying female infant than a crying male infant. Such differences in patterns of interaction might lead to self-fulfilling prophecies: infants come to behave in ways that are consistent with adult expectancies. Mameli argues that a similar dynamic might be at work when parents interpret early infant behavior as intentional communicative acts: infants begin to act in ways that confirm such interpretations, and this helps "bootstrap" the capacity for intentional communication in human infancy (2001, pp. 617–619). In both of these cases, argues Mameli, folk psychological behavioral interpretation functions to shape infant minds rather than read them.

Mameli sees mindshaping as a kind of "niche construction" (Laland et al., 2001). Niche construction is a relatively new concept in biology. The idea is that evolution does not always consist in adapting to a prespecified environmental niche through genetic selection. Often species construct environmental niches that are a better fit for their current genes. This might involve nothing more elaborate than imprinting on a new source of food or shelter. For example, Mameli considers the hypothetical case of a species of butterfly that imprints on the plant on which it feeds after hatching. That is, mature butterflies tend to lay eggs on plants of the same species as those on which they hatched, recognizing them via some signal. Imagine that this imprinting mechanism is fallible: sometimes mature butterflies lay their eggs on the wrong species of plant. Once, when this occurs, the deviant plant species fortuitously happens to be a better source of nutrition for that species of butterfly. The lucky butterfly has more descendants than those of its conspecifics that do not mistakenly lay eggs on the plant. These descendants imprint on the new plant, and the species' niche has been altered without any genetic selection: a new selection pressure arises because butterflies that lay eggs on the new plant do better than butterflies that do not make this "mistake." Imprinting is a form of nongenetic trait inheritance that can alter a species' niche in ways that feed back into genetic inheritance. Mameli's idea is that mindshaping via the mechanism of social expectancies is a human form of niche construction. We alter the selectional environment of subsequent generations by shaping their minds in ways that affect the social niche in which they find themselves.

Sterelny (2012) argues that distinctively human social cognition drove such social niche construction in human evolution.[11] He considers two different models of the evolution of social cognition in the human lineage. In both views, the central problem that human social cognition must solve is cooperation. In the received view—the Machiavellian intelligence hypothesis—the problem of cooperation can be solved only by detecting and preventing "free riders" from taking advantage of the cooperative efforts of others. But this sets up an arms race pitting better deception against better deception detection. The result is runaway selection for better mindreading. Suppose, for example, that a mutant with better mindreading ability is introduced into a prehuman population. The mutant uses her skill to successfully deceive her conspecifics, accumulating more survival-related resources, living longer, and having more offspring. Soon better mindreaders dominate the population. But since hominid biological success depends crucially on social interactions, this amounts to a dramatic alteration of the hominid niche. Where previously it was possible to succeed without mindreading virtuosity, this is now impossible. There are now strong selection pressures favoring good mindreaders. The mutant mindreader has not just adapted to a preexisting niche. She and her descendants have significantly altered the social niche to which subsequent generations must now adapt.

Sterelny favors a different model of the interaction between human social cognition and social niche construction. In his view, the key sociocognitive innovations in the human lineage are capacities for high-fidelity transmission, preservation, and elaboration of information across generations. As with Machiavellian intelligence, such capacities are plausible responses to the problem of cooperation, though to a different aspect of this problem. Sterelny argues that detecting and dissuading free riders was not an important problem among small bands of social foragers early in our lineage. Coordination was more important: advanced planning and on-the-spot adjustment to prey were necessary to successfully hunt the large fauna that early humans and their immediate precursors hunted with their relatively crude weapons. But such coordination required effective communication and training, possible only through high-fidelity cultural learning. Cooperative hunts yielded such nutritional boons that strong selection pressures favored a capacity to transmit and preserve information through cultural learning. This dramatically altered the social niche for subsequent generations. Individuals who were not good cultural learners could not benefit from group hunts and were at a major selectional disadvantage.

As I argue in chapter 4, in examining the evolution of distinctively human mindshaping, I think that Sterelny's picture of social niche construction in the human lineage is closer to the truth than the picture suggested by the Machiavellian intelligence hypothesis. For now, however, the important lesson is that evolutionary change in hominid social cognition can have dramatic feedback on hominid evolution: it results in an alteration of arguably the most important component of the hominid niche, that is, social circumstances, thereby creating new selection pressures. Mindshaping plays an important role in this process. If individuals are rewarded for conforming to social expectancies of the kind discussed by Mameli, or other kinds related to the cooperative projects highlighted by Sterelny (e.g., coordination and communication conventions passed down through cultural learning), then this constitutes the construction of a new social niche to which subsequent generations must adapt. Such niche construction can thereby result in selection for new genes, for example, encoding more cooperative behavioral dispositions.

As I intend to use the term, "mindshaping" refers to the kinds of phenomena discussed by Mameli, together with numerous other human social behaviors. Here are some examples: distinctively human imitation, peda-gogy, normative judgment and norm enforcement, the institution of social roles, and self-constituting narratives. An important goal of this book, espe-cially chapter 2, is to show that such behaviors, often treated as unrelated, all share important properties related to mindshaping and niche construc-tion. All such human practices aim to get a target to match the behavior of some model, and this, I argue, is the essence of mindshaping. Nonhu-man species show only the rudiments of some kinds of mindshaping, for example, a limited capacity to imitate. On the other hand, human beings are obsessive mindshapers. It is now well established by studies of very young infants that human beings are wired to be receptive to pedagogical instruction (Csibra & Gergely, 2009) and "overimitate" (Nielsen & Toma-selli, 2010) models, eagerly acquiring even noninstrumental behaviors, that is, behaviors that are not essential to securing typical goals like acquiring a favored food. We seem to engage in mindshaping, both as shapees and as shapers, for its own sake. As I argue in chapter 2, when it comes to social behavior, our species is best distinguished from others by the complexity, subtlety, variety, and broad scope of human mindshaping, and the inordi-nate amount of time and resources we devote to it. Chapter 4 addresses the evolution of such mindshaping, arguing that it constitutes a kind of *targeted* social niche construction, making successful human social interaction, on cooperative projects especially, significantly more computationally tracta-ble than it would be otherwise.

Thus although Mameli's notion of mindshaping is my point of depar-ture, I defend an expanded version of the concept. It applies to a far greater variety of human practices than Mameli (2001) envisions. Furthermore, although I agree with Mameli that mindshaping functions as a method of social niche construction, I emphasize that distinctively human mind-shaping makes possible a kind of social niche construction that is qualita-tively distinct from those available to other species. In Mameli's example of the butterfly accidentally imprinting on a more nutritious plant, the niche construction is a fortuitous by-product of traits selected for effects that have nothing to do with niche construction. Butterfly imprinting on plant species is selected for its nutritional effects on offspring. It then indirectly affects niche. But mindshaping practices like imitation, peda-gogy, norm enforcement, the institution of social roles, and narrative self-regulation are directly targeted at social niche construction. This is not to say that practitioners consciously conceive of themselves as constructing social niches for subsequent generations. The point is, rather, that such behavioral traits are selected for their effects on the social niche, making populations more cooperative, homogeneous, and predictable. So, I argue, distinctively human mindshaping is crucial to explaining the success of the hominid sociocognitive syndrome because it constitutes a way of bringing social niche construction under control: unlike other species, we obsessively engage in practices whose raison d'être is social niche construction. Unlike fortuitous niche construction that occurs as a by-product of traits selected for other reasons, human mindshaping enables *targeted* social niche construction.[12] This is key to understanding mindshaping's crucial role in the evolution of the human sociocognitive syndrome.

5   Cooperation

Compared to other primates and, indeed, most other vertebrates, humans are an uncommonly cooperative species (Sterelny, 2003, 2007, 2012). There is no doubt that cooperation is central to our relative biological success. We depend on cooperation to secure all our biologically significant goals: feeding, defense against predation and other threats, mating, reproduction, and care of offspring. Although some nonhuman primate species engage in rudimentary forms of cooperation, like monkey hunting among some chimpanzee populations (Boesch, 1994), nothing comes close to matching the breadth, scope, sophistication, pervasiveness, and centrality of cooperative projects among humans. Cooperation is so fundamental to the human way of life that we often fail to notice how much depends on it; we take it for granted like the proverbial fish in water. For example, sophisticated communication is possible only against a background of cooperation. Language is impossible without truth telling and trust, requiring cooperative tendencies unmatched by other hominids. Overwhelming evidence indicates that the disposition to cooperate is a universal human trait. Cross-cultural experiments involving economic games played for real money show that human beings of all cultures tend to favor equitable distributions of goods (Henrich et al., 2006). Developmental psychologists have shown that even very young children are default cooperators (Tomasello, 2009). Few claims are as well established in the social sciences as the claim that pervasive cooperation is a universal and distinctively human trait.

Thus it is fair to conclude that cooperation is one of the central functions of human social cognition. We need to be good mindreaders, mindshapers, and communicators because these proficiencies are necessary for successful cooperation, the key to our biological success. This basic premise, forcefully defended in recent years by Kim Sterelny (2003, 2007, 2012), looms large in the arguments of this book. In particular, chapter 4 argues that human cooperation cannot be explained by sophisticated mindreading. For this reason, since cooperation is one of the central functions of human social cognition, mindreading is not its most important component. Instead, I argue in chapter 4 that sophisticated mindshaping is the key to understanding how human cooperation is possible.

Despite its clear importance to the human species, the evolution of cooperation is notoriously difficult to explain. The reason is simple: it is easy to take advantage of overly cooperative agents. Imagine some protohuman hominid population no more cooperative than contemporary chimpanzees. Next imagine introducing a mutant into this population who is more cooperative. Perhaps the mutant shares food spontaneously. It is clear that such a mutant is unlikely to leave many offspring relative to her conspecifics. Other things being equal, the mutant will secure fewer net calories than her conspecifics, leaving her at a competitive disadvantage when it comes to securing mates, caring for offspring, and defending against predation. So it is hard to see how the kind of pervasive, default cooperation that characterizes our species can ever get off the ground. Even if this could be explained, this would lead to another puzzle: how can such cooperation remain stable in a population? Imagine that a mutant is introduced into a population of default cooperators. The mutant is a "free rider": she takes advantage of the fruits of others' cooperative efforts without doing her share. She secures all her caloric needs without expending the energy or incurring the risk associated with hunting or foraging. She takes advantage of offspring care offered by her cooperative conspecifics without reciprocating. Other things being equal, such a mutant would have more offspring than any of her conspecifics, and after several generations, her descendants would dominate the population.

Researchers have proposed a number of well-known solutions to these puzzles. The most well-confirmed model appeals to inclusive fitness or kin selection (Hamilton, 1964). It is worth sacrificing one's own biological prospects to cooperate with genetically related conspecifics. This occurs because selectively helping those who carry one's own genes helps ensure that those genes are passed on, including the genes for helping one's genetic relatives. Such kin selection explains most cooperation observed among nonhuman species. It is why many species of insects include classes of individuals willing to sacrifice their lives for the "queen" (Cronin, 1991). It is also why mammalian mothers go to extraordinary lengths to provision and protect their offspring. However, it is obviously insufficient to account for human cooperation, which involves trusting and forgoing advantages for genetically unrelated, and often completely unfamiliar, individuals.

Proposed solutions to the puzzle of cooperation with genetically unrelated individuals appeal to various kinds of reciprocity. The simplest variety, direct reciprocity, involves keeping track of whether or not an individual has cooperated in previous interactions. Perhaps the most famous example of this kind of reciprocity comes from computer simulations of interacting agents (Axelrod, 1984). Simulated agents would play the "prisoner's dilemma"[13] game against each other in tournaments, accumulating points, depending on their record of victories and defeats. Although in a one-shot prisoner's dilemma the uncooperative agent always comes out on top, this is not necessarily the case in iterated versions. One of the most successful simulated agents implemented the so-called "tit for tat" strategy: when interacting with another agent for the first time, "tit for tat" always cooperates, but on subsequent interactions with that agent, "tit for tat" does whatever that agent did in the previous interaction: cooperates if it cooperated, defects if it defected. Such computer simulations show that cooperation can be rewarding if agents interact repeatedly with each other. However, it is generally acknowledged that keeping track of numerous interactants' histories of cooperation is too cognitively demanding to explain cooperation among unrelated individuals in hominid populations (Stevens & Hauser, 2004; Henrich, 2004; Stevens et al., 2005). Also, subsequent computer simulations show that "tit for tat" does not do well against more sophisticated though less cooperative strategies (Dugatkin, 1997).

In response to such problems with simple direct-reciprocity models of cooperation, more complex versions of reciprocity have been proposed. For example, in "indirect reciprocity," the population of interactants also speaks a language that can be used to report on particular individuals' reputations for cooperation (Nowak & Sigmund, 2005). Cooperation is motivated by the long-term advantages of gaining a reputation for cooperation. Even if one never interacts with a particular individual again, or if one cannot remember whether or not the individual cooperated in previous encounters, it is worth cooperating because the individual with whom one cooperates will then communicate one's reputation as a cooperator to other members of the population, making them more likely to cooperate with the original agent in the future. The problem with this proposal is that communicating reputation is itself a cooperative act (Henrich, 2004). What is to stop one's interactants from spreading false rumors about one's cooperative inclinations? So-called strong reciprocity is another model proposed to avoid the problems raised by direct and indirect reciprocity (Henrich, 2004). Strong reciprocity is the disposition not just to cooperate but to punish, at a cost to oneself, uncooperative behavior in others. This raises the costs of uncooperative behavior and reduces the relative costs of cooperative behavior (Sigmund, 2007). However, like indirect reciprocity, strong reciprocity presupposes a form of cooperation that it cannot therefore explain. The reason is that costly punishment is itself a cooperative act: one incurs the cost of punishing the uncooperative, thereby making life easier for cooperative individuals who do not punish (Henrich, 2004). Such "second-order free riders" would eventually drive strong reciprocators to extinction.

Thus the remarkable cooperativeness of human beings remains a recalcitrant puzzle. The various proposed solutions reviewed here have been significantly tweaked in recent years to avoid the obvious problems I have briefly reviewed. Chapter 4 looks at such models in greater detail and argues that ultimately, dispositions to shape minds and have our minds shaped to respect prosocial norms are central to explaining the evolution of human cooperation.

6   Complex Communication

The final component of the human sociocognitive syndrome is complex communication. Public language is, of course, the best example of this; however, there are others, for example, music, ritual, and dance. Other species communicate, and sometimes their communicative behaviors can be highly complex, for example, birdsong. But human communication stands out because it marries extremely complex structure with extremely flexible use. For example, the recursive syntax of human language can generate well-formed formulas of arbitrary complexity. At the same time, such arbitrarily complex structures express a generally systematic semantics. We can use language to encode messages about almost anything, including facts that are not perceptually salient, or indeed that could not be perceptually salient, like subatomic structure. Such general expressive capacity is nonetheless systematic. There is a finite set of strict rules for pairing semantics with expressions, allowing for the well-ordered construction of an infinite variety of messages.

These rules permit the combination of arbitrarily diverse contents into unified expressions. For example, human language meets Gareth Evans's "generality constraint" (1982): one can combine any subject with any predicate. This is why we can communicate metaphorical messages, like "Light is a wave," which play an important role not just in poetry and literature but in science as well. Even the structurally most sophisticated examples of nonhuman communication, like birdsong, are extremely impoverished in the variety of messages they can convey. Birdsong, for example, is used almost exclusively to advertise male fitness in the context of courtship displays (Fitch, 2004).

The attempt to explain how a communicative system as structurally complex and semantically flexible as human language evolved has had a notoriously controversial history. Few evolutionary puzzles have generated as great a diversity of underconfirmed just-so stories. The received view sees language as a tool for externalizing thought (Pinker & Bloom, 1990). According to this view, the thought of our nonlinguistic precursors already had the structural complexity and semantic flexibility of human language. At the same time, sharing such thought had potentially dramatic, positive effects on fitness. So human language evolved as an adaptation for sharing thought, inheriting its structural complexity and semantic flexibility from the thought it evolved to express. This intuitively compelling picture fits well with the received "mindreading as sociocognitive linchpin" theory. Language is seen as a tool selected primarily for enhanced mindreading: for helping individuals learn each other's thoughts, where these are understood as constituted independently of the linguistic means used to express them. Furthermore, language use presupposes already extremely sophisticated mindreading abilities, especially the capacity to recognize communicative intentions, including which belief a speaker intends to express. To put it succinctly, according to the orthodox understanding of language evolution, language evolved as a way of enhancing the kind of sophisticated mindreading that made it possible in the first place (Origgi & Sperber, 2000).

A variety of problems undercut this intuitively very compelling picture. Most obviously, it presupposes a solution to the problem of cooperation. Sharing one's thoughts is a cooperative act. An honest communicator shares information that can be used against her without receiving anything in return. How can a disposition for honest communication win out against deceptive strategies? Another, related problem is a version of the holism problem that arises for all forms of sophisticated mindreading. If interpreting another's utterances requires inferring her communicative intentions and, in particular, the beliefs she wants to express, how is this possible if any belief is compatible with any behavioral evidence, given appropriate modifications of background propositional attitudes? If another's utterances are supposed to be evidence of her beliefs, thereby enhancing mindreading, how is the problem of uncooperative or otherwise inappropriate background intentions, for example, intentions to deceive, mitigated?

Finally, evidence strongly suggests that the thought of our closest non-human relatives is not structurally complex and semantically flexible in the way that language is. The kinds of thoughts they have to communicate do not require a language as powerful as human language. There is reason, therefore, to conclude that our last common ancestor with them also lacked thought with the structure and semantic flexibility of human language. And it is difficult to imagine how such thought can have evolved between the time of the LCA and the origin of our own species, with, presumably, the capacity for acquiring human language. So how can this capacity have evolved as a tool for expressing such thought? In fact, as Chomsky and his heirs point out, most thoughts that humans need to communicate to gain biological advantage do not require such a complex and semantically flexible system of communication. Speakers of pidgins and other languages constructed on the fly by interactants who do not share a public language (what Klein & Perdue [1997] call the "basic variety") do very well in their pragmatic collaborations. So if language was selected for the communication of biologically significant information, why all the apparently excess capacity? If the thought of our prelinguistic precursors, like that of contemporary chimpanzees, lacked the structure and semantic flexibility of contemporary language, then why did a communicative system as structurally complex and semantically flexible as human language evolve?

As I argue in chapter 5, the key to resolving these puzzles is conceiving of language as a mindshaping device, rather than as a mindreading device. I stress the continuity between language and other structurally complex yet semantically less precise forms of human communication, like music, dance, and ritual. We have increasingly compelling evidence that music, dance, and ritual can play an extremely direct role in enhancing cooperation (Wiltermuth & Heath, 2009; Kirschner & Tomasello, 2010). They also play an obvious role in distinguishing group members from nonmembers. It is widely assumed that such between-group distinctions play an indispensable role in making group selection possible, and group selection is key to understanding the evolution of human cooperation. Music, dance, and ritual can function to increase within-group homogeneity and between-group differences. They do so by shaping the minds of participants to be more alike. Furthermore, such forms of communication do not presuppose the kind of structurally complex, flexible thought that mirrors contemporary human language.

Accordingly, music, dance, and ritual are ideally suited to play the role of a kind of "missing link" between contemporary human language and non-human communication systems. The structural analogies between music and other rhythmic behaviors and contemporary language are significant (Lerdahl & Jackendoff, 1996). Such affinities have led some to propose that song and dance are indeed precursors to full-blown human language (Darwin, 1871/1981; Okanoya, 2002; Mithen, 2006; Fitch, 2010). So a musical protolanguage, employed in ritual, can show how creatures incapable of thought that mirrors the structural complexity and semantic flexibility of contemporary language could nonetheless use complex communicative behaviors to shape each other in ways that enhanced cooperation and mutual interpretability. We can then conceive of contemporary language as a highly refined descendant of such early mindshaping, cooperation- and interpretation-enhancing communicative systems. For example, whereas our prelinguistic precursors could use only relatively imprecise rhythmic rituals to commit to vaguely defined social roles, we are now able to use language to commit to courses of behavior of arbitrarily precise specificity, for example, the role of a believer that p, where p stands for any declarative sentence expressible in language. We can then use language to share and read each other's thoughts because we use language to make commitments to behavior that constitute such thoughts.

This, in any case, is the picture I defend in chapters 5 and 7. Language is key to understanding sophisticated mindreading *not* because it evolved as a way of externalizing independently constituted thoughts that share its structure and semantics, like the propositional attitudes; rather, language makes possible sophisticated mindreading because it helps constitute such thoughts by enabling us to commit to behavior consistent with claims we make.

7   Two Pictures of the Evolution of Human Social Cognition

The view that I criticize is intuitively compelling. It is hard to explain how human beings manage to anticipate each other's behavior with the precision and reliability necessary to explain our cooperative and communicative feats, without assuming that we are extremely proficient mindreaders. In this picture, the first and most important evolutionary step in the direction of the human sociocognitive syndrome was the emergence of a population of natural psychologists of unparalleled skill. Before we could shape each other to be more cooperative, before we could communicate using a language of unmatched syntactic complexity and semantic flexibility, we must have been able to reliably infer, based on behavioral evidence, the propositional attitudes responsible for each other's behavior. After all, how can you shape people to be more cooperative and more communicative without first understanding what and how they think?

Despite its intuitive appeal, I think this picture is fundamentally wrong. Inferring another's propositional attitudes based on her behavior is a computationally intractable task, unless she has already been shaped to be cooperative and easily interpretable. Such shaping does not require prior mastery of human psychology. As with other evolved capacities, gradual and piecemeal accumulation of dispositions to mindshape that happened to work in the contingent ecological contexts in which our ancestors found themselves gave rise to more humanlike cooperative and communicative practices. Such gradual development did not require deep psychological insights. Instead, motivations to mindshape coupled with modestly enhanced versions of the intentional stance employed by contemporary chimpanzees were sufficient to give rise to complex cooperation and communication. These then made possible sophisticated mindreading by providing culturally shared frameworks that interactants used to shape their thoughts and behavior to be easily interpretable. That, in any case, is what I seek to establish in the chapters ahead.

2   The Varieties of Mindshaping

1   Mindshaping: Definition and Taxonomical Overview

Before defending a theory of the evolution of human social cognition in which mindshaping plays the central role, it is necessary to further clarify what mindshaping is. Mindshaping takes a variety of forms, including imitation, pedagogy, norm cognition and enforcement, and language-based regulative frameworks, like self- and group-constituting narratives. Many nonhuman species engage in rudimentary precursor forms of mindshaping as well. Given the variety of its forms, there is a risk that they have nothing interesting in common. Indeed, many of the phenomena I call "mindshaping" have been intensely studied in recent years, in isolation from each other, without any attempt to draw them together under a common rubric. This is a mistake. These phenomena have important properties in common, properties that are key to understanding how the human sociocognitive syndrome evolved. I begin this chapter with a definition of mindshaping, meant to capture its central properties, that is, those that explain its central role in the evolution of the human sociocognitive syndrome. The definition makes clear that human varieties of mindshaping have in common mechanisms for making human minds and behavior more homogeneous and hence easier to predict and interpret. The definition also accommodates the diversity of human mindshaping and its nonhuman precursors. In particular, the definition identifies variables that, later in the chapter, I use to taxonomize the different varieties of mindshaping, in ways that highlight their roles in human evolution.

Before formulating the definition, it is necessary to make clear some background assumptions. Given the agenda of this book, mindshaping, even its sophisticated, distinctively human varieties, cannot presuppose sophisticated mindreading. That is, it cannot presuppose the attribution of full-blown propositional attitudes; after all, it is supposed to explain how reliable, full-blown propositional attitude attribution is possible.[1] On the other hand, some characteristic of distinctively human mindshaping must explain why the human sociocognitive syndrome evolved only once, in our lineage. So the taxonomy I construct here must identify properties that set distinctively human mindshaping apart, and explain how it drove the evolution of the human sociocognitive syndrome. It is tempting to distinguish human from nonhuman mindshaping in terms of sophisticated mindreading; as noted in chapter 1, the received view that we are such accomplished mindshapers because our mindshaping is guided by accurate and sophisticated knowledge of each other's minds is extremely intuitive. However, we must resist this tempting view because, as I argue in chapter 3, it is based on a misguided assumption: that reliably accurate propositional attitude attribution is possible independently of sophisticated mindshaping practices that make interactants more easily interpretable to each other. So the trick in what follows is to show why distinctively human mindshaping is so special without assuming that it is guided by a sophisticated theory of mind. In subsequent sections, reviewing specific examples of distinctively human mindshaping, this will be a constant burden: I argue that none of these examples of mindshaping presuppose sophisticated, reliable propositional attitude attribution.[2]

In light of these worries, it is important to flag, from the start, two specific components of mindshaping, as understood here. These are (1) that it *aims*[3] at something, that is, shaping minds; and (2) that it requires *representing* that which it aims to accomplish, that is, shaping minds in a specific way. The idea that mindshaping aims at a goal or has a purpose or performs a function can be construed in ways that undermine the central thesis of the book: that sophisticated mindreading presupposes sophisticated mindshaping. The reason is that one way a process can come to aim at a goal is through conscious, deliberate guidance by a mind. But if that is how sophisticated, distinctively human mindshaping comes to have its goal, then it is hard to see how it does not presuppose sophisticated mindreading. How can someone aim to shape mind X without first having concepts of X's current state, the desired state of X, and the means by which the difference between these two states can be eliminated? Thus if mindshaping comes to aim at its goal as the result of deliberate guidance by a mind, it will need to employ sophisticated representations of minds and states of mind; such a conception of mindshaping risks undermining the project of this book.[4]

Fortunately, we have ways of understanding notions like "goal," "function," "purpose," "aim," and "representation" that do not presuppose sophisticated cognition. In the following, the goals, functions, purposes, or aims that help constitute mindshaping are understood *teleofunctionally*, that is, in terms of what the mechanisms associated with mindshaping were selected for in evolution. This understanding of purpose or function has been most thoroughly explored, elaborately formulated, and exhaustively defended in the work of Ruth Millikan (1984, 1993). Although there are legitimate worries that Millikan's notion of "proper function" cannot fully explain propositional attitude content (Zawidzki, 2003), such worries are tangential to the present project. Millikan's central notion of proper function—roughly, the properties for which a state or process was selected in evolution—is sufficient to underwrite *a* notion of goal, and *a* notion of representation, whether or not these notions do justice to the sophisticated kinds of thought of which adult humans are capable. For the purposes of this project, it is sufficient that Millikan has formulated and adequately defended notions of "goal" and "representation" that do *not* presuppose deliberate, conscious intentions or propositional form. Millikan's theory of function and representation is tailor-made for the sorts of low-level neural representations (like cognitive maps) and goals (like finding mates and prey) in terms of which I elucidate mindshaping. By adopting Millikan's approach, the definition of mindshaping can avoid presupposing sophisticated mindreading. Although this definition requires specifying the goals and representational states of certain mechanisms, these are not to be understood as presupposing conscious, deliberate reasoning about minds. Following Millikan, they will presuppose only that these mechanisms are products of natural selection for certain proper functions, guided by neural, maplike representations of relevant facts that constitute normal conditions on the performance of these functions (Millikan, 1984).

With these caveats in hand, it is now possible to define mindshaping as a relation among four relata: a model, a target, a mechanism, and a set of respects in which the target can match the model. Mindshaping occurs when a mechanism aims to make a target match, in relevant respects, a model. The target is always a mind, that is, the categorical basis for some set of behavioral dispositions that characterize an agent. The mechanism can be some pattern of activity in an individual brain, as in basic forms of imitation, where the target's own neurally based mechanisms function to bring about a match between target and model. However, it can also involve complex patterns of extraneural activity that include the behavior of multiple agents, as in pedagogy or guided imitation, where a teacher can help the target match the model. The model can be an individual agent, but it can also be something more abstract, like a possible pattern of activity, or even a purely fictional agent. The respects in which the mechanism aims for the target to match the model are properties of the model that the mechanism can represent or track.

Mindshaping has one further component: it must involve more than aiming at just a onetime behavioral match between some target and model. For example, many species of animals engage in deceptive behavior aimed at changing the behavior of a competitor, like a conspecific competing for food or a predator hunting for offspring. But such deceptive behavior by nonhuman species is never aimed at changing a behavioral disposition. The goal is just a onetime behavioral modification, for example, a mother bird distracting a predator from her nest, or a subordinate chimp distracting a dominant chimp away from a food cache. Such behavior should not count as mindshaping because no mind is being shaped: aiming at a onetime behavioral modification is different from aiming to shape a behavioral disposition. So a mindshaping mechanism is one that aims to make a target's *behavioral dispositions* match, in relevant respects, some model.

To state the definition formally, mechanism X mindshapes target Y to match model Z in relevant respects R, S, T, … , if and only if (1) effecting such matches is X's "proper function," in Millikan's (1984) sense; (2) X is performing its proper function, that is, causing Y to match Z in respect to R, S, T, … ; (3) Y is a mind, understood as a set of behavioral dispositions or the categorical basis for them; (4) X's performance of its proper function is guided by representations of R, S, T, … ; and (5) Z is or is somehow derived from an agent other than the agent to which Y belongs. Applying this to a particular case, consider imitation. In imitation, the mechanism (X) is a neural process in the imitator, selected in evolution for its role in making novices match expert behavior. The target of imitation (Y) is the imitator's own mind; that is the mind that imitation aims to shape. The model in imitation (Z) is an expert whom the imitator copies. The relevant respects (R, S, T, …) are, for example, the model behaviors that the imitator aims to copy. As explained hereafter, other varieties of mindshaping assign very different sorts of objects and processes to some of these variables. For example, in pedagogy, the mechanism (X) includes not just neural processes in the mindshaping target (i.e., the novice's mind) but also neural processes in teachers helping the target learn, as well as extraneural factors, like artifacts and institutions, selected (perhaps via cultural evolution) for their roles in assisting pedagogy. As will become clear, other examples of mindshaping assign more exotic objects to the role of model (Z): in some forms of norm internalization or narrative self-constitution, the model (Z) might be a "virtual" agent, like a fictional character or a normative ideal, the behavior of which the mindshaping mechanism (X) aims to get the target mind (Y) to match.

Before continuing, let me clarify the motivations for some of the clauses in the definition. Clause (3) is meant to rule out deceptive behavior common among nonhuman species, of the kind discussed earlier, on the grounds that deceptive behavior aims to match not a mind but a onetime behavior to a model. Clause (4) is meant to rule out certain examples of social learning common in nonhuman species that are not under cognitive control. For example, young rats can learn what to eat simply by developing a preference for odors that they smell on their mother's breath (Galef, Wigmore, et al., 1983). The mechanism appears to be simple, involving no representation of the feeding behavior that the young rats end up matching.[5] Certain odors that young rats happen to smell on their mother's breath just happen to be marked as desirable. Such mechanisms are too widespread in the animal kingdom and too unsophisticated to count as examples of the kind of mindshaping that can explain what is unique about human social cognition. Any mechanism that can help explain this should be at least minimally cognitive, that is, involve a representation of the respects in which it aims to match a target to a model. Otherwise, entirely noncognitive processes, like natural selection, would count as varieties of mindshaping, thereby diluting the usefulness of this notion.[6]

Finally, (5) ensures that mindshaping always has a social dimension. This is important because, without this clause, certain forms of individual learning, possibly widespread among mammals, would count as mindshaping, again diluting the usefulness of this notion relative to the project of explaining what is distinctive about human social cognition. For example, suppose some forms of individual learning work as follows: the learner imagines herself engaging in a new behavior and then tries, through practice, to match this model. It is important to distinguish between cases where the imagined new behavior is derived from another individual, giving the learning a social dimension, and cases where it is entirely the product of individual imagination. Given the work to which the notion of mindshaping is put hereafter, there must be a social dimension. Otherwise mindshaping could not work to homogenize populations, making their members more easily mutually interpretable.

Note that the definition does not make mindshaping dependent on mindreading. A mindshaping mechanism must function to match target to model in certain respects, and the mechanism must represent these respects. But the respects in which the mechanism functions to match target to model can be entirely behavioral; the goal can be to make the target disposed to behave in ways that match a pattern of behavior. There is no need to represent or track states of mind. Therefore this notion of mindshaping is minimal enough in its commitments to sociocognitive capacities to play the role I envision for it: as the basis for, rather than a product of, sophisticated mindreading.

The definition puts substantial constraints on mindshaping. Not just any mechanism that aims to modify behavior counts. However, the definition is also flexible enough to accommodate a wide variety of cognitive mechanisms. These can be distinguished from each other along several dimensions. The most obvious consists in the respects in which mindshaping mechanisms aim to match target to model. These can vary as widely as the model behaviors that a target can come to match. As explained hereafter, there are interesting differences among species in the *aspects* of model behaviors that mindshaping mechanisms can make targets match. For example, mindshaping mechanisms available in humans and other primates enable targets to match the goals of models, as well as certain abstract properties of model behavior, like recognizing computer screen icons independently of their location and selecting them in a specific sequence to obtain a reward (Subiaul et al., 2004). However, it appears that only human mindshaping mechanisms enable targets to routinely match the fine-grained bodily motions by which models accomplish their goals or implement their abstract behavioral competencies (Horner & Whiten, 2005; Nielsen & Tomaselli, 2010).[7] As I argue in chapters 4 and 5, this difference between the kinds of mindshaping we share and fail to share with nonhuman species provides an important clue to the evolution of the human sociocognitive syndrome.

Another important dimension along which mindshaping can vary consists in the identities of the model, target, and shaping mechanism. In basic imitation, a form of mindshaping of which some nonhuman species are capable, the shaping mechanism is part of the target's mind/brain, and the model is another individual; that is, the target mind shapes itself to conform to the model's behavior. In some distinctively human forms of imitation, like guided imitation, the shaping mechanism includes guidance from a teacher (Sterelny, 2012). Such socially distributed shaping mechanisms are even more apparent in pedagogy and other distinctively human forms of mindshaping. In such examples of mindshaping, the model can be a behavior of the teacher, but it can also be the behavior of a third party, or even of a fictional exemplar. Other variations are possible as well. In some cases of human mindshaping, the model can be a representation of a possible yet unobserved pattern of behavior on the part of some other individual, as when a Christian asks, "What would Jesus do?" Such examples suggest another dimension along which mindshaping varies: the model's ontological status. In the most widely studied examples of nonhuman mindshaping, like imitation and various approximations of it, the model is always an actual individual, usually a higher-status conspecific, like a parent. However, human mindshaping involves a much greater variety of models, including fictional characters, imagined patterns of behavior, and normatively ideal agents. Finally, the motivations driving mindshaping can be either extrinsic or intrinsic, and variation along this dimension is important to distinguishing between varieties of mindshaping that are distinctively human and those that are not. As I explain hereafter, only human varieties of mindshaping are intrinsically motivated; in other words, achieving a match between target and model is its own reward. In nonhuman varieties of mindshaping, motivation is always extrinsic: achieving a match between target and model is a means to some further end, like more efficient foraging.

Thus, in the following, I construct a taxonomy of naturally occurring varieties of mindshaping based on four dimensions: (1) the respects in which targets and models are made to match; (2) the identities of target, model, and mindshaping mechanism; (3) the ontological status of the model; and (4) whether the mindshaping is extrinsically or intrinsically motivated. No doubt mindshaping varies along other dimensions.[8] However, these four dimensions are particularly important to identifying what is distinctive about human mindshaping and explaining its central role in the evolution of the human sociocognitive syndrome.

The next three sections address three different clusters of closely related examples of mindshaping: (1) various kinds of imitation, some occurring in both human and nonhuman populations, and some restricted to our own species; (2) various examples of pedagogy and other forms of socially assisted learning; and (3) various mechanisms of conformism, including (i) automatic and unconscious conformist dispositions studied by social psychologists, like the "chameleon effect," (ii) norm cognition and enforcement, and (iii) the use of narratives and other linguistic devices in self- and group constitution. Each section briefly reviews pertinent empirical evidence and classifies the highlighted example of mindshaping in terms of the four dimensions discussed earlier. In addition, for each example of mindshaping, I suggest some plausible mechanisms for implementing it, arguing that it is independent of sophisticated mindreading and, especially, full-blown propositional attitude attribution.[9] The chapter's final section highlights the properties that distinguish exclusively human mindshaping from varieties we share with other species.

2   Human and Nonhuman Imitation

Imitation has been the most intensely studied variety of mindshaping in recent years, especially among comparative and developmental psychologists. The received view of imitation characterizes it as more than mere behavior matching. The focus has been imitative *learning*, where the target acquires a *novel* behavior from a model, rather than simply mimicking model behavior that is already in the target's repertoire (Thorndike, 1898; Tomasello & Call, 1997; Subiaul, 2007). However, the novel/familiar distinction is problematic. All familiar imitation is novel in some respects, if only in the context in which the model performs the imitated behavior. For example, if one bird learns from another that pecking at a green panel triggers access to food, the pecking is familiar, but the context—pecking at a green panel in the context of a new experimental apparatus—is novel. At the same time, even examples of novel imitation consist in behaviors comprising some components that are not novel to the imitator. For example, if a chimpanzee learns from another that poking a hole with a stick can help extract termites, it is likely that the act of poking with a stick is familiar. Some have argued that the novel/familiar distinction is phylogenetically significant, dividing species into advanced or primitive imitators based on whether or not they can copy only familiar behavior or novel behavior as well (Visalberghi & Fragaszy, 2002). However, given the slipperiness of the distinction between familiar and novel behavior, this line of argument is not promising.

Tomasello et al. (1993) propose a highly influential characterization of the distinction between human and nonhuman forms of social learning. They argue that only human beings are capable of *true* imitation, understood as matching not just the goal of a model's behavior but also the means by which the model accomplishes her goal. Whereas other species are capable of copying the goals of models or mimicking behavioral patterns without understanding the goals at which they aim, only human beings can understand behaviors as means aimed at goals and acquire both from models. The reason for this, Tomasello et al. (1993) argue, is that human beings are better mindreaders: they can track both the goals of others and the means by which they try to accomplish them, while nonhuman social learners cannot.[10] More recently, in response to growing experimental evidence, Tomasello has softened his stance on this. He now claims that chimpanzees can track some states of mind, like goals and perceptions (Call & Tomasello, 2008), and that they are capable of more elaborate forms of imitation than he had once supposed (Tomasello et al., 2005). However, he still argues that only humans are capable of "rational imitation," which requires appreciating that the means chosen by the model to secure a goal constitute a rational plan involving means–ends reasoning. He thinks the psychological basis for this difference is partly cognitive and partly motivational. Unlike chimpanzees, human beings are motivated to share mental states with each other, including goals and the detailed intended means for securing them. Furthermore, unlike chimpanzees, human beings can represent each other's detailed intended plans for securing a goal.

The view defended most recently by Tomasello and colleagues suggests that a uniquely human mindreading component distinguishes human imitation: representing another's detailed intended plan for securing some goal. However, even Tomasello is ambivalent on this claim. He admits that the behavioral evidence does not rule out that chimpanzees have similar mindreading capacities yet simply are not motivated to share mental states in the way that humans are (Tomasello et al., 2005, p. 690). Furthermore, evidence suggests that both chimpanzees (Call & Tomasello, 1998; Call et al., 2004) and autistic children (Aldridge et al., 2000; Carpenter et al., 2001) are capable of distinguishing intended from accidental behaviors. Since autistic children are widely assumed to be severely impaired in sophisticated mindreading (Baron-Cohen, 1995), it seems that an agent can be sensitive to the intentions of others without sophisticated mindreading competence. Finally, in a battery of tests of social and physical cognition performed on large numbers of human children, chimpanzees, and orangutans, Tomasello's Leipzig group discovered that chimpanzees are far more humanlike in their capacity to detect intentions than in their capacity for social learning (Herrmann et al., 2007).[11] These data suggest that the key difference between chimpanzees and humans is not cognitive but motivational: chimpanzee mindreading is roughly comparable to the mindreading of young human children, but young human children seem more motivated to use such capacities to learn from others.[12]

Work in developmental psychology is also ambivalent about the role of sophisticated mindreading in imitation. A series of classic studies shows that human children selectively imitate only intended behaviors, and not accidental ones (Meltzoff, 1988, 1995; Carpenter et al., 1998; Carpenter, Call et al., 2002; Gergely et al., 2002). In Meltzoff's original (1988) experiment, fourteen-month-old infants were shown an adult model performing a familiar task in a novel manner: turning on a "light box" by touching the box with her head rather than her hand. Infants imitated the head touch, though the goal was more easily achieved by means of a hand touch. Carpenter et al. (1998) had adult models mark intended and unintended behaviors verbally with the exclamations "There!" and "Whoops!" respectively. Children imitated only the behaviors marked as intentional. Gergely et al. (2002) report a particularly dramatic illustration of this effect. They redid Meltzoff's original head touch experiment with the following variation: some adult models touched the light box with their heads while their hands were otherwise occupied, and other adult models touched the light box with their heads while their hands were free. In the former case, infants responded by using their hands to touch the light box, but in the latter case they responded by using their heads. It appears that the infants understood that the hands-occupied models intended only to turn on the light and could not use their hands because they were otherwise occupied, so the infants copied turning on the light in the most efficient way available to them: a hand touch. In contrast, they understood that the hands-free models intended to use their heads, specifically, to turn on the light, so the infants copied this action.

It is important not to overestimate the degree of mindreading required by such sophisticated imitative behavior. Indeed, even Meltzoff (2005) cautions that "the 18-month-olds appreciate the goal-directedness of a human action (an unsuccessful attempt), but this does not mandate that infants ascribe the mature adult notion of intention as a first-person experience in the mind of the actor" (p. 63). And Gergely et al. (2002) interpret their results as showing only that infant imitators assume their models choose the most rational means to their ends. Thus when a model turns on the light box with her head while her hands are otherwise occupied, the goal must be to turn on the light box by whatever means are available. However, when the model turns on the light box with her head while her hands are free, the goal must be to turn on the light box with her head. But this need not imply any mindreading, understood as reasoning about the psychological processes driving the model's behavior. It might simply rely on a heuristic for parsing behavior in ways that make components of it that are worth learning salient (Csibra & Gergely, 2006, 2009). In fact, as noted in chapter 1, Gergely, Csibra, and colleagues explicitly invoke a heuristic akin to Dennett's intentional stance, which they call the "teleological stance": a framework for interpreting an agent's behavior guided by the assumption that the agent is rational (Gergely & Csibra, 2003). Such an interpretive framework is not meant as a model of psychological processes; it is a framework for interpreting *behavior*, not mindreading.

Finally, in all such experiments, the difference between intended and accidental behaviors must be *marked behaviorally*. For example, Carpenter et al. (1998) had adult models mark intended and unintended behaviors verbally with the exclamations "There!" and "Whoops!" respectively. There is a host of observable distinctions between intended and unintended behaviors, for example, eye direction, "effortful" facial expressions followed by "triumphant" versus "disappointed" facial expressions, and verbal or other vocal expressions of effort, success, and failure. Such behavioral signals may be sufficient for infants to classify acts in terms of their intended effects, without making the additional inference that these intended effects are internally represented by the adults they observe. Indeed, many theorists impressed with the recent literature on "mirror neurons"[13]—a plausible neurophysiological mechanism underlying both human and nonhuman imitative capacities—argue that the primordial sociocognitive capacity with which infants begin does not include the representation of the distinction between self and other (Hurley, 2005a; Gallese, 2005; Gordon, 2005). Actions are classified in a common representational format; that is, instead of attributing intentions to others (i.e., mindreading), infants observing adult actions simply classify them together with their own similar actions as acts aiming at specific goals. That human infants appear capable of imitative learning in a so-called ghost condition, in which a behavior is demonstrated not by a human model but simply by the automated motion of relevant objects, as though manipulated by a ghost (Thompson & Russell, 2004; Huang & Charman, 2005), suggests that they are indeed classifying behaviors by what they are supposed to achieve, rather than attributing hidden, mentally represented intentions to human models.[14]

Thus the distinction between human and nonhuman imitation does not seem to consist in guidance by more sophisticated mindreading. In what, then, does the distinction consist? We have considerable evidence that human imitation and nonhuman imitation differ primarily in (1) the aspects of model behavior that can be matched by an imitator, and (2) the motivations of the imitator. Most nonhuman imitation involves a target matching either only the goals of the model or some abstract properties of model behavior that remain constant across a variety of behavioral implementations (Subiaul, 2007). Also, nonhuman imitation is always extrinsically motivated: nonhuman species treat matching a model's behavior as a means to securing a further goal, like obtaining food, rather than as an end in itself (Zentall, 2006, p. 348). In contrast, human imitation is often intrinsically motivated; that is, behavioral matching is its own reward. Also, it often aims to match the detailed behavioral means by which models accomplish their goals or implement abstract cognitive capacities.

Many bird and primate species can learn, from observing models, to deploy familiar behaviors in new contexts to secure some highly valued goal, like food. For example, Japanese quail that observe a conspecific peck at an apparatus in a certain way to receive food are likely to replicate this behavior (Zentall, 2006). Another example of mindshaping that appears to be relatively widespread in nonhuman primates is "cognitive imitation" (Subiaul et al., 2004). Although rhesus macaques do not appear capable of acquiring fine-grained motor skills from observing a model, they can imitate more abstract aspects of a behavior. For example, they can learn, from observing another, the sequence in which qualitatively distinct computer screen icons must be touched to earn a food reward. In each trial, the icons appear in randomly selected locations on the screen, so what is acquired is not a fine-grained motor plan, as the sequence of hand motions required in each trial differs. In fact, rhesus macaques cannot learn from each other a comparable sequence of precise *locations*; they learn only sequences of qualitatively distinct icons, independently of their locations. For this reason, Subiaul et al. (2004) call this "cognitive" as opposed to "motor" imitation: what is acquired is an abstract sequence of qualitatively distinct behavioral targets, not a concrete sequence of behaviors. Nevertheless this counts as mindshaping, as defined earlier, because the imitator must represent the aspects of model behavior that she comes to match.

The capacity to imitate fine-grained sequences of behavior appears to be restricted to humans and nonhuman great apes. In an important study, Horner and Whiten (2005) compared young wild-born chimpanzee with three- to four-year-old human performance on learning to use a tool to retrieve a reward from a puzzle box. The subjects were tested in "opaque" and "transparent" conditions. In the opaque condition, the mechanism by which the tool retrieved the reward from the box was obscured. In the transparent condition, the mechanism was visible. In each case, a model demonstrated a two-step procedure, involving the tool, for retrieving the reward. However, the first step was irrelevant: it played no role in the mechanism by which the food was retrieved. In the opaque condition, this was not apparent, since subjects could not see the mechanism, and so they were expected to assume that the first, irrelevant step played a role in retrieving the reward. In the transparent condition, the fact that the first step was irrelevant was apparent. The results of the experiment are striking. In the opaque condition, both human children and young chimpanzees imitated the model's two-step procedure exactly. However, in the transparent condition, human and chimpanzee performance diverged dramatically. The chimpanzees immediately recognized the irrelevance of the first step and retrieved the reward in the most efficient way possible, using only the second step. But the human children continued to imitate the two-step sequence.

Thus although nonhuman great ape species are capable of matching the precise behavioral means by which a model secures a goal,[15] they do so only when there is no other, more efficient way of securing the goal. The contrast with human children is striking: even if a model behavior is shown to be irrelevant to securing a goal, human children copy it.[16] In fact, in another study, Nielsen and Tomaselli (2010) show that children compulsively "overimitate" adult models; that is, they replicate precise behavioral means to ends, even when explicitly told that these means are not necessary, and when the adult model is no longer present and hence provides no incentive like pleasing an authority figure. A natural interpretation of these data is that human children, unlike nonhuman primates, find matching model behaviors *intrinsically motivating*: unlike nonhuman primates, human children do not condition their fidelity on instrumental payoff. Thus human imitation differs from nonhuman imitation in at least two related respects: humans are far more prone to imitate the precise behavioral means by which models accomplish goals, and human imitation appears to be intrinsically motivated. Whereas some nonhuman primates are capable of relatively high-fidelity imitation when it is the only known way of securing a further goal, like a food reward, human children will imitate whether or not the imitated behavior is instrumentally necessary. If human children find matching model behavior intrinsically rewarding, it is not surprising that they tend, by default, to engage in much finer-grained behavioral imitation than nonhuman primate species that are not similarly motivated.

This brief review of the empirical literature on imitation suggests that this widely studied form of mindshaping fits nicely in the taxonomical scheme proposed earlier. In imitation, the targets are the imitator's mind or behavioral dispositions; the model is another concrete, nonfictional individual; the mechanism is some pattern of activity in the imitator's nervous system, possibly involving mirror neurons; and the respects in which the target is shaped to match the model correspond to properties of model behavior to which imitation mechanisms (e.g., mirror neurons) are sensitive. In nonhuman species, these tend to be the goals of the model behavior, or certain abstract properties of it, as in the "cognitive imitation" of which rhesus macaques are capable. In human beings, and much less frequently in nonhuman great ape species, the specific behavioral means by which goals are secured or cognitive capacities are implemented are also among the respects in which targets are made to match models. However, in human beings, especially children, such fine-grained imitation is the default, while in nonhuman great apes it is evident only when there is no other way of securing some goal. The motivation behind nonhuman imitation appears to be entirely extrinsic: imitation occurs only to the extent that it helps secure some further goal. In contrast, human imitation often appears to be intrinsically motivated: behaviors shown to have no instrumental significance are nonetheless imitated.

Finally, the many varieties of imitation, even the more sophisticated human varieties that are sensitive to the distinction between intended and unintended behavior, do not appear to presuppose sophisticated mindreading skills. Instead imitators appear attuned to certain behavioral markers that distinguish behaviors that are worth imitating from those that are not. Even chimpanzees and autistic children, with their impoverished mindreading skills, distinguish between intended and unintended behaviors; indeed, autistic children can selectively imitate intended behaviors (Carpenter, Pennington et al. 2002). Neural mirror mechanisms appear capable of effecting behavioral matches without attributing mental states to the model, let alone full-blown propositional attitudes. In short, the sizable and continually expanding literature on imitation is consistent with the basic thesis of this book: imitation is a kind of mindshaping that takes a distinctive form in the human species but does not presuppose sophisticated mindreading. It is therefore a good candidate for the palette of mindshaping phenomena that make possible the human sociocognitive syndrome.

3   Pedagogy and Other Forms of Socially Assisted Learning

Unlike imitation, pedagogy is a form of mindshaping in which the mechanism effecting matches between target and model includes the activity of agents other than the target. Our species appears to be the only one capable of such mindshaping (Tomasello et al., 1993; Premack & Premack, 1996; Csibra & Gergely, 2006, 2009).[17] Pedagogy comes in a variety of forms, and some kinds of socially assisted learning do not quite fit this category, like collaborative learning among peers, for example, in group projects among schoolchildren (Tomasello et al., 1993). The kind of pedagogy with which most contemporary human beings are familiar—formal, institutionalized training in preparation for entry into the workforce—is probably a relatively recent and atypical form of pedagogy.[18] As Sterelny (2012) argues, a better model for the kind of pedagogy that likely characterizes most historic human populations likens it to apprenticeship. Novices learn from masters in structured environments, largely by observing masters at work. Masters modify their activity in ways that make it easier to copy, employ simple language to draw novice attention to appropriate components of the skill they teach, and provide negative or positive feedback. But such instruction does not rely on formal, language-heavy methods, as in contemporary scholastic contexts.

Sterelny argues that such pedagogical contexts in human prehistory likely selected for better mindreading: masters who were more sensitive to their apprentices' cognitive deficits and dispositions were likely better at modifying their own activity in ways that made their skills easier to acquire (2007, p. 726; 2012, p. 145). Assuming that effective pedagogy improved the biological success of masters and apprentices, such selection pressures would produce better mindreaders. This idea appears to be in tension with the agenda of this book, since it suggests that at least one distinctively human form of mindshaping—pedagogy—depends on distinctively human forms of mindreading. However, the tension is only apparent. First, the sorts of mindreading that Sterelny argues improve pedagogy do not require the attribution of full-blown propositional attitudes. Such mindreading consists only in sensitivity to behavioral dispositions: a capacity to appreciate what novices are or are not able to *do*, and a capacity to learn what sorts of modifications of demonstrated behavior, and what sorts of positive or negative feedback, are most effective at altering novice dispositions in the direction of skill mastery (Csibra & Gergely, 2006). Second, even if the mindreading selected for in pedagogical contexts is distinctively human, it is an effect of, rather than a precondition for, mindshaping, for two reasons. First, the kind of mindreading that Sterelny has in mind is selected for only once pedagogy has become part of the human or protohuman social niche (Csibra & Gergely, 2006; Sterelny, 2012, p. 145). Thus distinctively human mindshaping drives distinctively human mindreading in evolution. Second, pedagogy can be adaptive only in the context of populations that are already cooperative. Otherwise, teachers risk jeopardizing the adaptive advantages of superior skills. Without cooperative practices, novices can use skills acquired from teachers against them, for example, by outcompeting them for scarce food resources. So, as Sterelny acknowledges, improved mindreading selected for its pedagogical benefits is possible only in populations that have already solved the problem of cooperation. But, as chapter 1 suggested and as chapter 4 will argue at length, cooperation is unlikely to evolve in populations without widespread, humanlike mindshaping practices. Finally, as a growing body of evidence in developmental psychology indicates, teachers are often surprisingly passive and unwitting partners in the "natural pedagogy" (Csibra & Gergely, 2009) that characterizes interactions between young infants and caretakers.

The view of imitation, pedagogy, and other forms of mindshaping I defend in no way implies that objects of mindshaping are passive tabulae rasae. On the contrary, strong evidence suggests that targets of mindshaping are active coparticipants in this process, in many cases the more important coparticipants. All human mindshaping requires the cooperation of complex cognitive mechanisms in its targets. This perspective is well illustrated in the recent work of the developmental psychologists György Gergely and Gergely Csibra. In a series of ingenious experiments, they have mounted a persuasive case that natural human pedagogy in early infancy is driven almost entirely by cognitive processes in infants, which take advantage of certain pedagogical cues that their caretakers often unwittingly emit. Csibra and Gergely (2006) interpret Gergely et al.'s (2002) version of the Meltzoff head touch experiment, described earlier, as showing that human infants automatically interpret such adult behavior as pedagogical. In particular, when an adult makes eye contact with an infant, the infant interprets this as a signal that what will follow is important, *new* information that she should retain. In the head touch experiment, when the model's hands are occupied, the new information is turning on the light by the most efficient means available; but when the model's hands are not occupied, the new information is turning on the light with one's forehead. Infants acquire this information after three brief exposures lasting a total of twenty seconds (Meltzoff, 1988) and retain it for a week, which further strengthens the hypothesis that they interpret such interactions as pedagogical, that is, as indicating something important and novel to be retained. This view is further supported by the fact that a majority of infants do not copy the same behavior if it is not preceded with eye contact (Gergely, 2011, p. 82). According to Csibra and Gergely (2006), this shows that infants interpret eye contact as an "ostensive" act, establishing that the adult intends to communicate important information imminently.

Topál et al. (2008) give another dramatic example of such default pedagogical expectations on the part of infants. They argue that such expectations explain the well-known "preservative error" observed in human infants. After retrieving an object multiple times from the same location in which an adult has placed it, ten-month-old infants cannot then retrieve it from a new, occluded location to which they observe the adult move the object. The standard explanation of this error appeals to an alleged inability to inhibit a routine response in the light of new information. However, Topál et al. (2008) show that the preservative error can largely be eliminated if the adult does not attempt to communicate ostensively with, or engage the attention of, the infant subject when placing the object in the original location. Topál et al. (2008, p. 1833) argue that infants interpret such attempts at ostensive communicative engagement as *instructions*: in such bouts of "natural pedagogy," infants assume that the adult is conveying "generalizable information about properties of the objects (toys or containers) for the infant to learn … communicative demonstration … generates a semantic (and potentially long-term) memory trace that biases infants to search at the old location when they no longer have access to the decayed memory trace of the current location" (p. 1833). Without the communicative demonstration accompanying placements of the object in the original location, infants are at chance when deciding whether to reach for the original or the new location, presumably because no long-term semantic memory trace is formed concerning the original location.

Csibra and Gergely (2006, 2009) review a host of other puzzling phenomena that are naturally explained by their "natural pedagogy" hypothesis: (1) infants attend selectively only to human faces in an upright position, although this is not the most typical orientation they experience in early life, for example, when breast-feeding; (2) infant preferences for facelike stimuli are extinguished when the contrast polarity is reversed from black on white (as in dark pupils against the white sclera of the eyes) to white on black; (3) infants follow adult gaze only when it is preceded by eye contact; (4) infants follow gaze to the first object that intersects the line of sight, though they tend to be hopelessly inaccurate at identifying the object of the adult's attention without help; (5) even neonates attend preferentially to stimuli that are contingent on their own behavior, for example, as when adults mimic the turn-taking structure of conversation in suspending their infant-directed activity until infant activity stops, a phenomenon called "protoconversation" (Trevarthen, 1998); and (6) mothers in a variety of cultures automatically modulate their vocalizations in distinctive ways that seem to capture infant attention better than normal adult vocalization, a phenomenon called "motherese." Csibra and Gergely interpret all such phenomena as functioning to facilitate pedagogical interactions, which, according to Csibra (2010), have a three-part structure: ostensive signals like eye contact signal that the adult intends to communicate information; referential signals, like shifts in gaze, signal the object about which the adult intends to impart new information; and a relevance assumption helps the infant extract the novel information that the adult intends to impart, for example, that a light box can be turned on with one's forehead. According to Csibra and Gergely, infants are innately predisposed to interpret interactions with adults in such ways.

Csibra and Gergely (2006, p. 270) explicitly deny that such pedagogical assumptions involve sophisticated mindreading on the part of the infant. According to them, infants are born expecting adults to be cooperative and omniscient sources of valuable information, not minds with their own subjective perspectives on the world (ibid.). The communicative intentions to which infants must be sensitive are not full-blown propositional attitudes of the kind attributed in sophisticated mindreading, because their relations to behavior are not holistically mediated: they have very reliable connections to very narrow classes of observable behavior. Otherwise there would be no way that computationally frugal sociocognitive mechanisms, of the kind infants likely employ in bouts of natural pedagogy, could arrive at reliable interpretations. In fact, if Csibra and Gergely are right about the evolutionary importance of natural pedagogy, it is likely that ostensive signals like eye contact have evolved to be reliable indicators of pedagogy-enabling communicative intentions. If this is the case, then ostensive and referential signals can reliably signal future behavior without requiring the attribution of the propositional attitudes that they express. And this seems to be the case in natural pedagogy: infants need only associate certain highly distinctive observable behaviors (e.g., lingering eye contact contingent on infant reciprocation followed by shifts in gaze to salient objects) with the future behavior that they reliably indicate, that is, demonstration of relevant, generalizable, novel information. If infants are merely attuned to reliable behavioral patterns, rather than engaged in sophisticated mindreading, then this explains the fact that they interpret all such adult behavior as pedagogical, even when adults do not intend it this way, as in Topál et al.'s (2008) explanation of the preservative error.

Csibra and Gergely do argue that adult models must engage in mindreading and metacognition to accurately gauge what infants do not know and compare it to what they do know (2006, pp. 260–261). However, as I argued earlier in response to an analogous point made by Sterelny (2007, p. 726; 2012, p. 145), even if such distinctively human mindreading enhances pedagogy, it is an evolved response to already established pedagogical practices in the socioecological niche, and it seems to involve nothing more than a sensitivity to relevant behavioral dispositions rather than propositional attitudes. So it is not an embarrassment to the mindshaping-as-linchpin view. Furthermore, many of the results on which Csibra and Gergely draw belie their assumption that adults need to be good mindreaders to be good teachers. Adults might make eye contact with infants simply because adults find this rewarding, and because they automatically treat infants as mature communicative partners without taking their immature perspective into account. The adult models in the preservative error experiment do not take themselves to be imparting new information that they know infants have not yet mastered, thanks to sophisticated mindreading. Establishing eye contact is just a means to get the infant's attention. As Mameli (2001) notes in his pioneering discussion of mindshaping, adults might simply treat infants as mature communicators by default, despite evidence to the contrary, with this assumption gradually becoming a self-fulfilling prophecy.[19] If infants are born disposed to treat behavior that is typical of adult communication—for example, eye contact, gaze shifts to objects of interest, and turn taking—as pedagogical, whether or not adults conceive of it that way, infants will be able to exploit such behavior to learn important information from adult caretakers. It is likely that adults engage infants in modulated versions of typical adult communicative interactions, and infants have evolved to interpret signals that characterize such interactions as pedagogical, that is, as indicating that novel information worth retaining will follow.

Besides such low-level pedagogy that characterizes interaction with very young infants, more sophisticated varieties of pedagogy become available as human children mature. Drawing on the Vygotskyan tradition (1962), Tomasello, Kruger, and Ratner (1993) argue that adults act as "cognitive scaffolds" for their offspring, engaging in interactions that children then internalize and use to regulate their own behavior. This may start with the kinds of basic interactions on which Sterelny (2012) and Csibra and Gergely (2006, 2009) focus, and then, as the child acquires linguistic competence, graduate to full-blown instructed learning of the kind highlighted by Tomasello, Kruger, and Ratner (1993). Vygotskyans see such socially distributed pedagogical interactions as "zones of proximal development" in which novices can accomplish tasks that they cannot yet accomplish alone. Cognitive development consists in the gradual internalization of such initially social activity. The evidence strongly suggests that children who engage in self-directed speech gleaned from such interactions while solving tasks on their own are more successful (Diaz & Berk, 1992). Tomasello, Kruger, and Ratner (1993, pp. 500–502) also note such a dynamic in interactions among school-aged peers. Here the zone of proximal development is collaborative problem solving by groups of children without an adult teacher. Remarkably, such collaborations often enable solutions to cognitive tasks of which none of the children are capable on their own (ibid.). Once such socially mediated solutions are experienced, children proceed to internalize the dialogic interactions that make them possible, and learn to solve the problems on their own. Although calling such collaborative learning "pedagogical" may be a stretch, since no teacher is involved, it does constitute a kind of mindshaping in which the mechanism is socially distributed, as with pedagogy.

These verbally mediated forms of socially distributed mindshaping are considerably more sophisticated than the natural pedagogy on which Csibra and Gergely (2006, 2009) focus. It is thus tempting to argue that they require sophisticated, distinctively human mindreading, and perhaps even full-blown propositional attitude attribution.[20] However, there are reasons to resist this temptation. First, though in the minority, a number of theorists argue that such language-mediated interactions, and, in particular, the processing of narratives, are preconditions for sophisticated mindreading (Clark, 1998; Nelson, 2007; Hutto, 2008; Astington, 1990; Astington & Jenkins, 1999; de Villiers & de Villiers, 2000; Bermúdez, 2003a, 2009). Second, although acquiring linguistic competence requires sensitivity to communicative and referential intentions (Bloom, 2000), there is no need to conceive of such capacities in terms of sophisticated propositional attitude attribution. As we saw in the discussion of the selective imitation of intended behavior, chimpanzees and autistic children, neither of which are capable of sophisticated mindreading, can nonetheless distinguish intended from unintended behavior. Furthermore, autistic children selectively imitate intended behavior (Carpenter, Pennington, et al. 2002). And if Csibra and Gergely (2006) are right, such capacities do not require reasoning about models' mental states but rely on built-in assumptions concerning the significance of ostensive signals like eye contact, referential signals like shifts in gaze, and judgments of relevance based on a rationality assumption. Competence at linguistic communication might likewise require little more than such basic capacities to parse behavior. I address this issue in more detail in chapters 5 and 6, which focus on the roles of mindshaping and mindreading in the phylogeny and ontogeny of human linguistic competence. For now, I note only that many theorists argue that linguistic competence makes possible, rather than presupposes, sophisticated mindreading like propositional attitude attribution.

Where, then, do the various kinds of pedagogy fall in the mindshaping taxonomy? The diverse assortment of pedagogical behaviors we have just reviewed ranges from infants taking advantage of adults' communicative signals, to adults modulating their skillful behavior in ways that make it easier to acquire, to adults providing explicit instruction and other cognitive scaffolds that enable children to solve tasks they cannot solve alone until they internalize such scaffolds, to peers collaborating on problems they cannot solve alone until they internalize such collaborations. In all these examples of pedagogy, the target is the novice's mind, and the mechanism is socially distributed: it involves both dedicated neural mechanisms in the target and certain patterns of behavior on the part of those from whom the target is acquiring new information. The model is usually a pattern of behavior in which the target's teachers engage. In early infant "natural pedagogy," it is whatever novel behavior a teacher performs immediately after engaging the infant's attention with an ostensive signal like eye contact. In more sophisticated forms of pedagogy, it may include instructions, together with the behaviors that execute them, that characterize the target's zone of proximal development, and that the target eventually internalizes.

There appears to be a great deal of flexibility regarding the respects in which pedagogy can make a target match a model. Infants seem to focus on whatever novel, generalizable behavior follows ostensive and referential signals, including completely outlandish acts like turning on a light with one's forehead. In the kind of guided apprenticeship highlighted by Sterelny, novices can learn whatever masters make appropriately salient. Vygotskyan internalization seems similarly flexible: whatever instructions and behaviors contribute to socially mediated solutions to some problem can eventually be internalized. As for the model's ontological status, typically in pedagogy the target acquires the behavior of one or more actual, concrete individuals, not of a fictional character or normative idealization. The motivation to engage in pedagogical interactions appears intrinsic: infants appear to find acquiring new information in this way rewarding in itself, not because of its utility relative to other ends.

In many respects, therefore, pedagogy is a lot like distinctively human imitation: intrinsically motivating, shaping the target to match the behavior of a concrete, nonfictional model, and highly flexible in which respects the model behavior is matched. The key difference is that the mechanism of pedagogy is socially distributed. If Csibra and Gergely (2006, 2009) are right, pedagogy's most important component is in the mind/brain of the target; however, the models play crucial roles as well, engaging and directing the target's attention, modulating their behavior to make it easier to acquire, for example, by speaking in "motherese," and otherwise scaffolding their targets' learning environments, for example, through verbal instructions.

4   Mechanisms of Conformity in Human Populations

As I argue in chapter 4, making human groups more homogeneous is crucial to the sorts of cooperative and coordinative feats that are distinctive of human and protohuman socioecology. Also, as I argue in chapter 3, homogeneity can improve the reliability of fast and frugal social cognition. Mechanisms of conformity capable of imposing such homogeneity on human populations are similar, in some respects, to the kinds of distinctively human imitation and pedagogy I have already discussed. As with any mindshaping, they aim to effect matches between targets and models in certain respects. However, mechanisms of conformity differ from imitation and pedagogy in a crucial respect. The latter two forms of mindshaping have a variety of adaptive, nonsocial effects, for example, rapid acquisition of tool use or foraging expertise. Mechanisms of conformity do not necessarily have such adaptive, *nonsocial* by-products; their entire raison d'être is to maintain the kind of social homogeneity on which, as I argue in chapters 3 and 4, effective, sophisticated mindreading, cooperation, and coordination rely. I focus on three different kinds of conformist mechanisms: (i) low-level, unconscious, and automatic matching behavior like the "chameleon effect" (Chartrand & Bargh, 1999); (ii) norm cognition and enforcement;[21] and (iii) the regulative use of language, for example, narrative and law, in group and self-constitution. Although these mechanisms differ dramatically along several dimensions, their basic aim is the same: to ensure conformity and homogeneity among members of human groups.

(i) Unconscious, Automatic Behavioral Conformity

A series of powerful yet counterintuitive experimental results in social psychology suggests that, while interacting with each other, human beings automatically, unintentionally, and unconsciously match each other's nonfunctional behaviors. Such matching behaviors include postures, mannerisms, gestures, facial expressions, and accents. In a typical experiment illustrating such phenomena, a subject is asked to interact with a confederate of the experimenter on some routine task. The confederate deliberately engages in certain behaviors, and the experimenter measures the likelihood that the subject will also engage in these behaviors. For example, in one of Chartrand and Bargh's (1999) classic studies of the so-called chameleon effect, subjects interacted with two different confederates in two separate, consecutive, ten-minute tasks in which the subject and confederate collaborated on describing a photograph. During the collaborations, each confederate engaged in different nonfunctional behaviors: for example, shaking her foot, rubbing her face, or smiling. Subjects were significantly more likely to engage in such nonfunctional behaviors when confederates engaged in them than when they did not. No evidence indicated that subjects were aware of such mimicry. Chartrand and Bargh term such phenomena the "chameleon effect" because they are entirely unconscious and automatic matching responses to social circumstances, analogous to a chameleon's automatic chromatic matching response to the surface on which it finds itself.

Such matching responses are not restricted to ongoing, observable model behavior. Bargh et al. (1996) found that priming subjects with stereotypes can elicit behavior that matches the stereotype. For example, subjects primed with words connoting rudeness versus politeness in ostensibly unrelated tasks were more likely to behave in ways that conformed to these character traits: when primed with words connoting rudeness, they were more likely to interrupt conversations than a baseline control, while the opposite was true when primed with words connoting politeness. In a second experiment, Bargh et al. (1996) found similar effects when subjects were primed with stereotypes of the elderly using words like "Florida," "sentimental," and "wrinkle": though none of the primes connoted slowness or weakness, subjects walked more slowly down the hallway after leaving the experiment than they did when primed with words connoting no stereotype. Dijksterhuis and van Knippenberg (1998) showed that even cognitive performance can be affected by such primes: subjects primed with traits or stereotypes connoting intelligence versus stupidity performed differently on a subsequent general knowledge task, analogous to the game Trivial Pursuit. When primed with positive traits like "intelligent" or stereotypes like "professor," subjects performed better than they did without the prime. When primed with negative traits like "stupid" or stereotypes like "soccer hooligan," subjects performed worse than they did without the prime.[22]

Such phenomena provide clear examples of mindshaping that is independent of sophisticated mindreading.[23] Chartrand and Bargh (1999) argue that the mechanism that implements the chameleon effect involves a direct perception-behavior link, with no mediating processing: merely observing a behavior in another primes performance of the same behavior. They relate this idea to a tradition derived from William James's principle of "ideomotor action" (1890), according to which merely thinking of a behavior makes it more likely that the thinker will engage in it. Numerous theorists have since pursued this basic idea, arguing that it results from a principle of "common coding" (Lashley, 1951), according to which the brain uses the same representational resources in perceiving and interpreting behavior and in producing behavior. Lashley uses the common coding principle to explain the rapid acquisition of both receptive and productive language competence in children. Prinz (1990) generalizes Lashley's idea to all behavior, arguing that the same coding system is used for perceiving a behavior in others as for producing that behavior. Prinz reasons that this common code cannot be used simultaneously in the service of perception and behavior, and this idea has some experimental support (Müsseler & Hommel, 1997). Some theorists have argued that mirror neurons are the neural basis for the common coding model (Rizzolatti & Arbib, 1998; Hurley & Chater, 2005).

The chameleon effect occupies an interesting position in the mind-shaping taxonomy proposed earlier. Although unconscious, automatic, and unintentional, and hence arguably not as "high level" as some forms of imitation and pedagogy, in other respects it is extremely flexible. For example, while in most examples of imitation or pedagogy the model is typically a concrete individual, in the chameleon effect, the model can be an abstract stereotype. The chameleon effect in human beings also seems dramatically more flexible than imitative learning in nonhuman species. It can involve matching the fine-grained details of a wide variety of behaviors, not just goals or abstract routines, as in most nonhuman imitation. The mechanisms involved are clearly restricted to the target's brain, involving mirror neurons or other "ideomotor" or "common coding" resources. It is difficult to determine the motivations driving the chameleon effect because the behavior is automatic and unconscious. Individuals who do not even acknowledge matching the behavior of a model can hardly be queried about their motivations for doing so. However, evidence suggests that the function of such behavior is a kind of "social bonding." Chartrand and Bargh (1999) argue that the chameleon effect acts "as a kind of natural 'social glue' that produces empathic understanding and even greater liking between people, without their having to intend or try to have this happen" (p. 897).

The chameleon effect provides a particularly significant source of empirical support for the mindshaping-as-linchpin view. It enables sophisticated behavior matching that appears to be distinctive of human beings. However, the matching involves an automatic, unconscious perception-behavior link with no apparent need for mindreading of any kind. The mechanisms underlying the chameleon effect are hypothesized to involve the common coding of behavioral interpretation and behavioral regulation: the same representations are used both to interpret the behavior we see in others and to direct our own behavior. This is central to the notion of mindshaping at work in this book: because our interpretive frameworks are simultaneously regulative frameworks, fast and frugal behavioral interpretation has a greater chance of being reliable. Our interpretations of how we and others act are simultaneously instructions for how we and others are supposed to act, and this keeps our behavior in line with our interpretive expectations. Finally, as I discuss at greater length in chapter 4, evidence indicates that the evolutionary raison d'être of the chameleon effect is the facilitation of coordination and cooperation: people who mimic each other's nonfunctional, fine-grained behaviors, for example, walking in rhythm, tend to trust each other more (Wiltermuth & Heath, 2009; Kirschner & Tomasello, 2010).[24]

(ii) Norm Cognition and Enforcement

Social scientists from a variety of fields, ranging from anthropology to sociology to economics, have long appreciated the role that norms can play in making possible cooperation and coordination in human populations (Boyd & Richerson, 1985; Richerson & Boyd, 2005; Henrich, 2004; Henrich & Henrich, 2007). Chapter 4 addresses this literature in more detail, focusing on mathematical models that suggest that the willingness to incur a cost to punish counternormative behavior can play a central role in promoting within-group homogeneity necessary for group selection for cooperative dispositions. Recently this theoretical framework has received some empirical support from two sources. First, in cross-cultural experimental studies involving economic games played for real money, anthropologists have discovered that members of diverse cultures are willing to pay a monetary cost to punish counternormative behavior (Henrich et al., 2005, 2006). Second, developmental psychologists are documenting the remarkably early developing normative sensibilities of human children (Rakoczy et al., 2008a, 2008b; Rakoczy & Tomasello, 2009). Such data have recently been integrated into a general framework for understanding human normativity as a natural phenomenon (Sripada & Stich, 2006).

Henrich et al. (2005, 2006) conducted behavioral experiments focused on the "ultimatum game" in fifteen small-scale societies. The ultimatum game involves two players and has the following payoff structure. One player is given a sum of money and must propose a distribution of this sum with the second player. The second player can choose to accept or reject the first player's proposal. If the proposal is accepted, the money is distributed in the way that the proposal specifies. If the proposal is rejected, neither player gets any money. If all that human beings care for is money, then the second player should accept any offer greater than zero, no matter how small. The reason is that rejecting an offer leaves both players with nothing, and any positive sum is better than nothing. However, this is never observed in any culture. Although the fifteen cultures studied by Henrich et al. (2005, 2006) vary widely in the distributions that players routinely accept, no subject from any of these cultures accepted the smallest possible offer.

These experimental results are noteworthy for several reasons. First, in the experiments, interactions between players are one-shot and anonymous. This means that players need not fear that their behavior during one interaction will have repercussions on later interactions. So the kind of motive that drives "direct reciprocity" models of cooperation, discussed in chapter 1, that is, worry about future interactions with individuals one has slighted, cannot explain this behavior. Second, because they reject minimal offers and, as a result, receive no money, players are willing to incur a monetary cost to "punish" proposed distributions that are counternormative. In fact, minimal offers are rarely made because players who propose distributions know that counternormative ones are likely to result in such punishment (Henrich et al., 2010, p. 1481). Thus we have strong empirical evidence that human beings across a variety of cultures are willing to incur costs to enforce certain norms of resource distribution. This is predicted by influential models of the evolution of cooperation, which claim that such costly punishment is necessary for the kind of intragroup homogeneity that makes group selection for prosocial behavioral dispositions possible (Henrich, 2004).[25]

Developmental psychologists have charted the course of development of these sorts of normative attitudes in children. A recent study shows that (1) 8.5-month-old infants selectively prefer characters who act positively toward prosocial individuals and negatively toward antisocial individuals, and (2) young toddlers act positively toward prosocial others and negatively toward antisocial others (Hamlin et al., 2011). Numerous other studies suggest that children show sensitivity to norms and dispositions to punish counternormative behavior from as young as three years (Rakoczy et al., 2008a, 2008b). These behaviors have universal and culturally specific components. Every psychologically normal human being acquires the norms of her culture (Sripada & Stich, 2006). In addition, human beings of all cultures see norms as intrinsically motivating; that is, they are motivated to conform to norms not as means to further ends but as ends in themselves (Sripada & Stich, 2006). Children of every culture react to counternormative behavior with punitive emotions like anger (Sripada & Stich, 2006; Edwards, 1987). These assumptions about norms do not need to be taught; once a child acquires a norm from her culture, she automatically reacts to violations of it with punitive emotions and behavior, and she automatically treats it as intrinsically motivating. However, substantial variation exists in the content of the norms that children can acquire. For example,

Sripada and Stich (2006) document significant variation even in norms that are often taken to be universal, like incest taboos.[26]

Their intrinsic motivating force is the key feature of human norms. Human beings are motivated to comply with norms and to punish non-compliance not as instrumental means to further ends but as ends in themselves. Sripada and Stich are careful to note that actual cases of norm compliance or punishment may have mixed motives: one might find a behavior both intrinsically motivating and, coincidentally, instrumental to other ends. However, the evidence strongly suggests "that humans display an independent intrinsic source of motivation for norm compliance [and punishment of noncompliance], and thus that people are motivated to comply with norms *over and above (and to a substantial degree over and above)*, what would be predicted from instrumental reasons alone" (Sripada & Stich, 2006, p. 285). Evidence comes from studies of game behavior, like the one described earlier, in which subjects respect resource distribution norms though they gain no personal benefit, as the games are onetime interactions between anonymous individuals. Sripada and Stich (2006) also cite evidence that people typically "internalize" the norms of their culture, leading to "a lifelong pattern of highly reliable compliance" (pp. 285–286), independent of coercion or even the threat of coercion. Compliance with such internalized norms might be an effect of moral emotions like guilt and shame (Frank, 1988; Tomasello, 2009, pp. 42–43; Chang et al., 2011). The punishment of noncompliance also seems intrinsically motivated. First, punishment is inherently risky, since the object of punishment might retaliate; so knee-jerk dispositions to punish can jeopardize other goals, suggesting that motivation to punish is intrinsic rather than instrumental. Second, the anthropological literature suggests that punitive emotions, like anger and outrage, as well as punitive behavior, like ostracism, gossip, and sometimes physical violence, are cultural universals (Boehm, 1999). This suggests that human beings are innately predisposed to emotion-mediated, intrinsically motivated punishment of counternormative behaviors.

Following Sripada and Stich (2006), I have focused primarily on moral norms. But, as Carruthers (2006, pp. 261–263) points out, the capacity to internalize epistemic and semantic norms is also important to, and distinctive of, human social cognition. Such norms are particularly relevant to the distinction between System 1 and System 2 processing: human reasoning is sometimes unconscious, rapid, automatic, and based on relatively immutable and largely innate mechanisms (System 1); but it can also be conscious, deliberate, slow, and based on culturally acquired epistemic norms (System 2) (Stanovich, 1999; Kahneman, 2011).[27] It is possible that the culturally acquired epistemic norms that drive System 2 reasoning are acquired, stored, and executed using mechanisms similar to those Sripada and Stich propose for moral norms (Carruthers, 2006, p. 261). Carruthers also notes an important feature of the human norms system: it treats norms as simultaneously intrinsically motivating and truth evaluable (p. 204). More typical motivational states, like desires, cannot be evaluated for truth, nor can they contribute to truth-preserving inferences. The desire that I eat chocolate can be neither true nor false, and it cannot serve as a premise in a theoretical inference. However, the norm that lying should be avoided can be true or false and can serve as a premise in a theoretical inference. According to Carruthers, this unique property of norms—that they can be both intrinsically motivating and truth assessable—is key to understanding distinctively human cognitive flexibility. Unlike nonhuman species, we can acquire entirely novel, intrinsic motivations based on theoretical inferences to normative claims. A lion could never reason itself to vegetarianism, but human beings can because norms—such as an injunction against meat eating—can be both intrinsically motivating and justified by theoretical, truth-preserving inferences.

Given this broad overview of human norm cognition and enforcement, where do such phenomena fall in the mindshaping taxonomy? Like pedagogy, norm cognition involves both mindshaping mechanisms at work within the brains of shaping targets, and socially distributed mechanisms, like moral pedagogy or punishment. Unlike pedagogy and other forms of mindshaping I have discussed, the models to which such mechanisms match targets are typically not concrete individuals. This is because normatively ideal human beings are extremely rare. As Stich (1993) suggests, the models are often fictional figures, such as characters in parables.[28] Thus we can distinguish norm-based mindshaping from other varieties by the ontological status of its models: they tend to be virtual rather than real. In the dimension of motivation, norm-based mindshaping is clearly intrinsically motivated. Finally, norm-based mindshaping can make targets match models in an indefinite variety of respects. Norms govern almost every aspect of human behavior.

As with sophisticated, language-based pedagogy, it is tempting to assume that norm-based mindshaping presupposes sophisticated mindreading. Evidence suggests that punishment of counternormative behavior is sensitive to the intentions with which the behavior is performed (Cooper et al., 2010). However, as with the communicative intentions on which Csibra and Gergely's (2006, 2009) "natural pedagogy" relies, there is no need to conceive of such sensitivity to intentions as the attribution of sophisticated propositional attitudes. Reliable behavioral signals of intention can be a sufficient basis for making normative judgments, without attributing full-blown propositional attitudes to norm transgressors. Furthermore, when it comes to acquiring and internalizing norms and then complying with them, there is no apparent need for propositional attitude attribution.[29] Norm-based mindshaping aims to match a target's dispositions to the *behavior* of a (typically virtual) model.

(iii) The Regulative Use of Language

Numerous theorists stress the importance of language-based narrative in the acquisition of sociocognitive competence by human children (Sterelny, 2003, p. 222; Nelson, 2007; Hutto, 2008). The focus of such views is restricted to the role of narrative in facilitating the acquisition of mind-reading competence. For example, according to Hutto (2008), to learn how to attribute propositional attitudes, children need exposure to narratives that make salient the way circumstances can give rise to specific propositional attitudes in persons who witness them, and the way different propositional attitudes conspire with each other, and with other properties of persons, like personality, to yield behavior. Although this use of narrative to facilitate the acquisition of sociocognitive competence clearly counts as an example of mindshaping—in particular, pedagogy—I think an exclusive focus on it seriously understates the mindshaping role of language-based narrative. In particular, such views ignore the important role that narrative plays in self-regulation.

Any view that neglects the role of narrative in self-regulation[30] leaves mysterious the reliability of timely propositional attitude attribution. As I argue in chapter 3, there is bound to be tremendous variability among individuals in the sorts of propositional attitudes that similar circumstances activate, and in the sorts of behaviors to which similar propositional attitudes lead. How can exposure to generic narratives in childhood equip us with a fast, frugal, and reliable folk psychology in the face of such variation? The key to answering this question is to recognize a second role for narrative in the shaping of young minds. Narratives do more than merely equip us with generic knowledge of folk psychology; narratives help constitute the minds that such knowledge enables us to track. They do this because they perform a crucial regulative role in human psychology. Human beings, from childhood through adulthood, actively regulate their own behavior so that it conforms to the normative requirements of self-constituting narratives (McGeer, 2001, 2007). This phenomenon can explain how exposure to narratives in childhood can play a role in making possible reliable and timely behavioral interpretation. When children of a culture master the narratives that it affords, what they learn are systems of self-regulation that prevail in that culture (Sterelny, 2012, p. 163). Because children of the same culture are exposed to the same narratives, the problem of individual variation is mitigated. Since everyone masters the same small class of narrative types, and everyone uses at least some of these narrative types to regulate his or her own behavior, the kind of homogeneity on which, as I argue in chapter 3, reliable and timely behavioral interpretation depends comes along for free. The psychological phenomena for which exposure to narratives prepares us are partly constituted by those narratives, due to their role in self-regulation. It is therefore unsurprising that folk psychological competence scaffolded in development through exposure to narratives afforded by a child's culture makes possible reliable and timely behavioral interpretation.[31]

The notion that the human self is constituted by a self-regulating narrative has grown in influence in recent years (Flanagan, 1991; Dennett, 1991a, 1992; Fivush, 1994; Velleman, 2000; Ross, 2007; Tekin, 2011). Dennett's (1991a, 1992) basic idea is that the linear, sequential, digital structure that self-directed speech imposes on human cognitive processing implements a kind of cognitive control: the tumult of parallel processing in the brain is organized into coherent, linear sequences of thought, systematically serving long-term goals. Rather than have our attention captured by stimuli that we happen to encounter, triggering different neural subsystems in incoherent bouts of activity, we can control our neural processes by generating a linear stream of self-directed speech that takes narrative form. Human brains construct conscious selves through such self-regulating narratives: conscious selves are abstract, fictional authors to which human brains attribute such narratives.

Ross (2007) emphasizes the social functions of such narrative self-constitution. He argues that this use of language makes possible the solution of otherwise insoluble coordination problems. Without the digital, sequential structure that self-constituting narratives impose on the human nervous system, and hence human behavior, we are simply too hard to predict. Because we are intrinsically motivated to adopt and govern our thought and behavior by narratives afforded by our culture, we can drastically reduce, and hence make manageable, the space of interactions in which we engage: we restrict the games we can play with each other by adopting culturally afforded narratives as self-regulating regimes. Because such narratives are public, the culturally available games are known by our likely interactants, and coordination is dramatically facilitated.[32] For example, one's self-regulating narrative might include one's status as a responsible parent. This immediately generates a set of culturally determined expectations that guide one's behavior and others' responses to it. Of course, no human brain hews to such rigid categories automatically. It takes a kind of cognitive self-discipline to restrain sometimes unruly and difficult-to-classify neural activity in ways that make one's behavior conform to publicly available narratives.[33]

Intriguing research with so-called split-brain patients (Gazzaniga, 1995a, p. 1393) suggests a neural mechanism for implementing such narrative-driven self-regulation. It is possible to treat severe epilepsy by severing the corpus callosum, the band of nerve fibers that connects the two hemispheres of the brain. Experiments with such patients show that the two hemispheres function independently of each other and appear capable of extremely different kinds of thinking. For example, it is possible to induce standing in a sitting split-brain subject by flashing the word "walk" in her left visual field, to which her left, complex-language-encoding hemisphere has no access. The right hemisphere knows enough language to trigger compliance with the one-word command. When such subjects are asked why they stand up, they immediately confabulate a self-interpretation, for example, "I'm going into the house to get a Coke," and proceed to comply with this completely false self-interpretation. Presumably, when the subject's left hemisphere processes the question, it cannot access the correct answer and so quickly confabulates a culturally afforded self-interpretation, on which the subject proceeds to act. Gazzaniga (1995b) argues that the left hemisphere, in which the capacity for complex language is implemented in most human beings, acts as a kind of "interpreter." It is constantly weaving behavioral and introspectively available evidence that the brain generates into coherent narratives, using the public categories encoded in language.

Because the narratives and categories that individuals use to regulate and constitute their conscious selves are cultural products, they also play a role in group constitution. In fact, it is hard to disentangle the group- and self-constituting functions of such narrative self-regulation. This is because, as Ross (2007) makes clear, the reason we need such self-constituting narratives is to make social coordination possible: without conformity to publicly known narratives, anticipating an individual's behavior in real-world interactions is extremely difficult. So the narratives we use to regulate and constitute ourselves must be widely known to our likely interactants, that is, our cultural group. For this reason, they also play an important role in constituting group identity. The palette of narratives from which I can choose is one that has made coordination within the cultural group to which I belong possible; hence it helps define what it is to be a member of this group. This is why so many important components of self-constituting narratives typically involve ethnic, religious, political, and other culturally specific identities.

It also explains why human beings are typically disposed to pay tremendous costs to maintain such culturally specific identities. This is clearest in the case of minorities or otherwise politically dominated cultures. Individual members of such groups are willing to go to great lengths to resist assimilation and maintain the integrity of their culturally specific, group-constituting narratives. Consider the remarkable robustness of precommunist eastern European cultural identities through close to fifty years of Soviet domination, or strong, persistent separatist movements like the one in the French Canadian province of Québec, or even religiously motivated terrorism around the world. All such phenomena make evident the high intrinsic value that human beings place on cultural identity. Ross (2007) suggests an explanation: we need self-constituting narratives to make possible otherwise impossible feats of coordination. So these narratives must be public knowledge to our likely interactants, that is, members of our culture. We therefore have strong incentives to maintain the integrity of the culturally afforded narratives we have been socialized to inhabit: they are our principal tools for getting along, and getting along with others is central to human biological success.

Thus, although an important part of the mechanism that makes possible mindshaping via narrative self-regulation is implemented in individual brains—for example, Gazzaniga's interpreter—this mechanism also comprises important, socially distributed components. When one is taught a language, one acquires a set of culturally specific narratives and categories. Foundation myths and other narratives make salient how one is supposed to act to coordinate successfully with members of one's culture. Subtle normative sanctioning, involving often little more than others' (un)willingness to interact, can shape individuals to respect culturally afforded narratives. And in contemporary industrialized cultures, such narrative-based group constitution is supplemented with other linguistic, regulative frameworks, like the law.

Such language-based self- and group-constituting regulative frameworks are, in many ways, the pinnacles of human mindshaping. As I argue in chapter 7, they are central to understanding the role of sophisticated propositional attitude attribution, that is, the attribution of mental states with linguistically specifiable contents, in distinctively human mindshaping.[34] In terms of my mindshaping taxonomy, language-based self-constitution involves both internal neural mechanisms, like Gazzaniga's interpreter, and socially distributed mechanisms, like pedagogy and normative sanctioning centered on group-constituting narratives. The target is, as always, an individual mind; however, in this sort of mindshaping, as in norm-based mindshaping in general, the model is typically virtual rather than actual. Although there are always actual individuals who excel at exemplifying culturally afforded narratives, for example, national heroes, no actual individual can be a perfect exemplar. More typically, the models are protagonists of myths and other narratives to which members of a culture are constantly exposed from early childhood (Sterelny, 2012, p. 163). More formalized, language-based regulation, like the law, implicitly appeals to virtual models like the ideal citizen. The tremendous costs that human beings are willing to incur to maintain the integrity of self- and group-constituting narratives make clear that the motivations driving this variety of mindshaping are intrinsic: although its functions involve facilitating social coordination, individuals do not conceive of it as furthering this or any other end; rather, they see conforming to, and maintaining the integrity of, self- and group-constituting narratives as ends in themselves. Finally, like other forms of distinctively human mindshaping, self- and group-constituting narratives are highly flexible in the respects in which they can make targets match models. However, given their role in social coordination, such narratives will tend to highlight behavior that is predictable, easily interpretable, and facilitates social coordination, at least among members of one's culture. It will also highlight behavior that maintains the integrity of culturally afforded narratives against conflicting narratives from other cultures: this explains the extreme costs that human beings are willing to pay in defense of culturally afforded narratives.

5   Distinctively Human Mindshaping

No doubt I have left out many varieties of mindshaping, and I have failed to note significant dimensions along which they vary. But this chapter has already gone on long enough. The varieties of mindshaping explored in it, and the dimensions along which it has classified them are sufficient to give a taste of the power, pervasiveness, and significance of distinctively human mindshaping. Humans engage in mindshaping to a far greater degree than other species. But that is just the tip of the iceberg. In addition, distinctively human mindshaping is distinguished from the rudimentary varieties we share with other species in terms of four properties. First, distinctively human mindshaping is extraordinarily flexible in how it matches targets to models, including not just goals and abstract behavioral sequences but the fine-grained behavioral means by which they are implemented. Virtually any behavior type of which human beings are capable can serve as a model for distinctively human mindshaping. Second, many varieties of distinctively human mindshaping, like norm acquisition, pedagogy, and narrative self-regulation, rely on socially distributed mindshaping mechanisms. Third, distinctively human mindshaping is largely intrinsically motivated: we try to match models because we find this rewarding in itself, not as a means to other ends. Finally, unlike nonhuman mindshaping, much distinctively human mindshaping involves matching the behavior of "virtual" models: fictional characters or ideal agents, for example. Thus distinctively human mindshaping has the following profile: it is intrinsically motivated; the mechanisms that implement it are often socially distributed; the models are often virtual, nonactual individuals; and the respects in which models can come to match targets include any aspect of any behavior of which human beings are capable. Table 2.1 summarizes this taxonomy.

In chapter 4, I suggest and defend a phylogenetic hypothesis about distinctively human mindshaping: I try to explain how and why mindshaping with this particular profile evolved and has remained stable in human populations through the present day. However, before turning to this subject,

Table 2.1

Variety of mindshaping	Behavioral properties copied: Fine or coarse grained?	Motivation: Intrinsic or extrinsic?	Mechanism: Exclusively neural or distributed?	Model: Real or virtual?	Biological range: Shared or distinctively human?
1. Goal imitation	Coarse grained	Extrinsic	Exclusively neural	Real	Shared
2. Cognitive imitation	Coarse grained	Extrinsic	Exclusively neural	Real	Shared
3. Overimitation	Fine grained	Intrinsic	Exclusively neural	Real	Distinctively human
4. Pedagogy	Both	Both	Distributed	Both	Distinctively human
5. Chameleon effect	Both	?	Exclusively neural	Both	Distinctively human
6. Norm following	Both	Both	Distributed	Virtual	Distinctively human
7. Narrative self-constitution	Both	Both	Distributed	Virtual	Distinctively human

I devote chapter 3 to motivating the mindshaping-as-linchpin view. This chapter's discussion of the varieties of mindshaping has not addressed the issue of phylogenetic priority in any detail; the received view that the evolution and continued stability of the human sociocognitive syndrome rely overwhelmingly on sophisticated mindreading, perhaps with some supplementary support from mindshaping practices such as those described earlier, is entirely compatible with the evidence reviewed in this chapter. Chapter 3 is devoted to a thorough critique of the received view, showing why sophisticated mindreading is unlikely to be reliable, and hence unlikely to be viable, independently of the sorts of mindshaping practices described in the present chapter.

3   Mindreading and the Challenge of Computational Tractability

1   Preamble

The aim of this chapter is almost exclusively critical. It raises formidable difficulties for the view that sophisticated mindreading is the linchpin of the human sociocognitive syndrome. Section 2 focuses on the biological uniqueness of human mindreading: the apparent fact that we are the only species capable of attributing full-blown propositional attitudes, with tenuous, holistically constrained causal influence on behavior. Consensus has it that propositional attitudes play an important role in guiding the behavior of all primates. Furthermore, many primate species are intensely social and thus are subject to selection for capacities to predict conspecific behavior rapidly and reliably. However, we appear to be the only species that attributes full-blown propositional attitudes to this end. This is a serious puzzle for the received view.

Section 3 addresses the central problem for the received view: holism. Because any observable behavior is compatible with any finite set of propositional attitudes, accurate propositional attitude attribution that is timely enough to make a difference to behavioral prediction in dynamic, quotidian contexts appears to be computationally intractable. This might explain why full-blown propositional attitude attribution is so rare in the natural world, but it also raises the difficult problem of explaining why and how it evolved in the human lineage. I consider two influential approaches to addressing problems of computational tractability: modularity and fast and frugal heuristics. Section 3 argues that neither succeeds in explaining how propositional attitude attribution can be simultaneously reliable, timely enough to help with real-world behavioral prediction, and computationally tractable. The key problem is that we have good reasons to expect human populations to be too cognitively heterogeneous for computationally cheap propositional attitude attribution to be reliable. This suggests a role for mindshaping: cognitive homogenization that increases the reliability of social cognition.

Sections 4 and 5 address possible objections to the line of argument pursued in section 3. In section 4, I consider and refute reasons for thinking that human populations might be cognitively homogeneous enough for fast and frugal mindreading to work even in the absence of mindshaping. In section 5, I address the fact that so few theorists appear concerned regarding the implications of holism for the reliability and tractability of propositional attitude attribution (Carruthers, 2006, 2009a; Nichols & Stich, 2003; Goldman, 2006). The best explanation is that they countenance the possibility of attenuated propositional attitudes for which the holism problem does not arise, owing to their relatively straightforward and transparent links to observable behavior. I argue that even if such attenuated propositional attitudes do exist, attributing them to predict the behavior they cause is otiose, since we have far simpler means of tracking such behavior. Section 6 concludes the chapter, suggesting some ways in which mindshaping can help homogenize human populations and hence improve the reliability of fast and frugal social cognition.

2   How Does Sophisticated Mindreading Contribute to Biological Fitness?

In chapter 1, I characterized sophisticated, distinctively human mindreading in the following way. It involves the ability to track the propositional attitudes of one's conspecifics *as such*, where these are understood as mental states with extremely tenuous causal connections to observable stimuli and behavior. The reason propositional attitudes have such a tenuous connection to observable evidence is holism: any finite set of propositional attitudes is compatible with any finite set of observable evidence because a propositional attitude's relations to stimuli and behavior depend on other background propositional attitudes. In other words, as Quine (1960) might put it, an agent's beliefs face the tribunal of experience as a whole, not piecemeal, and an agent's beliefs and desires direct behavior in concert, not individually.

This holism is no accident; it is central to our conception of the propositional attitudes. The reason is that propositional attitudes are supposed to *rationalize* behavior as well as causally explain it.[1] In other words, they show how an agent's behavior is a rational response to the evidence available to her given her goals. But, as Quine showed, evidence requires interpretation: two incompatible beliefs can be equally rationally justified by the same evidence given different background beliefs. This is just a consequence of the nature of nondemonstrative inference, which is one of the most important capacities for which we need propositional attitudes. A rational, inference-mediated response to a stimulus depends on background beliefs. For example, the defendant's fingerprint on the murder weapon is evidence of guilt only if no other information defeats this inference, such as a watertight alibi. Unlike in demonstrative inference, where new premises cannot overturn a valid inference, in nondemonstrative inference, which implements justification of beliefs by empirical evidence, beliefs formed on the basis of evidence can be overturned by previously unavailable beliefs. Practical inference is similarly holistic. Inference to a rational decision based on a finite set of beliefs and goals can be overturned by the addition of new beliefs or goals.[2]

It is instructive to contrast this feature of the propositional attitudes with the behavior of "lower-level" mental states, like emotions and sensations, of the kind that some nonhuman mindreaders appear able to track (Parr, 2001). Such mental states have a far closer connection to observable behavior and stimuli because their tokening in response to stimuli and their effects on behavior are not mediated by inference. Unlike the propositional attitudes, emotions, sensations, and other nonpropositional mental states are not supposed to be rationally justified by the stimuli to which they are responses, nor are they supposed to rationally justify behaviors to which they lead. A kick in the shin leads to pain no matter what one believes, and pain leads to distinctive behavior, in all nonhuman animals and most humans, no matter what one believes and desires.[3] This is one reason why holism is not as serious a problem for the kind of low-level mindreading of which some nonhumans appear capable: they track mental states with much more reliable connections to observable stimuli and behavior, because these mental states are not typically involved in inferences that rationalize behavior given a set of evidence and goals.

Assuming the explanatory framework articulated in chapter 1, to explain the evolution of sophisticated mindreading, one must explain how such a trait could invade and remain stable in a population of individuals who lack it. This raises the following question about the evolution of sophisticated mindreading: how might the capacity to attribute full-blown propositional attitudes, with their tenuous, holistically mediated connection to observable stimuli and behavior, have invaded a population of individuals who did not have this capacity? In other words, why might a mutant capable of attributing full-blown propositional attitudes, introduced into such a population, outcompete its other members, leaving more offspring with the same capacity, leading to an eventual takeover of the population by sophisticated mindreaders?

There is an obvious answer to this question. It is widely assumed that contemporary nonhuman primates and the last common ancestor (LCA) we share with them token(ed) propositional attitudes, like beliefs and desires, whether or not they can (or could) attribute them to each other. These propositional attitudes play(ed) an important role in guiding their behavior. It follows that if being better at predicting the behavior of conspecifics gives an individual certain adaptive advantages, then a mutant capable of accurately representing its conspecifics' propositional attitudes should have an advantage over the other members of a population, all of whom lack this capacity. Unlike the rest of the population, the mutant would be sensitive to a class of mental states that play an important role in guiding behavior, and this sensitivity would make her better than the rest in performing tasks that require predicting behavior. Since it is well established that contemporary primates, and hence probably the LCA, depend(ed) on predicting each other's behavior for much of their biological success, it appears obvious that a mutant capable of attributing propositional attitudes would outcompete other members of a population, leaving more descendants who would eventually come to dominate the population. The mutant and her descendants would be better at deception, coalition formation, and other sociocognitive feats relevant to biological fitness.

This line of reasoning is not as compelling as it seems. For one thing, it seems to suggest that, for any species capable of tokening propositional attitudes, in which there are strong biological rewards for accurately predicting conspecific behavior, strong selection pressures should favor the evolution of sophisticated mindreading. But this description seems to characterize many mammals, including all nonhuman primates. Take our cleverest nonhuman cousins: canids, cetaceans, and primates, for example. Surely all these classes of animals token beliefs and desires. Similarly, many varieties of these classes of animals tend to be highly social, depending on sophisticated social coordination for survival and reproductive success. Yet, as far as we know, none are capable of attributing full-blown propositional attitudes.

Here is one reason sophisticated mindreading is not as widespread as one might expect. The foregoing characterization of the adaptive value of sophisticated mindreading focuses exclusively on its benefits. But cognitive capacities, like any biological trait, have costs as well as benefits. Sophisticated mindreading is no exception. In particular, due to the holism problem, attributing propositional attitudes should be computationally more demanding than tracking behavioral regularities or mental states that are closely tied to behavior. If any finite sequence of observable behavior is in principle compatible with any finite set of propositional attitudes, given appropriate adjustments to background propositional attitudes, then discovering a conspecific's propositional attitudes should be more computationally demanding, requiring more time and energy, than tracking behavioral regularities or mental states closely tied to observable behavior.[4] So it is not obvious that a mutant capable of attributing propositional attitudes would have an advantage over other members of a population who lack this capacity. Her predictions would not be as timely and energetically efficient as those of her fellows, even if, given enough time and computational resources to accurately attribute propositional attitudes, she might be able to predict conspecific behavior better than her fellows. Furthermore, if most conspecific behavior relevant to a particular individual's biological success is under the control of easily tracked, nonpropositional mental states closely tied to observable behavior, then an animal should gain little from the capacity to attribute full-blown propositional attitudes with tenuous, holistically constrained ties to observable behavior. Why go to all that trouble if most conspecific behaviors relevant to an individual's survival and reproduction can be predicted just as well by tracking behavioral dispositions or lower-level mental states, like sensations and emotions, with unproblematic ties to observable behavior?

It is a familiar point that ideal epistemic and rational agency is not necessarily adaptive. This is why no species other than our own has developed deep theories of the hidden nature of the physical environment. It is computationally overly demanding, relative to the kinds of tasks for which most species manipulate items in their physical environment, to accurately model their true, hidden natures, for example, the fact that they decompose into unobservable particles. Typically, selection pressures favor bounded epistemic and rational agents capable of efficiently acquiring no more information than is directly relevant to adaptively significant problems. In fact, in the domain of social cognition, natural selection might actually favor individuals who are more easily interpretable in social interaction, rather than building more sociocognitive capacity into interpreters (Godfrey-Smith, 2002; Sterelny, 2003). It might do so by bringing social behaviors under the control of easily tracked mental states, like emotions. For example, facial expressions in primates provide remarkably reliable signals of emotions. The problem of predicting conspecific behavior is made more tractable not by providing interpreters with a more powerful theory of mind but by making targets of interpretation easier to interpret using low-cost computations capable of tracking observable behavioral dispositions, like correlations between facial expressions and subsequent behavior.

Such reasoning might explain why the capacity to attribute full-blown propositional attitudes is extremely rare in nature, restricted, as far as we know, to our own species. However, at the same time, it makes the evolution of this capacity in the human lineage even more mysterious. Why is our own species such a glaring exception when it comes to social cognition? Like many other species, our behavior is determined by propositional attitudes. Like many other species, predicting conspecific behavior is key to our survival and reproductive success. Yet in other species, this problem appears to be solved not by attributing full-blown propositional attitudes but by making behavior relevant to social interaction easy to interpret based on behavioral cues. In our own species, by contrast, consensus has it that we solve the problem by accurately attributing full-blown propositional attitudes, despite the computational costs of this practice.[5] This suggests that something very strange happened in the hominid lineage from which we descend.

There are a few ways to defuse this puzzle. First, one might argue that human beings are the only animals that token what I have been calling "full-blown propositional attitudes." Despite appearances, other animals do not have beliefs and desires; or, at least, they do not have beliefs and desires of the same kind as we do. If that were true, we would have a straightforward explanation for the fact that sophisticated mindreading is restricted to our species. There is simply nothing to be gained from attributing full-blown propositional attitudes to individuals of other species because they do not token them. This strategy is not without its proponents. For example, Hutto (2008) argues that attributing propositional attitudes cannot be the basis for nonhuman social cognition because nonhuman species cannot token propositional attitudes, as this requires mastery of a public language. In fact, Hutto argues that most real-world human social cognition does not require attributing propositional attitudes because most of our quotidian behavior is not caused by propositional attitudes. Rather, like nonhuman species, most of the time we make do by tracking subtle behavioral regularities, what Hutto calls "intentional attitudes": attitudes apparent in behavioral patterns of whole persons, as opposed to hidden mental states like propositional attitudes.

Even if Hutto is right, this offers no comfort to the received model of the evolution of distinctively human mindreading. If tokening propositional attitudes depends on mastering a public language, then sophisticated mindreading cannot be the linchpin of the human sociocognitive syndrome. Somehow, complex communication, together with the cooperation and mindshaping on which it depends, must be possible independently of propositional attitude attribution.[6] Furthermore, the claim that tokening propositional attitudes requires mastering a public language is grist for the mindshaping mill, since if true, it would constitute a dramatic example of mindshaping playing a central role in human social cognition.

But to defuse the puzzle of human mindreading, one need not endorse Hutto's claims about the propositional attitudes, which, after all, fly in the face of consensus among comparative psychologists (Gallistel, 1990) and many philosophers (Allen & Bekoff, 1997; Bermúdez, 2003a; Carruthers, 2006, 2009b). One might grant that contemporary nonhuman species do not token the sorts of propositional attitudes that human beings routinely attribute. Nevertheless one could argue that contemporary nonhuman species do token mental states that deserve to be called propositional attitudes (Allen & Bekoff, 1997). Furthermore, one could argue that now extinct hominid species in our lineage tokened increasingly complex propositional attitudes, and human mindreading is the product of selection for increasingly sophisticated mindreading aimed at tracking such increasingly sophisticated mental states.

This proposal has a number of problems. First, if one grants that contemporary nonhuman species token attenuated versions of the propositional attitudes, one still needs to explain why none of them seem capable of tracking even such mental states in each other. Some evidence suggests that chimpanzees might be able to track false perceptions in each other (Krachun et al., 2009). However, we have no evidence of a nonhuman species tracking anything like a false belief in another agent. A second problem with this proposal consists in characterizing the difference between the sorts of propositional attitudes that humans and nonhumans can token. I assume that a central property of the propositional attitudes is their tenuous, holistically constrained connection to behavior. And this, I argue, raises the central puzzle about the evolution of distinctively human mindreading: accurate attribution of such propositional attitudes risks computational intractability. Thus if the proposal is that other species do not face this problem because they token only attenuated versions of the propositional attitudes, this attenuation must consist in their being more directly tied to behavior. But how closely tied to behavior can a mental state be but still count as a propositional attitude?

Suppose some creature has a neural representation of some terrain, of a kind that is often termed a "cognitive map" (Gallistel & Cramer, 1996). Could this count as a kind of attenuated version of a human belief? Carruthers (2006) goes so far as to argue that insects, like honeybees, have beliefs by virtue of using such cognitive maps to guide behavior aimed at radically different goals, for example, locating nectar or locating the hive. Evidence also suggests that such maps can be formed in response to radically different stimuli: observing a terrain firsthand or observing other bees perform their famous "waggle dance," which codes for nectar location. Because the same cognitive map can be formed in response to radically different stimuli and can guide behavior aimed at radically different goals, Carruthers claims that such maps must be products of, and contribute to, inferential processes and hence count as beliefs. To my ear, this stretches the commonsense notion of belief unacceptably. Of course, this notion is vague, and one could argue that bee belief is a limiting case. But it sounds odd to credit a creature with the belief that P, when only two ways exist to form this belief, and the belief can direct only two kinds of behavior. There is a strong intuition that beliefs and other propositional attitudes, composed as they are of concepts subject to Evans's generality constraint,[7] must be sensitive to an indefinite range of evidence and be capable of supporting an indefinite range of action.

A third problem with the proposal that nonhuman animals token only attenuated versions of the propositional attitudes, and human mindreading was selected for tracking more sophisticated propositional attitudes in our now extinct hominid ancestor species, is explaining the evolution of sophisticated propositional attitudes independently of the evolution of sophisticated social cognition. If the chimpanzee-like LCA lacked full-blown propositional attitudes and hence selection pressures for humanlike mindreading, what selection pressures led to the evolution of full-blown propositional attitudes in the human lineage? If the evolution of sophisticated mindreading was driven by the need to track such mental states, then there must be some explanation for why they evolved only in the human lineage. But it is difficult to see what selection pressures distinctive of the human lineage could have driven the evolution of the full-blown propositional attitudes. By all accounts, the physical environment of our ancestors in the human lineage did not differ significantly from the physical environments of numerous other contemporaneous species (Sterelny, 2007). So either they all evolved full-blown propositional attitudes, in which case the puzzle of human mindreading remains, or the evolution of full-blown propositional attitudes in the human lineage raises a further puzzle. One could argue that the social complexity of ancestral populations in the human lineage must have been much greater than that of other species, and this selected for full-blown propositional attitudes. But then such social complexity must be possible without sophisticated mindreading, since before such social complexity evolved, there would have been no full-blown propositional attitudes for sophisticated mindreading to track. And it is hard to see how social complexity can be maintained without cooperation, mindshaping, and complex communication.[8] So, in this view, these components of the human sociocognitive syndrome would be present before the evolution of sophisticated mindreading. This is in obvious tension with the mindreading-as-linchpin view.

Another way of defusing the puzzle of human mindreading—the fact that full-blown propositional attitude attribution evolved only in the human lineage—is to deny the significance of this kind of mindreading. For example, Gallagher (2001, 2008; Gallagher & Hutto, 2008) and Hutto (2008) argue that the kind of embodied understanding of behavioral patterns of which human infants are capable, sometimes called "primary and secondary intersubjectivity" (Trevarthen & Hubley, 1978), explains not just the sociocognitive competence of human infants and nonhuman primates but also the vast majority of adult human social cognition. Because full-blown propositional attitude attribution is such a rarefied phenomenon, even among humans, it is not surprising that it evolved in no other lineage. But this still leaves the puzzle of why a capacity for full-blown propositional attitude attribution evolved at all. Even those who claim that most adult human social cognition depends on some form of embodied intersubjectivity, rather than on attributing propositional attitudes, admit that we sometimes attribute propositional attitudes (Hutto, 2008; cf. Spaulding, 2010). Thus two closely related puzzles remain: why do we do it, and how do we do it? Presumably we would not do it if it were not reliable; yet, as I argue in the next section, it is hard to see how it can be both reliable and computationally tractable.

These puzzles are not necessarily irresolvable. Perhaps there is a way of explaining why sophisticated mindreading—the capacity to attribute full-blown propositional attitudes—emerged only in the human lineage. Perhaps it is because full-blown propositional attitudes emerged only in the human lineage, for some reason. Or perhaps it is because, though other species token full-blown propositional attitudes, for some reason, the benefits of attributing them are not sufficient to support strong selection pressures for sophisticated mindreading. Perhaps there is some mysterious feature of our lineage's ecology that significantly increased the benefits of attributing propositional attitudes to conspecifics. Or maybe our ancestors were just lucky. In this view, the capacity to attribute sophisticated propositional attitudes has always been a potential boon to any species that tokens them. However, the lucky mutations that made this capacity possible occurred only in the human lineage. And these watershed events triggered the evolutionary dynamic that led to the human sociocognitive syndrome. Even if we accept these promissory notes, the central problem remains: how can the attribution of full-blown propositional attitudes, with their tenuous, holistically constrained connections to observable behavior, be computationally tractable enough to give sophisticated mindreaders the competitive advantages they needed to take over protohuman populations?

3   How Can Sophisticated Mindreading Be Made Computationally Tractable?

Philosophers and psychologists assume that human beings are, on the whole, proficient mindreaders. That is, it is commonly assumed that human beings accurately attribute propositional attitudes to each other, in everyday contexts, quickly enough to make a difference to predicting behavior. This assumption is plausible for at least two reasons. First, it seems intuitively true. People take themselves to know a good deal about what others, particularly those with whom they interact regularly, are thinking. Second, many philosophers and psychologists assume that our theory of mind is a product of natural selection. Given the dramatic feats of interpersonal coordination of which all human populations (and few, if any, nonhuman populations) are capable, it is reasonable to conclude that dramatic improvements in social cognition were selected for in our lineage (Carruthers, 2006, p. 154). Presumably they included an improved capacity to attribute mental states. Given that mindreading appears to be implemented in recently expanded and energetically expensive brain areas (Gallagher & Frith, 2003), and that we devote a lot of time and energy to interpreting the behavior of our fellows (Dunbar, 1998), it makes biological sense to infer that human mindreading is, on the whole, accurate enough to pay for itself by contributing to successful behavioral prediction and coordination.[9]

Despite this persuasive line of argument, it is nevertheless puzzling *how* accurate mindreading is possible. Just as in other cognitive domains, mindreading tasks that *seem* trivial, prima facie, start to look intractable when one tries to spell out, in detail, how a mechanism might accomplish them. Artificial intelligence (AI) researchers have long puzzled over such problems in modeling human competence in nonsocial domains. For example, intuitively simple tasks, like keeping track of which routine changes in the physical environment are relevant to an agent's goals, are notoriously difficult to accomplish by artificial computational systems. This is the well-known "frame problem" in AI (Ford & Pylyshyn, 1996). As Dennett (1978, pp. 125–126) points out, the frame problem is philosophically interesting because it reveals the true complexity of everyday human cognitive competencies that we take for granted because of the phenomenological ease with which we execute them. Similarly, the phenomenological ease with which we accurately mindread conceals seemingly intractable computational complexity.

Take, for example, the tasks of accurately attributing propositional attitudes, and then accurately inferring behavioral predictions from such attributions. As I have noted, due to their holistic connection to behavior, any finite sequence of behavior by a target of interpretation seems compatible with indefinitely many distinct, finite sets of propositional attitudes, as long as appropriate adjustments are made to the target's other propositional attitudes. Since our interpretations of others are always based on finite behavioral evidence, this fact threatens to turn the task of accurately attributing propositional attitudes into an intractable search problem. Similarly, any finite set of propositional attitudes seems compatible with indefinitely many distinct, future behavioral sequences, as long as appropriate adjustments are made to the interpretive target's other propositional attitudes. This threatens to turn behavioral prediction on the basis of propositional attitude attributions into an intractable search problem. Thus the very mindreading tasks that we have good phenomenological and evolutionary reasons to think we excel at seem intractable when we begin to speculate about how we might accomplish them.

This problem has not gone unnoticed in recent work on the mechanisms underlying mental state attribution. For example, Nichols and Stich (2003) acknowledge that "typically there are endlessly many possible sets of beliefs and desires that would lead … to [any behavior]" (p. 139). Goldman (2006) is similarly puzzled: "[There is] an excess of state combinations that might yield a given upshot. How can a cognitive system handle them all? Can it limit the search space?" (p. 184). Apperly (2011, pp. 118–119) also draws attention to this problem. In the next two subsections, I consider and reject two common strategies for dealing with such problems.

3a   Why a Theory of Mind Module Cannot Help

"Modularity" is the classic response to issues of computational tractability. If the human mind/brain deploys *encapsulated* computational modules, with *prespecified, domain-specific* databases, tractably searchable by *dedicated* processes, then, it is often claimed, problems of computational tractability can be avoided (Carruthers, 2006, pp. 44–45). The idea is that when confronting some domain-specific problem, such as predicting the behavior of another person, the human mind/brain need not search all information to which it has access. Such problems trigger activity in dedicated, domain-specific modules—in the case of the social domain, the theory of mind module—which are informationally isolated from other parts of the mind/brain, making the search for solutions exponentially more tractable. However, it is not clear that modularity can help in the case of social cognition.

First, presumably any propositional attitude attribution consistent with an observed sequence of behavior would have to be generated by the theory of mind module: after all, any such attribution is composed of folk psychological concepts. So the problem of the computational intractability of attributing mental states with tenuous, holistically mediated connections to behavior would arise *within* an adequate theory of mind module (Sterelny, 2003, p. 209). The reason is that an indefinite number of propositional attitude attributions are consistent with any observed sequence of behavior. Second, because human beings can have beliefs about, and desires for, almost anything they can represent, any information represented by the entire mind/brain can be relevant to the task of propositional attitude attribution. Any information an interpreter possesses about some situation, for example, an event like a party, might be relevant to determining what her interpretive target believes or desires about the situation. For example, knowing that my interpretive target loves to dance at parties, the nonpsychological information that there will be no dancing at the party is relevant to attributing to her likely propositional attitudes, like the desire to leave the party early. In arguing for essentially this point, Currie and Sterelny (2000) give the example of detective work: figuring out who committed a crime and for what reasons, and predicting the criminal's next move, are precisely the kinds of problems that a dedicated, informationally encapsulated module cannot solve. The reason people enjoy detective fiction is that they have no way of knowing in advance what sorts of information might be relevant to cracking a case.

Fodor (1983) introduced the notion of computational/cognitive modules, contrasting them with "central systems," which, he argued, are responsible for most belief fixation or retrieval in human beings. Unlike modules, central systems are, according to Fodor, "isotropic"; in other words, any information is potentially relevant to belief fixation or retrieval. He focuses on examples from science, such as how information about fluid behavior turned out to be relevant to fixing beliefs about the behavior of light in nineteenth-century physics. Arguably, much everyday reasoning is similarly isotropic. There does not seem to be a way of prespecifying what kinds of information might be relevant to selecting among products in a supermarket, or deciding whom to date, and so on, in the way there would need to be were such problems tractable by encapsulated modules.

If Fodor is right that most human belief fixation and retrieval are isotropic, and therefore a product of nonmodular central systems, then a general case can be made against the reliability of a theory of mind module. A central goal of theory of mind is to determine what beliefs are likely operative in another agent. But if Fodor is right, the processes by which an agent fixes or retrieves her beliefs are isotropic and therefore nonmodular. It seems unlikely that the interpretive task of discovering what belief another agent is likely to token in a certain context can be accomplished with an encapsulated module, if the first-order tasks of fixing or retrieving that belief cannot be (Apperly, 2011, p. 122). The reason is that discovering what belief an interpretive target is likely to token in a certain context seems to require understanding *how* the target fixes or retrieves her beliefs. If these processes are isotropic, and attributing beliefs is modularized, this seems to imply that a module can somehow model isotropic processes—a rather unlikely possibility.

It is possible to deny that accurately attributing beliefs requires understanding how interpretive targets fix or retrieve their beliefs. Perhaps there are reliable enough behavioral signals of belief tokening.[10] However, given the holism problem, that is, the compatibility of any finite sequence of behavior with any finite set of beliefs, this seems unlikely. It seems more plausible that, in deciding which beliefs to attribute to an interpretive target, we attempt to infer the most reasonable doxastic response to her evidential context; however, this is precisely the kind of belief fixation/ retrieval problem that Fodor claims is isotropic. In fact, as Alechina and Logan (2010) have recently shown, even an extremely simplified formal model of belief attribution runs into serious difficulties with computationally bounded interpreters, that is, agents with memory limitations that can execute only a limited number of logical operations on their own beliefs at a time. The problem is that even if an interpreter begins with an accurate picture of her target's current beliefs, the interpreter has no way of knowing which beliefs the target will erase from memory and which operations she will perform on the remaining beliefs in the future. According to Alechina and Logan, the only way to mitigate this problem is for interpreters to know their targets' reasoning strategies, that is, the beliefs they prefer to retain and the operations they prefer to perform on them. This seems very close to the kind of reasoning that Fodor argues is isotropic; hence, if Fodor is right, Alechina and Logan's argument shows that accurate belief attribution requires modeling isotropic processes, a feat of which Fodorian modules should be constitutionally incapable. Furthermore, besides figuring out how her target solves the belief fixation/retrieval problems she faces, the interpreter must also determine what information the target likely has access to, and by what problems the target is most motivated—problems the target need not solve. This compounds the problem facing the interpreter: not only must she, in effect, solve the same isotropic belief fixation/retrieval problems as her target, but she must also determine the parameters governing her target's solutions. Thus the problems of computational tractability that arise for theory of mind do not appear to admit of a strict modularist solution.

3b   Why Fast and Frugal Theory of Mind Heuristics Do Not Seem to Help

Fodorian modularity is an extreme solution to the problem of computational tractability, which seems unhelpful in many domains, particularly social cognition. However, other kinds of modularity may evade some of the problems that have been raised for Fodorian modularity. Recently Carruthers (2006) has defended a kind of modularity that is *not* based on a prespecification of the *kind* of information that might be relevant to solving tasks in some domain. Instead Carruthers argues that the problem of computational tractability can be solved using content-neutral, "fast and frugal heuristics" (2006, pp. 53–59; Gigerenzer et al., 1999). Because such heuristics are content neutral, they have no limits on the kinds of information they can consult. This is promising in the case of mindreading, since, as we have seen, almost any kind of information can be relevant to this task. However, computational tractability is maintained by fast and frugal heuristics because strict limits constrain the *quantity* of information they can consult.

Consider "Take the Best," a well-known fast and frugal heuristic. It requires that one recall criteria previously used to distinguish between alternatives in some domain, determine which criterion distinguished best, and use that criterion on one's current decision. For example, when asked which of two German cities is larger, one might recall that, previously, having a professional soccer team distinguished best between larger and smaller cities, and so one asks which, if either, has a professional soccer team. If neither or both do, one then proceeds to the next best criterion. To avoid intractable search, "Take the Best" has a "stopping rule" that suspends search if it cannot arrive at an answer after a small number of iterations (Gigerenzer et al., 1999; Carruthers, 2006, p. 55). Such heuristics can easily be adapted to theory of mind tasks. For example, one can conceive of belief attribution as the problem of determining which of two incompatible belief attributions are appropriate for a given interpretive target. A theory of mind version of "Take the Best" could look at successful past belief attributions in similar contexts as a guide to interpreting behavioral evidence. Suppose that the interpreter is trying to determine whether or not her target believes she is untrustworthy. If, in the past, unsteady eye contact distinguished best between the target's tokening the belief that the interpreter is untrustworthy and the target's failure to token this belief, then "Take the Best" should lead the interpreter to either attribute or withhold attribution of this belief based on the current target's form of eye contact.

Fast and frugal heuristics combine computational tractability with openness to a wide variety of potentially relevant information. For example, although "Take the Best" is restricted to considering only information that a particular agent has recently consulted, when reasoning about a certain domain, this restriction is content neutral. It includes different information for agents with different histories of reasoning about a domain. There is no reason why, for a different agent reasoning about relative population sizes of German cities, "Take the Best" could not consult relative crime rates instead of the presence of professional soccer teams (Carruthers, 2006, pp. 55–56). Analogously, a different interpreter deploying "Take the Best" in the belief attribution task described in the previous paragraph might focus on fidgeting rather than eye contact as a sign of the target's belief about the interpreter's trustworthiness. Such heuristics are computationally tractable because they restrict search based on an agent's current epistemic context, including relevant recent searches, not because they restrict search based on the content of the relevant domain, for example, social, physical, and so on. So there is no need to prespecify the kinds of information likely to be relevant to each domain. This mitigates the problem that Currie and Sterelny (2000) raise for modular theory of mind. "Take the Best" can consult any type of information in a theory of mind task. But only information that has recently been useful on similar tasks is consulted on any particular occasion.

Unfortunately this proposal seems unlikely to work for theory of mind tasks. The problem is that fast and frugal heuristics work only in domains characterized by extreme homogeneity. Unlike more sophisticated statistical learning algorithms, such heuristics make no attempt to ensure that the sample from which they generalize is unbiased. Strategies that *happen* to have worked for a particular agent in the recent past are taken to be appropriate for current and future problems. Such contingent regularities can safely be assumed in certain extremely homogeneous, well-behaved domains. However, there is every reason to deny that the social domain is like this (Sterelny, 2003).

Ironically, if human beings rely on fast and frugal heuristics to fix their beliefs, then the dependence of such heuristics on the idiosyncratic background assumptions of particular individuals is likely to make discovering their beliefs computationally intractable for fast and frugal *theory of mind* heuristics. This is because such social cognition would require quickly and frugally uncovering the idiosyncratic background assumptions on which one's interpretive targets rely. But fast and frugal theory of mind heuristics can depend only on what has worked for the *interpreter* in the recent past, and there is no reason to think that this is any guide to the idiosyncratic background assumptions of a new interpretive target. For example, suppose, as before, an interpreter is trying to determine whether or not a target believes she is untrustworthy. Unbeknownst to the interpreter, the *target's* fast and frugal heuristics for *determining trustworthiness* require the target to engage in rapid eye movements to evaluate body language and other signals of trustworthiness; the efficacy of such visual body scanning constitutes an idiosyncratic background assumption based on the target's successful past attributions of trustworthiness. The interpreter employs her fast and frugal theory of mind heuristic: she checks for steady eye contact and finds it lacking, thus concluding that her target believes she is untrustworthy. This would be a mistaken belief attribution, since the interpretive target is merely trying to ascertain the interpreter's trustworthiness and has not yet established whether or not she is trustworthy. Thus belief attribution based on fast and frugal heuristics risks unreliability because such heuristics cannot take into account the idiosyncratic background assumptions on which interpretive targets' fast and frugal heuristics depend to fix their first-order beliefs, in this case, about trustworthiness.

Furthermore, as Sterelny (2003, p. 229) emphasizes, human beings appear to have strong biological incentives to behave in ways that are unpredictable relative to heuristics that their potential competitors have previously used to predict them. If unsteady eye contact previously led an interpreter to attribute to her target the belief that she is untrustworthy, then if the target wants the interpreter to think otherwise the next time they interact, the target might make steady eye contact whether or not she believes the interpreter is trustworthy. Interpretive contexts are often competitive, and it is plausible that interpretive targets often intentionally corrupt the behavioral signals on which their interpreters rely, especially when maintaining opacity gives them a competitive advantage. Finally, there are good reasons to think that individual variation among human beings is extreme compared with other species: we have unmatched capacities for creative cognition and conation that involve random processes heavily dependent on idiosyncratic learning history (Carruthers, 2006, pp. 208, 218, 222, 231, 288–289), and extreme phenotypic plasticity is likely a human adaptation to extremely variable physical and social environments (Sterelny, 2003, pp. 216–217). So we have every reason to suppose that fast and frugal heuristics, the reliability of which relies on extreme homogeneity in the domains to which they apply, cannot support reliable social cognition.

Perhaps more specific mindreading heuristics can evade some of these problems. The most influential models of fast and frugal social cognition appeal to some kind of simulation (Goldman, 2006). Interpreters save on the computational costs of interpretation by simply projecting, in some sense, their own decision procedures onto others. But the accuracy of such simulation heuristics obviously depends on extreme homogeneity in human populations: interpreters and their targets must prioritize problems in similar ways and make decisions based on similar information and heuristics. And as we have seen, good reasons exist to doubt that such homogeneity characterizes human populations.

Thus the computational tractability of reliable and timely propositional attitude attribution remains mysterious. Neither of the two most prominent approaches to mitigating problems of computational tractability appears promising in this context. Nevertheless we do spend a lot of time and energy attributing propositional attitudes, so there must be some adaptive justification for this. Furthermore, there is no denying the phenomenology of propositional attitude attribution: it certainly seems as though we reliably and rapidly attribute propositional attitudes all the time. The holism problem seems to be merely a philosopher's problem: although any finite sequence of behavior is *logically* compatible with any finite set of propositional attitudes, in real life it is plausible that all sorts of nonlogical constraints on propositional attitude attribution help mitigate this problem.[11] However, the arguments I have just considered suggest that these constraints are not *psychological*: nothing within the heads of interpreters can help adequately constrain propositional attitude attribution. The suggestion explored in the rest of this book is that the constraints are *sociological*. We are able to interpret each other's behavior accurately and rapidly because most of our interactants are products of the same cultural mindshaping influences as ourselves (Apperly, 2011, pp. 29, 160). We tend to interact with people who have been subject to the same kinds of pedagogy, who have tried to imitate the same kinds of role models, and who seek to conform to the same norms as ourselves. For this reason, our fast and frugal interpretations are typically accurate: the cognitive homogeneity on which they depend is a product of sociocultural mindshaping practices. But before I turn to a more detailed exploration of this idea, I want to address some ways that proponents of the mindreading-as-linchpin view might resist my skepticism about mindshaping-independent, fast and frugal social cognition. First, in section 4, I turn to arguments that human populations should be cognitively homogeneous enough without mindshaping for fast and frugal social cognition to be reliable. Later, in section 5, I consider the possibility that some propositional attitude attribution might not face the holism problem because there are attenuated propositional attitudes with relatively transparent relations to observable behavior.

4 Human Cognitive Homogeneity

Human cognitive heterogeneity is easily overstated. Despite our many differences, human beings are characterized by a great deal of cognitive homogeneity, even independently of similar histories of mindshaping. It is arguable that most human beings share the vast majority of their propositional attitudes. This is most apparent from the infinite number of trivial dispositional beliefs shared by every normal human being, for example, that the sun rises in the east, winter tends to be colder than summer, night tends to be darker than daytime, the moon is more than one meter away from the earth, the moon is more than 1.1 meters away from the earth, and so on. The idea that our conceptual schemes largely overlap has garnered consensus since Davidson (1973) first proposed it.[12]

Models of human social cognition have exploited this point to show how mindreading can be simultaneously reliable and computationally tractable. For example, Nichols and Stich (2003) argue that because most people share most of their beliefs, belief attribution is simplicity itself: interpreters need only begin with the default assumption that their interpretive targets share their beliefs. As evidence of exceptions to this assumption accumulates, they can tinker with the beliefs they attribute, but such tinkering does not appear to raise the sorts of worries about computational tractability that I raise earlier. Goldman has similarly based his simulationist model of human mindreading on the assumption that people are cognitively very much alike (1989, 2006). One of his key early arguments in favor of "simulation theory" models of mindreading is that they make mindreading computationally more tractable than "theory theory" models, according to which human interpreters know and deploy psychological generalizations (1989). If we simply use our own cognitive resources as models of those of others, then we need not employ theories of how these resources work to arrive at reliable propositional attitude attributions and behavioral predictions. But, as Goldman acknowledges, this works only if people are substantially alike cognitively. And he provides numerous arguments in support of this claim (1989, 2006).

It is clear that the reliability of low-cost mindreading depends on cognitive homogeneity. Furthermore, Davidson, Goldman, and many others may be correct that human populations are characterized by substantial mindshaping-independent cognitive homogeneity. However, this is still not enough to explain the reliability of computationally fast and frugal mindreading. The reason is that, by all accounts, accurately tracking dispositional beliefs and other widely shared mental states is not sufficient for sophisticated mindreading to earn its keep. Mindreading earns its keep by reliable behavioral prediction. And it is not the case that agents who share most of their dispositional propositional attitudes, and who "carve" up the world into similar categories based on similar conceptual schemes (Goldman, 2006, p. 178), tend to behave similarly in similar circumstances. The reason is that trivial background dispositional beliefs and desires, and the conceptual schemes on which they draw, are not *direct* determinants of behavior. Behavior is determined by *occurrent* mental states directly implicated in action guidance. Two agents who share most of their dispositional propositional attitudes and the conceptual scheme from which they derive may nevertheless attend to very different components of this shared cognitive background. Very different beliefs and desires may be actively guiding their behavior. For simulation or "Take the Best" or any other fast and frugal heuristic to function as a reliable mechanism for *predicting behavior*, extreme homogeneity must exist in *occurrent* mental states directly guiding action. And it is far from obvious that human populations are characterized by this kind of cognitive homogeneity. In fact, it is a common observation that individuals are often animated by radically different occurrent mental states.

A great deal of evidence suggests that we are often terrible at attributing occurrent, action-guiding desires not just to others but even to our future selves. Both Nichols and Stich (2003, pp. 137–138) and Goldman (2006, pp. 166–167) draw on research in behavioral economics showing that human interpreters are frequently wrong in attributing motivations to others and their future selves. In particular, in experiments concerning the so-called endowment effect, Van Boven and Loewenstein (2003) showed that human interpreters are systematically wrong about what they or others will prefer under different conditions. In other work, Loewenstein showed similar unreliability in predicting behavior guided by "hot cognition" or "cold cognition" when the interpreter is not in a comparable state (Loewenstein,

2005; Goldman, 2006, p. 167). For example, addicts in a coldly rational, sober state are notoriously bad at predicting their future susceptibility to temptation (Loewenstein, 2005). Nichols and Stich (2003, pp. 72–73) draw on well-established findings in social psychology to argue that human interpreters are surprisingly unreliable at predicting motivation and behavior in unfamiliar situations. For example, they are shocked to learn the amount of pain they and others are willing to administer when told to do so by a scientific authority figure in the context of a staged experiment (Milgram, 1963). According to Goldman (2006, pp. 166–167), such data support simulation theory, as interpreters seem to project motivations and behavioral dispositions they take themselves to have onto their interpretive targets (including their future or counterfactual selves), although no theoretical basis for such projection exists.[13] However, these data also call into question Goldman's assumption that human cognitive homogeneity ensures that simulation is a reliable form of mindreading. Apparently, even different time slices of the *same* individual are not cognitively homogeneous enough to ensure reliable behavior prediction. The so-called curse of knowledge (Birch & Bloom, 2007) suggests similar unreliability in the attribution of occurrent beliefs. Even adult interpreters have trouble taking into account the fact that their interpretive targets often do not know what they know.

Such findings throw doubt on the reliability of fast and frugal mindreading not just because they show us to be unreliable judges of each other's motivations. The problem runs much deeper, because it is becoming increasingly clear that all cognition is deeply determined by motivation (Damasio, 1994; Glimcher, 2004). What an individual is likely to perceive or remember, and which dispositional belief she is likely to activate on a particular occasion, depend on the individual's motivational state. The reason is that cognitive states and processes depend for their activation on *attention*, and attention is overwhelmingly a motivational phenomenon. Two individuals, or even two time slices of the same individual, with substantial overlap in dispositional mental states, can be put in the same situation but behave in very different ways due entirely to differences in motivation. What a person perceives about a particular situation depends on what she attends to, and this depends on what she is motivated by. A hungry person notices different things about a kitchen than a sated person.

Because motivation affects attention, it also affects depth of encoding. Two cognitively similar yet motivationally different individuals might look at the same scene and remember it entirely differently because they attend to different aspects of it and therefore encode different aspects with sufficient depth to form memories. Similarly, as a host of experimental evidence conclusively demonstrates, motivation can affect memory during retrieval as well. Elizabeth Loftus (1996) has devoted her career to showing how the context of memory retrieval, including motivationally salient features like the behavior of authority figures such as police officers, can alter how events are remembered. Such contextual effects on memory are not only related to motivation. Just the way a question is asked can prime responses in ways that cause dramatic misremembering. And, as Neisser and Harsh (2000) show in their classic study of so-called flashbulb memory, the experiences that intervene between encoding and recalling a high-visibility event, like the explosion of the space shuttle *Challenger* in 1986, alter the way the memory is recalled.

Such experimental findings show that even significant cognitive homogeneity cannot explain how fast and frugal mindreading heuristics help human beings reliably predict each other's behavior. The reason is that, against this background of cognitive homogeneity, humans have a great deal of individual variation in motivation, experiential history, and hence attention, perception, and memory. What good is it to an interpreter that her interpretive target carves the world with the same conceptual scheme as she does, and shares many of her dispositional beliefs, if all of this is compatible with radically different behavior, depending on her motivations and the cognitive processes they determine, like attention, perception, and memory? What good is it to an interpreter that both she and her interpretive target witnessed the same high-visibility event five years earlier, if the idiosyncratic experiences that each had in the intervening time lead to dramatic variation in the way the event is remembered? Shared background cognitive homogeneity can support fast, frugal, and reliable behavioral prediction only if differences in motivation, attention, and memory can be detected and factored in. But as the experimental evidence reviewed by Nichols and Stich (2003) shows, we are surprisingly bad at attributing discrepant or counternormative motivations, and hence other motivation-dependent occurrent mental states.[14] After all, what evidence can we draw on? Gaze direction does not help, since a person may be looking at the same object as her interpreter but attend to radically different aspects of it. Body language is hard to interpret due to the holism problem: radically different sets of occurrent propositional attitudes are compatible with the same body language. This is why it is difficult to detect deception. Expressions of belief and other mental states in a public language (Nichols & Stich, 2003, pp. 91–92) are also potentially unreliable due to the possibility of deception. In any case, complex communication is impossible without sophisticated cooperation and mindshaping,[15] so it cannot constitute an evidence base for sophisticated mindreading before the evolution of the other elements of the human sociocognitive syndrome.

The evidence just reviewed suggests that the motivation-driven dynamics of attention and memory are a constant threat to the homogeneity of occurrent, action-guiding propositional attitudes: even if all human beings share a conceptual scheme and the majority of their dispositional beliefs, the factors that determine what aspects of this shared background individuals attend to and by which they are guided can vary considerably. It is plausible that one of the central raisons d'être of mindshaping is to mitigate the risks of such variation, to keep each of us from spinning off into idiosyncratic unintelligibility. For example, concern with status, or strong dispositions to conform, can ensure that individuals ignore motivations that might be atypical relative to a context.

Some practices may aim at ensuring that individuals attend to and remember similar features of public events. For example, Hirst and Manier (2008) describe the phenomenon of "collective memory," in which members of a group or culture co-construct narratives in an attempt to create common memories of high-profile events, like the attacks of 9/11. Such group-memory-constituting narrative construction is a plausible mechanism for mitigating the dramatic interpersonal variation in flashbulb memory documented by Neisser and Harsh (2000). Because memories of high-profile events are altered by the circumstances of their frequent subsequent retrieval, individuals often remember the same event incorrectly and idiosyncratically. Recollecting such events in group contexts and collectively integrating them into group-constituting narratives is a way of mitigating such potential heterogeneity: a great example of mindshaping working to make fast and frugal social cognition more reliable by homogenizing human populations. In general, one of the most effective ways of counteracting potential cognitive heterogeneity is through public language. If one is unsure whether or not one's interactants are attending to the same aspect of a shared cognitive background, one can always ask them. But, of course, this presupposes mindshaping. It works only if one's interactants are shaped to respect norms of communication, like honesty. More fundamentally, it works only if one's interactants acquire the same language in infancy, another form of mindshaping.

Thus we have strong reasons to doubt that human cognitive homogeneity suffices, in the absence of mindshaping, to support reliable fast and frugal social cognition. One possible response to these concerns points to the likely demographics of the ancestral human and protohuman populations from which we descended. According to one influential view, our mindreading and other cognitive capacities were selected for in the so-called environment of evolutionary adaptiveness (EEA) (Tooby & Cosmides, 1990), widely thought to involve small, widely dispersed bands of hunter-gatherers in the Pleistocene. Perhaps the problem of heterogeneity in occurrent cognitive states was not as acute in that context, and hence fast, frugal, and accurate propositional attitude attribution might have been possible at the time in which it likely evolved. Most individuals with whom an interpreter had to interact would have been extremely familiar, and many would have been genetically related and subject to similar learning histories.[16] However, I think this suggestion underestimates the severity of the problem of heterogeneity of occurrent mental states. No matter how small, familiar, and closely related one's band of interactants, the fact remains that they are often motivated by very different agendas, and hence attend to different aspects of commonly perceived situations, and remember commonly experienced events differently. If they are human, then, if Carruthers is right, they fix their first-order beliefs using idiosyncratic-experience-dependent, fast and frugal heuristics. In addition, they often engage in creative cognition and conation dependent, if Carruthers is right, on random sampling of idiosyncratic experiences that happen to be attentionally salient in specific contexts. This should raise the same sorts of problems for reliable tracking of occurrent, action-guiding cognitive states in ancestral populations as humans face today. After all, who isn't frequently mystified by the behavior of family members with whom one interacts on a daily basis for years? Indeed, the experimental findings from behavioral economics and social psychology highlighted by Nichols and Stich (2003), Loewenstein (2005), and Milgram (1963) show that we are terrible at predicting even our own future occurrent mental states, let alone those of familiar others.

The suggestion that sophisticated mindreading was possible for our Pleistocene ancestors because they lived in small, widely dispersed bands of familiar individuals raises other problems as well. First, if it is true that most interactants were highly predictable due to their familiarity, then it is hard to see why such populations would need sophisticated mindreading to meet their sociocognitive needs. If one interacts with the same individuals, on the same sorts of projects, in the same environment, for years, then behavioral signals should be sufficient to predict future behavior. This is, arguably, why contemporary nonhuman primates do not need sophisticated mindreading to successfully interact. Furthermore, even if the homogeneity of small ancestral populations made fast and frugal yet sophisticated and reliable mindreading possible, this still leaves the sociocognitive feats of later human populations, up to the present day, unexplained. Although today most human beings routinely interact with unfamiliar individuals on a daily basis, we are still amazingly good at coordinating with each other, and we still spend a lot of time attributing propositional attitudes, suggesting that this practice is reliable enough to pay for itself. So the persistence of successful coordination and propositional attitude attribution into modern times, in circumstances vastly different from those of our Pleistocene ancestors, cannot be explained by appeal to the alleged cognitive homogeneity of those ancestors.

The conclusion remains: without mindshaping, we are not, nor have we likely ever been, cognitively homogeneous enough, especially in our occurrent, action-guiding mental states, to explain how fast and frugal, sophisticated propositional attitude attribution can be sufficiently reliable to be selected for and remain stable in human populations.[17] If the reason we track full-blown propositional attitudes is because doing so helps us predict each other's behavior, then we have no idea of how or why it helps us predict each other's behavior, independently of mindshaping.[18]

5   Tracking "Attenuated" Propositional Attitudes

If the foregoing arguments are cogent, then computational intractability poses a serious problem for the received view of human mindreading. However, many proponents of the received view do not seem to share these concerns. For example, the foregoing material draws on Carruthers (2006) to support the contention that the human social domain is unlikely to be homogeneous enough to allow fast and frugal theory of mind heuristics to accurately track propositional attitudes. If we typically use fast and frugal heuristics to fix our first-order beliefs, this should make them difficult to track using fast and frugal theory of mind heuristics, since there is bound to be significant, idiosyncratic variation in the first-order beliefs we fix. In addition, the foregoing also draws on passages in which Carruthers stresses the unpredictability of creative human cognition and conation (2006, pp. 288–289, 330–301). However, these arguments pit Carruthers against himself: he is sanguine about the reliability of human theory of mind (2009a). What explains this? Given all the relatively obvious problems with computationally frugal yet reliable propositional attitude attribution, why is this not of greater concern?

One reason is that, as noted earlier in the chapter, theorists mean different things by "propositional attitudes." Throughout this book I assume that their tenuous, holistically constrained relation to behavior is a central property of the propositional attitudes. Clearly Carruthers does not share this view. He thinks that even bees have beliefs about the spatial locations of hives and food sources, though such beliefs are responsive to only a limited variety of evidence and can influence only a limited variety of behavior (2009b). For Carruthers and most others, a mental state counts as a propositional attitude if it meets two criteria: (1) it has satisfaction conditions that can fail to be satisfied, for example, as beliefs have truth conditions that fail to obtain when the beliefs are false; and (2) it can be formed in response to more than one type of stimulus and can influence more than one type of response. So, according to this view, the capacity to track propositional attitudes requires only that the interpreter appreciate that (1) her interpretive target can get things wrong, (2) a possibly narrow range of different types of stimuli can trigger the same type of mental state, and (3) the same type of mental state can influence a possibly narrow range of different types of behavior. Given these minimal conditions on sophisticated mindreading, the problem of computational tractability seems to lose its bite. Since even chimpanzees (Call & Tomasello, 2008) and very young infants (Onishi & Baillargeon, 2005) appear[19] to have some capacity to track mental states that fail to be satisfied, and some mental states that can fail to be satisfied may be triggerable by only a small set of distinct stimuli and capable of influencing only a small set of distinct behaviors, the capacity to track such mental states should not be computationally intractable.

This line of argument has a number of problems. First, it still leaves unanswered why propositional attitude tracking evolved only in the human lineage. Our closest and by most accounts cleverest and socially most sophisticated nonhuman cousins, chimpanzees, can track false perceptions, at best (Krachun et al., 2009). We have little evidence that they can track mental states that are triggerable by distinct types of stimuli or influence distinct types of behavior. But if this task is not as computationally demanding as the foregoing arguments assume, and if the potential benefits of tracking such mental states are significant, as they must be for chimpanzees, given their famously Machiavellian social dynamics (de Waal, 2000), then the fact that such mindreading did not evolve in any lineage other than our own is even more puzzling.

A second problem concerns the explanatory scope of this proposal. Suppose it is true that our precursors could track propositional attitudes triggerable by only a small set of distinct stimuli and capable of influencing only a small set of distinct behaviors. This then triggered the evolution of the human sociocognitive syndrome. It remains the case that contemporary humans appear also able to track far more sophisticated propositional attitudes with far more tenuous, holistically constrained connections to observable stimuli and behavior. So the problem of computational tracta-bility must have been solved somehow in the human lineage.

Carruthers (2006, 2009a) distinguishes between System 1 and System 2 mindreading, which is relevant to this problem. System 1 mindreading is fast, automatic, unconscious, and likely innate. Because of these qualities, it can likely track only relatively "transparent" (Sterelny, 2003, p. 219) aspects of the social domain, like mental states with a narrow variety of connec-tions to observable stimuli and behavior. System 2 mindreading is slow, deliberate, conscious, and acquired from one's culture. Such mindreading, like other System 2 capacities (e.g., science), can be used to track "opaque" aspects of the social domain, including propositional attitudes with tenu-ous connections to observable stimuli and behavior. At best, therefore, the problem of computational tractability need not arise for System 1 track-ing of propositional attitudes with limited, stable, and predictable con-nections to observable stimuli and behavior. But this still leaves unsolved the puzzle of System 2 tracking of the kinds of propositional attitudes we routinely attribute using language: beliefs, desires, and other mental states with tenuous, holistically constrained connections to observable behavior and stimuli.[20]

However, if System 1 tracking of such attenuated propositional atti-tudes is computationally tractable, then this may jeopardize the thesis of this book. It is possible that such computationally tractable propositional attitude tracking triggered the evolution of the human sociocognitive syn-drome. This made possible more complex culture, which gradually drove the evolution of more complex kinds of propositional attitudes. As a result, selection pressures developed for increasingly sophisticated mindreading. But this capacity gradually ratcheted up from the initial System 1 capacity to track attenuated propositional attitudes, so computational tractability never posed a problem. In such a story, it would be plausible to conclude that mindreading was the linchpin of the human sociocognitive syndrome.

However, this story is implausible for the following reason. If a men-tal state has only a small number of stable and predictable connections to stimuli and behavior, then it is not clear that it is worth tracking the mental state rather than merely tracking the correlations between stimuli and behavior that the mental state mediates. Consider, for example, visual attention. In many of their real-world social interactions, chimpanzees appear capable of tracking the visual attention of their conspecifics; they seem to know what other chimpanzees see. For example, when a chimpan-zee sees another look at a space that she herself cannot see due to some obstacle, she will look behind the obstacle to see what the other is looking at. This seems to indicate that chimpanzees appreciate that others are subjects of visual attention. This interpretation has some experimental support. For example, Hare et al. (2000) showed that subordinate chimpanzees take into account whether or not a food reward for which they are competing with a dominant chimpanzee is visible to the dominant chimpanzee. They are far more likely to retrieve the food when they know it is not visible to the dominant chimpanzee. But it is far from clear that such behavior indicates a capacity to track the mental state "seeing." The reason is that visual attention has such reliable links to observable behavior that there is no need to attribute the mental state to predict the behavior it influences.

Chimpanzees need only determine whether or not another has a direct line of sight to some object to predict how the other will behave with respect to that object (Povinelli & Vonk, 2003, 2004; Penn & Povinelli, 2007; Lurz, 2009). Suppose a chimpanzee wants to avoid conflict over a food item with a dominant individual. If the dominant individual does not have a direct line of sight to the food item, this is a highly reliable indicator that conflict can be avoided. The opposite is the case if the dominant individual has a direct line of sight to the food item. But "direct line of sight" is not a mental state. Attributing it involves extending an imaginary line in the direction that the interpretive target is looking, and seeing whether or not it intersects with an item of interest. So chimpanzee interpreters can arrive at highly reliable behavioral predictions without going to all the trouble of attributing mental states. The lesson is that when it comes to mental states with highly reliable and direct connections to narrow ranges of behavior, like visual perceptions, it is not obvious that tracking the mental state helps with behavioral prediction. If the behavioral accompaniments of the mental state, for example, direct line of sight in the case of visual perception, are reliable enough predictors of future behavior, then these behavioral accompaniments are all that interpreters need to track. What is true of visual attention is presumably also true of the kinds of attenuated propositional attitudes to which *reliable* System 1 mindreading would be restricted.

The contrast with full-blown propositional attitudes is dramatic and instructive. There are no highly reliable and direct connections to narrow ranges of behavior for mental states like the *belief* that there is food in a certain location because such beliefs can be triggered in an indefinite number of ways: through smell, vision, memory, testimony, and so on. So, for example, although direct line of sight is necessary for an individual to have a visual perception of food location, it is not necessary for an individual to have a belief about food location because the belief can be triggered in some other manner, like remembering a previous visual perception. It follows that tracking direct line of sight is not a good surrogate for belief tracking: an individual *without* direct line of sight to a location with food might still believe there is food there. For this reason, predicting behavior caused by a belief, as opposed to a perception or an emotion or any other low-level mental state with direct and reliable connections to narrow ranges of behavior, requires attributing the belief; no acceptably reliable behavioral surrogates exist for such mental states, as direct line of sight is for visual perception. But nonhuman animals cannot attribute mental states like belief, and they appear to have no reason to track simpler mental states like perceptual states or attenuated propositional attitudes, since tracking such states does not appear to improve on the reliability of simple behavior tracking.

This line of argument is not convincing to everyone. For example, Whiten (1996) argues that tracking simple mental states like perceptions and desires is more efficient than tracking behavior. The reason is that, even in the case of such simple mental states, there is a many-to-one mapping from observable behavioral evidence to mental state types, and a one-to-many mapping from mental state types to behaviors. Whiten argues that it is more efficient to compress all this information under a mentalistic category, or "intervening variable" (Whiten, 1996, p. 283). Rather than storing pairwise correlations between different behavior types, it is computationally more efficient to treat different behaviors as indicating that the interpretive target is in a single mental state, and to predict subsequent behavior based on attribution of this mental state. For example, attributing the desire for food on the basis of a wide variety of behavioral cues (like constant monitoring of the food, grooming those with the food, trying to grab the food, threatening lower-ranked individuals approaching the food, picking up any scraps of food possible, following those with food, etc.) can support the following behavioral predictions: the interpretive target will take unguarded food; she will guard food once she has it; she will groom as a ploy to steal food; she will be friendly in exchange for food, and so on (p. 286). Surely this open-ended range of behavioral predictions requires the attribution of a mental state. The only alternative seems to be independent correlation between each of an open-ended range of behavioral signals of a mental state, and each of an open-ended range of behavioral consequences of a mental state, and this does seem highly inefficient.

This line of argument is not convincing. In the case of the desire for food,[21] it is not clear why such a mental state need be represented at all. Presumably, in the wild, chimpanzees always desire food, or at least they display a narrow range of reliable behavioral symptoms of this desire.

Therefore behaviors that indicate an individual's visual perception of food, that is, anything that establishes a direct line of sight, should be reliable evidence that the food is at risk of being retrieved by the individual. Given that chimpanzees are constantly monitoring each other's lines of sight, as soon as evidence indicates that a direct line of sight to a food item has been established, an interpreter can automatically anticipate food-related behavior. The form this behavior will take depends on situational factors, such as how far the interpretive target is from the food, which other individuals are in the vicinity, their lines of sight and locations relative to the food, and so on. However, there is no reason why such situational factors need to be supplemented with attributions of mental states to support reliable behavioral predictions. Interpreters need only assume that their interpretive targets choose the most efficient means of retrieving food to which they have a direct line of sight, given salient situational constraints. As noted in chapter 1, this is a variant on Dennett's (1987) "intentional stance": perhaps chimpanzees simply parse observable behavior into goals and rationally and informationally constrained means of achieving them. Empirical evidence supports this idea (Wood & Hauser, 2008). As argued in chapter 1, this does not require attributing mental states, that is, mental representations of goals and means for achieving them with causal influence over behavior. It involves only tracking of behavioral patterns (Dennett, 1991b).[22]

There would be an advantage to attributing intervening mentalistic variables if chimpanzee behavior were typically guided by enduring mental states the evidence for and behavioral consequences of which can be separated by significant time lags. Then it would pay to store information about mental states to help anticipate behavior in the future. The reason is that such mindreading would obviate the need to remember the relevant behavioral details for a long period of time: behavioral evidence could be interpreted mentalistically, as indicating an intervening variable like desire for food, or fear of another individual, or knowledge of the location of food, and only this would have to be remembered to anticipate behavior after a long delay. But what evidence do we have that chimpanzee behavior and interpretation are like this? If chimpanzee behavior is primarily determined by salient, immediately perceivable objects, like food items that are obvious both to interpreters and to their targets, rather than enduring mental states triggered long before the behavior to which they lead, then interpreters gain nothing from long-term representations of their targets' mental states. One need only track behavioral evidence of goals and information access, which have highly reliable behavioral signatures. If chimpanzees' behavior is almost entirely determined by what they perceive in the here and now,

then coding it in terms of mentalistic intervening variables provides absolutely no advantages.

Suppose an interpreter sees that her target has a direct line of sight to
a food item. And suppose a variety of behaviors are compatible with this.
What is the advantage of first attributing a mental state like visual attention? The interpreter still needs to decide among the variety of behaviors
compatible with visual attention: exactly the same variety of behaviors
compatible with direct line of sight. So, assuming that chimpanzee behavior is usually determined by salient objects in the here and now, it seems
more efficient to make predictions based directly on behavioral clues available in the here and now, without the extra step of inferring intervening
mentalistic variables. That different behavioral clues in different situations
can lead to the same behaviors is irrelevant to the context of a specific interpretive task; in these different situations, interpreters will employ different
behavioral correlations, opportunistically retrieving relevant behavioral
regularities on the fly, so to speak.

Furthermore, I think arguments such as Whiten's assume a false
dilemma: either chimpanzees are sensitive only to behavior types that
human experimenters distinguish, or they are sensitive to the mental states
for which these different behavior types provide evidence (Sterelny, 2003,
pp. 66–67, 215). Whiten (1996) does not consider a number of alternatives.
For example, perhaps chimpanzees compress behavioral information into
functional rather than mental categories (Sterelny, 2003, pp. 66–67). That is,
they may arrive at similar predictions based on the different behavior types
associated with, for example, visual attention, not because they conceive of
them all as indicating that the interpretive target *visually perceives* the food
item but because they conceive of them all as indicating that the interpretive target is unlikely to let them retrieve the food item. The equivalence
between the different behaviors of an interpretive target consists in their
(in)compatibility with the interpreter's projects, that is, their similar functional significance to the interpreter. So looking directly at a food item,
looking at it over one's shoulder, looking at it from the left or from the
right, are treated the same by subordinates not because they indicate that
the dominant sees the food but because they are all equally incompatible
with the subordinate retrieving the food unscathed. The categories with
which the subordinate interprets the dominant's behavior are something
like "(in)compatible with my plan to retrieve the food," rather than "sees/
does not see food."[23]

Consider an analogy: My computer engages in many different behavior
types to which I react similarly. Whether the screen suddenly goes dark or

turns bright white or starts flickering rapidly, or the track pad or keyboard is suddenly unresponsive, my reaction is always the same: reboot. Does this mean that I attribute to the computer some internal, unobservable state that all such behavior types indicate? Is this the only alternative to storing a separate correlation between every possible indicator of malfunction and my reboot response? This false alternative ignores a far simpler option. All these different behavior types have in common nonfunctionality relative to my projects: they make my computer useless to me. And I know one response that pretty reliably solves this problem: rebooting. None of this requires me to know or even guess what sort of internal state such different computer behaviors might indicate. Similarly, chimpanzees might learn from experience that a variety of observable conspecific behaviors all have the same functional import; for example, to the subordinate chimp, the various ways a dominant chimp has of noticing food all indicate that retrieving the food unscathed is unlikely. All these behaviors afford potential aggression, so the subordinate reacts similarly in each case: by avoiding the food.

Finally, it is important not to underestimate the power of intelligent behavior reading. The social cognition of our closest and cleverest nonhuman primate relatives involves constant monitoring of behavior throughout social interactions. As one individual approaches another, for example, they are constantly monitoring the real-time dynamic patterns of behavioral response. So it is almost never the case that interpreters need to make behavioral predictions based on incomplete data. They are fully aware of a constantly updated stream of behavioral data, and the task of behavioral prediction amounts to pattern completion: settling on the most likely development of the behavioral pattern they are in the process of witnessing. The real-time behavioral dynamics made available by such constant monitoring put significant constraints on future behavior. For example, once a shadow of hesitation has briefly appeared in an antagonist's facial expression, an interpreter immediately knows that certain future behaviors, such as determined aggression, are rendered less likely. The interpreter has no need to attribute an intervening mental state. An analogy to database search engines is instructive here. Consider the Internet search engine Google, for example. As one begins typing a search string, Google automatically suggests completions of it, so that one need not finish typing; one need only select one of the candidate completions suggested by the search engine. As one types more letters, that is, offers more behavioral evidence, the set of candidate completions shrinks because the more one types, the fewer commonly entered strings are compatible with what one types. Does this mean that Google can read minds? Assuredly not. Google "knows" that the more letters one types, the fewer completions are possible. This knowledge is based on statistical regularities gleaned from millions of other searches by millions of other users. But why can't behavioral interpretation in humans and nonhumans be based on a similar procedure? As an interpreter observes an increasingly extended pattern of behavior in a target, the set of feasible behavioral completions of this pattern, based on past observations of this target and others, shrinks, making possible increasingly reliable behavioral prediction. No attribution of mediating mental states seems necessary.[24]

Thus, even if there are attenuated propositional attitudes, with direct, reliable connections to narrow classes of behavior, it is not obvious that tracking such propositional attitudes themselves offers any advantage over tracking the behaviors, or perhaps some higher-order, perceptually accessible behavioral invariants that they share (like line of sight), and relating these to judgments of functionality relative to the interpreter's projects. Carruthers's System 1 mindreading is supposed to be fast, efficient, innate, and not under conscious control. Hence such mindreading can be accurate only for mental states with direct, simple, reliable connections to narrow classes of observable behavior. As we have seen, the more tenuous the connection to behavior, the more computationally costly and hence ecologically implausible the mindreading. But given this, there seems to be no reason to track such mental states. Subtle attunement to behavioral patterns would seem a much more efficient means of behavioral prediction for System 1 sociocognitive capacities.[25]

In any case, these sorts of considerations shift the burden of proof. Even if propositional attitude attribution would be computationally tractable in the case of attenuated propositional attitudes, this does not show that such propositional attitude attribution is likely to evolve. The reason is that, in the case of propositional attitudes with direct, reliable connections to narrow classes of behavior, nothing seems to be gained from attributing the propositional attitudes: as argued earlier, tracking the functional significance of subtle behavioral patterns should suffice to reliably anticipate how those patterns will be completed. To explain how propositional attitude attribution might have evolved, proponents of the received view need to evade the following dilemma. It seems that propositional attitude attribution is too intractable if it is meant to track full-blown propositional attitudes with tenuous connections to behavior; yet if it is meant to track attenuated propositional attitudes with direct, reliable connections to narrow classes of behavior, it seems otiose: behavior tracking can work just as well. Propositional attitude attribution, it seems, can be useful only if there are cases of behavioral prediction that occupy a kind of "middle ground" between mere behavior tracking and intractable propositional attitude attribution. There need to be situations where the costs of mere behavior tracking (e.g., unreliability and storing numerous behavioral correlations) outweigh the costs of propositional attitude attribution (e.g., unreliability due to holism). As far as I know, no one has yet shown that such situations are likely to have constituted an important selection pressure in hominid evolution.[26]

Furthermore, even if one can identify ecologically plausible types of social interaction in which System 1 attribution of attenuated propositional attitudes can improve on subtle behavior tracking while avoiding the pitfalls of holism, this still leaves unsolved the mystery of full-blown propositional attitude tracking. The connections between such mental states and behavior remain too tenuous to allow for computationally tractable yet reliable tracking. Yet we still devote a lot of time, energy, and neural resources to attributing full-blown propositional attitudes. Why do we do this, and how is this possible?

6   The Way Forward: Mindshaping as Human Homogenizer

I end the chapter by proposing a sketch of how I think humans solve the problems I have reviewed here. I propose that the kinds of mindshaping mechanisms and practices that chapter 2 argued are prevalent in, and distinctive of, human populations work to homogenize them, thereby making fast and frugal interpretation more effective.

Suppose human beings have an automatic default disposition to compare their own behavior to that of others, monitoring for any discrepancies. If the other is higher status, discrepancies tend automatically to issue in attempts at self-modification: one tries to change one's dispositions such that one's behavior better matches that of the high-status model (Henrich & Gil-White, 2001; Henrich, 2009). If the other is lower status, discrepancies tend automatically to issue in attempts to modify the other: one tries to change the other's dispositions, as in teaching offspring or punishing norm transgressors, such that the other's behavior better matches one's own. Assuming that judgments of status are largely homogeneous in a population, such mindshaping dispositions would tend to further homogenize populations, counteracting the "centrifugal forces" causing individual variation. And such homogeneity would render fast and frugal interpretation more reliable. For example, the "Take the Best" heuristic would be more likely to work. In a population of similarly socialized individuals, decision strategies that happen to have worked well in recent interpretive contexts are more likely to work in new circumstances. Similarly, variations of the simulation heuristic would also be more reliable: procedures that interpreters use in their own decision making would be more likely to be used by their interpretive targets as well.

Solutions to problems of computational tractability that arise for theory of mind, I want to urge, lie not *within* human mindreaders but *outside* them. Rather than deploy intractably sophisticated theories of each other's minds, we use a variety of mindshaping practices to ensure that our fellows are sufficiently familiar so that fast and frugal heuristics can help us accomplish our sociocognitive goals (Apperly, 2011, pp. 29, 160). We teach our children to behave in ways that make them easier to interpret (Bruner, 1983; Mameli, 2001; McGeer, 2007). We sanction those who behave in ways that are harder to interpret (think of the damage to status that often results from weakness of the will or absentmindedness). We display unconscious, automatic, and irresistible tendencies to conformity, such as the chameleon effect (Chartrand & Bargh, 1999). Such practices shape the sociocultural environment in ways that make behavioral interpretation significantly more tractable by fast and frugal heuristics than it would otherwise be.

This, in any case, is the argument in the following chapters. In particular, chapter 4 argues that the sorts of interactions that likely distinguished protohuman and human ancestral populations from other species, that is, elaborate bouts of cooperation, are possible only thanks to the cognitive homogeneity that results from sophisticated practices of mindshaping. This will *not* suffice to explain the evolution of sophisticated mindreading. The reason is that, given sufficiently homogenized populations, behavior tracking from the intentional stance should be sufficient to permit coordination. Chapter 7 focuses on this issue. It explains the role that full-blown propositional attitude attribution plays in the increasingly elaborate mindshaping and communicative practices that emerged in ancestral human populations and remain with us today.

4   Mindshaping and the Phylogeny of Human Cooperation

1   The Challenge of Human Uniqueness

Chapter 2 identified four properties that are unique to human mindshaping: it is intrinsically motivated, maximally flexible in the aspects of model behavior it can make targets match, often involves socially distributed mechanisms, and often involves nonactual models, like fictional characters or idealized agents. Chapter 1 also reviewed the widely acknowledged unique properties of human mindreading, cooperation and communication. No other species appears capable of attributing full-blown propositional attitudes. No other hominid species is as cooperative as ours. And no other species communicates using a language with the syntactic complexity and semantic flexibility of human languages. It is clear, therefore, that the human sociocognitive syndrome must be the product of an exceedingly rare evolutionary process. Some biological traits have evolved multiple times in different lineages, for example, wings, fins, and eyes. Such traits are products of selection for functions related to extremely stable properties of environments that many different species share, such as motion through water or air, or detecting and identifying distal objects based on the light they reflect. The same cannot be said for the human sociocognitive syndrome. Although our ancestors shared their physical environment with many other mammals, they were the only ones to evolve this set of capacities. Sterelny (2012, p. 6) concludes from this that human evolution was driven largely by "internal" dynamics: human evolution is the product of positive feedback loops of our own making. Some idiosyncratic sequence of events in our prehistory triggered a cascade of mutations that so altered significant, and especially social, aspects of our environment that it sent our lineage on a highly idiosyncratic trajectory, culminating in the human sociocognitive syndrome.[1]

Sterelny's explanation for the unique evolutionary trajectory culminating in the human sociocognitive syndrome focuses on the emergence of a lifestyle heavily dependent on cooperation. At some point in the history of our lineage, our ancestors began to depend on each other for basic survival and reproduction in ways unlike any other known hominid. They could not meet their basic nutritional needs, could not ensure that their offspring were nurtured and protected, and could not protect themselves against predators without the cooperation of numerous other individuals. This much, Sterelny takes as a given. Controversy emerges when one tries to fill in the details of how the requirements of cooperation explain our unique evolutionary trajectory. Sterelny considers two models: the Machiavellian intelligence hypothesis (MIH) and the cooperative foraging hypothesis (CFH).

The MIH is a natural ally of the mind*reading*-as-linchpin theory of the human sociocognitive syndrome, to which the view I defend in this book presents an alternative. The basic idea is the following. As noted in chapter 1, the evolution of cooperation is difficult to explain due to the "free rider" problem. In a population where most individuals cooperate at some cost to themselves, for example, by contributing to a public good like defense against predators, incentives will arise to take advantage of this public good without incurring the costs of contributing to it.[2] An individual engaged in such free riding could incur all the benefits of cooperation while incurring none of the costs. This should make the free rider more biologically successful: she should secure more calories, attract more mates, incur fewer risks vis-à-vis predators, and produce more offspring. Eventually the population should come to be dominated by such uncooperative individuals. An obvious way to prevent this is policing. If group members are good at detecting free riders, then they can exclude them from the spoils of cooperative endeavors. However, this sets up an incentive to avoid detection. Free riders who can fool the group should have an advantage. It is obvious how sophisticated mindreading might emerge from such dynamics. Both detecting free riders and avoiding such detection would improve dramatically with improved mindreading. If one can tell that an individual has no *intention* of contributing to a public good, then one can prevent her from taking advantage of it. If one can tell that an individual *suspects* that one has no *intention* to contribute to a public good, then one can engage in deceptive behavior aimed at changing the individual's mind.

This theory has the potential to explain both the internal positive feedback loop that generated our unique evolutionary trajectory, and the various properties that distinguish the human sociocognitive syndrome that it produced. The linchpin, according to this theory, is sophisticated mindreading. For cooperation to be viable, free riders need to be policed.

But such policing requires better mindreading and sets up selection pressures for even better mindreading supportive of deception by free riders. This triggers a coevolutionary arms race between deceiving free riders and deception-detecting police. This arms race alters the protohuman sociocognitive niche dramatically, nudging human cognitive evolution onto its highly idiosyncratic path. The path leads to the other components of the human sociocognitive syndrome: police and free riders use their enhanced mindreading to shape each other in increasingly human ways. For example, police set up increasingly humanlike systems of norm enforcement, which free riders learn to manipulate to their own advantage in increasingly humanlike ways. Language emerges as a way of signaling mental states, like cooperative intentions, or of faking such signals.

This is a familiar and highly influential story. However, Sterelny (2007, 2012) is not convinced. He argues that this standard story drastically overestimates the significance of the free rider problem relative to the likely demographics and lifeways of early humans and their immediate precursors. According to Sterelny's cooperative foraging hypothesis (CFH), these populations subsisted on kills of extremely formidable megafauna, accomplished with very crude weapons—mainly spears for jabbing, but, importantly, no accurate projectile launchers that individuals could use to bring down prey alone. Such hunts could succeed only with sophisticated cooperation and coordination; however, Sterelny argues that the cooperative component of such endeavors was unlikely to have been problematic. Meat from a kill would be distributed on the spot to all participants, so everyone would know that each contributor was getting his fair share. The coordinative and informational demands of such hunts, on the other hand, would pose extraordinary challenges. Knowing how to track, ambush, and bring down megafauna through the coordination of numerous individuals using only crude weaponry is no easy trick. Sterelny argues that it is possible only through reliable information sharing across and within generations.

To preserve and elaborate on ecological knowledge necessary for tracking, ambushing, and successfully killing megafauna, early humans and their immediate precursors needed traditions of reliable information transmission across generations. Only such practices could give rise to the preservation, accumulation, and refinement of such sophisticated knowledge.[3] In addition, to coordinate during hunts, early and protohuman populations would need to deploy subtle, flexible, yet efficient systems of communication. Thus, according to Sterelny's CFH, selection operating on such populations would have favored cooperative information sharers, rather than Machiavellian mindreaders. The cognitive capacities initially favored in such circumstances would have been social learning capacities: high-fidelity imitation and the kind of master-and-apprentice-style pedagogy discussed in chapter 2. Better mindreading might then evolve as a way of improving such already established mindshaping practices: in chapter 2, I also noted Sterelny's conjecture that pedagogy would improve as masters became better at reading their apprentices' minds. The evolution of language could also be explained along these lines: there would be selection for increasingly effective means of communicating culturally accumulated information to novices, and of coordinating and planning hunts.

Sterelny (2012) grapples with an obvious flaw in this picture. As noted in chapter 1, reliable communication itself presupposes cooperation and affords opportunities for free riding based on deception. Why would masters allow novices to learn skills from them without some kind of guarantee that the novices would not later use these skills against them? On what basis could hunters trust each other's signals in the context of planning and coordinating hunts? It seems that, rather than offering an alternative to the MIH, the CFH actually presupposes it. Reliable information sharing seems impossible without sophisticated policing against deceptive free riders, and this should set up the coevolutionary spiral leading to sophisticated mindreading described earlier. But Sterelny argues persuasively that, given the demographics and lifeways that likely characterized early human and protohuman populations, there was a much cheaper way to prevent the corruption of communicative practices: the *public* sharing of information (2012, pp. 136–139). If information transmission is many-to-many, then profitable deception is highly unlikely.[4]

How might we adjudicate between the MIH and the CFH? Sterelny's CFH is obviously a better fit for the thesis of this book. In this view, the evolution of the human sociocognitive syndrome is driven largely by the requirements of efficient and reliable mindshaping, for example, imitation and pedagogy required to preserve, accumulate, and improve ecologically significant information across generations. However, as Sterelny realizes (2012, p. 101), such arguments for the CFH and against the MIH have their limits. First, just because free riding was not incentivized in *some* of the socioecological circumstances that likely characterized early and protohuman populations, there may well have been other circumstances that were more conducive to free riding. Just living in groups large enough to allow for (1) adequate predator defense, (2) cooperative child rearing, (3) robust and high-fidelity intergenerational information transmission, (4) public information pooling sufficient to prevent deceptive free riding, and (5) group hunting of megafauna with primitive weaponry would seem to create diverse and numerous opportunities for free riding.[5] For example, after meat from a kill was distributed and no longer open to public scrutiny, opportunities for theft would arise. If hunting parties involved only males, couldn't an unscrupulous male feign injury and then take advantage of unguarded mates? Once food was distributed, wouldn't a market emerge, where individuals could trade meat for other goods, such as sex, tools, and so on? Such interactions would be open to Machiavellian manipulation in a way that the more public ones on which Sterelny focuses would not be.[6]

A second set of problems arises with Sterelny's positive view: his model does not seem to account for some of the key features that distinguish the human sociocognitive syndrome. Recall that, as argued in chapter 2, human mindshaping is distinguished from nonhuman varieties by (at least) the following four properties: (1) it is intrinsically motivated, (2) it often involves socially distributed shaping mechanisms, (3) it is extremely flexible in the aspects of model behavior that shaping mechanisms can make targets match, and (4) models are often nonactual individuals, like fictional characters or idealized agents. Sterelny's theory might account for (2); indeed, he stresses that master-apprentice interaction would be selected for in his scenario.[7] However, it is hard to see how the other properties of uniquely human mindshaping are explained by his account.[8] Furthermore, Sterelny's CFH does not account for the other unique properties of the human sociocognitive syndrome. Why would it predict sophisticated, full-blown propositional attitude attribution? After all, Sterelny himself stresses that the kind of mindreading that could help masters teach apprentices involves nothing more than sensitivity to (limitations on) behavioral capacities (2012, pp. 145–146). And why would the CFH predict the evolution of a communication system with the syntactic complexity and semantic flexibility of human language? Sterelny stresses that the communication system needed for the kinds of information pooling on which he focuses would not approach the complexity of contemporary human languages (pp. 36, 139–140). Communication among cooperative foragers could easily be restricted to short sequences of attention-directing signals, devoted to topics related to hunting, tool manufacture and use, and knowledge of natural history—hardly sufficient to explain the evolution of a recursively structured language capable of expressing information about any domain.

To be fair, Sterelny intends the CFH only as a model of how the human sociocognitive syndrome got off the ground, so to speak. He gestures toward more complex selection pressures related to what he calls the "broad-spectrum revolution" (BSR) of roughly 100,000 to 40,000 years ago (2012, pp. 4, 90, 180). I think these developments are far more important to explaining the distinctive features of the human sociocognitive syndrome than the earlier ones highlighted by the CFH. Accordingly, in the following, I treat the CFH as a plausible theory of how a broadly chimpanzee-like species might have initially become more cooperative and capable of reliable and pervasive information sharing. The next three sections focus on the sorts of selection pressures that likely resulted from the social-niche-altering developments of the BSR, arguing that these can explain the distinctive features of the human sociocognitive syndrome noted in chapter 1 and chapter 2. In particular, I argue that these new selection pressures made behavioral anticipation substantially more challenging because they exacerbated cognitive heterogeneity due to economic and demographic factors such as division of labor. In such circumstances, our ancestors could no longer rely on the cheap means of free rider prevention that they relied on earlier, in the context of cooperative hunting of megafauna. This naturally suggests that the sorts of dynamics proposed by the MIH took hold, leading to an evolutionary arms race favoring increasingly sophisticated mindreading, but I offer arguments against this idea in section 2. In sections 3 and 4, I argue that sophisticated mindshaping practices were the key to stabilizing cooperation and coordination in the new circumstances ushered in by the BSR. Section 5 reviews empirical evidence supportive of Sterelny's conjectures as well as my supplements.

2   Grappling with Heterogeneity: Why Machiavellian Mindreading Can't Help

According to Sterelny (2012, pp. 90–93), a cluster of related developments gave rise to the BSR. First, after thousands of years of hunting by early humans, populations of megafauna began to dwindle. Second, presumably as a response to this decline, our ancestors developed more sophisticated weaponry, such as accurate projectile launchers, capable of bringing down larger numbers of smaller prey more efficiently. Third, also in response to the decline of megafaunal populations, our ancestors began to specialize in diverse, narrow foraging niches. Some became expert at tracking and hunting smaller mammals, others became expert at harvesting various marine fauna, and so on. These kinds of specialization gave rise to a sophisticated division of labor. Fourth, increasing population densities brought separate groups increasingly into contact with each other. Given specialized foraging, such contact likely gave rise to trade among individuals unfamiliar to each other: when one group's foraging niches were underproductive, for example, due to seasonal fluctuation, they could compensate by trading goods for food from another group whose foraging niches happened to yield a surplus at that time. But such frequent intergroup contact also likely gave rise to competition between groups. As noted in chapter 1, evidence points to the existence of long-distance trade routes from as long as 100,000 years ago (McBrearty & Brooks, 2000).

Because of these features, the BSR undermined the conditions that had made cooperation relatively cheap in earlier populations. Hunting was no longer communal, so public food sharing among all members of a group after a kill could no longer block free riding. The division of labor undermined public pooling of information among all members of a group. Information relevant to a particular foraging niche would need to be pooled only among the small minority who specialized in it. Such balkanization of information sharing jeopardized some of the cognitively cheap mechanisms of free rider prevention that had made earlier cooperation possible.[9] Finally, interaction with other human groups likely increased intercourse with unfamiliar individuals. Such intercourse obviously afforded more opportunities for deception than the more communal and parochial interactions to which earlier populations were restricted.

Understanding how our post-BSR ancestors addressed the deceptive free rider problem in the wake of the collapse of the earlier cooperative foraging lifeways is key to understanding how the human sociocognitive syndrome acquired its distinctive profile (Sterelny, 2012, p. 180). As noted earlier, this *seems* like precisely the set of circumstances that would trigger the kind of mindreading arms race suggested by the Machiavellian intelligence hypothesis. However, these considerations do not vindicate the MIH. On the contrary, post-BSR cooperation and coordination relied primarily on sophisticated mindshaping that mitigated the need for sophisticated mindreading. In defense of this claim, let me begin with three arguments against the MIH, specifically, against the assumption that sophisticated mindreading can help solve problems of coordination and cooperation in cognitively and motivationally heterogeneous populations. I will follow this, in sections 3 and 4, with an explanation of how sophisticated mindshaping can solve such problems.

The first argument against the MIH draws on the lessons of chapter 3. Sophisticated mindreading appears to be extremely difficult and hence time and energy consuming. The general reason for this, as argued in chapter 3, is holism: it is extremely difficult to read propositional attitudes off of finite bouts of behavior because any finite sequence of behavior is compatible with any finite set of propositional attitudes, if appropriate adjustments are made to background propositional attitudes. This problem takes specific forms in the circumstances that likely followed in the wake of the BSR. First, given the increasing cognitive and motivational heterogeneity brought about by more extreme divisions of labor, interactants would bring diverse cognitive and motivational resources to their interactions, compromising fast and frugal sociocognitive heuristics for the reasons discussed in chapter 3. Second, given the increasing incentivization of deception and free riding conjectured by Sterelny, interactants could no longer rely on the presence of cooperative background motivations in formulating reliable behavioral interpretations quickly and frugally. Everyone would have an incentive to modify his or her behavior so as to make it less easy to interpret using heuristics that had worked earlier (Sterelny, 2003, p. 53). As Sterelny puts it, this would make the social domain "translucent," and hence not easily negotiated using either modularized or fast and frugal social cognition (2003, p. 219; 2012, p. 9). Finally, given increased intergroup intercourse, individuals would interact with increasing numbers of unfamiliar individuals possibly motivated by covert antipathy. This would make fast, frugal, and reliable mindreading in such contexts a near impossibility. All such interpretive problems would be compounded in many-to-many interactions, where each interactant would have to simultaneously attribute mental states to numerous other individuals.[10]

The second argument against the mindreading-as-linchpin perspective of the MIH draws on an obvious fact about contemporary human social cognition. Human beings rarely attribute, and are, on the whole, not very good at attributing, "higher-order" mental states. We often think about what others are thinking; that is, we often attribute "first-order" mental states. And sometimes we think about what others think that we are thinking; we occasionally attribute "second-order" mental states. But as anyone will acknowledge, thinking about orders of intentionality higher than this is rare, difficult, and unlikely to be reliable (Skyrms, 2009). To my knowledge, there has been only one rigorous empirical study of human performance on such tasks. As part of a study relating theory of mind ability to causal-explanatory styles in normal adults, Kinderman et al. (1998) compared performance on the attribution of increasingly higher orders of intentional states to performance on the attribution of comparably complex nonpsychological states.[11] Subjects read stories that required the attribution of higher orders of intentionality, as well as complex nonpsychological causal sequences, and were then tested for recall of such attributions with forced-choice questions. Only recall of attributions of the lowest order of intentionality, for example, attributions of belief about nonpsychological states of affairs, showed error rates comparable to recall of correspondingly complex nonpsychological attributions. Recall of attributions of second-order intentional states (e.g., she believes that he desires X), third-order intentional states (e.g., he hopes that she believes that he desires X), and especially fifth-order intentional states (e.g., she suspects that he desires that she believes that he hopes that she wishes that X) showed significantly more errors than recall of comparably complex nonpsychological facts. Oddly, while recall of attributions of fourth-order intentional states was less reliable than recall of comparably complex nonpsychological attributions, the difference did not reach significance. Kinderman et al. conclude that the attribution of higher orders of intentionality shows a great deal of variation in normals and probably places strong demands on domain-general capacities like executive functioning, working memory, and attention.

That attributing higher-order intentional states, or at least recalling such attributions, seems so much more error prone and interpersonally variable than comparably complex nonpsychological attributions seems to rule out the possibility that the attribution of higher-order intentional states was a socioecologically crucial capacity in human prehistory, which led to selection for some kind of module dedicated to Machiavellian mindreading. This provides evidence against the MIH because, according to this hypothesis, deception and deception detection triggered an evolutionary arms race, leading to ever more sophisticated mindreaders. Furthermore, the kind of mindreading that deception and deception detection are likely to incentivize is precisely the kind that human beings seem to find extremely challenging. To effectively deceive, one must think about what others are thinking; and to detect deception, one must think about what others think one is thinking. Furthermore, to avoid having one's deception detected, one must think about what others think one thinks they are thinking, and so on. So if the MIH is true, and an evolutionary arms race between deception and deception detection drove the evolution of the human sociocognitive syndrome, then not only should we be sophisticated and accurate mindreaders, but our mindreading should make thinking about mental states of indefinitely higher orders intuitive, easy, and reliable. But this flies in the face of everyday experience and empirical facts.[12]

The final argument against the MIH draws on well-known problems that arise in the context of game theoretic modeling of coordination problems. It turns out that better mindreading cannot help with coordination or cooperation.[13] Even if deception and other forms of free riding can somehow be prevented, the success of cooperative endeavors is not guaranteed because coordinating on a specific cooperative course of action out of many alternatives is not a trivial accomplishment. For example, in the "Hi-Lo" game, two interactants must coordinate on the same response for each to secure the highest payoff: both must pick "Hi" (Bacharach, 2006). If both pick "Lo," they each get a lower payoff, and if their picks do not match, neither gets anything. The "Stag Hunt" game raises a similar coordination problem (Skyrms, 2003). If both interactants choose to hunt stag together, they each receive the highest payoff, bringing in the most meat. If both choose to hunt hare separately, they each receive a lower payoff—less meat. If one chooses to hunt stag but the other chooses to hunt hare, the stag hunter gets nothing, and the hare hunter gets the smaller amount of meat. In such interactions, cooperation is not a problem: there is no incentive to defect, because unlike in games where interests conflict (e.g., the prisoner's dilemma), cooperation yields the highest rewards for both interactants. However, cooperation can still fail due to a lack of coordination: each interactant must somehow determine that the other will act as she does—play "Hi" if she plays "Hi," or hunt stag if she hunts stag—to reap the potential benefits of cooperation. The problem is predicting what one's interactants will do in situations where the relative payoffs of one's actions are contingent on their actions.

There *seems* to be an obvious role for mindreading to play in such situations, even though, as will become apparent, this is an illusion. If each interactant could just read the other's mind, the problem should disappear. This solution appears highly intuitive. Consider Bacharach's "Hi-Lo" game again. As he points out, in everyday life this type of interaction is a trivial accomplishment: every normal adult human being chooses "Hi," confident that her interactant will as well (2006, pp. 35, 42–45). And such confidence is vindicated. Surely, one might argue, this is because we are reliable at gauging each other's preferences, beliefs, and intentions: each other's propositional attitudes. David Lewis explicitly endorses this assumption in his seminal analysis of conventions as equilibriums in such coordination games:

We may achieve coordination by acting on our concordant expectations about each other's actions. And we may acquire those expectations … by putting ourselves in the other fellow's shoes, to the best of our ability. If I know what you believe about matters of fact that determine the likely effects of your alternative actions, and if I know your preferences among possible outcomes and I know that you possess a modicum of practical rationality, then I can replicate your practical reasoning to figure out what you will probably do, so that I can act appropriately. … In the case of a coordination problem … one of the matters of fact that goes into determining the likely effects of your alternative actions is my own action. In order to figure out what you will do by replicating your practical reasoning, I need to figure out what *you* expect *me* to do. ... To replicate your reasoning, I may have to replicate your attempt to replicate my reasoning. ... This is not the end. I may reasonably expect *you* to realize that, unless I already know what you expect me to do, I may have to try to replicate your attempt to replicate my reasoning. So I may expect you to try to replicate my attempt to replicate your attempt to replicate my reasoning. So my own reasoning may have to include an attempt to replicate your attempt to replicate my attempt to replicate your attempt to replicate my reasoning. And so on. (Lewis, 1969, pp. 27–28)

Here Lewis seems to endorse a simulationist model (Goldman, 2006) of mindreading as the central component of solutions to coordination problems: by adopting the perspective of the other, each interactant can discover the other's occurrent, action-guiding propositional attitudes and predict what the other will do. Of course, as Lewis notes, such mindreading potentially triggers an infinite regress of propositional attitude attributions: when interactants read each other's minds, assuming that their epistemic perspectives are symmetrical, as all game theoretic models do, they will discover only that the other is trying to read *their* mind, *not* what the other intends to *do*. Lewis does not see this as an insurmountable problem; however, as Gilbert (1996, pp. 27, 42, 49–50, 136–139) and Bacharach (2006, pp. 44–47, 61, 162) argue, classical game theory does *not* have the resources to explain how we get past it.

The problem is that, in coordination problems, the rational decision is conditional on one's interactant's decision. Consider the well-known example of reconnecting an interrupted phone conversation. If both parties try to call, they will fail, as the lines will be busy. It is best if one calls while the other waits. However, how does each party determine which role to play? The rational choice depends on the other party's choice. Of course, there could be an antecedent, verbal agreement to the effect that, for example, the party who initiated the original call should initiate reconnecting if the call is interrupted. However, since using a conventional language raises precisely the same sort of coordination problem, it is unavailable as a solution to the problem of how coordination arises in the first place. Suppose we appeal to mindreading here, as Lewis does. If one party tries to read the other party's mind, she will *not* discover whether the other party intends to initiate the reconnection or wait instead. Rather, she will discover that the other party's decision is conditional on her decision, and hence that the other party is trying to read her mind in an attempt to determine this. But since the parties are equally rational and in symmetrical epistemic circumstances, the other party will discover exactly the same facts about the first party: that she is trying to read her mind, and so on. This launches a regress: A will phone back only if B believes that A will phone back, but B believes that A will phone back only if A believes that B believes that A will phone back, but A believes that B believes that A will phone back only if B believes that A believes that B believes that A will phone back, and so on.

Lewis (1969) tries to show how varieties of salience, like precedent, might block this kind of regress. Perhaps when the parties had tried to reconnect interrupted phone conversations before, they succeeded by luck when the initial caller initiated the reconnection while the other party waited. The memory of this fortuitously successful coordination should make similar courses of behavior salient in later circumstances of a similar nature, and both parties should know this and hence know what roles to play. But, as Gilbert argues (1996, pp. 27, 42, 49–50), this fails to solve the problem. It is rational to follow precedent or to opt for some otherwise salient course of behavior only on condition that one's interactant opts for the complementary course of behavior. But since one's interactant is in exactly the same situation, she will intend to pursue the complementary course of behavior only on condition that one intends to do one's part. So when the interactants read each other's minds, they discover only that each will do her part in the salient course of behavior if the other will, but never what the other will actually do.

The problem is that game theory—as a species of rational choice theory—attempts to show that each interactant has a *reason* to choose to play her part in a coordinative equilibrium. It is not enough that each interactant happens, by luck, to choose to play her part due to some nonrational factor. Suppose, for example, that one interactant in a "Hi-Lo" game displays an involuntary facial tic only when she is about to choose "Hi," and the other somehow knows this. The other will then have a reason to pick "Hi" when she sees the first produce the facial tic, but only because the interaction ceases to be of any interest from a game theoretic perspective: it is no longer an interaction between two agents whose behavior is determined by reasons; it is more like an interaction between a single rational agent and a nonrational phenomenon. If what is at issue is determining the right course of action to achieve coordination between two rational agents in symmetrically epistemic circumstances, then accurate mindreading seems to be of no help.

It is reasonable to question the relevance of rationalistic, game theoretic models of coordination to actual, real-world feats of human coordination. After all, it is a commonplace that we are not ideally rational. Can't we just "satisfice" somehow, for example, by learning each other's nonrational behavioral dispositions and taking advantage of them to predict each other's behavior in ways that permit actual coordinative success?

Perhaps something along these lines is correct. However, this jeopardizes the Machiavellian intelligence hypothesis, for it suggests another reason why sophisticated mindreading offers little help in explaining cooperation. Imagine an evolving population in which sophisticated, powerful, and accurate mindreaders are rapidly becoming dominant. As they edge out less sophisticated mindreaders, they begin to interact exclusively with their mindreading equals, since there are fewer and fewer others left. However, as this happens, their coordinative projects must come to a standstill. When they encounter their mindreading equals, they cannot predict what they will do, since accurate mindreading reveals only that others are trying to read *their* minds. Since their decisions are contingent on knowing what the others will do, and they never discover this because the others' intentions are also contingent on knowing what they will do, they never come to any decisions.

Thus, for at least three reasons, the MIH cannot explain the success of human cooperation in the wake of the BSR. According to the MIH, better mindreading can help solve cooperative dilemmas by enabling agents to better detect free riding and deception, and by allowing cooperatively disposed agents to coordinate on complementary courses of action. But, as we have seen, this claim is unlikely to be true. First, it offers no solution to the holism problem, that is, the problem of inferring an agent's mental states based on observations of finite bouts of behavior. Second, it predicts that human reasoning about higher-order mental states should be intuitive, easy, and reliable; but this claim is empirically false. Third, even putting the problem of cooperation to the side, sophisticated, accurate mindreading is not sufficient to explain successful coordination among cooperatively inclined individuals. The reason is that successful coordination requires that each interactant first determine what the other will do, but accurate mindreading reveals only that the other is trying to determine what the first will do, and this launches a regress of mindreading that appears to have no rational limit. I turn now to a discussion of some recent models of cooperation and coordination that show how sophisticated mindshaping can solve the kinds of cooperative and coordinative dilemmas that sophisticated mindreading appears incapable of solving.

3   Conformism and Costly Punishment: How Mindshaping Explains Human Cooperation

The puzzle of human cooperation decomposes into two component problems: (1) how cooperation is incentivized above free riding and deception, and (2) how agents incentivized to cooperate successfully coordinate on complementary cooperative acts when choosing from a range of alternatives, many of which are not complementary. I think that sophisticated mindshaping has played crucial roles in solving both of these problems and continues to play these roles today. In this section, I focus on models of how cooperative dispositions and practices that incentivize cooperation might emerge and remain stable in human populations. In section 4, I turn to models of how practices necessary to successful coordination emerge and remain stable in populations of individuals who are already cooperatively disposed.

As we saw in section 1 of this chapter, there are good reasons to conjecture that our distant ancestors—the first humans and their immediate precursors—were likely disposed to cooperate and trust each other before the BSR. The question is how such cooperative dispositions remained stable after the BSR, which degraded various public information-sharing practices on which honest communication and cooperation had depended previously (Sterelny, 2012, p. 180). As populations became more heterogeneous due to increasing division of labor, and interactions with unfamiliar individuals increased due to increasing population density and intergroup encounters, greater risks of deception and free riding arose. However, according to recent models of the evolution of cooperation, a combination of mindshaping practices could mitigate such risks (Henrich, 2004).

The key notion behind such models is group selection (Sober & Wilson, 1998; Boehm, 1996; 1999, chap. 9; Sterelny, 2003, pp. 125–127; 2012, pp. 173–196). Classical evolutionary theory assumes that natural selection operates only on individual organisms. Genetic mutations are expressed in phenotypic traits of individual organisms. If such mutations hinder the individual's reproductive prospects, they are selected against. If such mutations help the individual's reproductive prospects, they are selected for. It is difficult to see how selection operating solely on individual organisms could give rise to and maintain the stability of cooperative dispositions. As I have noted, free riding often pays off at the individual level. Sterelny's characterization of the socioecology of pre-BSR hominins suggests that dependence on cooperative hunting of megafauna made cooperation worthwhile at the individual level. So selection operating on individual hominins may have favored cooperative dispositions in such circumstances (Sterelny, 2012, p. 180). But after the BSR, these circumstances no longer obtained. Once the information commons was balkanized, selection operating on individuals began to favor deception and other forms of free riding. These were easier to get away with, so individuals who had such "countersocial" dispositions were favored. Group selection could potentially mitigate such selective pressures. According to the hypothesis of group selection, selection sometimes operates on groups of organisms rather than just individual organisms. That is, we can conceive of groups as units that vary in their properties. Properties that promote the stability and survival of groups should then be favored by selection over properties that do not. It is plausible that groups whose members have strong cooperative dispositions, including honest signaling, remain more stable than, and successfully compete with, groups whose members lack such dispositions. For this reason, the hypothesis of group selection predicts that even in circumstances where free riding and deception are favored at the individual level, such as post-BSR human prehistory, groups consisting of members with such dispositions would be at a disadvantage relative to groups consisting of members with more cooperative, honest, and, in general, "prosocial" dispositions.

Here is how group selection can operate. First, groups with more prosocial members should be better at solving the sorts of cooperative problems on which human survival and reproductive success depend. Imagine a post-BSR human group whose members are generally honest with each other. When they signal commitment to a course of behavior, they do not renege. When members specializing in different foraging niches or artifact production practices trade with each other, they agree and conform to equitable terms. Members resist temptations to mate with others' mates. Reciprocity in cooperative child rearing is the default. Everyone contributes equitably to predator defense. Such a group would have obvious advantages over groups consisting of less prosocial members. Honest signaling would promote better coordination in group endeavors, like hunts, artifact construction, and warfare. Honest trading would promote more efficient distributions of goods. Conformity to restrictions on mate access would ensure that investment in offspring is genetically rewarded. Reciprocity in child rearing and cooperation on predator defense would promote the reproductive success of all members. Most importantly, the savings in time, energy, and resources required for constant vigilance against free riders should favor groups with more prosocial members over groups with less prosocial members. So even without direct intergroup competition, groups with more prosocial members should survive longer and grow larger than groups with less prosocial members. Thus, in the long run, more individual members of the species should belong to such prosocial groups and hence possess such prosocial dispositions.

The second way in which group selection can operate is through direct intergroup competition, as in warfare or resource extraction. Groups in close proximity to each other should, inevitably, compete for scarce resources. Those with more cooperatively disposed members should have advantages in extracting more of such scarce resources, and in more direct forms of competition like warfare. Facing an enemy in battle raises the free rider problem in a particularly acute way. The temptation to defect to save one's skin is strong. Groups defended by fighters who do not renege on their martial commitments obviously have advantages over groups defended by more self-interested fighters. In the long run, groups consisting of members with more prosocial dispositions should outcompete groups with less prosocial members, both militarily and economically.[14] The relative success of such cooperative groups might even encourage members of less cooperative groups to voluntarily assimilate.[15] Groups left standing by such selective processes would consist of individuals with prosocial dispositions. This is how group selection can explain the stability of cooperative dispositions even in circumstances, like those faced by post-BSR human populations, where free riding and deception appear to be favored at an individual level.

However, the hypothesis of group selection has a serious problem. It assumes that variation among individuals is much smaller within than across groups.[16] Selection can operate on groups only if variation exists between groups. But what is to stop less prosocial individuals from invading groups consisting of more prosocial individuals? This can occur in numerous ways. First, given that members of different human groups all share the same genetic endowment, if countersocial dispositions are possible for one human group, they are possible for all human groups. So any group consisting of prosocial individuals is constantly at risk of invasion by countersocial individuals because their offspring carry the genetic potential for countersocial dispositions expressed in less prosocial groups. Furthermore, what is to stop countersocial members of other groups from joining prosocial groups and free riding on their cooperative dispositions? For group selection for prosocial dispositions to work, there must be mechanisms that protect against invasion by countersocial individuals—either offspring with countersocial genetic potential or individuals from other, less cooperative groups.

This is the first role that robust forms of mindshaping can play. Imitation, pedagogy, and other mechanisms of conformism should ensure intergroup homogeneity and intergroup variation. Offspring born in prosocial groups would have their genetically determined countersocial dispositions dampened through pedagogy and a bias to conform to the behavior of the majority of their group mates. Individuals invading from other groups would also tend to conform to majority behavior. If Sterelny is right about the dispositions of pre-BSR humans, such conformist dispositions should still have been present in post-BSR human populations and should have made intergroup variation possible. Members of less cooperative groups would also have conformed to the countersocial behaviors that character-ized such groups. The intergroup variation induced by such conformity is precisely what is required for group selection to operate. Groups with pro-social members would have been favored in such circumstances.

Unfortunately it is not clear that this is sufficient to explain group selec-tion for prosocial dispositions. The reason is that dispositions toward con-formism were at risk in the post-BSR world. In the information commons of the pre-BSR world, it paid to conform: everyone needed to acquire broadly the same skill set to participate in group hunts of megafauna and receive one's fair share of the kills. However, in the post-BSR, balkanized infor-mation commons, one could not simply conform to the majority because there was no uniform skill set that everyone had to acquire to prosper. One had to selectively imitate individuals whose specialized skills one reckoned were favored in the circumstances. Such selective imitation would naturally give rise to a *prestige bias*: more successful individuals would be imitated more.[17] However, the prestige bias jeopardizes the intergroup variation and intragroup homogeneity on which group selection depends. The reason is that free riders introduced into a generally prosocial population should, at first, be highly successful. After all, they reap the rewards of public goods without incurring any of the costs and risks associated with contributing to them. So the prestige bias should lead individuals to imitate clever free riders. This should dampen any prosocial tendencies in any group, thereby decreasing intergroup variation with respect to such traits. This would jeop-ardize group selection for prosocial tendencies.

According to Henrich (2004), one way such effects of the prestige imita-tion bias can be mitigated is through another mindshaping practice that appears to be widespread across the full range of human populations: costly punishment. As I noted in chapter 2, strong evidence from both a variety of small-scale, traditional societies and contemporary industrialized soci-eties indicates that human beings are strongly disposed to incur material costs to punish behavior that induces counternormative distributions of material goods (Henrich et al., 2005, 2006).[18] Furthermore, human infants appear favorably disposed toward the punishment of antisocial characters (Hamlin et al., 2011). Henrich (2004) argues that such costly punishment can explain how variation in prosocial dispositions across different groups could arise and remain stable enough for group selection to operate and favor groups with more prosocial members, even in the face of the prestige bias.

Here is the idea. If a sufficient proportion of a group's members are disposed to incur costs to punish nonconformist behavior, then the intragroup homogeneity and intergroup variation necessary for group selection should be maintained. The reason is that punishment raises the costs of nonconformist behavior. So, for example, in a population with prosocial norms, free riders will not have an advantage, and hence will not gain in prestige, if enough members are disposed to incur the costs (e.g., potential physical harm) of punishing their transgressions. Such punishment increases the costs of counternormative behavior, so norm violators do not have any advantages when it comes to securing resources and hence are not imitated as the result of prestige bias. Costly punishment, in itself, does not necessarily favor the evolution of prosocial norms (Boyd & Richerson, 1992). In some groups, *cooperators* might be punished. However, it should promote the kind of intragroup homogeneity and intergroup variation necessary for group selection to get off the ground. Then groups that punish countersocial behavior should have an advantage, and cooperative dispositions should remain stable and spread.

The problem with this suggestion, as noted in chapter 1, is that it spawns a "second-order free rider problem" (Henrich, 2004). Since punishment is costly, prosocial individuals who do not punish have an advantage over prosocial individuals who punish. Such nonpunishing cooperators do not incur the costs of punishment, but they take advantage of those who punish free riders who might take advantage of them. So nonpunishing cooperators do better and, given the prestige bias, tend to be imitated more than costly punishers. Eventually populations are dominated by nonpunishing cooperators and thus once more become susceptible to invasion by free riders. Henrich responds to this problem by proposing a recursive hierarchy of costly punishment: not only are free riders punished, but the failure to punish a free rider is itself punished, as is the failure to punish failures to punish free riders, and so on.[19] Henrich thinks that distributing the task of costly punishment through such a recursive hierarchy can reduce the costs of punishment. The reason is that higher-order transgressions—that is, failures to punish lower-order transgressions—should be less common than lower-order transgressions, so the cost of punishing transgressions diminishes as one ascends the punishment hierarchy. This raises the costs of the lowest-order transgressions, like basic free riding, without overly burdening punishers. The cost of punishing a free rider is made tolerable because second-order punishment ensures a greater cost to failing to punish her.[20]

So the costs of counternormative behavior can be raised without unduly burdening first-order punishers if the costs of punishment are socially distributed through a recursive hierarchy of punishment.[21]

It is possible that such sophisticated recursive hierarchies of punishment were unlikely in human prehistory. However, other mechanisms with similar effects are also possible. For example, Sterelny (2003, p. 131) suggests that forming punishment coalitions against norm flouters might serve to enforce prosocial norms. Given strong enough conformist tendencies, if enough members of a group sanction an offender, through ridicule, for example (Boehm, 1993, p. 230), then other group members should join in. Growing evidence suggests that neural mechanisms in contemporary human populations are capable of implementing such conformist formation of punishment coalitions.

In a recent study, Klucharev et al. (2009) scanned brain areas related to a task that induced conformism in judgments of facial attractiveness. While their brains were being scanned, subjects were asked to rate the attractiveness of different female faces presented in random order and were then informed about group ratings of the same faces. Later they were unexpectedly asked to rerate the faces, again in random order, during an unrelated behavioral task. The second set of judgments showed a clear conformist effect: subjects changed their judgments in the direction of the group rating. The result was expected based on decades of research on conformism by social psychologists (Cialdini & Goldstein, 2004). The interesting twist in this study concerns the differences in neural activation induced by discrepancy between individual and group attractiveness judgments. When the judgments differed, neural areas known to play a role in reinforcement learning were activated. These areas are hypothesized to provide an error signal when an individual makes a prediction that is not borne out. This signal is thought to drive individual reinforcement learning. Klucharev et al. (2009) show that failure to conform to group judgments is treated in the same way as a prediction error on a purely individual task.

Given Klucharev et al.'s evidence that conformism is mediated by the same neural mechanisms as reinforcement learning, deviation from group judgments appears to automatically generate an error signal and hence to act as a form of punishment. So, returning to the role of conformism in norm enforcement, once a tipping point in punishment by group members is reached, nonpunishers themselves should experience a kind of punishment—the neurally generated error signal—as a result of their failure to conform. Thus such conformism can actually implement a recursive hierarchy of punishment: those who fail to punish are themselves punished simply because of the error signal associated with a failure to conform. Such dynamics can support a kind of "ganging up" on norm flouters that would have the same effect as Henrich's (2004) recursive hierarchy of punishment (Sterelny, 2003, p. 131).[22]

Once such sophisticated norm-enforcing mindshaping practices are present in a population, even less costly mechanisms of conformism should arise. In Sterelny's terms, such punishment regimes constitute a drastic alteration of the socioecological niche: hierarchically distributed or coalition-based punishment ensures that counternormative behavior incurs costs, so those who flout norms can no longer acquire prestige and hence lose their status as models. In such circumstances, individuals who are disposed to conform to norms should be favored: they can avoid the costs of being punished. This sets up selection pressures favoring conformists. Those with genetic mutations that predispose individuals to conformism should come to dominate the population. Alternatively, parents can now improve their inclusive fitness by teaching offspring to conform to cultural norms. If a group's norms include reliable communication, supported by costly punishment, then individuals disposed to communicate truths should be favored. This would make possible yet another mechanism for enforcing conformity to norms: indirect reciprocity. As noted in chapter 1, this is the idea that individuals can have an incentive to cooperate even if they cannot keep track of whether or not their interactants reciprocate because it pays to have a reputation as a cooperator passed on through gossip. Given norms supporting reliable communicative practices, individuals would have an incentive to gain a reputation as cooperators, and they could rely on gossip to spread such reputations. Finally, the development of prosocial emotions should also flourish in such circumstances. Given the costs of flouting norms, individuals who conform without thinking should have advantages. As many have remarked, guilt, shame, and other emotions are plausible proximal causes of norm-respecting behavior (Frank, 1988; Chang et al., 2011). In circumstances in which such behavior is advantageous, like groups with recursive hierarchies of punishment, such emotions could emerge and become stable. Given the costs of failures to punish in such circumstances, emotions that encourage punishment, like resentment, should likewise emerge and become stable (Price et al., 2002).[23]

Thus it seems that mindshaping can explain the stability of cooperation in the post-BSR world where mindreading fails.[24] Sophisticated mindshaping practices—pedagogy, imitation, conformist biases, and recursive hierarchies of costly punishment—can give rise to the intragroup homogeneity and intergroup variation on which group selection depends. Groups with cooperatively disposed members should have an advantage in such circumstances. Sophisticated mindreading need play no role in this. As I made clear in chapter 3, mechanisms of conformism, including the chameleon effect, imitation, and rudimentary pedagogy, do not require sophisticated mindreading like full-blown propositional attitude attribution. Costly punishment is likewise, in the first instance, a response to counternormative *behavior*, not propositional attitudes.[25] Explaining the continued stability of cooperative dispositions in the post-BSR world entirely in terms of such mindreading-independent mindshaping evades two of the problems I raised for the MIH: since cooperation can be stabilized without mindreading, there is no need to solve the holism problem, and human incompetence at attributing thoughts of indefinitely higher orders is no longer puzzling. I now turn to the third problem: explaining coordination.

4   The Construction of Plural Subjects: How Mindshaping Explains Human Coordination

Assuming that the array of sophisticated mindshaping practices described in the previous section kept our post-BSR ancestors cooperative, how did they manage the coordination problems that cooperative endeavors raise? Assuming, for example, that individuals, on the whole, wanted to help others hunt stag, how did they know when and where to meet for a stag hunt? Assuming that individuals, on the whole, wanted to help their fellows defend against invaders, how did they know what role to play in strategies of collective defense? From a contemporary perspective, such problems seem trivial. The reason is that we take for granted a sophisticated, elaborate, conventional language: we can simply *tell* each other what to do, where and when. However, deciding on a public, conventional system of communication is precisely the sort of coordination problem that is at issue. So this cannot be assumed in an account of the origins of successful coordination.

In Sterelny's cooperative foraging hypothesis, it is clear that pre-BSR hominin populations must already have solved this problem. Hunting megafauna with primitive weaponry obviously requires sophisticated capacities for coordination. As Sterelny emphasizes, such capacities must have depended on the intergenerational transfer, accumulation, and refinement of cultural knowledge relating to natural history, tool manufacture, and hunting strategies. So pre-BSR populations must also have solved the coordination problems raised by constructing public, conventional communication systems. However, although Sterelny provides persuasive arguments for the claim that pre-BSR hominin populations must have solved such coordination problems, he does not provide enough detail about *how* they solved such problems. He devotes most of his energy to explaining how cooperation could be stabilized without policing and Machiavellian mindreading. But he neglects another plausible role for mindreading: perhaps it was used for solving coordination problems. Hurley (2005b) defends this hypothesis.

According to Hurley, the key to understanding how human beings solve coordination problems is to reject what she calls "the exogenous units assumption" of classical game theory. This is the assumption that "carving" a strategic interaction into units of activity (typically individual human agents) is *not* itself subject to instrumental reasoning; rather, units of activity must be treated as a given—as an input to the process of reasoning to a decision, rather than as an output of this process. So, for example, in standard analyses of the "Hi-Lo" game, the game is set up such that two agents are involved with the following pattern of interdependent preferences for each agent: Hi-Hi > Lo-Lo > Hi-Lo = Lo-Hi.[26] In classical game theory, this description is treated as a given: it is input into the reasoning process that is supposed to yield a preference-maximizing decision. However, as Bacharach (2006) argues persuasively, this way of describing the situation raises a serious problem. Neither agent appears to have any reason to pick "Hi" or "Lo" because her decision is contingent on the other matching her pick, and she has no reason for thinking that the other will, for either alternative. This is puzzling because the solution to such problems is obvious to any normal human being.

Following Bacharach, Hurley thinks the key to this solution involves redescribing the situation. Rather than conceiving of it as a coordination dilemma for two individual agents, we must conceive of it as a straightforward preference maximization problem faced by one *plural* subject. The way to allow for this is to jettison the exogenous units assumption. Rather than simply accept the description of the situation as a problem of getting two separate agents to match responses, encountering this situation should trigger, as part of the process of instrumental reasoning in which each agent engages, a redescription of the situation as a maximization problem faced by a single plural subject. Each agent should then see that "Hi-Hi" yields the highest total preference satisfaction for the plural subject, and thus have reason to do her part in this group response. This solves the problem, avoiding the regress threatened by the original description of the situation.

Bacharach and Hurley's suggestion is plausible, but what role does Hurley see for mindreading? She argues that good mindreaders should be better able to identify viable coordination partners than bad mindreaders. If you can tell whether a potential interactant approaches coordination problems similar to the "Hi-Lo" game with a plural subject strategy, then you should do better in selecting coordination partners. Drawing on computational models of cooperation and coordination explored by Regan (1980), Howard (1988), and Danielson (1992), Hurley argues that successful coordinators employ "meta-heuristics"—heuristics for interacting that depend on mirroring or otherwise uncovering the heuristics of potential interactants. Crucially, what matters is not predicting behavior—which is possible without mindreading—but identifying the strategy that a potential interactant brings to coordination problems. According to Hurley, our ancestors were preadapted for such mindreading thanks to the kind of arms race of deception and deception detection conjectured by the MIH and described earlier. As products of such a history of selection, our ancestors were well poised to identify the strategies each brought to interactions, and hence were capable of selecting partners who treated coordination problems like "Hi-Lo" as straightforward preference maximization problems for plural subjects.

Although transforming coordination problems like "Hi-Lo" into straightforward maximization problems for plural subjects is a promising explanation of human coordination, Hurley's suggestion about mindreading's role in this process is problematic. She offers no solution to the three problems for mindreading approaches to cooperation and coordination raised in section 2. First, given the holism problem, how can an agent determine whether or not a potential interactant really intends to engage in the plural subject strategy? Second, if we really are such good mindreaders, as the result of a coevolutionary arms race between deception and deception detection, why are we so bad at attributing higher-order thoughts? Third, in Hurley's own terms, the best coordination strategy is not blind commitment to reasoning as part of a plural subject but a commitment to such reasoning that is contingent on one's partner's commitment to such reasoning. So the coordination strategy she urges is not "*Always* reason as part of a plural subject aiming to maximize preference satisfaction" but "*If* my partner intends to reason as part of a plural subject aiming to maximize preference satisfaction, then I should reason in a complementary way." But, given this, what does accurate mindreading reveal? Only that a potential partner intends the plural subject strategy if I do. But I intend the plural subject strategy only if she does. So the mindreading regress described in section 2 arises for Hurley's proposal as well.

These problems could be avoided if there were some way of raising the likelihood that most of one's potential interactants were unreflectively disposed to engage in the plural subject strategy. The problem with Hurley's proposal is an instance of the more general problem raised for fast and frugal mindreading in chapter 3: unless human populations are cognitively homogeneous, fast and frugal social cognition is unlikely to be reliable. But, as chapter 3 argued, we have reasons to doubt that human populations are sufficiently homogeneous, independently of mindshaping. If Hurley is right and coordination depends on accurate yet fast and frugal mindreading, then her proposal as it stands fails to explain successful human coordination. The key to solving this problem is appreciating the role of mindshaping in making human populations more cognitively homogeneous than they would otherwise be.

If most members of one's group are shaped, from a young age, through imitation, pedagogy, conformism, and costly punishment, to apply the plural subject strategy to coordination problems as a kind of default, then mindreading should not even be necessary for coordination to succeed. Two separate lines of argument support the antecedent of this conditional. First, assuming that group selection is central to the explanation of human cooperation and coordination, we can safely conclude that mindshaping mechanisms succeed in homogenizing human populations with respect to the plural subject strategy. Groups that failed to do this would not coordinate as well and hence would lose out in intergroup competition. Second, many influential discussions of plural subject formation and other successful coordination strategies appeal to mindshaping mechanisms of various kinds, including imitation, conformism, and normative attitudes.

Using computational models, Brian Skyrms (1996, 2003) has explored this sort of noncognitive approach to coordination in detail. These models explore "replicator dynamics"—patterns of change that occur when traits, including coordination strategies, are replicated. Both biological and cultural evolution can be modeled in this way. In biological evolution, genes encoding traits are passed between generations. In cultural evolution, patterns of behavior spread through imitative learning. Skyrms's models show how various forms of coordination, including stag hunts and communication conventions pairing signals with messages, can evolve through replicator dynamics if certain conditions are met. These conditions involve ensuring that similar strategies are likely to interact with each other, for example, that agents disposed to hunt stag are more likely to interact with other stag hunters than with hare hunters (1996, pp. 21, 59–62; 2003, pp. 24–25, 40, 108). In this respect, Skyrms's models confirm Hurley's conjecture that coordination problems can be solved if agents using similar strategies, e.g., the plural subject strategy, are more likely to interact. However, in Skyrms's models, mindreading is unnecessary for such pairing of the like-minded. Instead the imitation that drives cultural replicator dynamics, together with certain properties of agents' environments, like neighborhood structure (2003, pp. 40–41), ensure that only the like-minded are likely to interact, thereby ensuring the evolution and stability of successful coordination.

When we turn specifically to the plural subject strategy advocated by Hurley and Bacharach as a solution to coordination problems raised by interactions similar to the "Hi-Lo" game, it is clear that plural subject formation requires mindshaping. Like Hurley, Bacharach argues that such coordination problems can be solved only by conceptualizing them as problems facing plural subjects: instead of asking what "I" must do, each interactant must ask what "we" must do and answer this question using what Bacharach calls "team reasoning," which identifies each individual's role in maximizing utility for the team (2006, pp. 121–127). Bacharach understands such plural subject formation as a mechanism not just for transforming the payoffs that define coordination problems but also for transforming agency and modes of reasoning (2006, pp. 90, 135–137). Clearly, then, in Bacharach's view, plural subject formation requires mindshaping. However, he has little to say about how this occurs, treating it as a primitive human psychological disposition outside the domain of game theory. For Bacharach, features of certain interactions simply trigger what might be called "we"-construals rather than "I"-construals of the interactions (pp. 73–90, 141). But much more can be said here.

In her discussion of plural subjects, Gilbert (1996) emphasizes the importance of various kinds of subtle normative pressures to the formation of plural subjects. Consider, for example, the case of walking together (pp. 179–186). For two individuals to walk together, it is not sufficient that each desires to walk with the other, nor even that they both have common knowledge of each other's individual desires to walk in each other's presence. The reason is that individuals have the option of changing their minds regarding what they want to do. Intuitively, if two people are walking beside each other because each individually wants to, and then one changes her mind and stops while the other keeps going without complaint, we would not call such a situation "walking together" (p. 182). If the two are truly walking together, one party's sudden, unwarned, and unexcused stop entitles the other party to an "offended rebuke" (pp. 16, 180–184, 432–435). This is because, according to Gilbert, walking together is a joint action proceeding from a joint intention, which is a psychological attitude attributable to the plural subject consisting of the two walkers:

walking together requires *us* to desire to walk together, not each to desire this separately. Among other things, forming the plural subject of a psychological attitude, like intending, preferring, or believing, requires, according to Gilbert, a *commitment* that no member of the plural subject can *unilaterally* surrender (p. 10). Commitments to joint intentions, and so on, can be suspended only with the consent of all parties to such commitments, and any unilateral shirking of the commitment entitles the other parties to rebuke or otherwise sanction the culprit.[27]

In some respects, Gilbert's account of plural subjects presupposes cognitive capacities that are too sophisticated given my aim of explaining the phylogeny of the human sociocognitive syndrome in terms of mindshaping. For example, Gilbert makes it a necessary condition on making the sort of joint commitment on which plural subjects are based that the parties to the joint commitment have "common knowledge" of each other's intentions to make the commitment (1996, pp. 55, 293–294). Common knowledge is typically understood in terms of highly sophisticated mindreading: for you and me to have common knowledge that P, each of us must know that the other knows that P, that the other knows that the other knows that P, and so on. Since knowledge presupposes belief, common knowledge appears to presuppose a capacity to attribute beliefs of indefinitely higher orders. If this is a necessary condition for joint commitment, then entering a joint commitment entails attributing indefinitely iterated hierarchies of belief. However, it is possible to make sense of Gilbert's central insight that plural subjects are constituted by joint commitments enforced through normative attitudes, like those triggering offended rebukes, without presupposing such sophisticated mindreading.

Wilby (2010) argues that common knowledge need not be understood in terms of complex sociocognitive capacities. Instead it might be treated as a primitive relational property shared by two or more persons, in terms of which phenomena like joint action can be explained. In fact, Wilby argues persuasively that common knowledge is *itself* better understood as the irreducible psychological state of a plural subject, not to be analyzed in terms of the psychological states of its individual members. This perspective can help avoid what Wilby calls "the problem of mutual [i.e., common] knowledge: how can one characterise mutual knowledge without being committed to an infinite regression of mental states?" (2010, p. 86). This is a problem because we desperately need a psychologically realistic characterization of mutual/common knowledge, since its importance in human coordination is phenomenologically and empirically obvious. However, standard analyses, in terms of infinite iterations of knowledge attributions (Schiffer, 1972), fail to explain how mutual/common knowledge can play such an important role, due to their psychological implausibility.

In general, it is not obvious that the sorts of *behaviors* that Gilbert argues are necessary for individuals to constitute plural subjects *require* sophisticated mindreading. Certainly, team reasoning of the kind Bacharach thinks is key to solving coordination problems like "Hi-Lo" can be triggered by much lower-level capacities. Recall chapter 2's discussion of the chameleon effect. Human beings appear to automatically and unconsciously match the behaviors of their interactants. Chartrand and Bargh (1999) argue that such behavior matching serves a social bonding function; human beings feel a special connection to, or belonging with, each other as a result of behavior matching. In a recent study, Wiltermuth and Heath (2009) showed that the connection between behavioral synchrony and cooperation is extremely direct. They had groups of strangers move objects and sing or walk either in rhythm or out of rhythm with each other. Immediately afterward they engaged them in ostensibly unrelated tests, involving various interactive games that afforded obvious opportunities for free riding. Subjects who moved objects or sang or walked in rhythm were significantly more likely to cooperate with each other. In addition, the synchronized participants were far more likely to report that they trusted, and felt connected to and on the same team as, their partners.[28]

Comparative and developmental psychology also provide a wealth of evidence that plural subject formation may be a distinctively human yet cognitively unsophisticated disposition. For example, in a highly suggestive study, Warneken et al. (2006) identified significant differences between eighteen- and twenty-four-month-old human infants and human-raised chimpanzees on collaborative tasks involving reward retrieval or playing a social game. Only the human infants would collaborate on playing social games; however, the differences in behavior on collaborative reward retrieval are perhaps even more telling. When the adult experimenters unexpectedly stopped collaborating, *all* the human subjects yet *none* of the chimpanzee subjects produced communicative attempts to reengage the adults. Clearly, even very young children understand social interactions as joint, cooperative undertakings, while even human-raised chimpanzees do not. These attempts to reengage are reminiscent of Gilbert's "offended rebukes" at the unilateral reneging of commitments to joint intentions and agency, as in walking together. However, as I argue in chapter 6, it is clear that children this age are incapable of the kind of sophisticated mindreading presupposed by Gilbert's analysis of joint action.

This result fits a robust pattern in distinctively human sociocognitive development. Recent evidence suggests that joint music making among four-year-olds increases subsequent spontaneous cooperative and help-ful behavior (Kirschner & Tomasello, 2010), providing developmental evidence for the cooperative effects of behavioral synchrony discovered in adults by Wiltermuth and Heath (2009). Such rhythm-induced coop-eration seems to depend on basic capacities for coordination on joint rhythmic action, apparent in children as young as two and one-half years (Kirschner & Tomasello, 2008). Thus the evidence strongly suggests that, from a young age, human beings display cognitively unsophisticated dis-positions that make cooperation and coordination possible. Furthermore, this sociocognitive profile appears to distinguish humans from other primates.[29]

Parts of human nervous systems together constitute individual human subjects. However, no evidence indicates that parts of human nervous sys-tems conceive of themselves as doing this under conditions of common knowledge, nor is this necessary. Similarly, there seems to be no a priori reason why individual human subjects need to conceive of themselves as forming plural subjects, under conditions of common knowledge, to succeed in doing so. What appears, from the perspectives of individual subjects belonging to a group, as routine, conformist, or norm-respecting behavior may, from a broader perspective, function to implement a plural subject constituted by these individual subjects, without their awareness. The cognitive capacities needed to support such normative regimes need not involve sophisticated mindreading: the sorts of normative attitudes discussed in chapter 2, directed solely at behavior, should suffice. Mem-bers of a plural subject need only expect, in the normative sense (Gilbert, 1996, p. 75),[30] that each plays her role in some activity, without conceiv-ing of the activity as constituting a plural subject. Even common knowl-edge can be understood in this way: instead of representing what each believes and knows, members of a plural subject need only expect, in the normative sense, that everyone will behave in ways that are compatible with (witnessing) salient public performances that implicitly count as commitments to do one's part in some joint activity. Those who fail to behave in such ways can be tacitly sanctioned, for example, via reductions in status, without their sanctioners making any assumptions about what they know or believe.

Thus it is clear from a variety of discussions of human coordination—from philosophical, modeling, and economics perspectives—that various mechanisms of mindshaping are key to solving coordination problems.

Furthermore, we have no obvious reason to suppose that such mechanisms depend on a prior capacity to attribute full-blown propositional attitudes. It is also clear that human populations engage in a plethora of pedagogical practices aimed at teaching the kind of "team reasoning" that Bacharach thinks is central to the effectiveness of the plural subject strategy in solving coordination problems. Across cultures, members engage in group rituals from a young age (Senft & Basso, 2009). This is exactly what the mindshaping account predicts. Rather than rely on sophisticated mindreading to detect other team reasoners, human groups shape their members to be default team reasoners, ensuring that, when faced with coordination problems, they are likely to encounter like-minded interactants. If most of one's neighbors approach "Hi-Lo"–type coordination problems with the plural subject strategy, because most have been subject to the same mindshaping regimes, and all are subject to sanctions if they fail to do their parts in plural subjects, then one need not deploy sophisticated mindreading to detect the like-minded; simple membership in one's community is enough to ensure a high likelihood of coordinative success.

The differences between the mindshaping approach I advocate and Hurley's mindreading approach illustrate the differing background commitments behind mindreading-first and mindshaping-first theories of human sociocognitive evolution. Hurley's view is clearly wedded to an individualist and cognitivist conception of the evolution of human social competence. Coordination is a problem that individuals must solve using sophisticated sociocognitive, neural mechanisms. These mechanisms are products of selection operating on individuals in a coevolutionary arms race pitting deceivers against deception detectors, leading to Machiavellian mindreading. In the alternative, mindshaping-first view that I advocate, coordination admits of a more distributed solution. Mindshaping practices that happen to prevail in groups construct social niches in which solutions to coordination problems emerge automatically due to default interaction strategies that most group members are shaped to follow. Enhanced individual sociocognitive capacities are not necessary, just the motivational conditions on successful mindshaping: conformity bias, resentment-based dispositions to engage in costly punishment, and motivations to shape offspring through rudimentary pedagogy. Coordination emerges not because individuals are preselected to be good mindreaders but because groups with better mindshaping practices that ensure that most members engage in superior coordination strategies by default have selective advantages over other groups. Coordination is an effect of the complex coevolution of properties at various levels of organization, including appropriate mindshaping dispositions in group members and more abstract group-level properties, like neighborhood structure. It need not be an individual cognitive achievement produced by selection operating on individuals.[31]

This perspective also makes good on a suggestion made in chapter 1: that human niche construction differs from niche construction in other species in being directed or purposeful, rather than a mere by-product of social capacities selected for other reasons. For example, according to the MIH, social cognition leads to niche construction because with better mindreaders, the social tasks facing subsequent generations are altered. However, better mindreading is not selected for such niche-altering effects. In the alternative defended here, many distinctive human sociocognitive capacities are selected for their niche-altering effects. Our mindshaping dispositions are adaptive because they make human social life easier to navigate, allowing for successful coordination on cooperative projects. So niche construction, for human beings, is not just a by-product of capacities selected for other reasons; it is the raison d'être of our mindshaping practices.[32]

5   Evidence for and Lacunae in the Mindshaping Account of Human Cooperation and Coordination

The foregoing is a complicated just-so story explaining the evolution of human cooperation, in which varieties of mindshaping, of the kind reviewed in chapter 2, play a central role. As noted in chapter 1, such just-so storytelling plays an important role in cognitive science. When trying to explain human social cognition, for example, it is necessary to establish what human social cognition is for. To do this in an empirically responsible way, one must formulate hypotheses about what human social cognition was selected for. Such hypotheses face daunting lacunae in evidentiary support, given the paucity of data about the cognitive traits of our distant ancestors. Nevertheless we do have some data, and some hypotheses accord with the available data better than others. Much contemporary work on human social cognition assumes that it aims at accurate mindreading. Allegedly, all the other boons of human social cognition can be traced to this capacity: our impressive feats of cooperation and coordination all depend on our ability to read each other's minds accurately. In this chapter, I have defended an alternative to this account. Accurate mindreading that is fast and frugal enough to help with coordination and cooperation is ecologically implausible due to the holism problem. Little evidence suggests that contemporary human beings have the kind of facility with Machiavellian mindreading that the MIH predicts. And it is unclear how accurate mindreading can help solve coordination and cooperation problems given the regress of propositional attitude attributions it seems to generate. In contrast, various mindshaping mechanisms, including conformism, imitation, pedagogy, and costly punishment of counternormative behavior, can induce the intragroup homogeneity and intergroup variation that are necessary for group selection to operate, resulting in selection for groups whose members are generally cooperatively disposed. Furthermore, such mindshaping practices can also yield solutions to coordination problems, including the formation of plural subjects described by Hurley (2005b), Bacharach (2006), and Gilbert (1996).

How does this just-so story fare relative to the kinds of evidence reviewed in chapter 1? Is it compatible with what is known from the fossil record, the archaeological record, and studies in comparative psychology, neuroscience, and genetics? Sterelny's cooperative foraging hypothesis is supported by strong correlations in the fossil data between the arrival of human beings in geographic areas and subsequent declines in megafauna in those areas (Burney & Flannery, 2005). These data focus on relatively recent extinction events (in the last 50,000 years), whereas Sterelny's CFH dates our ancestors' reliance on this foraging strategy much earlier. However, evidence suggests that megafaunal hunting probably dates back over one million years. Sterelny (2003, p. 137) argues that evidence of central place provisioning of food, including hearths indicating the use of fire, points to lifeways dependent on group hunts. Such evidence dates back to over 500,000 years (Wrangham, 2009, pp. 83–88). But even stronger fossil and anatomical evidence indicates that cooked food, and hence presumably hunting, are extremely old adaptations in the hominin lineage. Wrangham dates them to the evolution of *Homo erectus* from the habilines, between 1.9 million and 1.8 million years ago:

In the evolution of *Homo erectus* from habilines, we find the largest reduction in tooth size in the last six million years of human evolution, the largest increase in body size, and a disappearance of the shoulder, arm, and trunk adaptations that apparently enabled habilines to climb well. Additionally, *Homo erectus* had a less flared rib cage and a narrower pelvis than the australopithecines, both features indicating that they had a smaller gut. There was a 42 per cent increase in cranial capacity. *Homo erectus* was also the first species in our lineage to extend its range beyond Africa: it was recorded in western Asia by 1.7 million years ago, Indonesia in Southeast Asia by 1.6 million years ago, and Spain by 1.4 million years ago. The reduction in tooth size, the signs of increased energy availability in larger brains and bodies, the indication of smaller guts, and the ability to exploit new kinds of habitat all support the idea that cooking was responsible for the evolution of *Homo erectus*. (2009, p. 98)

Of course, cooking does not necessarily imply group hunting of megafauna. However, given the dramatic increase in cranial capacity in *Homo erectus* and the substantial energetic requirements of large brains, populations that relied on cooking would have been incentivized to develop reliable and plentiful sources of nutrient-rich foods. Learning how to hunt increasingly larger game would have been an obvious solution to this problem. Furthermore, such hunting provides a natural explanation of the remarkably distant and broad migratory patterns of *Homo erectus*: they were following the migratory patterns of the megafauna on which they had come to rely.

Sterelny's conjectures regarding more recent hominin evolution—in particular, the broad-spectrum revolution (BSR)—are also strongly supported by the fossil record. First, there is broad consensus that the relatively stereotyped pre-BSR Acheulean tool kit began to be replaced with more geographically diverse and complex tool kits, including multipart structures designed for specialized foraging niches and totemic ornamentation, by 50,000 years ago (Mithen, 1996). Second, growing evidence suggests that an important feature of this period of human evolution is increasing contact between unfamiliar individuals, a development to which Sterelny traces the emergence of ethnic markers (2012, pp. 54–55), and which motivates my mindshaping-based account of cooperation and coordination. According to Powell et al. (2009), demography was a "major determinant" of the increased symbolic and technological complexity of late Pleistocene human populations (90,000 years ago in sub-Saharan Africa and 45,000 years ago in Europe). Mellars (2005) traces the technological, economic, and social adaptations of the BSR to increased interaction and competition between local populations that resulted from demographic changes.

There is controversy about how long this transformation took and how recently it occurred. Mithen (1996) argues for a relatively recent and rapid shift, but McBrearty and Brooks (2000) claim that this perspective is an artifact of Eurocentric bias. None of these disputes, however, bear on the main point: Sterelny's hypothesis that archaic *homo* depended on large-scale cooperative hunts, and that this foraging strategy was replaced in the last 100,000 years by more specialized, niche-specific foraging, employing a far more sophisticated tool kit, is based on relatively uncontroversial data. It is also uncontroversial that, according to the fossil record, hominin brain expansion correlates with such shifts in foraging technology. Thus the assumption that archaic *homo* was distinguished from other primates by a dependence on highly sophisticated cooperative foraging is not in serious dispute. What is disputed is what form of social cognition supported this unusual (for primates) lifestyle. To choose between the mindreading-centered Machiavellian intelligence hypothesis (MIH) and the mindshaping-centered alternative explored here, it is necessary to examine evidence of cognitive capacities from contemporary human populations.

The key distinctions between the mindreading-centered MIH and the family of mindshaping-centered alternatives discussed here consist in the importance of group selection, plural subject formation, and the mindshaping dispositions and practices that support these capacities, like conformism, imitation, pedagogy, and norm enforcement. If sophisticated cooperation was made possible by sophisticated mindreading, then group selection is unlikely to have played as important a role in the evolution of cooperation as I have argued. If people were good at detecting potential free riders or poor coordination partners, then group selection for prosocial dispositions would not be necessary to ensure that one's potential interactants were good bets: individuals could figure this out for themselves. However, if sophisticated mindreading was extremely difficult in the circumstances in which our ancestors developed sophisticated cooperation and coordination, and if it was unlikely to help in cooperation or coordination due to the regress problem, then group selection seems to be the only way of increasing the likelihood that prosocial interactants would interact with each other. This predicts that contemporary human beings should show acute sensitivities to group membership, as well as the kinds of mindshaping dispositions that can induce the intragroup homogeneity and intergroup variation necessary for group selection. Evidence from studies of contemporary human populations strongly supports this hypothesis.

A number of recent studies of the neural basis for social cognition in contemporary human adults support a group selectionist, mindshaping-driven model of human capacities for coordination and cooperation. For example, Mitchell et al. (2006) showed that different neural areas are active in tasks thought to require the interpretation of others' behavior in terms of mental states—what they call "mentalizing"—depending on whether or not the interpreter perceives the others to be like her or not. While those perceived to be like the interpreter are interpreted using the same brain areas as those used in self-interpretation, those perceived to be unlike the interpreter are interpreted using different brain areas. This suggests that the brain distinguishes between in-group and out-group social interactions, in line with the group selectionist hypothesis defended earlier. The Klucharev et al. (2009) study discussed earlier, showing that brain areas known to produce error signals in individual learning are also activated by failures to conform to group judgments, also supports the mindshaping story proposed here. Also relevant is new evidence regarding neural processing related to social rejection: this activates brain areas known to be involved in physical pain (Kross & Berman, 2011).

In addition, as noted in chapter 2, impressive cross-cultural data show that human beings are willing to pay material costs to punish counternormative distributions of goods (Henrich et al., 2006). Furthermore, behavior that seems of a piece with such attitudes is apparent in human children as young as 8.5 months (Hamlin et al., 2011).This seems consistent with the case for egalitarian distribution norms among hunter-gatherer societies that Christopher Boehm has been making for decades (1993, 1996, 1999, 2004). Boehm details the various means of punishment by which such norms are enforced, including public criticism, ridicule, and ostracism of norm violators. If, as Boehm assumes (1999, p. 198), contemporary hunter-gatherers are good models of prehistoric human populations, the kind of punishment that Henrich (2004) argues is necessary to give rise to group selection for cooperative dispositions was likely present in prehistoric populations. It is difficult to determine whether or not the kinds of recursive punishment hierarchies to which Henrich (2004) appeals are also present among contemporary hunger-gatherers or were present in prehistoric human populations. But, as argued earlier, perhaps they are not needed. Strong dispositions to conformism, of the kind implemented by the brain areas identified by Klucharev et al. (2009), can support a kind of ganging up on norm flouters: once a critical number of high-status group members initiate sanctions, others in the group will contribute due to their strong dispositions toward conformism; for instance, they will join in mockery and ridicule to not feel left out.[33]

Earlier I criticized Sterelny's cooperative foraging hypothesis for failing to explain certain distinctive properties of the human sociocognitive syndrome. The CFH does not explain three of the properties of distinctively human mindshaping highlighted in chapter 3: (1) its intrinsic motivation, (2) its flexibility concerning the aspects of model behavior it can make targets match, and (3) its use of nonactual models, like fictional characters or idealized agents. Furthermore, Sterelny's proposal fails to explain why distinctively human mindreading involves the attribution of full-blown propositional attitudes or the structural complexity and semantic flexibility of human language. Are the foregoing proposals regarding the role of mindshaping in maintaining cooperation and coordination in the post-BSR world any better at explaining these distinctive features of the human sociocognitive syndrome?

They appear to do a better job with regard to some of them. For example, given the importance of conformity to group selection, and the importance of interacting only with the like-minded to successful coordination, it is not surprising that human mindshaping is intrinsically motivated and maximally flexible in the aspects of model behavior it can make targets match. Unlike the goal of mindshaping identified by Sterelny's CFH—acquiring information necessary for successful cooperative foraging—the goal of mindshaping in the story defended in the previous sections is conformity itself. Mindshaping is not a means to some further end, like becoming a better hunter. Rather, its goal is simply matching the behavior of others. This is what makes possible the intragroup homogeneity and intergroup variation on which group selection relies. Furthermore, matching even nonfunctional behaviors is a signal of like-mindedness and hence promotes interaction with viable coordination partners. This explains phenomena like the chameleon effect, and Wiltermuth and Heath's results linking cooperation and "team-spiritedness" to behavioral synchrony. In Sterelny's account, targets should try to match only the aspects of model behavior relevant to the skill they are trying to acquire, such as wielding a spear. And they should be motivated to imitate only to the extent that it enables them to acquire such skills. Like the chimpanzee imitation described in chapter 3, imitating the means to such goals should be incentivized only if better means are not apparent.[34] But if, as I have argued, conformity in itself is key to group selection and successful coordination, then intrinsically motivated mindshaping that is maximally flexible in the aspects of model behavior it can make targets match begins to make sense. Thus the foregoing proposals about the role of mindshaping in post-BSR cooperation and coordination can explain two properties of distinctively human mindshaping for which there is a wealth of evidence.[35]

The role for mindshaping articulated and defended in this chapter also has the potential to help explain why distinctively human mindshaping often treats nonactual individuals, like fictional characters or idealized agents, as models. Assuming the presence of a language in which such nonactual models can be publicly represented, groups that mindshape their members to match the behavior of fictional characters or idealized agents should have advantages over groups that treat only actual individuals as models. The reason is that nonactual, or "virtual," models can be imitated by much larger and more geographically dispersed groups. Groups limited to shaping their members to match actual individuals with whom all are familiar would inevitably be limited in their size and geographic range: there are only so many people who can be familiar with and model their behavior on the same living role models. In contrast, groups capable of constructing virtual models, using narratives like myths, for example, could spread their cooperative and coordinative norms far more widely. Their members could count on cooperative and coordinative success even with individuals they have never met, from geographically distant origins, given that they all model their behavior on the same virtual agents encoded in narratives with which they are all familiar. It is plausible that this is the role of foundation myths or accounts of the lives of heroes in contemporary human groups. Whether or not I've ever met you, if we've both been shaped from a young age to approximate the behavior of some fictional character, or some mythologized version of a historical figure, then we are likely to be like-minded enough to successfully coordinate on cooperative equilibriums. If we have both spent much of our lives regulating our conduct based on questions like "What would Jesus do?" then our expectations about each other's behavior are more likely to be accurate, and our interactions are more likely to succeed. Assuming that, all else being equal, larger, more geographically dispersed groups have competitive advantages over smaller, geographically limited groups, group selection should promote conformity to virtual models.[36]

This explanation of the importance of virtual models to distinctively human mindshaping contains a glaring lacuna, however. The hypotheses I defend about the roles of mindshaping in cooperation and coordination are no better than Sterelny's CFH in explaining how the human sociocognitive syndrome came to include a system of communication with the complex structure and flexible semantics characteristic of human languages. The kinds of narrative-based virtual models that play an important role in distinctively human mindshaping are possible only once such a language is on the scene. But the received view of the phylogeny of human language sees it as dependent on sophisticated mindreading (Origgi & Sperber, 2000; Bickerton, 1998, 2000, 2002). And the hypotheses I defend, like Sterelny's CFH, say nothing about this either. Distinctively human mindreading involves, as chapter 1 argued, the capacity to attribute full-blown propositional attitudes with tenuous connections to observable stimuli and behavior. However, the foregoing account of the role of various kinds of mindshaping in cooperation and coordination does not identify any role for such mindreading. In fact, I have argued that effective mindshaping mitigates the need for sophisticated mindreading: to the extent that potential interactants are likely products of similar mindshaping, they are likely to conform by default to complementary interaction strategies and norms, so sophisticated mindreading appears unnecessary to successful coordination. Although the story defended here seems to account for two components of the human sociocognitive syndrome—cooperation and sophisticated mindshaping—it is silent on the other two components: sophisticated mindreading and complex communication.

Furthermore, this story also neglects an important feature of post-BSR human socioecology: increasing contact among competing groups. Although the sorts of mindshaping described here might explain cooperation and coordination among group members, they say little about how such feats were possible among members of different groups. Yet, as noted earlier, increased contact among members of different groups after the BSR is one of the reasons coordination and cooperation became more problematic than they had been. This constitutes another glaring lacuna in the foregoing account.

These three unexplained features of distinctively human social cognition and socioecology—sophisticated communication, sophisticated mindreading, and interaction with unfamiliar individuals from different groups—are closely related to each other. Chapters 5 and 7 explain how they are related, and how the requirements of cooperation and coordination with unfamiliar individuals drove the evolution of structurally complex and flexible communication systems, which, in turn, made possible the attribution of full-blown propositional attitudes, with tenuous connections to observable behavior, that distinguishes sophisticated human mindreading.

5 Sophisticated Mindreading and the Phylogeny of Language

1 Preamble

It is a commonplace in contemporary philosophy and cognitive science that mastering a language presupposes sophisticated mindreading (Grice, 1989; Sperber & Wilson, 1995, 2002; Bloom, 2000, 2002). This is in obvious tension with the perspective defended in this book. In particular, chapter 2 issued multiple promissory notes regarding the independence of language-involving mindshaping practices, like norm formulation, recognition, and enforcement and narrative self-constitution, from sophisticated mindreading. Such independence is important for the project of this book because if distinctively human mindshaping relies on sophisticated mindreading, then mindreading *is* the linchpin of human social cognition, as the received view maintains. Given the widespread assumption that complex language presupposes sophisticated mindreading, it is particularly challenging to explain how language-involving mindshaping can be independent of sophisticated mindreading.

The goal of this chapter is to undermine two lines of argument for the claim that complex language presupposes sophisticated mindreading. First, I tackle a general argument for this view based on the claim that the production and interpretation of linguistic acts require inferring intentions and other propositional attitudes of and by interlocutors. The basic idea is that the meanings of most linguistic acts are too indeterminate to be straightforwardly decoded, and so interpretation requires inferring what specific interlocutors believe or intend in the context of communicative exchanges. Second, I tackle arguments based on claims about the phylogeny of syntactically complex language. According to these arguments, syntactically complex language could not evolve in populations that were not already capable of sophisticated mindreading. There is a third line of argument for the claim that mastering a complex language presupposes sophisticated mindreading, based on the ontogeny of linguistic competence. For example, Bloom (2000, 2002) argues that children could not acquire the semantics of nouns without the capacity to attribute sophisticated referential intentions to their caretakers. I tackle this line of argument in chapter 6, which is devoted to the ontogeny of mindshaping and mindreading.

All these lines of argument are animated by a picture of language according to which it is a mindreading device: the point of language is to make publicly available independently constituted thoughts. This is the central assumption of received theories of linguistic communication and language evolution. In the course of responding to these lines of argument, I defend alternative theories of linguistic communication and language evolution that see language as primarily a mindshaping tool. According to these theories, linguistic communication is primarily about conforming to and tracking *appropriate* conditions on and consequences of linguistic acts, and language evolution was driven by the need to express *commitments* to appropriate (e.g., group-beneficial and cooperative) courses of behavior. Thus the point of language is to regulate behavior,[1] rather than to offer a window into the independently constituted mental states of interlocutors.

2   Sophisticated Mindreading and Human Language

The traditional understanding of how sophisticated mindreading and human language interrelate sees the former as necessary for the latter. That is, one cannot acquire or use human language without first being capable of sophisticated mindreading, especially the reliable attribution of full-blown propositional attitudes, including higher-order intentions and beliefs. As Grice famously argues, a truly communicative act requires not only that the speaker intend to inform her audience but also that the speaker intend that the audience recognize this informative intention and acquire the information on the basis of recognizing this informative intention. Grice proposes these conditions as part of an attempt to provide a philosophical analysis of human communication and its chief currency, what he calls "non-natural meaning" (Grice, 1989). Nonnatural meaning is what human conversation communicates, and it is distinct from "natural meaning," which exists wherever one event carries information about another, such as in "smoke means fire." Grice wants to distinguish cases where agents might inform each other using relations of natural meaning from cases of true communication, involving nonnatural meaning. For example, suppose I am under investigation for a crime and I want to throw the authorities off my scent. I might frame my neighbor by leaving some incriminating evidence in his garage. My intention is to inform investigators of something—to induce a belief in them. But this involves no communicative intention. I am simply manipulating relations of natural meaning—between the presence of incriminating evidence and responsibility for a crime—to induce a belief in an audience. Grice's analysis of communication consists in identifying what more is involved in true communication.

His proposal appeals to sophisticated mindreading. In truly communicative acts, the speaker must intend not just to change the mental state of an audience, for example, induce a belief. In addition, the speaker must intend that this mental state change as a result of the audience recognizing that the speaker intends to change their mental state in a specific way: the "communicative intention" (Sperber & Wilson, 1995, p. 29). The idea is that in true communication, the audience must recognize not just the message that the speaker is trying to convey but also *that* the speaker is trying to convey a message. Both speaker and audience require sophisticated mindreading abilities to pull this off. The speaker must be able to think about the audience's beliefs so that she can change them by providing new information, and she must also be able to think about the audience's beliefs about her own intentions so that she can ensure that they change their beliefs on the basis of recognizing the speaker's intention to inform them. The audience must be able to recognize both the speaker's intention to inform them and the information the speaker intends to convey, to acquire the information on the basis of recognizing the intention. In fact, according to more recent versions of the Gricean analysis, the mindreading presupposed in linguistic communication is substantially more sophisticated than this. In response to counterexamples to the sufficiency of Grice's original analysis, a number of theorists have argued that linguistic communication requires the capacity to attribute intentions of indefinitely higher orders. As Avramides (1989) explains:

there is a diagnosable pattern in these challenges to the sufficiency of the analysis. In each case genuine communication is frustrated because of an element of deceit ... there is a pattern in the moves to counteract them [too] ... with the appearance of further counterexamples ... simply add to the existing set of intentions, n, the further intention, n+1, that A recognize S's (n–1)th intention. Adding such a condition will restore each time the missing ingredient that transforms a case of someone's merely getting something across to another into a genuine case of communication by eliminating a particular deceit. (p. 50)

Thus, there are reasons to favor baroque versions of the Gricean analysis according to which even straightforward linguistic communication presupposes highly sophisticated mindreading.

The Gricean analysis of nonnatural communicative meaning has had a deep influence on the cognitive science of human language and communication. Influential theories of both the ontogeny and the phylogeny of human linguistic communication presume that these phenomena presuppose the kind of mindreading to which the Gricean analysis of communication appeals. For example, Gergely and Csibra propose a Gricean analysis of infant communicative competence as part of their "natural pedagogy" hypothesis, discussed in chapter 2. Csibra (2010) argues that very young infants are capable of recognizing the kinds of second-order communicative intentions to which the Gricean analysis appeals.[2] Bloom (2000, 2002) argues that children could not learn the referents of nouns without a capacity to attribute referential intentions to their caretakers. Origgi and Sperber (2000) argue that language evolution presupposes sophisticated mindreading as well.

This picture is not incompatible with the evolutionary scenario sketched in chapter 4. It is possible that the kinds of mindshaping practices that made cooperation and coordination possible also made fast and frugal propositional attitude attribution possible. Full-blown language then evolved in the way that Origgi and Sperber suggest.[3] However, many have objected to the view that language evolution and acquisition presuppose sophisticated mindreading abilities, in particular, the capacity to attribute full-blown propositional attitudes of higher orders (Millikan, 1984, pp. 61–62; 2005). The central problem with this view concerns its psychological plausibility. Children seem to be able to acquire linguistic communicative competence long before acquiring the capacity for sophisticated propositional attitude attribution. The phylogenetic time course seems similarly unaccommodating. As I argued in chapter 3, it is unlikely that our last common ancestor with chimpanzees could attribute full-blown propositional attitudes, and it is difficult to identify selection pressures that could have driven the evolution of this capacity before the evolution of language. As chapter 4 argued, the Machiavellian intelligence hypothesis is inadequate in a number of respects. If the arguments in chapter 4 are on the right track, evolution in the human lineage favored easy interpretability, given group selection for cooperative dispositions and the various mindshaping practices that made this possible. This suggests that interpreting communicative acts should be so easy that it does not require sophisticated mindreading, especially not the attribution of full-blown propositional attitudes of higher orders.

In an effort to save the Gricean approach from these problems, Sperber and Wilson (1995, 2002) propose a stripped-down version, according to which, in any act of communication, the communicator tokens two intentions: an informative intention and a communicative intention. The informative intention is to *make manifest* to the audience a set of assumptions.[4] The communicative intention is to *make mutually manifest* among communicator and audience that the communicator has this informative intention. According to Sperber and Wilson (1995, p. 39), assumptions are manifest to a cognitive agent when they are perceivable or inferable by that agent. So, in Sperber and Wilson's theory, communicators need not attribute nested intentions to each other. A communicator need only alter her audience's "cognitive environment"—roughly, the features of her physical environment that she has the cognitive capacity to represent—such that the communicator's intentions are *inferable* by the audience. When a communicative intention is made mutually manifest between communicator and audience, both *can infer* that the communicator has a communicative intention, that the audience recognizes this, that the communicator recognizes that the audience recognizes this, and so on. However, neither communicator nor audience need actually engage in such psychologically unrealistic attributions of intentions of arbitrarily higher levels. The communicator need only alter the audience's cognitive environment in a way that makes such mutual knowledge inferable by both.

Although this mitigates some of the psychological implausibility of the more baroque versions of the Gricean model, it is still unclear how communicators and their audiences can pull off the mindreading feats necessary to make communicative intentions mutually manifest. According to Sperber and Wilson (1995, 2002), the key to this is the principle of relevance. Roughly, an item of information is relevant to a cognizer to the extent that it minimizes the "distance" between the cognizer's current state and her epistemic and pragmatic goals. Minimizing this distance depends on two factors: (1) whether or not processing the item of information will help the cognizer achieve her goals, and (2) the processing *effort* required to achieve these goals using the item of information. The more the item helps in achieving the goals, and the less effort it takes to process it, the more relevant the item is. Given that this principle of relevance governs all human cognition, it can be exploited to facilitate communication. In particular, a speaker can make her communicative and informative intentions mutually manifest by producing signals she takes to be relevant to her audience. Such signals constitute alterations of the audience's cognitive environment in ways that make the speaker's intentions perceivable or inferable. Assuming that successful communication is among the audience's goals, the speaker need only produce signals that are relevant to this goal, that is, help the audience understand the speaker's intentions with minimal processing.

Despite this stripping down of the mindreading capacity presupposed by Grice's original theory, Sperber and Wilson (1995, 2002; Sperber, 2000), and those who use their framework to interpret infant communicative competence, endorse the basic Gricean insight: communication requires metapsychology and metarepresentation. To communicate, human beings must attribute representational mental states to their interlocutors, in particular, propositional attitudes like intentions and beliefs. How else could we judge which sorts of communicative signals our interlocutors are likely to find relevant? However, as we saw in chapter 3, this assumption has a serious problem. Due to the holism problem, the timely and accurate attribution of propositional attitudes appears to be computationally intractable. Most human conversation occurs seamlessly in dynamic interactions, leaving little time to infer the propositional attitudes that best explain observed behavior. So it remains mysterious how human communicators can accurately attribute propositional attitudes in a timely enough fashion to communicate as seamlessly as we do.

3   Mindreading versus the Intentional Stance

Sperber and Wilson (1995, 2002; Sperber, 2000) are sensitive to issues of psychological plausibility and computational tractability. These are among the primary motivations for their version of the Gricean theory of communication. A close reading of their work suggests that the notions of metapsychology and metarepresentation to which they appeal are ambiguous: it is not clear whether they intend these to require full-blown attribution of propositional attitudes *as such* or merely some deflationary, behavior-based surrogate. In chapter 1, I distinguished between "high-level" mindreading, involving the attribution of propositional attitudes *as such*, and "low-level" mindreading, involving the tracking of abstract behavioral patterns, which I characterized as adopting Dennett's intentional stance. High-level mindreading requires attributing unobservable mental causes that represent contents under individually variable modes of presentation and influence behavior only indirectly, via interaction with numerous other mental states. Low-level mindreading requires parsing bouts of behavior into goals and informationally and rationally constrained means of achieving them. The evidence strongly suggests that very young infants and nonhuman animals are capable of low-level mindreading, but not of high-level mindreading. The question is: when Sperber, Wilson, and researchers influenced by them claim that human communication presupposes metapsychology and metarepresentation, do they mean high-level or low-level mindreading, as I have characterized them?

Although they often refer to communicators as inferring intentions and beliefs, suggesting the former interpretation, in some passages they seem to assume the low-level interpretation. Here is Sperber (2000) explaining how children might come to understand "conversational implicatures" without attributing full-blown propositional attitudes:

> The *conclusion* of such a process of interpretation is an attribution of a meaning to the speaker and, hence, a metarepresentation. Nevertheless, the *premises* in the inference process need not be metarepresentational. This procedure, therefore, can be followed by a relatively unsophisticated metarepresenter, for instance by a young child. (p. 133)

One might add that, in the case of very young infants engaged in Gergely and Csibra's natural pedagogy, even the conclusion need not be a meta-representation: they need only notice the objective, worldly informa-tion to which adults intend to draw their attention, without in addition understanding that the adults are representing this information. Also, in the case of typical, quotidian adult communication, such a deflationary understanding of the metapsychology that supports interpretation seems more compatible with how smooth, seamless, and dynamic it typically is. Thus there appears to be some question about the sophistication of the metapsychology that Sperber and Wilson think is presupposed by human communication: does it require high-level mindreading (i.e., attribution of propositional attitudes *as such*) or low-level mindreading (i.e., adopting the intentional stance)? In addition, whatever Sperber and Wilson's intentions, there appears to be some reason to favor the low-level view.

The details of Sperber and Wilson's theory certainly seem to suggest that human communication presupposes sophisticated metapsychology. Recall that their key notion is relevance: speakers must choose their com-municative acts carefully, based on assessments of what their audiences find relevant. To judge whether or not a signal will be relevant relative to a given audience, the speaker must establish what motivates the audience, to what the audience is likely attending, what is likely fresh in the audience's memory, what sorts of cognitive heuristics the audience is likely to deploy in the present context, the audience's mood, and other elements of the audience's cognitive background. Sperber and Wilson assume, plausibly, that the audience is usually motivated to engage in successful communi-cation, so perhaps this can be taken for granted by the speaker. However, human beings are rarely motivated by just one goal at any particular time.

Any communicative interaction takes place against the background of other projects in which interlocutors were engaged before communication. These are likely to have consequences for what sorts of information they will find easier to process, what is likely to be fresh in their memory, what sorts of heuristics are likely to be primed, and their general mood. And if Sperber and Wilson are right, all these factors determine what the audience will find relevant, and hence which modifications of their cognitive environment are likely to further their cognitive goals while minimizing processing.

If you are trying to communicate with me, and unbeknownst to you, I have just heard some terrible news, or I am famished, or I have just had an unpleasant memory triggered, or I am in an uncooperative mood, such factors may compromise your ability to produce signals that are relevant to me. So in one interpretation of Sperber and Wilson's theory, any successful communication presupposes that the speaker is capable of some fairly sophisticated natural psychology: she must be able to gauge her audience's mood, attention, recent memories, primed heuristics, and so on. It is difficult to see how such mindreading could be reliable enough to explain the seamlessness, rapidity, and reliability of human communication in dynamic interactions even with unfamiliar individuals: consider the indefinitely large range of factors that might influence the audience's mood, motivation, attention, memory, inferential dispositions, and other variables that determine relevance. Such problems are compounded by the fact that a speaker's audience often involves multiple individuals, for each of which, in this interpretation of Sperber and Wilson's theory, the speaker would have to determine what counts as relevant.

The sorts of mindshaping mechanisms and practices I discussed in chapter 3 might go some way toward mitigating these problems. If we are socialized to be motivated similarly in similar contexts, to use similar heuristics in similar contexts, to remember the same events similarly, and, most importantly, to cooperate in communicative contexts, then speakers might get away with expending minimal effort in determining their audience's motivational, emotional, attentional, and cognitive states. If there are normative practices that sanction audience members who bring inappropriate motivations, moods, or dispositions to communicative contexts, speakers should not need to expend too much effort in determining whether their audiences are primed for the communicative signals they are likely to produce. This much is *compatible* with an interpretation of Sperber and Wilson's theory in which communication presupposes sophisticated mindreading. However, once such an important role for mindshaping is granted, a more deflationary understanding of the mindreading presupposed by communication becomes viable: to the extent that such mindshaping mechanisms and practices succeed in making a speaker's likely audiences maximally receptive to her communicative acts, successful communication should be feasible in the absence of sophisticated mindreading. If speakers can rely on the fact that audience members are likely to be socialized to be in mental states relative to which communicative acts that speakers tend to perform are maximally relevant, then no sophisticated mindreading appears to be necessary for successful communication. This is a specific version of a more general point for which I argued in chapter 3: the more familiar one's interpretive target, the less mindreading seems necessary, since their behavioral dispositions in familiar contexts should be reliable enough guides.[5] Uniform mindshaping practices throughout the population with which one is likely to interact ensure that interactants unacquainted with each other may nonetheless be familiar enough to each other for cheap, behavior-tracking interpretive heuristics to work.

In their critiques of code-based models of communication (Sperber & Wilson, 1995, 2002; Origgi & Sperber, 2000), Sperber and Wilson appear to assume that the only alternative to a code-based model is a sophisticated mindreading model. However, given that the interpretive capacity posited by this model is supposed to support rapid, seamless, and successful communication among interlocutors who are often personally unacquainted with each other, it is not clear whether sophisticated mindreading offers any help. If mindreading involves the reliable attribution of mental states with propositional content to specific agents based on behavioral evidence, we have seen in chapter 3 why this is highly unlikely to be rapid and reliable enough. On the other hand, if the interpretive capacity involves generating generic normative expectations about what audiences *ought* to find relevant, then it is not clear that this counts as sophisticated mindreading. It seems that speakers need only form expectations about *appropriate* patterns of behavior, rather than about the likely mental states of their interlocutors. For example, in a birthday party scenario, the speaker needn't do any deep mindreading of any of the participants to know how they ought to interpret an utterance like "The cake looks delicious." She needn't attempt to determine what each member of her audience is likely to find relevant, based on the behavioral clues they emit, to have well-grounded expectations regarding how her utterance will be interpreted. The reason is that audience members have likely been socialized to find salient similar features of the cognitive environment constituted by a birthday party. Any person happily interacting with guests at a birthday party *should* express no puzzlement regarding the topic of utterances containing the word "cake," because everyone is *expected*, in the normative sense (Gilbert, 1996, p. 75), to treat the birthday cake as the most salient cake in this context. Furthermore, subtle normative sanctioning practices ensure such homogeneity: an absentminded audience member who asks "What cake?" is likely to be mocked and have his status as a potential interactant diminished.

So here is my proposal. Rather than conceive of the communicators' capacities to make mutually manifest informative and communicative intentions as metapsychological, that is, as involving sophisticated mindreading, or the attribution of unobservable mental states with propositional content and causal powers over behavior, we should conceive of these capacities as behavior reading guided by certain normative assumptions. In other words, such interpretive capacities are better characterized as adopting something like Dennett's intentional stance toward potential interlocutors than as trying to read their minds. Relative to robust enough mindshaping practices, human capacities for communication stand the best chance of being reliable, while at the same time supporting rapid and seamless communication in dynamic interactions, if they deploy something like a culturally specific,[6] communication-dedicated version of the intentional stance.

When a communicator chooses her words with the aim of maximizing relevance to the goal of making her informative and communicative intentions mutually manifest, she is guided not by hypotheses about the mental states of her audience but by assumptions about how her audience *ought* to react given the context and the audience's behavior. Audience behavior is interpreted as enacting the most rational means to goals at which it aims in the light of available information. There is no need to attribute representations of these means, goals, and information to the audience; simply parsing behavior and context in this way should suffice for the speaker to select maximally relevant signals, *if* audience and speaker are products of similar mindshaping practices.[7] The intentional stance is a simple interpretive strategy that, against the background of histories of similar mindshaping, can be extremely reliable and efficient *because* it is not deeply metapsychological. Interpreters and communicators can rely on such shared mindshaping backgrounds without knowing it; it is simply a brute fact that most of a speaker's likely interlocutors are products of the same mindshaping practices of which the speaker is a product, and her communicative and interpretive capacities can take advantage of this without her knowing it.[8]

4   A Defense of the Intentional Stance, Part 1

How plausible is this application of Dennett's intentional stance to the problem of interpreting and producing communicative acts?[9] As noted in chapter 2, the developmental psychologists Gergely Csibra and György Gergely sometimes invoke something like Dennett's intentional stance in their theories of sociocognitive development. Rather than attribute mental states, they sometimes argue that infants simply parse behavioral patterns into goals and means, guided by the assumption that behavior constitutes the most efficient means to a goal given available information (Gergely & Csibra, 2003). However, this perspective has recently been subject to a number of criticisms (Nichols & Stich, 2003, pp. 142–149; Goldman, 2006, pp. 54–68). Fortunately, I think these criticisms miss the mark.

Before defending the intentional stance, it is necessary to adopt a terminological convention. Dennett conceives of the intentional stance not just as the basis for quotidian interpretation but also as providing an analysis of what the folk mean by "belief" and "desire." For this reason, discussion of the intentional stance must refer to the attribution of beliefs and desires, or what I have been calling "sophisticated mindreading." However, as noted in chapter 1, Dennett's understanding of "belief" and "desire" is not widely accepted by theorists who see sophisticated mindreading as the linchpin of human social cognition. While propositional attitudes are typically seen as concrete, unobservable mental states that are causally responsible for behavior, Dennett sees them as abstract posits that help interpreters track rational patterns in observable behavior. To adopt the intentional stance, one need only be sensitive to certain abstract properties of bouts of behavior, for example, means–ends rationality; one need not conceptualize behavior as being caused by concrete, unobservable mental states. For this reason, as I argued in chapter 1, the intentional stance can serve as a characterization of the kind of low-level mindreading capacity that we share with at least some nonhuman primates. However, this introduces confusion into any comparisons between Dennett's views on the attribution of propositional attitudes and those of his rivals, since technically they disagree not just on *how* behavioral interpretation proceeds but also on *what* is attributed in interpretation: for Dennett, it is something like conformity to abstract, rational behavioral patterns, while for his rivals it is something like the tokening of clusters of concrete, unobservable mental states, causally responsible for behavior.

The following defense of the intentional stance must inevitably speak of the attribution of propositional attitudes, since this is how Dennett characterizes it. However, because Dennett does not intend such talk as implicating sophisticated mindreading, I adopt the following convention: terms referring to states attributed from the intentional stance are marked with an asterisk. The states referred to by such marked terms are not full-blown propositional attitudes, that is, they are *not* concrete, unobservable mental states, with holistically constrained causal influence on behavior, representing the world under individually variable modes of presentation; rather, they are abstract posits that help track rational patterns in bouts of behavior. In other words, I refer to Dennettian beliefs and desires as "beliefs*" and "desires*." These should be understood as types of information access and goals, respectively, that can be read off observable behavior, rather than as concrete, unobservable causes of behavior.

The most common criticism of Dennett's proposals is that, in characterizing the intentional stance as a way of interpreting behavior guided by the assumption that it is rational, he provides no substantive account of rationality. If the intentional stance is supposed to guide everyday behavioral interpretation, then it is unlikely to be guided by formally worked-out theories of rationality, of which most people are unaware. In fact, robust empirical results from social psychology show that human beings find inferences and behavior that violate rational norms quite natural. For example, we naturally think that an individual meeting a certain profile is more likely a feminist *and* a bank teller than merely a bank teller (Tversky & Kahneman, 1983). However, this violates norms of probabilistic reasoning: since a feminist bank teller is a bank teller, it cannot be more probable that she is the former than that she is the latter. Or consider the so-called paradox of the preface. An author modestly claims in the preface to her book that surely some of the book's claims are false, yet she believes them all. This seems to be manifestly contradictory, and thus irrational, though we find such authorial modesty quite natural. So it seems that if Dennett's theory of interpretation is correct, either we cannot attribute beliefs* and desires* in these cases, since the objects of interpretation fail to meet the rationality constraint, or attribution of beliefs and desires is independent of any assumptions about rationality.

The obvious response to this worry is that the folk have a false and inconsistent theory of rationality. One of the chief rivals of Dennett's intentional stance, the so-called theory-theory of mental state attribution (Gopnik, 1996; Leslie, 1994), must make a similar move. According to the theory-theory, the folk think of mental states as unobservable causes of behavior, individuated by laws connecting stimuli to mental states, mental states to each other, and mental states to behavior. But, as Nichols and Stich (2003) document, many folk assumptions about such causal relations are false. So it is unclear why Dennett's intentional stance is in any worse shape than the theory-theory. Both have to posit some false folk background theory to constrain mental state attribution. Just as Dennett has not provided many details about the content of the folk notion of rationality, referring to it vaguely as a "general-purpose term of cognitive approval" (Dennett, 1987, p. 97), the theory-theorist has not provided many details about the content of the alleged folk theory of psychology. For this reason, the criticism that Dennett is not clear enough about what the folk mean by rationality is unfair. Theory-theorists are not clear enough about what the folk mean by unobservable mental causes, either. Presumably both Dennett and the theory-theorist expect empirical work to fill in the details of folk assumptions about rationality or unobservable mental causes. In chapter 6, I discuss some recent empirical results in developmental psychology (Gergely, 2011) that suggest default assumptions about rationality employed by young infants.

The way to settle this dispute is to see whether or not folk attribution of mental states is normatively constrained. Presumably, if the folk are attributing causally potent, unobservable mental states, with no normative import, then they should *not* respond with criticism to behavior that is rationally incompatible with the states they attribute. A more appropriate reaction would be to adjust one's theory of the causes of behavior in light of counterevidence. On the other hand, if the states the folk attribute are normatively constrained, then responses to behavior that is rationally incompatible with attributed states should often involve criticism driven by normative attitudes like blame. Here I think the evidence favors Dennett. When a person does something irrational, that is, stupid by the lights of the folk, the reaction often expresses a normative attitude like blame or mockery. If A gives B grounds for attributing a belief* P, and then acts in ways that are rationally incompatible with P, B's reaction often takes the form of criticizing A, rather than revising the attribution, as one would predict if B were deploying a theory of the causes of behavior. If I say that there is at least one false claim in this book and then claim that I believe every claim in it, the appropriate response is that I am being irrational.[10] This shows that the belief* attributed on the basis of the first claim carries with it a presumption of rationality. If it were merely a theoretical hypothesis based on a causal law, then the interpreter's appropriate response would be to revise her theory's assumption that there is a causal relationship between saying that one conjunct in a long conjunction is false, believing this, and not believing the entire conjunction. But this is not how people react to such cases.

Here is the upshot: neither the theory-theory nor Dennett's intentional stance go into sufficient detail about the background folk theories that allegedly constrain mental state attributions. Dennett does not explain in sufficient detail what the folk mean by rationality, and theory-theorists do not describe in sufficient detail which causal laws the folk appeal to in their mental state attributions. However, Dennett's view does a better job explaining interpreters' reactions to behaviors that appear to contradict mental state* attributions. The intentional stance model predicts that mental state* attributors will express normative attitudes like blame in response to behavior that is anomalous relative to the states* they attribute, and I submit that this prediction is borne out in everyday life. Theory-theory provides no obvious explanation of this phenomenon.[11]

This line of reasoning raises another problem for Dennett's theory, however. The intentional stance requires that we attribute the beliefs* and desires* that make an agent's behavior come out rational. This means that we cannot attribute inconsistent sets of beliefs* and desires*. However, the point about our reaction to irrationality seems to rely on this possibility. The reason that we are inclined to chide the author of the paradoxical preface for being irrational is because we *can* attribute contradictory beliefs* to her: she believes* both that everything in the book is true and that the book contains at least one falsehood. But if Dennett is right, it seems that we could never attribute contradictory beliefs* to an agent, since belief* attribution is constrained by rationality: we must attribute only those beliefs* that make the agent's behavior come out rational. However, this problem is easily solved.

Although Dennett often speaks as though whole human persons are the typical objects of interpretation from the intentional stance, this is not essential to his view. The central point is that, to interpret a *pattern of behavior* in terms of propositional attitudes*, we must assume the behavior is rational, in other words, that it aims to achieve some goal via the most efficient means possible given available information (Dennett, 1991b). Although the relevant pattern of behavior *can* involve the entire biography of a whole human person, it *need not*. Cases of irrationality are easily dealt with from the intentional stance if we individuate the objects of interpretation at a finer grain than whole human persons. Thus incompatible sets of propositional attitudes* might make sense of different components of the same person's behavioral biography. In one short period of time, the author says that at least one claim she makes in the book is false. The intentional stance requires us to make sense of this behavior in terms of the belief* that at least one claim in the book is false: this is what makes the behavior come out rational. In another subsequent short period of time, the author says that she believes every claim she makes in the book. Relative to this bout of behavior, the intentional stance requires us to attribute the belief* that no claim in the book is false. Both attributions are constrained by the rationality assumption. The irrationality is apparent only when we consider these two behaviors as behaviors of the *same agent*. But if in the first instance the intentional stance takes patterns of behavior of various durations as the main objects of interpretation, then contradictory beliefs* at the level of whole human persons can be accommodated by the intentional stance. Once a pattern of behavior has been interpreted from the intentional stance, under the assumption of rationality, we can then choose to attribute the interpretation to the whole human person who engaged in the pattern of behavior. If we have already attributed other interpretations to this person based on other patterns of behavior in which she has engaged, then the possibility arises that the different interpretations are incompatible.[12]

Goldman (2006) raises some other problems for Dennett's proposal. First, he claims that it fails to provide a unified account of all mental state attribution, since it explains only how we attribute propositional attitudes*, and not how we attribute mental states that are not rationally constrained, like emotions or sensations. This does not strike me as a serious problem. No theory of mental state attribution, including Goldman's own (2006, pp. 43–45), provides such a unified theory. Everyone acknowledges that some mental states are better handled by simulation-type mechanisms, while others are better handled by theory-like mechanisms (Carruthers, 1996; Nichols and Stich, 2003). Every currently viable theory of mental state attribution is some kind of hybrid, so why not throw in rationality as a further heuristic?[13]

A more serious problem raised by Nichols and Stich (2003, pp. 147–148) is that we sometimes attribute propositional attitudes based on their non-rational causal links to behavior. For example, we might infer the true beliefs of a liar based on subtle cues like facial expressions or body language. Clearly, given the liar's beliefs and intentions, such behaviors are not rational. However, restricting the scope of the intentional stance can easily accommodate such cases. Perhaps it is true that we can pick up on signs of insincerity among close acquaintances or very young children. These are cases where relations between propositional attitudes and behavior are not problematically complex. But my interest is in successful interpretation of individuals with whom the communicator is not necessarily personally acquainted. This, after all, is the really tough case for Sperber and Wilson's theory: how can we reliably attribute propositional attitudes to complete strangers, on the basis of scant behavioral evidence, quickly enough to support the smooth, seamless, and dynamic communicative interactions of which strangers speaking the same language are typically capable? As Sterelny (2003, p. 219) puts it, in such cases the psychological domain is not "transparent": there are no strong correlations between behavioral evidence and mental state. Adopting the intentional stance, in the context of a history of similar mindshaping, can help in such cases of interpretation.

Finally, Goldman (2006, p. 65) complains that we cannot learn the rational norms governing propositional attitudes without first having some way of identifying them independently of those norms. This point paves the way for Goldman's own simulationist theory of propositional attitude attribution: if we first identify our own propositional attitudes by their phenomenology and then project these onto others (pp. 261–263), the problem is avoided, since there are phenomenological means of identifying propositional attitudes that are independent of their normative properties. Whatever the merits of Goldman's positive proposal, this criticism of the intentional stance counts equally against the theory-theory, according to which propositional attitudes are identified in terms of their causal roles: how can you determine a state's causal role without having an independent way of identifying it first (Zangwill, 2005)? So it is not a special problem for Dennett's theory. Furthermore, there is a response to Goldman's problem. We can identify *behavior and its public context* independently of the rationality assumption. We can then parse behavior into goals and means and assume that the means are the most efficient way of reaching the goals given contextually available information. The basic apparatus of the intentional stance requires only the ability to parse observable behavior and context, and the assumption that different segments of behavior bear rational relations to each other that are constrained by information available in the context. We can then attribute representations of these goals, means, and information to the agents performing the behavior, calling them "desires" and "beliefs," but this is not essential to assuming the intentional stance.

Thus the main critiques of the intentional stance fail to refute a suitably modest version of it, according to which it is one among numerous strategies for interpreting bouts of behavior of varying durations, by parsing them into goal states, and informationally and rationally constrained means for reaching those goal states. Many of the problems raised for the intentional stance can equally be raised for the theory-theory. However, the intentional stance has one advantage over the theory-theory: it explains the fact that mental state* attributions are often paired with normative expectations, as indicated by the fact that behavior incompatible with an attribution is often met with normatively charged reactions like derision, mockery, and other forms of criticism.[14]

We therefore have no reason to think that the interpretive capacities Sperber and Wilson identify as necessary for human communication involve sophisticated mindreading, that is, the attribution of propositional attitudes *as such*. Given how rapid, fluid, and effective communication can be, it is unlikely that it requires entertaining hypotheses about unobservable mental states. It is more likely that communication relies on assumptions about what is rational or appropriate given a certain context and observed behavior. Such assumptions should be enough for speakers to craft maximally relevant signals without any deep mindreading, assuming that a speaker's likely interlocutors are products of the same mindshaping regimes as she is. This establishes that standard cases of adult linguistic communication need not presuppose sophisticated mindreading. However, as I mentioned in section 1, more specific concerns along these lines have been raised for the phylogeny and ontogeny of linguistic competence. Origgi and Sperber (2000) argue that grammatically complex language evolved only because it aided sophisticated practices of mindreading that preceded it. Bloom (2000, 2002) claims that children can learn the referents of nouns only if they can read the referential intentions of their caretakers. I address Bloom's claim in chapter 6. In the next three sections, I explain how grammatically complex language could evolve independently of sophisticated mindreading.

5   The Phylogeny of Grammatically Sophisticated Language: Problems for Mindreading—First Accounts

Human language is distinguished from other forms of communication in a number of ways (Pinker & Jackendoff, 2005). Theories of the evolution of human language have tended to focus on its recursive syntax and the various semantic properties that it makes possible. Briefly, a recursive rule both generates and applies to items of the same type. Phonological rules are not recursive because they apply only to phonemes but generate strings of phonemes rather than other phonemes. However, syntactic rules are recursive. A syntactic rule that applies to a noun phrase can generate another noun phrase to which the same rule can be applied again. This makes possible the property of "discrete infinity" (Hauser et al., 2002): the syntactic rules governing human language can generate sentences of arbitrary length because the rules can keep being reapplied to their products.[15] No known animal communication system employs such recursive rules. Furthermore, evidence suggests that, unlike human beings, nonhuman primate species that are otherwise adept at detecting patterns of speech syllables *cannot* detect patterns generated by recursive rules (Fitch & Hauser, 2004).

Recursive syntax makes possible an important semantic feature of human language: spatiotemporally displaced referents can be specified to an arbitrary degree of precision. Human beings can communicate about specific persons, places, or things with which they have no acquaintance because they can use recursive syntax to generate descriptions of arbitrarily precise specificity (Bolender, 2007). This is why we can talk about the composition of the cosmos nanoseconds after the Big Bang, for example. Few animal communication systems are capable of communicating information about spatiotemporally displaced referents, and none seem capable of specifying them with the precision that recursive syntax makes possible. The famous "dance language" of honeybees can be used to communicate information about spatiotemporally displaced locations (Gould & Gould, 1988); however, the lack of recursive syntax compromises the precision with which bees can specify such locations. Furthermore, some member of the hive must have had direct acquaintance with a location to encode it in a honeybee dance. However, recursive syntax enables human language to communicate information about objects and events with which no speaker has ever been, or indeed ever *could* be, acquainted (Bolender, 2007), such as the Big Bang.

Domain independence is a further distinctive property of human language. Language can communicate information that is independent of any domain of activity to which it might be relevant. Nonhuman animal communication systems all seem restricted in the domains about which they can convey information. For example, the honeybee dance language is devoted exclusively to communicating information about location. Vervet monkey predator signals are used only to communicate information about predators. Birdsong is used almost exclusively to advertise fitness in the context of attracting mates. So information communicated by nonhuman animal communication systems seems highly constrained in the uses to which it can be put. The contrast with human language is dramatic. Information communicated by a sentence like "Jerry likes chocolate" can be used for an indefinite range of tasks: as part of a strategy for seducing Jerry, as part of a strategy for selling chocolate, as part of a strategy for poisoning or bribing Jerry, and so on. More typically, it can be treated as potentially useful information and "filed" away, in case it becomes useful in the future.

Domain independence is closely connected to another feature of human language and the thought it expresses. As noted in chapter 2, since Evans (1982), theorists have recognized that language and the conceptual thought it expresses are governed by the "generality constraint": to count as having mastered any word or the concept that it expresses, one must be capable of understanding sentences and entertaining thoughts that combine that word/concept with any other word/concept that one counts as having mastered. For example, to count as understanding the nouns "cat" and "dog" and the verb "chase," a speaker must be able to understand both the sentence "The dog chases the cat" and the sentence "The cat chases the dog." Furthermore, true generality also requires the capacity to understand even rather unlikely combinations of words/concepts (Camp, 2004). For example, if you count as understanding the terms "cat," "can of tuna," and "eats," you must be able to understand not just the sentence "The cat eats the can of tuna" but also "The can of tuna eats the cat." One of the advantages of representational systems that meet the generality constraint is that they enable us to represent situations or states of affairs that have never been perceived, and perhaps could never be perceived, like a can of tuna eating a cat. This is closely related to the human capacity for metaphorical thought and language. It also constitutes an extreme enhancement in the representational power of thought. Many of the scientific insights that constitute the pinnacles of human achievement begin with the formulation of metaphors made possible by a system of thought and language that meets the generality constraint. For example, the thought that light is a wave was a central insight of nineteenth-century physics.

It is also arguable that the generality constraint *makes possible* the domain independence of human language and the thought it expresses. In language, a representation of a particular individual or property places no restrictions on the tasks for which it can be used, because the generality constraint ensures that it can be combined with any other representation from any other domain. So, for example, a representation of a predator is not combinatorially restricted to representations having to do with predator defense or avoidance. If it is part of a representational system that meets the generality constraint, then it must be combinable with any other representation in the system, such as representations of food or family members. This allows the predator also to be represented as a potential meal or as having a mother, for instance. Such cross-domain thinking is unavailable to nonhuman species but is quite natural to human beings.

Given these biologically unique properties, explaining the phylogeny of the capacity for distinctively human language has always been extremely challenging. Like the peacock's tail, human language is an extreme outlier and tempts many to despair about providing a phylogenetic explanation of it (Chomsky, 2005). The classic approach to this problem adopts the traditional philosophical understanding of language as an expression of thought (Pinker & Bloom, 1990). According to this view, many of the problematic properties of language are actually properties of uniquely human thinking, inherited by language because it functions to communicate human thought. Thus language has recursive syntax, is domain independent, and meets the generality constraint because it evolved to express thought that is recursively structured, domain independent, and governed by the generality constraint. This approach has a clear affinity with the mindreading-first model of the evolution of the human sociocognitive syndrome: the point of language is to make mindreading easier, that is, to enable users to reveal their true, independently constituted thoughts.

The central problem with this view of language evolution is that there is absolutely no reason to suppose that the thought available to our nonlinguistic ancestors had the relevant problematic properties: recursion, domain independence, and full generality (Zawidzki, 2006). If our nonlinguistic ancestors did not wield a system of thought with these properties, then this jeopardizes the received theory of the evolution of language: we cannot explain how human communication came to be recursively structured, domain independent, and fully general by appeal to selection for the function of expressing thought with these properties. Furthermore, it becomes difficult to understand language as a tool for enhanced mindreading. If the minds of our nonlinguistic precursors contained a system of thought that was not recursively structured, domain independent, and fully general, then how can a communicative system with these properties be selected for helping with accurate mindreading? Wouldn't such an account predict a communicative system with properties that better reflected the thought available to our ancestors before the evolution of language?

There is a response available to the received view. The idea is that human thought and language coevolved (Pinker, 2003). The first "proto-languages" (Bickerton, 1990) lacked the problematic properties of human language and reflected the properties of our nonlinguistic precursors' system of thought. Bickerton (1990, 1995, 1998, 2000) argues that protolanguage lacked the recursive syntax, domain independence, and full generality of contemporary human language. Instead it consisted exclusively of lexical items—analogous to nouns and verbs—combined unsystematically into short, unstructured strings.[16] In this view, once such a protolanguage became widespread in prehuman populations, it somehow created selection pressures that led to more complex thought. This then selected for even more complex systems for communicating thought. After thousands of years of such coevolution, the results are recursively structured, domain independent, and fully general systems of thought and communication that work in a kind of symbiotic relationship. This picture is a substantial corrective to the traditional view of language as selected for the function of expressing thought. Although protolanguage may have been selected for this function, it then somehow led to selection for more complex thought. Thus language shaped thought as much as thought shaped language. Still, this picture remains wedded to the traditional idea that the function of language is to express thought. The protolanguage that was initially selected for this task had side effects, altering the protohuman social niche in a way that selected for more complex thought as a kind of by-product. Because, in this view, language functions primarily to express thought, such cognitive side effects quickly selected for more complex language capable of expressing the more complex thoughts they made possible. The basic idea behind this theory is still that language is primarily a mindreading technology: it enables us to reveal our true, independently constituted thoughts to our interlocutors and to learn theirs. For this reason, this theory is incompatible the perspective defended in this book. Before defending an alternative more compatible with this perspective, the following provides some independent motivation for it.

Any account of the evolution of language must explain why human language has the three problematic properties of recursive syntactic structure, domain independence, and full generality. As noted earlier, the second and third of these are closely related. The received theory of language evolution suggests a plausible account of how human language and thought came to be domain independent and fully general. Once protolanguage existed, it provided a common medium into which the domain-specific thoughts of early protolanguage users had to be translated. Once these internally segregated thought contents could be expressed in a common, public medium, protolanguage users gained a new domain-independent and fully general format for representing them. This is one clear sense in which the emergence of a protolanguage could have had systematic effects on the kind of thinking of which our precursors were capable (Dennett, 1991a; Carruthers, 2002, 2006). However, it is much more challenging to explain how the mere presence of a protolanguage could have led to the emergence of recursive structure in both thought and language. Without such structure, the mere capacity to concatenate symbols of a public medium, expressing internally segregated thoughts, would have been of limited utility; it could not support extended strings of such symbols, involving long-distance structural dependencies between them, capable of specifying contents with arbitrary precision. As Darwin puts it, a "complex train of thought can no more be carried on without the aid of words, whether spoken or silent, than a long calculation without the use of figures or algebra" (1981/1871, p. 57). To this, we might add that such complex trains of thought require complex syntactic structure to keep track of mutual dependencies among their components.

According to one influential proposal, recursive syntax is a by-product of theory of mind (Bickerton, 1998, 2000, 2002). If the Machiavellian intelligence hypothesis were true, and sophisticated mindreading capable of accurately attributing propositional attitudes of arbitrarily higher orders preexisted human language, then this proposal would be plausible. Propositional attitude attribution is recursive because attributing a propositional attitude itself requires tokening a higher-order propositional attitude. For example, to claim that Johnnie believes the Canadiens will upset the Capitals tonight, Joan must believe that Johnnie believes this. This is a second-order belief. Anyone attributing it to Joan would have to token a third-order belief. In this way, the capacity to attribute propositional attitudes can generate attributions of infinite depth, in the same way that recursive grammar allows for the generation of clauses of infinite depth. Since, in the received view, language use involves theory of mind anyway, it is not a stretch to claim that the recursion implicit in sophisticated propositional attitude attribution was somehow exapted to perform a communicative function: the recursive structure implicit in theory of mind came to structure protolanguage, yielding true human language.

Bickerton (1998, 2000) highlights one advantage of this proposal: it potentially explains how language gained its syntactic structure in a single rapid step. According to Bickerton, the greatest puzzle about the evolution of the syntax of contemporary language is that it does not seem compatible with the gradualist assumptions of Darwinian evolution: recursive syntax cannot have evolved piecemeal; a system of communication either has it or does not. So there must be some mechanism by which protolanguage acquired recursive syntax all at once, and exaptation of the structure implicit in sophisticated propositional attitude attribution is a plausible candidate.

Unfortunately, if the arguments of chapter 4 are on the right track, we have no reason to suppose that sophisticated theory of mind preceded the evolution of recursive language. Given the likely socioecology of early humans and their immediate ancestors, the Machiavellian intelligence hypothesis is false: there was no arms race between deception and deception detection that produced a capacity to attribute propositional attitudes of arbitrarily higher orders. As I argued in chapter 4, contemporary humans are not adept at attributing propositional attitudes of higher orders, and even if they were, it is mysterious how this capacity could help solve the coordination and cooperation problems at which human beings excel. Furthermore, there is no known case of an individual, human or nonhuman, with no competence in recursive grammar, who can nonetheless attribute propositional attitudes of indefinitely higher orders. So it is unlikely that recursive grammar is the product of exapting the structure of propositional attitude attribution to communicative functions.

As noted earlier, Origgi and Sperber (2000) also propose a role for sophisticated theory of mind in the evolution of grammatically complex language. The problem they address is how a mutant singleton capable of producing and understanding grammatically complex speech could have had an advantage over her conspecifics if she could not take advantage of these capacities, since none of her conspecifics shared them. The mutant would not need the capacity to understand grammatically complex speech, since no conspecific could produce it, and she would gain no advantage from producing grammatically complex speech, since no conspecific could understand it. This raises a serious bootstrapping problem: how could grammatically complex language ever get off the ground if mutants capable of it could have no advantages? Origgi and Sperber's response assumes that grammatically complex language evolved in populations that were already communicating using a nongrammatical protolanguage. Members of such populations routinely tried to infer the communicative intentions of their interlocutors based on ambiguous, unstructured strings of word-like signals. For example, an unstructured signal string roughly translatable as "John bring water lake" is massively indeterminate: Does it mean that John is to bring water to the lake or from the lake? Is it asking someone to bring water to John, or John to bring water to someone, or someone to bring John to the lake so that he can see the water? The ambiguity of such unstructured communication would have been a serious challenge to interpreters. According to Origgi and Sperber, a mutant who automatically parsed such unstructured communicative signals into grammatical categories might have an interpretive advantage. Suppose, for example, that the mutant parsed any communicative signal into a verb and fillers of certain thematic roles associated with it. For example, the mutant would automatically interpret "bring" as a transitive verb, requiring an agent (someone doing the bringing), a theme (that which is brought), and a goal (the place or person to which the theme is brought). According to Origgi and Sperber (2000), this would give the mutant an advantage over her conspecifics: she would be able to interpret their unstructured utterances more quickly and efficiently because her grammar module would require her to decide on the fillers of the thematic roles associated with particular verbs.

This proposal has a number of problems. First, it is unclear why this should represent any improvement over the kind of interpretive resources that must already exist in a population for a verb like "bring" to play *any* role in successful communication: any individual capable of understanding "bring," whether she wields a grammar or not, must realize that the verb requires an agent, a theme, and a goal. Perhaps the idea is that agrammatical interpretation is less efficient: while agrammatical interpreters must rely on time- and energy-consuming general-purpose interpretive heuristics to process communicative acts, in grammatical interpreters, much of this process is automatized within a dedicated module and hence is less time and energy consuming. However, it is not clear how a grammatical module that *automatically* interprets word strings in terms of thematic relations supplies interpreters with any advantages. A grammar-wielding interpreter still needs to figure out which thematic role each of the other words surrounding "bring" must be assigned. How is this task any easier than trying to figure out the message using general-purpose interpretive heuristics?

Finally, evidence strongly suggests that human beings succeed extremely well on pragmatic tasks requiring communication using entirely ungrammatical improvised languages. Bickerton (1990) offers historical pidgins and the language of two-year-olds as examples of this phenomenon. Jackendoff (2002) argues that these are both versions of the "basic variety" (Klein & Perdue, 1997). This agrammatical form of language, consisting of short strings of nouns and verbs, is also employed in linguistic communication among immigrant workers with no formal instruction in the languages of their host countries. These individuals communicate successfully with short, unstructured sequences of words drawn from the local language. The kinds of pragmatic ends for which communication originally evolved are served efficiently by the basic variety, despite its lack of any grammar, let alone a recursive one. So it is not clear what sorts of biologically basic communicative ends the elaborate, recursive structure of human language could possibly have been selected to help meet. It seems that human beings are perfectly capable of biologically significant communicative feats, like arranging fair trades, setting up meetings, communicating intentions and locations, without a grammatically complex language. Chomsky's (2005) skepticism about natural selection as the mechanism for the evolution of recursive syntax seems well grounded given these facts. It is unclear what survival and reproductive advantages speakers of a grammatically complex language would have over speakers of the basic variety. Thus the received theory of language evolution fails to explain the origins of grammatically complex language. Sophisticated mindreading, from which recursive structure could have been exapted, was not available before it, and it is unclear how grammatical complexity could have helped the kind of mindreading that may have supported protolanguage.

6   Costly Signaling in Human Prehistory

Variants of the received theory of language evolution all assume that the structure of language is related to the function of expressing thought. However, there are other possibilities. Perhaps language acquired its structure independently of any expressive function it may have played. This possibility is implicit in a number of hypotheses about language evolution. For example, in *The Descent of Man*, Darwin speculates that language originated as a kind of mating song, selected as a means of attracting mates by means of advertising biological fitness (Darwin, 1871/1981, pp. 56, 336–337). The model is birdsong, one of the most structurally complex forms of nonhuman communication. Although not fully recursive, some varieties of birdsong approach the structural complexity of recursive grammar (Okanoya, 2002). However, the explanation is not that birds have complex thoughts to convey; most birdsong conveys the same basic message: "Mate with me!" Rather, the explanation is that elaborate signaling is an effective means of advertising mate quality.[17]

Among songbirds, males with structurally more complex songs attract more mates and have more offspring. There are at least two different explanations for this. First, lengthy, complex songs are risky and energy intensive. Any male that produces them signals that he is able to incur the risk of selective targeting by predators and has excess energy to produce lengthy, complex songs and to evade the predators that his songs attract. This is an example of a costly, honest signal of mate quality: displaying such "handicaps" (Zahavi & Zahavi, 1997) is possible only for quality males, ones that can afford to risk predation and waste energy on producing elaborate songs. For this reason, complex birdsong serves as a reliable signal of mate quality; the more complex the birdsong of which a male is capable, the more excess energy he has.[18]

A second explanation for why more complex songs are better at attracting mates makes no appeal to the biologically beneficial traits with which complex birdsong might correlate. According to the theory of "runaway sexual selection," once a tipping point is reached in a population, such that a small plurality of females prefer more complex sexual displays, whether birdsong or plumage or some other advertisement, a positive feedback loop ensues, leading to eventual domination of populations by males capable of complex sexual display and females with a preference for it. The reason is the so-called attractive sons effect (Cronin, 1991, p. 203). Females attracted to males with a certain trait, such as the capacity for relatively complex birdsong, will tend to have both male offspring with the trait and female offspring attracted to it. If a population has a plurality of such females, the next generation will have more males capable of relatively complex birdsong, that is, the "attractive sons," and more females with a preference for it will mate successfully. The coupled traits—in this case, a male capacity for complex birdsong and a female preference for it—eventually come to dominate the population. Furthermore, given widespread female preferences for complex mating calls, male-on-male competition for mates can fuel the evolution of ever more complex birdsong.

If true, these accounts of birdsong constitute an existence proof for the evolvability of structurally complex communication independently of structurally complex thought. The key factor is a preference for complex communication. The handicapping model provides a good explanation for how this preference might initially appear in a population: complex communicative behavior is an honest, costly signal of genetic quality, so females with a preference for it tend to mate with high-quality males, producing more viable offspring than females without this preference. Once enough females have this preference, runaway sexual selection can give rise to positive feedback leading to a takeover of the population.

Fitch (2010) is similarly impressed that structurally complex communication has been shown to evolve in other vertebrate clades, independently of any thought-expressing function. He proposes the following phylogeny of human language:

> The acquisition of complex vocal learning occurred during an initial song-like stage of communication that lacked propositional meaning. ... This system of "bare phonology" provided a learned, complex, generative vocal communication system, with multiple units being combined into a hierarchical, but propositionally meaningless, signaling system. Thus, the sharpest distinction between humans and chimpanzees—vocal imitation—arose first, along with simple "phonological" aspects of syntax (sequencing, hierarchy, and phrase structure). This innovation satisfies the "evolvability" constraint, as Darwin argued, because of its frequent convergent evolution in other vertebrate clades, including birds, whales, and seals. (p. 503)

Like Darwin (1871/1981) and more recent theorists (Okanoya, 2002; Miller, 2001; Mithen, 2006; Zawidzki, 2006), Fitch thinks sexual selection contributed to this evolutionary trajectory. However, following Dissanayake

(1992), he thinks kin selection may have played a role as well: songlike communication may have helped mothers bond with, care for, and stimulate cognitive development in offspring.

Fitch sees these functions as explaining only the initial stage of language evolution, in which hominids first acquired the capacity for complex communication. Different dynamics that took hold later explain how this musical protolanguage acquired semantics (Fitch, 2010, pp. 503–504). However, it is implausible that sexual and kin selection alone can account even for the evolution of a meaningless, hierarchically complex, musical protolanguage. For one thing, it is not clear how kin selection for a role in child rearing can help explain why musical protolanguage became structurally complex: why should maternal care for, bonding with, and cognitive stimulation of offspring take on a structurally complex form? The great advantage of the sexual selection scenario is that it can explain the complex structure of human communication. However, unlike in bird species, there is little evidence that the human capacity for complex communication is the product of sexual selection. For example, the songbird model would predict gender dimorphism in the production of complex communicative signals, since, in most species, only males use them for sexual signaling. But there is no evidence of such gender dimorphism in human communication. Also, the capacity to produce and understand complex communicative signals does not appear to be linked to sexual maturity, unlike in songbird species: human children display this capacity long before puberty (Fitch, 2004, p. 287). Fortunately, the basic principle behind sexual selection for complex communicative capacities governs communicative contexts other than sexual advertising. For example, if a communicator needs to signal *commitment* to a group or to some cooperative endeavor, costly, honest signals are also apposite.[19]

A number of anthropologists and economists have argued that honest, costly signaling is important to cooperation and coordination in human populations. In a number of publications, the anthropologist Richard Sosis and colleagues have argued that religious ritual plays the role of a costly signal of commitment to a group (Sosis, 2003; Sosis & Alcorta, 2003; Ruffle & Sosis, 2007).[20] The idea is that engaging in elaborate, cognitively, emotionally, and physically taxing rituals signals one's commitment and reliability to other members of the group. Only individuals truly committed to the group would endure the costs of such rituals, and so participation in rituals signals the trustworthiness and reliability of individuals. Free riders are unwilling to invest in rituals, so such costly signaling can be used to weed them out. Sosis cites data about the longevity of various communities to support this thesis. For example, among nineteenth-century communes in the United States, a strong correlation holds between strict adherence to costly religious rituals and commune longevity (Sosis & Bressler, 2003). A similar correlation is apparent among Israeli kibbutzim: religious ones far outlast secular ones (Sosis & Ruffle, 2003). Sosis's ideas are modeled game-theoretically by the economists Bacharach and Gambetta (2001). They argue that the key problem in human cooperation and coordination—knowing whom to trust—is solved by signaling one's identity, including one's membership in a group. However, such signals are open to exploitation by mimics—individuals who bear no commitment to the group, and hence are untrustworthy, but mimic signals of group identity to gain and exploit the trust of group members. This puts pressure on trust-signaling sign systems: to weed out mimics, these systems become increasingly complex, such that only trustworthy group members can master them.

Sosis (2003, pp. 100–107) suggests that if commitment-signaling rituals reach a level of complexity and difficulty such that only group members in good standing can perform them smoothly and correctly, they constitute a highly efficient way of weeding out free riders without constant monitoring of behavior or elaborate mindreading aimed at detecting cheaters. Individuals who have been socialized to identify with a group since infancy and to participate in commitment-expressing rituals will treat even highly complex and demanding rituals as routine overtures to cooperative group activities: to group members, the rituals will not seem costly. Mimics, on the other hand, will see such rituals as costly, at least in the sense that they appear as a waste of time and hence require them to forgo other opportunities. So mimics will be less willing to invest the time and energy required to participate in such rituals. Thus communicative practices, like religious rituals, can function as honest, costly signals of commitment to groups and their cooperative projects. Such costly signals are honest in precisely the same way that birdsong is an honest signal of mate quality. Only genetically superior male songbirds can afford to divert energy from other functions, like fighting off parasites, and incur risks of predation to produce lengthy, complex songs. Similarly, in human populations, only reliable, well-socialized group members can engage in costly rituals to signal commitment to cooperative group projects because only such individuals will *see* the rituals as low-cost, routine overtures to group activities; outsiders will see the rituals as unnecessary, nonfunctional flourishes for which they are unwilling to incur opportunity costs.

If the arguments in chapter 4 are on the right track, the need to signal commitment to a group or to cooperative endeavors became more pressing with the broad-spectrum revolution (BSR). As Sterelny (2012) persuasively argues, before the BSR, free riding was not a serious risk because human and protohuman populations relied on collective hunts of megafauna. This ensured that all members of a group of interactants were well known to each other and had broadly similar skill sets and cognitive capacities. Public pooling of information made deception unlikely. The BSR gradually changed this socioecology over the last 100,000 years. A division of labor arose supporting specialized foraging by small subgroups. Group members were no longer as familiar to each other: there were no communal hunts of megafauna in which almost all participated that doubled as arenas for the public display of skill and reliability. Increasingly, individuals had to cooperate and coordinate with others of only cursory familiarity. They had to trade with specialists in foraging niches about which they knew little. They had to select mates from subgroups they could not observe daily. They had to cooperate in group defense or warfare with individuals whose reliability they had no personal knowledge of (Matthew & Boyd, 2011). As noted in chapter 4, Powell et al. (2009) and Mellars (2005) trace late Pleistocene technological innovations, which constitute the BSR, to demographic changes involving increasing contact among unfamiliar individuals. Studies of contemporary hunger-gatherer populations—often claimed to be good models of prehistoric human populations—also show a surprising degree of interaction among unrelated individuals (Hill et al., 2011).

As Caporael (2001) argues, as human populations grew in size and in specialized divisions of labor, individuals had increasingly to manage different degrees of affiliation corresponding to different levels in a hierarchy of groups. At the lowest level were affiliations based on daily, face-to-face interactions, such as family members and collaborators in specialized foraging. At the next level were affiliations based on less intimate yet still frequent interactions, for example, something corresponding to fellow "band members." Further up the hierarchy were affiliations based on tribal membership tested in relatively rare though regular interactions, such as seasonal gatherings organized for trade, the renewal of alliances, and mate selection.[21] Finally, at the highest level, involving the most tenuous form of affiliation, there likely occurred irregular, occasional interactions with members of other tribes, perhaps for the purposes of trade.[22]

Given such a socioecology, individuals could count on personal knowledge of potential interactants only at the lowest level of the hierarchy, that is, those with whom they had daily, face-to-face interactions. In such interactions the risk of free riding was likely low for the reasons that Sterelny (2012) argues it was low among megafaunal hunting bands before the BSR:

information about potential interactants was regularly, publicly available, and the public sharing of information made deception riskier and less rewarding. However, many of the most important interactions likely took place at higher levels of the hierarchy, with less familiar individuals. After the BSR, individuals likely came to rely on cooperative interactions with relative strangers for some of their most important biological needs: nutritional needs would be met largely by trading with band members specialized in different foraging niches, with whom face-to-face interactions were infrequent and sporadic; mate selection would be optimized through interaction with genetically unrelated individuals at rare though regular tribal gatherings; defense against other groups would be optimized by martial coordination and cooperation involving groups as large as possible, again requiring rare interactions with relatively unfamiliar members of the tribe. Thus it is likely that the changes in demographics and the rise of division of labor corresponding to the BSR made successful cooperative interaction with relative strangers crucial to human biological success.[23]

As noted in chapter 4, Sterelny (2012, pp. 54–55) sees the rise of elaborate symbolic culture as archaeological evidence of the BSR. The foregoing discussion of honest, costly signaling as an explanation of the evolution of structurally complex communication can explain this correlation. As individuals came increasingly to rely on cooperative interactions with relative strangers, they needed some system for signaling trustworthiness and commitment to cooperative group endeavors. As Bacharach and Gambetta (2001) argue, any such signal would be subject to undermining by mimics, so costly, hard-to-fake signals would emerge. These signals would work only if they adequately filtered out unreliable partners. If Sosis (2003) is right, potentially free-riding, inappropriately socialized individuals could be filtered out by complex signaling because such signaling would present to them as too costly while presenting to appropriately socialized individuals as routine, uncostly overtures to interactions. But such costly, honest signaling would do more than just filter out potential free riders. Cooperation requires not just willing but also able partners. So costly displays, for example, as parts of rituals, could also serve as honest signals of ability: individuals capable of better-quality performances would thereby showcase their superior skills at cooperative behavior. For example, those who were better at rhythmic synchrony in rituals would likely be better at coordination in hunts or warfare.[24] Given the importance of cooperation to human biological success, those who signaled superior cooperative motivations and skills thereby signaled superior mate quality, so such signals would double as sexual signals. Competition for inclusion in status-enhancing cooperative endeavors, as well as correlated competition for mates, would drive the evolution of increasingly complex signaling capacity.

The foregoing has focused on the capacity to *produce* complex signals; however, the capacity to *process* and *appreciate* such signals would also be favored in these circumstances.[25] Just as it is adaptive for female songbirds to discriminate more complex from less complex songs, and to favor the former, it would have been adaptive for potential cooperators to discriminate more complex from less complex overtures to cooperative endeavors, and to favor the former. If such costly signals were truly honest, that is, correlated with potential cooperation partner quality, then discriminating more costly from less costly signals and favoring the more costly was a means of selecting good cooperation partners and hence increasing the chances of successful cooperative endeavors. In general, costly signals evolve only if they provide benefits to both producers and consumers of the signals (Zahavi & Zahavi, 1997). It is therefore unsurprising that considerable overlap exists in the neural basis for productive and receptive communicative competence in human beings (Rizzolatti & Arbib, 1998).

Thus the proposal that the capacity to process complex communicative structures, similar to those employed in contemporary language, evolved as a means of transmitting costly, honest signals, analogous to birdsong, fits well with the likely cooperative and coordinative dilemmas faced by our post-BSR ancestors. Signaling that one possesses the motivational and cognitive capacities required to be trusted in large-scale cooperative projects involving relatively unfamiliar members of affiliations at different levels would often have been crucial to biological success in such circumstances.[26]

7 Language as Mindshaping Technology

This is clearly not a complete account of the evolution of language. Once language came to be acquired early and automatically by all normal human beings, it could no longer function as a costly, honest signal. Virtually all human beings are so good at language that deception is a constant threat. But the proposal here is not that language functions as an honest, costly signal. The proposal is that our capacity to produce and comprehend communicative signals with complex and even recursive structure is a product of selection, in prehistory, for costly, honest signals of commitment to groups and cooperative endeavors in ritualistic displays. Once this capacity became widespread in human populations, it could no longer function as a costly signal in and of itself; however, by then, it may have acquired all the other functions for which we use structurally complex language.

The crucial point is that this presents an alternative to the common view that structurally complex language reflects the structure of prior and independently constituted thought and arises only in the context of populations already capable of sophisticated mindreading. The alternative takes seriously the lessons of chapter 4 that sophisticated mindreading is unlikely to have helped with prehistoric coordination and cooperation, and post-BSR prehistoric populations had to solve the problem of cooperating and coordinating with unfamiliar individuals. In this alternative, complex structure was an attribute of human communication from early on, not because it reflected the structure of prior thought or mindreading but because, like birdsong, it was the product of selection for ever more costly, honest signaling. In the human case, though there may have been a sexual dimension to this, the primary pressure was the need to reliably signal commitment to groups and cooperative endeavors.

The picture of language that this suggests departs significantly from the orthodox conceptualization of language as a tool for transmitting independently constituted thoughts. According to the view proposed here, language descends from far less precise and intentional yet structurally complex forms of communication that are perhaps better conceived in "performative" terms. Such "protolanguage" likely involved rhythmic, dance- and songlike behaviors in the context of rituals that functioned to express commitment to, and competence at, various cooperative group endeavors. The messages conveyed by such performances were not explicitly and intentionally preformulated in the minds of performers. Just as a songbird does not intend to communicate the message "Mate with me!" with his song, participation in ritual does not require explicit intentions to communicate one's reliability as a cooperation partner. Motivations for participation were likely simple desires to conform or to gain status. But successful performances communicated, whether participants knew it or not, reliability in cooperative endeavors. For this reason, successful performances, and motivations to engage in such performances, were rewarded with the status accorded to reliable cooperation partners, as well as with consequent advantages in the mating market. Competition for such rewards, together with pressures to weed out free-riding mimics, selected for more complex communicative capacities, that is, the capacity to produce ever more complex performances in song and dance rituals. As human socioecology became more complex and the variety of cooperative endeavors multiplied, the capacity for ritual performance became more flexible: successful cooperators needed to master diverse rituals appropriate for different audiences and different cooperative projects. This selected for an increasingly domain-general capacity for ritualized communication.

Assuming that human populations already employed a structureless, "Bickertonian" protolanguage akin to the "basic variety" discussed earlier, for more straightforward, informative forms of communication,[27] the structurally complex, ritualistic, honest signaling could easily come to be integrated with it. The lexical units of the Bickertonian protolanguage would come to be arranged into complex structural patterns typical of ritualistic protolanguage, to yield something like syntactically structured means of transmitting information. Suppose, for example, that our prehistoric ancestors conveyed referential and predicative information using unstructured strings of lexical units, as Bickerton argues. At the same time, they engaged in structurally complex, rhythmic rituals, akin to song and dance, as honest, costly signals of commitment to, and competence at, cooperative endeavors. Given that these two systems would often use the same vocal or gestural media, it would be almost irresistible to integrate the two.[28] Given that the cooperative endeavors, commitment to which ritualistic protolanguage was supposed to signal, also involved transmitting referential and predicative information using lexical units, it would be surprising if such lexical units were *not* integrated into the complex structures of ritualistic communication.

Strong selection pressures likely favored the capacity to rapidly acquire such complex commitment-signaling forms of communication, so the Baldwin effect (Pinker & Bloom, 1990, pp. 722–723; Schull, 1990; Dennett, 1991a, pp. 184–187; Pinker, 2003, pp. 25–26) likely led to widespread virtuosity at producing and processing structurally complex communicative acts. The Baldwin effect is an evolutionary mechanism hypothesized to explain how difficult-to-acquire skills might, through natural selection, become increasingly easy to acquire, until they are almost innate. The idea is that if strong enough selection pressures come to bear on acquiring a skill quickly, individuals capable of acquiring it on the basis of minimal triggers should be favored. It is commonly argued that the relatively rapid time course of language acquisition in contemporary humans is a product of the Baldwin effect. As a result of its widespread mastery, complex communication likely lost its efficacy as a costly signal, since everyone was capable of it. However, by then it likely acquired all the other varied functions for which structurally complex, recursive language is maintained in contemporary populations: making explicit logical relationships, specifying referents with which no speaker is acquainted to arbitrary levels of precision, representing claims and thoughts of arbitrarily higher levels, taking advantage of full generality to formulate domain-independent, creative, analogical representations capable of encoding deep insights into phenomena, for example, that light is a wave, and so on.[29] Once language of this kind was present in the population, individuals were able to *commit* to courses of behavior that group norms deemed compatible with tokens of such structurally complex signals. Structurally complex language then became the ultimate mind*shaping* technology, making arbitrarily complex, flexible, and powerful forms of representation available to a lowly primate brain through the mechanism of commitment to linguistic items.[30] In chapter 7 I argue that the practice of undertaking and attributing such discursive commitments led to the emergence of sophisticated mindreading, that is, full-blown propositional attitude attribution.

Besides its compatibility with the mindshaping-as-linchpin model of the human sociocognitive syndrome, this picture of the evolution of language makes sense of numerous facts about the relation between linguistic structure and nonlinguistic, structured forms of communication like music, dance, and rhythmic behavior in general. The structural analogies between language and music have long been appreciated (Lerdahl & Jackendoff, 1996). Based on such structural analogies and significant overlap in brain areas devoted to language and music processing (Patel, 2008), Mithen (2006) argues that the primary form of communication among Neanderthals was a kind of rhythmic hybrid of speech and song—a kind of chanting or voicing of mantras. The view that language descended from such forms of communication also makes sense of obvious facts about the role of rhythmic performance in contemporary human populations. Like language, these forms of communication are cultural universals and appear early in development (Papousek, 1996). As noted in chapter 4, Wiltermuth & Heath (2009) showed that rhythmic synchrony induces trust among unfamiliar interactants in public goods games. Kirschner and Tomasello (2010) showed similar effects in four-year-olds making music together. Another tantalizing connection to recent evidence about the evolution of language concerns the genetic basis for structurally complex language. As mentioned in chapter 1, defects in the FOXP2 gene have been implicated in Specific Language Impairment, a disorder that affects the capacity to produce structurally complex utterances (Lai et al., 2001). The human version of this gene has undergone significant mutations in the last 100,000 years, corresponding roughly to the timeline of the BSR. In addition, avian versions of this gene are implicated in the capacity for complex, sexually selected birdsong (White et al., 2006). This evidence is congenial to the theory of language evolution defended here. Finally, the amount of energy and financial resources that contemporary humans are willing to invest in rhythmic performance is puzzling unless our capacity for producing and processing it is a deeply entrenched trait that played and perhaps continues to play an important adaptive role.

Data of this sort conflict with Steven Pinker's notorious suggestion that "music is auditory cheesecake" (1997, p. 534), meaning that music is a kind of nonadaptive epiphenomenon arising from the joint activity of other capacities that have adaptive explanations. If this is true, then how is it maintained in every single culture? Why are almost all human beings willing to devote substantial resources to music and other forms of rhythmic performance? Shouldn't there be selection against using up resources for such nonadaptive behaviors?[31] Why is the capacity for processing and producing rhythmic and musical performances present from such an early age—even before language is fully developed? Pinker appeals to analogous facts about language and other capacities to argue that they are selected for their adaptive value. Why deny this about rhythmic performance? The evidence supports views like Mithen's (2006) and Donald's (1991): music and rhythmic performance are more primitive forms of communication from which language derives, the currency of what Donald calls the "mimetic" culture of early human populations. Pinker's view is burdened with the assumption that communication is useful only to the extent that it transmits explicitly formulated messages from one mind to another, in other words, that communication can only be mindreading technology. But the proposal outlined here shows that very different forms of complex, structured communication can be adaptive.

8 Summing Up and Moving Forward

This chapter has shown that complex language does not necessarily presuppose sophisticated mindreading. Sperber and Wilson (1995, 2002) sometimes seem to claim that interpretive indeterminacy in human communication can be prevented only with the help of sophisticated mindreading. However, if the arguments in the first sections of this chapter are on the right track, then the capacity to adopt the intentional stance toward interlocutors who are products of similar mindshaping practices can do a better job at resolving interpretive indeterminacy in a timely manner. Various theories of the phylogeny of structurally complex language, according to which language is mindreading technology (Pinker & Bloom, 1990; Pinker, 2003) and sophisticated mindreading must have preceded it (Bickerton, 1998, 2000, 2002; Origgi & Sperber, 2000), are not the only, or even the best, games in town. Given the arguments in chapter 4, the proposal defended in this chapter, according to which structurally complex language is descended from a capacity for costly, complex, honest signaling of commitment to groups and cooperative endeavors, makes more sense.

The upshot is that we have good reasons to suppose that structurally complex language preexisted sophisticated mindreading. This cashes some of the promissory notes issued in chapter 3: varieties of mindshaping that involve language use, like norm institution, recognition, and enforcement or narrative self-constitution, need not presuppose sophisticated mindreading. It also paves the way for the argument in chapter 7: sophisticated mindreading is best understood in terms of the concept of discursive commitment (Brandom, 1994; Frankish, 2004). But before turning to this topic, I must address another line of argument for the view that linguistic competence presupposes sophisticated mindreading: the evidence from human cognitive development establishes this (Bloom, 2000, 2002). In the next chapter, I address this argument as part of a general survey of the ontogeny of human mindshaping and mindreading.

6 Mindreading and Mindshaping in Human Ontogeny

1 Preamble

The claim that sophisticated mindreading is necessary for linguistic competence is the ultimate challenge to the view defended in this book. The reason is that in chapter 7 I propose to explain sophisticated mindreading as the undertaking and attribution of discursive commitments. In pursuing this strategy, I am relating the mindshaping-as-linchpin theory of the phylogeny of the human sociocognitive syndrome to a prominent philosophical tradition that sees full-blown propositional attitude attribution in terms of (something like) discursive commitment (Ryle, 1949; Davidson, 1985; Dennett, 1978, chap. 16; Brandom, 1994; McGeer, 2007; Frankish, 2004; Hutto, 2008).[1] I think these two ideas—that mindshaping is the linchpin of the human sociocognitive syndrome, and full-blown propositional attitude attribution involves the undertaking and attribution of discursive commitments—have a natural affinity. The reason is that discursive commitment is a mechanism for mindshaping: to commit to a claim is to commit to normatively kosher courses of behavior, that is, those that are deemed compatible with the claim. For this reason, this understanding of full-blown propositional attitude attribution provides a way of understanding sophisticated mindreading in terms of the sorts of mindshaping mechanisms that I have argued were central to the phylogeny of the human sociocognitive syndrome.[2] Just as the sorts of costly, honest signals of commitment to groups or cooperative endeavors discussed in chapter 5 can explain how early humans made relatively crude commitments, today's more sophisticated discursive practices can explain

This chapter draws on material that was originally published under the title "How to Interpret Infant Socio-Cognitive Competence" in *Review of Philosophy and Psychology* 2 (2011): 483–497.

how we can make commitments as diverse and precise as the distinctions afforded by contemporary languages.[3]

Chapter 5 has already blunted some of the force of the claim that linguistic competence presupposes sophisticated mindreading. However, recent work in developmental psychology provides different evidence for this view. This evidence appears to show that human infants are capable of sophisticated mindreading long before they are capable of understanding or producing linguistic performances (Onishi & Baillargeon, 2005). Furthermore, empirical evidence strongly supports the claim that infants could never acquire a language without sophisticated mindreading (Bloom, 2000, 2002). This sort of evidence threatens any attempt to understand sophisticated mindreading, that is, full-blown propositional attitude attribution, in terms of discursive commitment or, indeed, any view that sees sophisticated mindreading as somehow parasitic on language (Davidson, 1975; Brandom, 1994; Hutto, 2008; Bermúdez, 2003a, 2009).

Since the project of this book concerns phylogenetic priority, evidence from human ontogeny is not directly relevant to my argument. It is possible that despite its alleged ontogenetic priority, sophisticated mindreading depended on prior discursive competence in phylogeny. Even if this were true, sophisticated mindreading might come to precede discursive competence in ontogeny. Because discursive competence would have had such profound effects on the human socioecological niche, it could have given rise to selection pressures favoring individuals born with a natural affinity for sophisticated mindreading. As I noted in chapter 5, the Baldwin effect can genetically entrench traits that are initially acquired only through protracted and difficult learning processes. If there is significant reward to rapid and early acquisition of a skill, selection pressures can favor individuals who find it easier to acquire the skill, to the point that individuals in whom the skill is triggered almost from birth come to dominate populations. If the capacity to make and track discursive commitments was important enough in human prehistory then, thanks to the Baldwin effect, there may have been selection for individuals precocious in this practice almost from birth. This may have made possible sophisticated mindreading in prelinguistic infants: perhaps individuals capable of attributing beliefs before discursive competence were quicker at acquiring it. In other words, ontogeny need not recapitulate phylogeny, so the phylogenetic hypothesis defended in this book does not directly contradict evidence that sophisticated mindreading precedes discursive competence in human ontogeny.

Nevertheless, if human infants are capable of full-blown propositional attitude attribution long before they can understand and produce linguistic performances, and if the former capacity is necessary for the latter capacity, then this is not good news for the mindshaping-first theory. In chapter 1, I noted that this theory is viable only if two claims can be established: sophisticated mindshaping is possible without sophisticated mindreading; and reliable, sophisticated mindreading depends on prior, sophisticated mindshaping. If discursive competence can be acquired only by sophisticated mindreaders, it is hard to see how prehistoric humans can have acquired it independently of sophisticated mindreading. And some of the most important varieties of sophisticated mindshaping cataloged in chapter 2 presuppose discursive competence. Thus recent developmental evidence of the priority of sophisticated mindreading to discursive competence is in tension with the mindshaping-first theory.

Fortunately, I do not think that the recent evidence from human ontogeny—as groundbreaking as it is—warrants either the conclusion that human infants can attribute full-blown propositional attitudes before acquiring a language or the conclusion that language acquisition in contemporary human ontogeny presupposes such sophisticated mindreading. The next four sections are devoted to making this case. Section 2 considers the growing evidence that very young infants can pass nonverbal versions of the false belief task (Onishi & Baillargeon, 2005) long before they have mastered complex language. For more than twenty years, developmental psychologists have assumed that passing the false belief task represents the best evidence of having mastered the concept of belief. Focusing on one study (Scott & Baillargeon, 2009), I argue that passing nonverbal versions of the false belief task, of which infants as young as thirteen months appear capable (Surian et al., 2007), is far from sufficient for mastery of the concept of belief. Section 3 defends a different interpretation of these results, according to which infants can adopt rudimentary versions of the intentional stance and hence expect the behavior of their interpretive targets to be rationally appropriate relative to goals and immediately available information. Section 4 defends the application of the intentional stance hypothesis to infant social cognition against a variety of objections, arguing that it explains recent developmental data better than its chief rivals: theory-theory and simulation theory. Section 5 tackles the claim that only sophisticated mindreading can explain how children acquire language (Bloom, 2000, 2002).

Section 6 turns to the evidence of dispositions toward mindshaping in very young human children. Some of this evidence shows that even prelinguistic infants are predisposed for receptivity to pedagogical interactions and imitation of fine-grained behavioral sequences. Evidence also shows that very young children are disposed to express normative attitudes toward violations of expectations related to human interaction, and to make behavioral predictions based on norms that define social roles, rather than on information about mental states or behavioral dispositions. Together, this evidence constitutes a persuasive case that human beings are predisposed from a very young age to engage in mindshaping, both as "shapees" and as shapers.

2   Infant Performance on Nonverbal False Belief Tasks Does Not Show Mastery of the Concept of Belief

Until about 2005, most developmental psychologists assumed that passing the standard false belief task (SFBT) was the most important milestone in the development of human sociocognitive competence. The SFBT comes in a variety of versions. The earliest version confronted children with two dolls, Sally and Anne. The child subject sees Sally handle an object she likes, like a toy or a piece of candy, in the presence of Anne. Sally then places the object in a location that all can see, like a drawer, and leaves the scene. With Sally gone, Anne takes the object and hides it in another location, like a cupboard in another part of the room. Sally returns, and the child subject is asked where Sally will look for the object. The correct answer is that Sally will look for the object where she believes it to be, that is, the drawer in which she left it. However, children provide this answer reliably only after the age of four. Before this, most children answer that Sally will look for the object where it actually is, that is, where they saw Anne put it: the cupboard. Other versions of the SFBT show similar results. For example, a child is shown a box of a well-known brand of candy from the outside and asked what is in it; the child responds with the name of the candy. However, unbeknownst to the child, the candy has actually been replaced with crayons. The box is then opened, and the crayons are shown to the child. The child is then asked what some other child, who has not seen inside the box, will think is in the box. Again, before the age of four, children tend to show a reality bias: they assume others will know the truth behind the appearance—that the box contains crayons, not candy. After four, children are suddenly capable of predicting others' responses based on their likely false beliefs.[4,5]

There are several reasons why the different versions of the SFBT were taken for such a long time to indicate a milestone in human sociocognitive development. First, many developmental psychologists assumed that the central feature of the concept of belief is that it is a potentially nonveridical mental state. Second, inspired by centuries of philosophy, many also assumed that the attribution of beliefs and desires was the most important component of human sociocognitive competence. Since passing the SFBT appeared to show an appreciation of nonveridical mental states, and thus mastery of the concept of belief, passing the SFBT was plausibly interpreted as *the* central milestone in human sociocognitive development. In addition, there is convergent evidence from psychopathology: most individuals with autism, known to have severe deficits in social cognition (Baron-Cohen, 1995), never pass the SFBT. Furthermore, that subjects do not pass the SFBT until four years of age, long after most children have mastered complex language, further supported this view. Sophisticated mindreading seems like something that should be difficult to acquire, and the evidence seemed to confirm this.[6]

In recent years, this consensus about the significance of passing the SFBT has been rapidly eroding. Since 2005 there has been a steady stream of data that appear to undermine the assumption that passing the SFBT is the earliest indicator of competence at full-blown propositional attitude attribution. Drawing on various methods for gauging the expectations of preverbal and nonverbal subjects, Onishi and Baillargeon (2005) ran a nonverbal version of the false belief task (NVFBT). The basic measure that such tasks employ is looking time. It is widely held that preverbal infants look longer at stimuli that violate their expectations. This makes possible a way of testing for the understanding of false belief in preverbal infants. One need only run two versions of the Sally-Anne task with different endings and see which triggers longer looking time. In one version, Sally returns to look for her toy or candy and goes directly to where it is. In another version, Sally returns to look for her toy or candy and goes directly to where she left it. Onishi and Baillargeon (2005) found that fifteen-month-old infants look longer when Sally goes directly to where the toy or candy is than when Sally goes directly to where she left it.[7] If longer looking time indicates violation of expectations, then fifteen-month-olds expect Sally to go to where she should think the toy or candy is, not to where it actually is. In other words, fifteen-month-olds appear to understand that Sally has a false belief about the location of the object she seeks.[8] Numerous investigators have found congenial results since Onishi and Baillargeon's initial study (Song & Baillargeon, 2008; Surian et al., 2007). Passing the SFBT does not appear to be the earliest indicator of competence at full-blown propositional attitude attribution, nor does this capacity appear to require discursive competence.

I do not agree with this interpretation of infant performance on versions of the NVFBT. I think the data can be reinterpreted in a way that makes clear that infants who pass versions of the NVFBT are not capable of full-blown propositional attitude attribution and hence not capable of sophisticated mindreading as I have characterized it in this book. But before I turn to this subject, I want to draw attention to an unjustified inference that is common in this literature, which can be traced to the original interpretations of performance on the SFBT. It is tempting to conclude from the newer data that infants master the concept of belief long before they show any mastery of complex language. After all, they expect agents to behave in certain ways depending on whether or not they have false beliefs; what more could there be to mastering the concept of belief? This line of reasoning inherits from the original interpretations of the SFBT the assumptions that potential nonveridicality is the central property of the concept of belief, and mastering the concept of belief is the key accomplishment in the ontogeny of human sociocognitive competence. Although these assumptions seemed innocuous when the evidence showed that expectations sensitive to false belief did not develop until relatively late, the earlier one pushes such competence, the less plausible such assumptions seem. Can it really be that fifteen-month-olds possess the full-blown concept of belief and hence have cleared the most important hurdle on the road to mature sociocognitive competence?[9]

This is clearly an overly rich interpretation of the NVFBT data. There is much more to the concept of belief than merely potential nonveridicality. First of all, mental states that are far less sophisticated than beliefs can be nonveridical, for example, perceptions. As noted in chapter 2, evidence suggests that even chimpanzees can appreciate nonveridical perceptions (Krachun et al., 2009), though it is widely acknowledged that they have no capacity to attribute false beliefs, and hence no concept of belief. So, clearly, an appreciation that an agent might be guided by a nonveridical mental state is not sufficient for a mastery of the concept of belief, and hence not sufficient for sophisticated mindreading, as I have characterized it.

Second, one of the central properties of belief, at least as philosophers have understood the concept, is its intensionality. The truth of a belief attribution depends on how the content of the belief is characterized. For example, someone may believe that Mark Twain wrote *Huckleberry Finn* without believing that Samuel Clemens wrote *Huckleberry Finn*, though Mark Twain and Samuel Clemens were the same person. To know how to attribute beliefs, one must be able to take into account not just what one's interpretive targets know but also how they represent what they know. At best, passing NVFBTs or even SFBTs requires sensitivity to what one's interpretive targets know. But it requires no appreciation of how they represent what they know, so passing these tests does not show mastery of the concept of belief (Apperly, 2011, pp. 16–17, 42–45, 150). In fact, as Apperly argues, evidence indicates that children who can pass SFBTs are not sensitive to the intensionality of belief, that is, the fact that different individuals can represent the same facts under different modes of presentation. For example, after using an eraser that looks like a die, even five- and six-year-old children judge that a puppet with only visual access to the die/eraser (and hence presumably no awareness that it is actually an eraser) would treat it as an eraser (p. 17).[10]

Third, the intensionality of belief is closely related to a property of the propositional attitudes on which I have focused since chapter 1: their tenuous, holistically mediated relation to observable behavior and circumstances. The belief with which an interpretive target responds to a stimulus depends on indefinitely many other propositional attitudes she tokens. The holism of beliefs and other propositional attitudes is closely related to their intensionality because how an agent represents the content of her propositional attitudes can be identified with how they combine with other propositional attitudes, that is, how other propositional attitudes mediate their tokening in response to stimuli or how other propositional attitudes mediate their influence on behavioral response.

Neither the SFBT nor the NVFBT tests for an appreciation of holism (Apperly, 2011, pp. 118–119). Even if Sally searches for her candy where she left it, this does not mean that she believes it is there. Perhaps she is searching for something else. Perhaps she believes Anne moved the candy but forgets this, absentmindedly, in the moment. Perhaps she believes Anne moved the candy to the cupboard, but also knows that she is part of an experiment testing whether a child can pass the false belief task and so pretends that she does not believe this. The possibilities are limitless. Until a child shows some appreciation of the many-to-many mapping between observable circumstances/behaviors and mental states, she has not mastered the full-blown concept of belief. Accordingly, an appropriate test for mastery of the belief concept would require children to show some hesitation when attributing beliefs based on limited evidence, and perhaps attempts to find more evidence to rule out competing interpretations. Hence the typical results of SFBTs and NVFBTs do not show that full-blown propositional attitude attribution is possible before full mastery of complex language.[11]

But this raises the question: what does preverbal infant performance on versions of the NVFBT show? Experimenters involved in these studies are often far more careful in interpreting the results than I have allowed. I have focused on overly rich interpretations based on assumptions inherited from the earlier SFBT paradigm. However, Scott and Baillargeon (2009), for example, sometimes characterize infant competence on versions of the NVFBT in terms of an appreciation or understanding of "reality-incongruent informational states" (p. 1172). This term is significantly less loaded than "false belief." However, it is clear from their discussion that Scott and Baillargeon intend the term to refer to something more sophisticated than just nonveridical perceptions. I do not think the evidence supports even this interpretation.

Scott and Baillargeon subjected eighteen-month-olds to the following version of the NVFBT. Initially, infant subjects were familiarized with the following scenario. On a table in front of the subject, there are two toy penguins, one of which is hollow and split in two, like a Russian matryoshka doll. The other is in one piece. Each penguin is in front of a shallow, open box. An adult faces the infant from across the table. A gloved hand reaches out from a draped opening to the side and places the two pieces of the split penguin in the box behind them, and the one-piece penguin in the box behind it. All penguin pieces remain visible because the boxes are shallow. The adult facing the infant from the other side of the table reveals a key in one hand. She places the key in the bottom part of the two-piece penguin and then assembles the doll, fitting the top piece snugly onto the bottom piece. When assembled, the two-piece penguin is indistinguishable from the one-piece penguin.

After this familiarization phase, the infants are ready for the test phase. There are two test scenarios: the false belief and the true belief scenarios. The false belief scenario begins with the adult absent. On the table in front of the infant are the disassembled two-piece penguin on one side and the one-piece penguin on the other. Instead of shallow boxes, each penguin has a solid cover behind it, of the kind you might place over a cake. The cover behind the two-piece penguin is transparent, and the cover behind the one-piece penguin is opaque. The gloved hand reaches out from the draped opening to the side, assembles the two-piece penguin so that it is indistinguishable from the one-piece penguin, and then places the penguins under their respective covers—the assembled two-piece penguin under the transparent cover and the one-piece penguin under the opaque cover. There are then two test conditions in which the adult from the familiarization phase returns, holding her key, apparently looking for the two-piece penguin in which to put it. In one condition, the adult reaches for the transparent cover. In the other condition, the adult reaches for the opaque cover. Infant subjects tend to look longer in the former condition. That is, in the standard interpretation of looking time, they expect the adult to reach for the opaque cover, concealing the one-piece penguin, rather than for the transparent cover, under which the two-piece penguin, assembled to *look* like the one-piece penguin, is visible. The results are reversed when the adult *witnesses* the manipulations of the gloved hand. In this true belief scenario, infants expect the adult to reach for the transparent, rather than for the opaque, cover.

Here is how Scott and Baillargeon (2009, 1192) interpret these results. The infants attribute to the adult a bout of practical reasoning to form expectations about how she will behave. The adult wants to place her key in the two-piece penguin. In the false belief condition, she falsely believes that the penguin under the transparent cover is *not* the two-piece penguin. This is because the adult is not present when the infants witness the gloved hand assemble the two-piece penguin to look like the one-piece penguin and place it under the transparent cover. Thus the infants conclude that the adult will first look under the opaque cover in an attempt to locate the two-piece penguin. This is why they look longer when the adult first reaches for the transparent cover; their expectations are violated.

According to a common alternative interpretation of such experiments, instead of attributing false beliefs, infants are merely sensitive to knowledge and ignorance (Perner & Ruffman, 2005). That is, infants assume merely that ignorant agents are far less likely than knowledgeable agents to succeed at tasks. This does not require the attribution of false beliefs; it is merely a behavioral generalization: if an agent has not witnessed an event relevant to her projects, then she is not likely to succeed at those projects. Scott and Baillargeon (2009) explicitly tested for this possibility with variants on the penguin scenario. In these tests, the scenario is essentially the same as for the false belief scenario in the initial test. The only difference is that, in one test, both covers under which the penguins are placed while the adult is absent are transparent, while in the other test they are both opaque. The knowledge/ignorance sensitivity hypothesis predicts that infants should look longer when the adult selects the correct option—the covered, assembled two-piece penguin—in both of these conditions. The reason is that the adult is absent during the manipulations of the gloved hand, so she does not witness them. According to the knowledge/ignorance sensitivity hypothesis, infants expect agents who have not witnessed events relevant to their goals to fail at achieving those goals. Thus even if both covers are opaque or transparent, infants should expect the adult to reach for the wrong one if she has not witnessed the gloved hand's manipulations. This means that infants should look longer when the ignorant adult reaches for the correct cover (the one with the two-piece penguin under it) than when she reaches for the incorrect cover (the one with the one-piece penguin under it). However, Scott and Baillargeon's results confute this prediction: infant looking times did not differ for correct and incorrect reaches when the penguins were both under transparent or both under opaque covers.

Scott and Baillargeon's (2009) results clearly show that eighteen-month-old infants know more than just that agents who do not witness events relevant to their projects are unlikely to succeed on those projects. They also appear to know how failing to witness specific information will affect agents' behavior differently in different conditions. Still, the results show, equally clearly, that these infants are *not* operating with the concept of *belief*. The reason is that, given their knowledge of what the adult they interpret has witnessed, the infants have no grounds to conclude that she falsely *believes* the one-piece penguin to be under the transparent cover in the original false belief scenario. In the familiarization phase, both the infants and the adult witness the two-piece penguin being assembled to look like the one-piece penguin. In fact, not only does the adult witness this, but the adult actually assembles the two-piece penguin to look like the one-piece penguin after placing the key in the bottom half. Given that the adult knows that the two-piece penguin can be assembled to look like the one-piece penguin, why would she come to believe, in the false belief scenario of the test phase, that the penguin under the transparent cover is *not* the two-piece penguin? When she confronts the scene, consisting of the assembled two-piece penguin under the transparent cover and an opaque cover, what she should believe is that the two-piece penguin might be under either of the covers. Furthermore, the infant subjects should know this because they see the adult assemble the two-piece penguin to look like the one-piece penguin during the familiarization phase.

This problem illustrates how the concept of belief requires an appreciation of the tenuous, holistically mediated connection between beliefs and observable circumstances or behavior. Not witnessing, in the false belief scenario of the test phase, the two-piece penguin assembled to look like the one-piece penguin is *not* sufficient grounds to attribute to the adult the *belief* that the penguin under the transparent cover is *not* the two-piece penguin. The reason is that the adult may have background information that defeats this inference. In fact, the adult does have such background information from the familiarization trial, in which the adult herself assembles the two-piece penguin to look like the one-piece penguin. The infant subjects witness this act during the familiarization trial. However, they appear to miss the relevance of this when forming expectations about how the adult will behave in the test phase. This means that they are not operating with the full-blown concept of belief.

3   Infants Adopt the Intentional Stance

How else might we interpret the infants' knowledge, then? One possibility is that they treat the familiarization trial as a kind of game: the adult is *supposed* to put the key in the penguin that is in two pieces. The reason they look longer, in the false belief condition of the test phase, when the adult reaches for the assembled two-piece penguin is because she is not playing by the rules of the game: she is reaching for a penguin that is not in two pieces. Perhaps the infants think: if you see no penguin in two pieces, look around for one before you reach for a penguin in one piece. No attribution of false beliefs appears necessary here. One problem with this interpretation is that infants *do* expect the adult to reach for the assembled two-piece penguin in the true belief scenario of the test phase: they look longer when the adult reaches for the opaque cover if she *witnesses* the two-piece penguin assembled to look like the one-piece penguin immediately before her decision. So the infants cannot be working with a *simple* rule to the effect that the adult is not supposed to reach for a penguin that is not in two pieces. But perhaps they are working with an only slightly more complex rule: the adult is not supposed to reach for a penguin that is not in two pieces *unless she has reason to*. Having just witnessed the two-piece penguin assembled to look like the one-piece penguin constitutes a reason that defeats the basic rule. This is why the infants expect the adult to reach for the assembled two-piece penguin in the true, but not in the false, belief scenario.

This line of thought suggests that, rather than attributing full-blown propositional attitudes, infants might instead track *rationally appropriate* patterns of behavior: they parse sequences of behavior into goals and rationally and informationally constrained means of achieving them. In other words, we can interpret Scott and Baillargeon's (2009) results as an application, by infants, of Dennett's intentional stance to the adult's behavior. Scott and Baillargeon's infants are clearly sensitive to what is rationally appropriate given the goal of placing the key in the two-piece penguin and information that is immediately available at the time. When the adult witnesses the two-piece penguin assembled to look like the one-piece penguin *immediately before* she must select a penguin in which to place the key, the infants expect her to pick that penguin. Given the adult's goal and the information to which she has immediate access, that is the most rational choice. However, when the adult does not witness the two-piece penguin assembled to look like the one-piece penguin *immediately before* she must select a penguin in which to place the key, infants do not expect her to pick that penguin. Relative to the goal of placing the key in the two-piece penguin, and the only information to which the adult has *immediate* access in *this* condition, that is, a penguin that looks to be in one piece under a transparent cover and an opaque cover, it is no longer rational to pick the visible penguin. Instead it is rational to look for the two-piece penguin under the opaque cover.

None of this requires attributing to the adult unobservable mental states with causal influence over behavior. It requires only an appreciation of what is rational relative to the goals of one's interpretive target, and the information to which she has immediate or very recent access.[12] Infants are better interpreted as deploying a specialized version of the intentional stance to relatively brief bouts of behavior. Witnessing relevant information immediately before performing a task affects what counts as rational because rationality is a function of goal and available information. So Scott and Baillargeon's (2009) results show only that infants expect agents to act rationally relative to their goals and immediately available information. This is not the same as attributing full-blown propositional attitudes with tenuous, holistically constrained relations to observable circumstances and behavior.

It is true that these infants appear to show a limited capacity to keep track of *differences* in the information to which they and other agents have access. Presumably, if an infant subject were required to place the key in the two-piece penguin, she would know to reach for the assembled two-piece penguin, even when the adult did not. However, this is not equivalent to understanding the concept of belief. Such tracking of information differentials seems entirely limited to the here and now, for example, whether or not interpreter and interpretive target witnessed the same event immediately before task performance. I think this is more usefully characterized as an imaginative ability to keep track of different perspectives (Hutto, 2008, pp. 194–195) than as an understanding of the full-blown concept of belief. Given that, as chapter 4 argued, human social cognition was selected for facilitating coordination in cooperative projects, it is not surprising that such skills are present from a very early age.

For example, to know what role one must play in a plural subject's pursuit of a goal, one must keep track of how one's own perspective differs from those of other members of the plural subject. To borrow an example from Bacharach (2006, p. 37), to play the appropriate role in furthering the goal of her team, a soccer player needs to take into account differences in the information to which she and her teammates have access. But such rapid, dynamic, embodied tracking of perspectives is not usefully conceptualized as the attribution of full-blown propositional attitudes with tenuous, holistically mediated connections to observable circumstances and behavior. Differences in access to information can be read directly off observable circumstances, like the current location of the ball and whether or not one's teammate is looking at it. In such coordinative contexts, mere behavioral rules relating observable circumstances and behavior (e.g., the location of the ball and the teammate's head position) to expectations of appropriate future behavior (the teammate is not ready for a pass) seem more apposite than the attribution of full-blown propositional attitudes.[13]

This understanding of Scott and Baillargeon's results as a kind of embodied, dynamic application of the intentional stance to brief bouts of behavior, the capacity for which was selected in evolution due to its role in facilitating coordination, makes great sense of another recent result involving preverbal infants. Buttelmann et al. (2009) showed that eighteen-month-olds take into account information differentials when deciding how best to help an adult achieve a goal. The experiment takes advantage of the well-documented fact that infants of this age are spontaneously cooperative: they grasp goals of others' behavior and actively try to help accomplish those goals. The experiment begins with an adult displaying a favorable attitude toward an object she is handling while she sits between two boxes. In front of the adult is a key that can be used to lock the boxes, and the infant knows this from earlier familiarization. The adult places the object in one of the boxes. After this there are two conditions, as usual in NVFBTs. In the true belief condition, the adult witnesses a second adult move the object from the box in which she placed it to the other box. While the first adult briefly looks away, the second adult locks both boxes with the key. The first adult then tries to open the box in which she originally placed the object, but she struggles with this, as the box has been locked. At this point, the infant is allowed or encouraged to help the adult.[14] In the false belief condition, everything proceeds in exactly the same manner, except the first adult leaves the scene before the object is moved to the second box and the boxes are locked. After this, she returns to the scene and tries to open the box in which she initially placed the object, as in the true belief condition. In the true belief condition, most infants try to help the first adult open the box she is trying to open, that is, the box in which she originally placed the object. In the false belief condition, most infants immediately go to the second box (in which, unbeknownst to the adult, her object has been locked), unlock the box, and retrieve the object for the adult.

It is tempting to attribute to these infants a sophisticated understanding of practical reasoning, according to which the infants know what the adults *believe* about the location of the object, and how these beliefs constrain their *desires*, given their observable behavior. Thus, in the true belief condition, because the adult believes the object has been moved, yet still tries to open the box in which she had put it, she must desire something other than retrieving the object. In contrast, in the false belief condition, because the adult believes the object has not been moved, her attempt to open the box in which she placed it indicates the desire to retrieve the object. However, a simpler interpretation is possible. The infants may be attributing to both adults, by default, the goal of retrieving the object, based on the favorable attitude they show it before the manipulations. So, by default, the infants assume the adults' goal is to retrieve the object, and intend to help in this endeavor. However, when the first adult witnesses the object moved to the other box yet persists in trying to open the first box, the only way to *rationalize* this behavior is by assuming the adult's goal has changed: she now seeks to open the first box not to retrieve the object but for some other reason, and so the infant helps with this. This interpretation of the infants' behavior does not require attributing to them the concept of belief. We can explain their behavior entirely in terms of an understanding of perceptions and goals. Agents pursue goals in which they have previously indicated interest unless they witness information that *should* lead them to adjust the means by which they pursue those goals, yet they fail to do so. The best way to rationalize such anomalies is to attribute to agents new goals.

I have already discussed evidence that infants automatically seek to rationalize agent behavior when attributing goals to it. Recall, from chapter 2, Gergely et al.'s (2002) update of Meltzoff's (1988) experiment on infant imitation. Meltzoff found that fourteen-month-olds imitate an adult who lights a light box by leaning over and pressing it with her forehead, though lighting it by hand is easier. Gergely et al. showed that this effect depends on whether or not the adult's hands are otherwise occupied. If they are not, infants interpret the forehead touch as the whole point of the demonstration and hence imitate the gesture, as in Meltzoff's original experiment. However, if the adult's hands are otherwise occupied, for example, wrapped in a blanket, infants interpret the forehead touch as the most efficient available means of lighting the light box and so assume *that* to be the whole point of the demonstration; hence, in this condition, they light the light box using the most efficient means available to them: by hand. Buttelmann et al.'s (2009) experiment seems to involve exactly the same kind of reasoning. In the so-called true belief condition, the adult witnesses her favored object moved, yet she persists in trying to access its original location. Infants automatically rationalize this behavior by attributing a different goal to the adult, just as infants in Gergely et al.'s (2002) experiment rationalized the apparently inefficient forehead touch as the whole point of the demonstration. In both experiments, what is shown is not a capacity to attribute full-blown propositional attitudes (i.e., unobservable mental states with tenuous, holistically mediated, causal influence on behavior) but an application of the intentional stance (i.e., an attempt to rationalize behavior relative to potential goals and information to which the interpretive target ought to have access). Rather than sophisticated mindreaders, infants are highly sensitive detectors of rationally appropriate patterns of behavior.

But there are rivals to the hypothesis that infant social cognition consists in applying the intentional stance: the so-called theory-theory and simulation theory. According to theory-theory, infants interpret systems as agents with beliefs and desires using something akin to the process by which scientists formulate hypotheses about the unobservable causes of observable behavior (Gopnik, 1996; Leslie, 1994).[15] Much as a cognitive scientist might posit unobservable cognitive and motivational states to *causally* explain the observable behavior of some animal, infants posit beliefs and desires to *causally* explain the behavior of other human beings and, indeed, all animate beings. According to simulation theory, infants interpret systems as agents with beliefs and desires by projecting onto them the beliefs and desires that would lead them to behave as those systems do (Gordon, 1996; Goldman, 2006). I now turn to a defense of the intentional stance hypothesis against these rivals.

4   A Defense of the Intentional Stance, Part 2

Here is what the intentional stance hypothesis predicts. From the time they begin to attribute agency, infants assume agents are rational, in some sense.[16] If a system appears to behave nonrationally or irrationally, infant interpreters either (1) withhold attributions of agency or (2) reinterpret the behavior in a way that makes it rational. Furthermore, given Dennett's (1991b) emphasis on patterns of behavior as objects of interpretation from the intentional stance, we should expect infants to be extremely generous in their attributions of agency. That is, all and only patterns of behavior parsable into goals and rationally and informationally constrained means of achieving them should trigger attributions of agency. It should not matter what the target of interpretation is made of or how it looks. In fact, it should not even matter whether there is a visible agent or not.[17] In contrast, the theory-theory predicts that infant interpreters should attribute unobservable mental states preferentially to paradigmatic agents, for example, all humans or animals, as parts of nomic/causal explanations of their behavior.[18] There should be no expectation that the behavior is rationalizable, as only nomic dependence of behavior on unobservable mental states is assumed. Finally, the simulation theory predicts that infant interpreters should reserve attributions of agency for systems that they judge to be, in some sense, like themselves. Furthermore, infants should be restricted to interpreting only *familiar* behavior, that is, similar to behavior of which they are capable. The reason is that simulation involves pretending to perform the interpretive target's behavior and projecting onto the target whatever mental states are triggered by such pretense. This is obviously impossible if the interpreter is incapable of anything like the target's behavior. I now review a variety of compelling evidence from developmental psychology that confirms the predictions of the intentional stance hypothesis and confutes the predictions of its two rivals.

Over the last fifteen years, the developmental psychologists György Gergely, Gergely Csibra, and their colleagues have amassed an impressive amount of evidence that very young human infants have a domain-specific capacity for tracking instrumental agency:

Infants are innately equipped with a *teleological action representation and interpretation system* (the "naive theory of rational action" or the "teleological stance") that can account for infants' early ability to infer, represent and predict the goal-directed actions that instrumental agents perform to realize some specific change of state in their environment. ... The teleological stance is a context-sensitive and inferential system of action interpretation that is guided by the principle of rational action ... according to which instrumental agents are expected to perform the most efficient means-ends action available to them within their situational constraints to bring about the goal state. Attributing and representing the outcome of an observed action as the goal is, therefore, a function of evaluating whether the action satisfies the criterion of efficiency of goal approach given the physical constraints of the situation. (Gergely, 2011, p. 79)

As with the various versions of the NVFBT, the principal measure in this paradigm is looking time, interpreted as tracking violation of expectations. Here the comparison is between looking time in response to inefficient goal-directed behavior and looking time in response to efficient goal-directed behavior. For example, an infant might be familiarized with a computer-generated agent jumping over an obstacle to reach a goal. Then the obstacle is removed. In one subsequent condition, the agent performs the same jump over the space where the obstacle had been, while in another subsequent condition, the agent goes directly to the goal. Infants look longer in the former than in the latter condition (Gergely & Csibra, 2003). Therefore they expect agents to choose the most efficient paths to their goals. There is evidence of such expectations in infants as young as six and one-half months (Csibra, 2008).

Thus the evidence strongly suggests that human infants interpret behavior as the most efficient means, given situational constraints, to accomplish a goal. This assumption governs not just expectations about behavior but also reasoning about what the point of a model's behavior is in imitative tasks, as shown by Gergely et al.'s (2002) update of Meltzoff's (1988) forehead-touch experiment. Goldman (2006, p. 66) argues that simulation theory can just as easily explain these results; however, this is implausible. The reason is that infants demonstrate such interpretive biases for behaviors of objects that are entirely unlike them, as well as for entirely novel behaviors. In the study that Goldman discusses, infants are interpreting the behavior of an animated circle on a computer screen. Csibra (2008) shows that six-and-one-half-month-old infants respond similarly to an inanimate box. Why would infants treat the behavior of computer-animated circles or inanimate boxes as similar to their own behavior?[19] Simulation theory seems to predict that human attributions of agency will be triggered by cues that an interpreter perceives as "like me." Gergely (2011, p. 87) cites a growing list of studies that refute this prediction:

Young infants are ready to interpret unfamiliar entities such as inanimate objects, abstract 2D figures, humanoid robots, unfamiliar human actions, and even biomechanically impossible hand actions ... as goal-directed as long as they show evidence of context-sensitive justifiable variation of action obeying the principle of efficiency of goal approach. In other words, what seems to be criterial for attributing intentionality and goal-directedness is evidence indicating the ability for *rational choice* among the accessible action alternatives by reliably performing the most efficient action available to bring about the goal state across changing environmental constraints.

In addition, the imitative behavior with the light box involves learning a behavior of which the infant is not yet capable. How can the infant simulate the goals of the adult agent and the means she selects if the infant is not yet capable of the behavior in which the adult engages?

Thus it seems that empirical evidence from developmental psychology favors the intentional stance hypothesis over simulation theory. But perhaps the theory-theory can equally accommodate these data? Not according to Gergely (2011). Various theory-theorists have proposed that agency is detected on the basis of context-independent cues, like self-propulsion or variability of movement or "(unjustified) equifinal target approach" (Gergely, 2011, pp. 86–87). However, no such cues are sufficient for the attribution of agency. Even a human hand grasping an object "is *not* interpreted as goal-directed ... if this outcome ... is achieved as the end result of unnecessary and therefore unjustifiable and inefficient preceding actions, as when a hand first opens a transparent empty box before grasping the target object that is *in front of* the box" (pp. 86–87). Such results are difficult to explain by the hypothesis that human infants attribute unobservable mental causes to systems they consider agents. If that were the basic principle of interpretation, wouldn't we expect infants to treat as agents systems that look like paradigmatic agents, such as humans, and then attribute goals to them as *nonrational* causal factors in the generation of any of their behavior? Contrary to this, and in line with the intentional stance hypothesis, it seems that all and only systems that pursue goals using the most rational and efficient means available given situational constraints are treated as agents. Furthermore, it does not seem plausible that infants treat the behavior of inanimate objects, geometric shapes, and human beings all as governed by the same kinds of unobservable causal factors.

The theory-theory is further undermined by evidence that infants can imitatively learn new goals and new means to goals they can otherwise accomplish from purely behavioral stimuli, involving no visible agent. In the so-called ghost condition, discussed in chapter 2, objects are manipulated to secure a goal as though by a ghost—with no visible agent. Infants can imitate in this condition (Thompson & Russell, 2004; Huang & Charman, 2005). If imitation requires treating an object as an agent and attributing unobservable mental causes to the object, as theory-theory seems to imply, to which object are infants attributing such unobservable mental causes in the ghost condition? In contrast, such evidence is entirely unsurprising in the intentional stance hypothesis, which sees agency detection and interpretation in terms of rationally and informationally constrained means of achieving goals, as primarily concerned with behavioral patterns, rather than the unobservable causes that animate concrete agents.[20]

Thus the evidence from early infant social cognition seems definitively to favor the intentional stance model of agency attribution over the theory-theory. It is particularly compelling that young, preverbal infants either treat apparently counternormative behavior as nonagentive or reinterpret it to accord with rational norms. Thus a hand grasping an object immediately after traversing an inefficient and hence counternormative path toward the object is *not* treated as agentive. On the other hand, when imitating the

light box forehead touch, infants appear to reinterpret an apparently inefficient and irrational behavior—turning on the light box with one's forehead
when doing so with one's hand would be more efficient—as maximally
rational: they treat the forehead touch as the whole point of the behavior.[21]
This suggests that interpretation by preverbal infants presumes that agents
conform to rational norms.[22] Behavior that does not is not treated as agentive. It is hard to see how the theory-theorist can explain this fact. If infants
attributed nonrational causes when they interpret agents, then why would
they refuse to treat apparently nonrational behavior as agentive or reinterpret it so that it turns out rational?[23]

   That agency and goal attributions by infants are completely indifferent
to the nature of the agent,[24] yet highly sensitive to whether or not the pattern of behavior constitutes the selection of the most efficient means to
accomplishing the goal, provides extremely strong grounds to favor the
intentional stance hypothesis over its rivals. It is unclear how either simulation theory or theory-theory can explain why infants can see agency in
geometric shapes, inanimate boxes, and patterns of motion among tools
manipulated by no visible agent (as in the ghost condition) but fail to see
agency in rationally unjustified human hand grasps of ordinary objects.
In contrast, these are not just easily explained by the intentional stance
hypothesis but explicitly predicted by it: Dennett proposed the intentional
stance as a way of seeing agency in an extremely broad variety of systems,
including thermostats, computer programs, simple organisms, and even
nature as a whole.[25]

   In chapter 5, I responded to prominent philosophical objections to
the intentional stance hypothesis. Here I want to consider some potential objections to my application of this hypothesis to the evidence from
human sociocognitive development. The most obvious worry is that I have
overstated the differences between the intentional stance hypothesis and
the theory-theory hypothesis. Dennett usually speaks of the intentional
stance as a method for attributing beliefs and desires.[26] This is exactly how
theory-theorists characterize infant sociocognitive feats. Furthermore, most
theory-theorists acknowledge that the laws interpreters assume link mental states to each other, to stimuli, and to behavior can double as rational
relations. Everyone acknowledges that belief attributions often rationalize
behavior. The difference between the intentional stance hypothesis and
the theory-theory is that, according to the former, this is the central role of
belief attributions, and according to the latter, belief attributions can but
need not rationalize behavior. Furthermore, I have drawn mainly from the
research by Gergely, Csibra, and colleagues in defense of the intentional

stance hypothesis. Yet these developmental psychologists often defend the view that very young infants are sophisticated mindreaders and attribute full-blown propositional attitudes from a very young age (Gergely, 2011).

Much of the evidence that supports the intentional stance hypothesis can also be interpreted as supporting the theory-theory. For example, infants might expect behavior to constitute the most efficient means to a goal because this is a causal/psychological law presumed by their innate theory of mind. My quarrel is not with the evidence but with this interpretation of it. Interpretations have implications, and even if the evidence does not clearly favor one interpretation over another, there are broader considerations with which the implications of one interpretation might be more compatible than those of others. If one interprets the evidence I have reviewed as the application of a theory of mind or as mindreading, this seems to have the following implications. Very young infants conceive of others as animated by causal factors in an unobservable realm, that is, their minds. These causal factors must be inferred from behavioral evidence. If what infants attribute are propositional attitudes, then, as I have argued since chapter 1, their connections to observable circumstances and behavior are extremely tenuous and holistically constrained. Hence the inferences infants make must be precarious. In general, talk of infants mindreading or deploying a theory of mind encourages the thought that they are confronted with the traditional philosophical problem of other minds: infants have direct evidence only of behavior and must make some kind of leap to think of their fellows as conscious, thinking subjects. Many theory-theorists explicitly conceive of infant mindreading in this way.[27]

These implications of "theory of mind" or "mindreading" talk strike me as a highly implausible characterization of infant sociocognitive capacities. Many researchers have already provided devastating objections to Gopnik's claim that infant sociocognitive competence can be understood by analogy to scientific inference to unobservable causes (Hutto, 2008, chap. 9; Goldman, 1992, pp. 106–107; Stich & Nichols, 1998; Sterelny, 2003, pp. 223–225). The evidence I have reviewed here and in previous chapters also makes clear that whatever infants are doing when they form expectations that interpretive targets pursue goals using efficient, rationally, and informationally constrained means, it does not seem to involve a precarious, careful, scientific inference to unobservable causes. They seem automatically to parse observable patterns of behavior into goals and rationally and informationally constrained means to achieve them. And contrary to the view that infants confront the philosophical problem of other minds, such patterns are perceptually available. A trajectory to a goal that involves an unnecessary hop over the space where an obstacle had been just *looks* inefficient.[28] There does not appear to be any need to engage in inference to unobservable mental states. Furthermore, the speed with which infants form such expectations, both in looking time experiments such as those described by Gergely and Csibra (2003) and in imitation experiments such as the Gergely et al. (2002) forehead-touch study, throws doubt on the theory of mind or mindreading interpretation. Can infants really manage a theoretical inference to causal factors inhabiting some unobservable realm within their interpretive targets so rapidly and dynamically?

The intentional stance interpretation of this evidence seems much more apposite. Dennett's original proposal was inspired by his teacher Gilbert Ryle's seminal book *The Concept of Mind*. The main thesis of that book is that the Cartesian notion of the mind as some unobservable, private, subjective nexus of mental states with causal influence over observable behavior is fundamentally confused. Intelligence, rationality, and other mental properties can be read directly off behavior, according to Ryle. In Ryle's terms, the theory-theory constitutes a classic Cartesian understanding of the mind: mental states and properties are never directly perceived and must be inferred from observed behavior. Dennett's intentional stance inherits Ryle's demystifying attitude toward our interpretive practices: agency can be read directly off behavior when interpreters adopt the intentional stance, parsing bouts of behavior into goals and rationally and informationally constrained means of achieving them. Philosophers have long dismissed such views (Chisholm, 1957; Putnam, 1965); however, philosophers are not primarily interested in how best to characterize infant sociocognitive competence. Rylean approaches to mature mentalistic concepts, like belief, might not constitute the best philosophical analyses of such concepts; however, the question of how best to characterize prelinguistic infant sociocognitive competence is completely independent of this. The evidence I have reviewed seems more compatible with Ryle's and Dennett's approach. Whether or not beliefs and other mental states are really dispositions to behavior, human infants seem to directly perceive rational relations among components of behavioral patterns: that is why, for example, they look longer at agents that take an inefficient path to a goal than at agents that take an efficient path. The same ability is apparent in their dynamic, on-the-spot reinterpretations of situations when behavior appears nonrational, such as when they interpret an adult model's forehead touch as the whole point of the behavior when her hands are free, yet not when her hands are otherwise occupied. Finally, the hypothesis that infants adopt the intentional stance is the best explanation of the fact that infants interpret any pattern of behavior by any object as agentive if it constitutes a rationally and informationally constrained, efficient means of achieving some goal, yet do not attribute agency to apparently nonrational human behavior.

Theory-theorists often assume a false dilemma: either interpretation involves attributing causally potent mental states inhabiting an unobservable, private realm, or it involves tracking concrete physical or behavioral properties. The latter disjunct is unlikely, since infants come to similar interpretations and expectations when confronted with behavior with radically different physical properties. As the work reviewed by Gergely (2011) shows, items as physically dissimilar as human hand gestures, computer-animated shapes, and inanimate boxes are all interpreted as agentive. But it doesn't follow from this that infants must be attributing unobservable, causally potent mental states. As I noted in chapter 3 when discussing the social cognition of nonhuman primates, a third alternative exists. As Sterelny (2003, pp. 66–67, 215) notes, interpreters might categorize physically disparate behaviors as instances of the same *functional* kinds. A variety of chimpanzee body postures might be classified not as indicating the mental state of seeing but as indicating a disposition toward preventing the interpreter from retrieving a food item. The idea that infants assimilate physically disparate behaviors to an abstract template according to which they constitute rationally and informationally constrained means of achieving goals is a variant on Sterelny's proposal.[29] Interpretive categories can be abstract without being mentalistic. Applying the intentional stance does not even require distinguishing one's own mind from another's. A behavior can simply be classified as the rationally appropriate thing to do, given certain informational constraints, with no commitment as to whether the agent performing the behavior represents it as such. As Hurley (2005a), Gordon (2005), and Gallese (2005) point out, infants might represent their own and others' behavior in a common format, as simply aiming to achieve a goal in the most efficient way possible, without attributing responsibility for the behavior to any particular agent, let alone unobservable causes within the agent.

A final advantage of the intentional stance hypothesis is that it provides a framework in which we can understand both the phylogeny and the ontogeny of sociocognitive competence in terms of gradual, incremental improvement. We begin with the rationality assumption: behavior is assumed to constitute the most efficient, rationally and informationally constrained means of achieving a goal.[30] This gives rise to expectations that are sometimes confuted. The response is reinterpretation that attempts to rationalize the anomalous behavior. For example, as in the forehead-touch experiment, the interpreter might search for a different goal that would make the behavior turn out rational. Or the interpreter might search for situational constraints she has overlooked. Or ultimately the interpreter might hit upon the idea of differences in information access. The principle that behavior constitutes rationally and informationally constrained means of achieving a goal can thus explain phylogenetic and ontogenetic milestones as discoveries of factors that excuse apparently counternormative, irrational behavior, allowing reinterpretations that make it come out rational. In human phylogeny, this process may ultimately have selected for the capacity to track differential information access almost from birth. In human ontogeny, this may lead to an increasingly sophisticated understanding of factors that induce false beliefs. In this regard, the intentional stance hypothesis is superior to alternatives that see dramatic discontinuities in the phylogeny and ontogeny of social cognition. Rather than posit conceptual revolutions modeled on the history of science (Gopnik, 2003, 2004), it explains these phenomena in terms of the natural, incremental development of one basic idea: that agents pursue their goals in the most rational way possible given certain constraints. The phylogeny and ontogeny of social cognition is explained entirely in terms of increasing sensitivity to the variety and complexity of such constraints, including differential access to information, disparate goals, and, eventually, false beliefs.

5   Propositional Attitude Attribution and Language Acquisition

Recent evidence concerning the role of mindreading in language acquisition suggests a final worry about the hypothesis that preverbal children employ a version of the intentional stance in their social cognition, rather than attributing full-blown propositional attitudes. Bloom (2000, 2002) has argued persuasively that human children could never learn what objects nouns refer to unless they were able to read the minds of adult speakers. Specifically, they must be able to attribute referential intentions to determine the referents of nouns adults use. However, none of the evidence cited by Bloom shows that first language learners must employ a theory of mind or attribute unobservable mental states with causal influence over behavior. Nor does the evidence show that first language learners must attribute full-blown propositional attitudes as I have characterized them: states with tenuous, holistically mediated connections to observable circumstances and behavior.

Bloom's evidence is meant to support the hypothesis that noun learning requires sophisticated mindreading over the hypothesis that first language learners merely associate objects to which they happen to be attending with words they hear simultaneously. The evidence clearly rules out the latter hypothesis. However, sophisticated mindreading is not the only alternative. Infant application of the intentional stance to patterns of behavior, together with their susceptibility to the kind of "natural pedagogy" (Csibra & Gergely 2006, 2009, 2011; Csibra, 2010) described in chapter 2, can explain the evidence just as well. Here is some of the most striking evidence that Bloom (2000, 2002) cites in favor of the hypothesis that language learning presupposes sophisticated mindreading.

First, children acquire word meanings very quickly and with a surprisingly low rate of error, although such learning often does not involve hearing a new word while attending to its referent. Bloom calls this "fast mapping." In Western cultures, it is common for parents to ensure that their children are attending to the correct referent when they introduce a new word, but this practice is entirely absent from many non-Western cultures, and even in Western cultures, many words are learned without such scaffolding. This makes the associationist model of word learning implausible. Far more plausible is the idea that children infer the referential intentions of mature language users when they utter words that are new to them.

Second, Bloom (2002, pp. 40–41) cites a number of studies by Dare Baldwin and colleagues (Baldwin, 1993; Baldwin et al., 1996) in which a new word is introduced to a child while she attends to some object. These studies showed that contiguity between word utterance and attention to an object is neither necessary nor sufficient for the child to map the word onto the object. If an adult utters the new word while she and the child are attending to different objects, the child looks at the object to which the adult is attending, and maps the word onto that object (Baldwin, 1993). So contiguity between utterance of a new word and its referent is not necessary to map the word onto the referent. If a disembodied voice utters a word while the child attends to an object, the child does not map the word onto the object (Baldwin et al., 1996). This shows that contiguity between new word and object is not sufficient for children to map one onto the other. These experiments appear to show that what matters for word learning are the referential intentions of mature word users, in other words, that language learning presupposes sophisticated mindreading.

A third line of evidence further supports this view. Bloom (2002, p. 41) describes a study on which he collaborated with Susan Birch, in which two-year-old children are shown two bags of toy animals. They are told that the experimenter is familiar with the animals in one bag and not with those in the other. The experimenter then removes one animal from each bag, places them in front of a box, covers her eyes, and asks each child subject to put "Jesse" in the box. Children automatically interpret the proper name as referring to the animal with which they are told the experimenter is familiar. Apparently children know that proper names are used to refer to objects with which one is acquainted. So children must understand which toy animal the experimenter is acquainted with, which requires some sophisticated mindreading.

In a series of similar studies, children appear to show that they employ sophisticated mindreading to infer that different words are likely to refer to different objects—the "bias against lexical overlap" or "mutual exclusivity" assumption (Bloom, 2002, pp. 43–45). When children are shown a familiar object and an unfamiliar object and then asked to point to the X, where X is a familiar term, they will automatically select the familiar object. When they are asked to point to the Y, where Y is an unfamiliar term, they will automatically select the unfamiliar object. This bias also occurs when children are told familiar versus unfamiliar facts about the objects, suggesting that this is a general interpretive bias related to communication, rather than a specific word-learning bias. For example, when told that one object was given to the experimenter by her sister, and then asked to point to the object with which dogs like to play (an unfamiliar fact), children point to the unfamiliar object. They do not respond this way when a newcomer, who was not present when the experimenter related the fact about his sister, makes the same request. So children appear to keep track of what different interlocutors know when interpreting their utterances.

Bloom draws out the seemingly obvious lessons of this research for the role of mindreading in communication and language acquisition. He attributes to child subjects the following kinds of sophisticated mindreading:

It is clear that he means me to point to one of the two objects. If he meant me to point to the object that his sister gave him, he would have referred to it in some way that would make sense to me—he would have asked for "the one my sister gave me," for instance. But he didn't; he used a novel fact. And so he doesn't want me to point to the first object.

The only remaining option is that second object, so this must be what the novel fact refers to. (2002, p. 44)

Such intuitive interpretations of the evidence as showing that language acquisition requires sophisticated mindreading are further confirmed by a fourth line of evidence, which demonstrates abnormal patterns of word learning in autistic children, known to be impaired in theory of mind (pp. 41–42).

Bloom makes a persuasive case that word learning is not a matter of simple association between words and potential referents. Furthermore, he is surely right that some fairly sophisticated social cognition is necessary for normal language acquisition in human children. However, none of the evidence he cites shows that this is best characterized as a kind of mindreading, or theorizing about mental states, or attribution of full-blown propositional attitudes. Little in Bloom's work suggests that he intends to claim that language learners employ sophisticated mindreading as I have characterized it here. His target is the associationist model of word learning that sees no role for social cognition in it. Bloom seems entirely neutral on how one should characterize the sociocognitive capacities that appear to underlie language learning (2000, pp. 60–61). The vocabulary of "mindreading" or "theory of mind" is often intended in a minimalist sense, that is, to refer to the sorts of interpretive capacities at work in early social cognition, however they are implemented. In fact, Bloom explicitly denies that the kind of social cognition necessary to acquire word meanings presupposes an understanding of false belief (p. 61). Nevertheless, as I argued earlier, different interpretations of the same evidence can have different implications. For example, treating infant social cognition as a matter of "mindreading" encourages the view that infants must solve the philosophical other-minds problem by engaging in precarious theoretical inferences to unobservable causes with tenuous influence over behavior. As I have argued, treating infant social cognition as an application of the intentional stance makes better sense of how rapid and dynamic it can be, and avoids the implausible implication that infants somehow solve the other-minds problem via precarious theoretical inferences.

The evidence discussed by Bloom is entirely compatible with the following interpretation. First-language learners may simply adopt the intentional stance in an effort to interpret the linguistic behavior of mature language users. All that is required is the assumption that the primary goal of mature language use is to make manifest or communicate information about salient referents. Utterances are then interpreted as the most efficient, rationally, and informationally constrained means of accomplishing this goal. Given the evidence I reviewed in chapter 2, supporting Gergely and Csibra's natural pedagogy hypothesis, it is clear that human infants are born with a bias to interpret certain adult behaviors as cues that important generic information about salient referents will be demonstrated imminently. It is plausible that as children mature, they pick up on a greater variety of such cues, including the production of wordlike stimuli. Hence when a mature language user produces such stimuli, this should trigger the assumption that she is about to demonstrate important generic information about salient referents. This assumption is supplemented with the sensitivity to information differentials that I discussed earlier, and the role it plays in constraining judgments of rational action. Since, in this case, the goal is a communicative one, the first language learner need only notice to what the mature language user is attending, to identify the referent of her word utterance. No speculation about unobservable states of mind appears necessary. No attribution of full-blown propositional attitudes with tenuous, holistically constrained causal influence over behavior appears required or even apposite. A capacity to parse observable behavior into communicative goals and rationally and informationally constrained means of achieving them seems a much more efficient way to achieve the fast mapping of new nouns to referents that Bloom identifies as one of the central puzzles of language learning.

6   Mindshaping in Human Ontogeny

The main burden of this chapter has been discharged. I have explained why recent evidence concerning the ontogeny of human social cognition does not jeopardize the thesis that sophisticated mindreading presupposes linguistic competence. This clears the table for the arguments in chapter 7: I can now argue that sophisticated mindreading, that is, the attribution of full-blown propositional attitudes, derives from the practice of undertaking and attributing discursive commitments, often modeled on those of characters in public narratives. But before I turn to this subject, let me close chapter 6 with a brief review of some compelling recent evidence regarding the role of mindshaping in human ontogeny.

I have already discussed the evidence supporting Gergely and Csibra's natural pedagogy hypothesis; this provides clear examples of human infants' readiness for mindshaping (see chap. 2). But the evidence does not end here. As chapter 2 also noted, older children seem disposed toward "overimitation": they copy even apparently nonfunctional behaviors of models engaged in salient tasks. Nielsen and Tomaselli (2010) show that, from about eighteen months, human children from diverse cultural backgrounds routinely copy arbitrary and unnecessary behaviors.[31] This disposition seems unaffected by age, differences in testing environment, or familiarity with adult model. Nielsen and Tomaselli argue that, though seemingly maladaptive, overimitation constitutes a universal human adaptation that is instrumental in the transmission of culture.

The picture of the phylogeny of the human sociocognitive syndrome defended in chapters 4 and 5 makes sense of this phenomenon. According

to this view, the most important skills that human children have historically needed to acquire from adult models consist in producing complex
communicative signals of commitment to groups and their cooperative
projects. As argued in chapter 5, the precise execution of such signals is
central to their function, that is, discriminating reliable from unreliable
cooperation partners. Given this, we should expect products of selection for
such capacities, that is, contemporary human children, to overimitate: historically the eventual social status of human children, and hence their biological success, have depended on copying precise bodily motions that were
components of communicative behaviors like ritualistic dance and vocalization. This explains why such overimitation distinguishes human social
learning from that of our closest primate cousins, chimpanzees (Horner &
Whiten, 2005).[32]

Gergely et al.'s (2002) forehead-touch experiment suggests a mechanism
by which human children implement overimitation. When they parse an
adult's behavior into goals and means, they are guided by the assumption
that the behavior constitutes a rationally and informationally constrained,
efficient means of achieving the goal. When one parsing fails to conform
to this expectation, they generate another, taking into account situational
constraints they may at first have overlooked. In this way, they can come
to see a behavior that *seems* inefficient at achieving some putative goal
(e.g., turning on a light box by touching it with one's forehead) as the
entire point of the behavior. This may be what is going on in overimitation.
Infants reinterpret behaviors that appear arbitrary and nonfunctional relative to putative goals as the true goals of their adult models.[33] This kind of
reinterpretation would have been adaptive if, as the arguments in chapter
5 suggest, many of the behaviors that adults modeled for their offspring in
human prehistory constituted complex, costly, honest, and arbitrary signals of cooperative and coordinative potential.

Thus the evidence from developmental psychology strongly suggests
that human infants are wired to be good targets of mindshaping, and specifically the kind of mindshaping one would expect in a species as obsessed
with communicating cooperative and coordinative potential as our own.
There is also strong evidence that human children are disposed, from a
young age, to track and enforce deontic status. I alluded to this evidence in
chapter 2, when I discussed Sripada and Stich's (2006) claim that children
grasp the import of moral norms from a young age, automatically evinc-
ing appropriate emotional attitudes in response to transgressions of moral
norms they acquire from their culture.[34] Here I want to briefly note some
dramatic experimental confirmations of this phenomenon. These studies

are interesting because they concern arbitrary, nonmoral norms invented to constitute completely novel games, as well as nonmoral norms governing speech acts.

In a series of studies, Hannes Rakoczy and colleagues have investigated two- and three-year-old children's reactions to a variety of norm violations. Rakoczy et al. (2008a) showed that three- but not two-year-olds spontaneously correct puppets that violate arbitrary norms governing the manipulation of an object in the context of a simple game. Children were told that a sponge, colored differently on each side, could be used for its typical function—wiping—when on the floor. However, when brought to a game table, it acquired a new function, related to a game that experimenters had made up: the sponge was to be thrown like a die, and depending on which side came up, one was then allowed to perform specific manipulations of other objects on the table. The experimenter explained these rules to the children with the puppet present. The puppet then left the scene, and the experimenter and child proceeded to play the game. There were then two test conditions in which the puppet returned and manipulated the sponge. In the first condition, the puppet used the sponge for its normal function—wiping—on the floor. In the second condition, the puppet did the same but at the game table. Three- but not two-year-old children showed a marked tendency to protest the puppet's behavior in the second condition, often using normative vocabulary like "No, you are not allowed to clean up here." Such protests were absent from the first condition, in which the puppet wiped with the sponge when it was on the floor. In another experiment, Rakoczy et al. (2008b) found similar results when game and nongame contexts were distinguished linguistically; that is, the experimenter introduced a verbal label for game-specific object manipulation and used the label to establish game versus nongame contexts. In the experimental condition, the puppet would produce the verbal label and proceed to manipulate the object in a counternormative way, to which three-year-old children responded with explicit normative protests, while two-year-old children showed a weaker tendency to order the puppet to stop. These results suggest that human children have and express normative expectations from a very early age.

Not only are two- to three-year-olds capable of quickly learning and enforcing arbitrary, novel norms in the context of game play, but a recent experiment suggests that they spontaneously express normative attitudes regarding the "direction of fit" (Searle, 1969) that distinguishes different kinds of speech acts from each other. Rakoczy and Tomasello (2009) showed that two-year-olds verbally corrected puppets whose behavior did not conform to commands issued by an adult. Three-year-olds showed even more sophisticated understanding of such communication norms. When the adult issued a command with which the puppet did not comply, like two-year-olds, the three-year-olds verbally corrected the puppet. However, when the adult issued an *assertion* with the same content, and the puppet's behavior did not match it, rather than correct the puppet, the three-year-olds corrected the adult. Thus from a very young age—indeed, from about the time that children begin to speak and pass important folk psychological milestones—they are already full-fledged norm learners and enforcers. That such explicit normative attitudes infect their *interpretive* capacities is particularly noteworthy, given the agenda of this book. From the time that human children have the requisite verbal capacities, they appear to correct interpretive targets when their behavior is incompatible with interpretations for which they give good grounds. An adult who produces an utterance in an assertive tone—thereby giving good grounds to interpret her as intending to tell the truth—is immediately corrected when the content of her assertion does not match the salient state of affairs. This is good evidence that our interpretive practices are bound up, from a very early age, with normative attitudes that can function to shape behavior to conform to expectations triggered by interpretations.

Recent studies by Charles Kalish and colleagues suggest that young children also show remarkable sensitivity to deontic properties, that is, rights and obligations, associated with social categories and use these properties to determine the likely mental states and behaviors of interpretive targets (Kalish & Shiverick, 2004; Kalish & Lawson, 2008). Kalish and Shiverick (2004) showed that five-year-olds are far more likely to predict behavior based on social rules than on individual preferences: they predict that individuals will do what is right rather than what they want. By eight years, this pattern is reversed. Kalish and Lawson (2008) showed that preschool-aged children treat deontic properties as more central to all social categories, including entirely novel, made-up ones, than psychological or behavioral properties. Older children and adults treat psychological properties as more important for some social categories. This pattern of results suggests that, in early childhood, human social cognition is largely based on normative expectations: preschool-aged children predict behavior based on norms that define social category membership.[35] This is gradually replaced by more psychologistic strategies in school-aged children and adults. Such results are unsurprising from the perspective I defend in this book. Given reliable, effective, and pervasive mindshaping practices, the assumption that people tend to do what they are obligated to do is a much more reliable heuristic than predicting behavior on the basis of mental state attributions.[36]

7   Summing Up and Moving Forward

The evidence I have reviewed in this chapter suggests the following picture of the ontogeny of human social cognition. There is no doubt that human infants are born with sociocognitive capacities that are not shared by our closest primate cousins. However, these capacities are not usefully characterized as better theories of mind or capacities for mindreading. Such characterizations suggest that human infants can somehow solve the philosophical other-minds problem by engaging in precarious theoretical inferences from observable behavior to unobservable, causally potent mental states. This perspective does not make sense of the rapidity and fluidity with which even very young infants can interpret behavior. The evidence is better accommodated by the hypothesis that, from a very young age, human infants employ a version of the intentional stance in their social cognition. They parse sequences of observable behavior into goals and rationally and informationally constrained means of achieving them. Parsings that confute the expectation of a rational fit between means and goals are immediately replaced with alternatives that are compatible with this expectation. This hypothesis explains both infant expectations, as measured by differentials in looking time, and infant dispositions to imitate adult behavior. Furthermore, it can also explain recent data from infant performance on nonverbal versions of the false belief task. All that these experiments show is that, from a remarkably young age, infants are able to take into account information differentials when forming expectations about what course of behavior is rational for a given agent. This is not equivalent to attributing full-blown propositional attitudes, understood as states of an unobservable, private mental realm, with tenuous, holistically constrained causal influence on behavior.

The minimalist intentional stance view of prelinguistic sociocognitive competence can also accommodate the data suggesting an important role for social cognition in language acquisition (Bloom, 2000, 2002). These data do not warrant the view that language acquisition presupposes the capacity to attribute full-blown propositional attitudes, so the project of the next (and final) chapter is not undermined: this capacity can be understood in terms of discursive competence. Rather, the data show that, in learning the referents of nouns, human children depend on the following assumptions: (1) adults pursue rationally and informationally constrained means to achieve their goals, and (2) certain stereotypic behaviors are reliable indicators that an adult's goal is to communicate important, novel, generic information about a salient referent.

Understanding early infant sociocognitive competence in terms of the application of a rudimentary version of the intentional stance suggests the following picture of human sociocognitive development: it consists in a gradually developing appreciation of the diverse and complex variety of constraints that govern the rational choice of means to ends. To this, we must add species-specific mindshaping tendencies. Unlike other species, human beings, from a very early age, interpret stereotypic adult behaviors as overtures to pedagogical demonstrations, overimitate the behavior of adult models, acquire and enforce ambient normative attitudes, and predict behavior based on deontic expectations associated with social categories. In short, the evidence from developmental psychology is more than merely *compatible* with the phylogenetic hypothesis defended in this book. The hypothesis that mindshaping is the linchpin of the human sociocognitive syndrome makes much better sense of this evidence than the view that sophisticated mindreading is the basis for distinctively human social cognition. I now turn to the final chapter, wherein I propose and defend a hypothesis about the role of sophisticated mindreading—the attribution of full-blown propositional attitudes—in our mindshaping practices.

7   The Role of Sophisticated Mindreading in Human Mindshaping

1   Preamble

In chapters 4 and 5, I proposed and defended a hypothesis about the phylogeny of three of the four components of the human sociocognitive syndrome: sophisticated mindshaping, cooperation, and complex language. I argued that none of them require sophisticated mindreading, understood as the attribution of full-blown propositional attitudes, with tenuous, holistically constrained causal influence over behavior. For the most part, these components of the human sociocognitive syndrome are products of changes in social motivations rather than social cognition. Our ancestors found themselves in a socioecological niche in which motivations to cooperate, learn from and conform to each other, and keep track of and enforce normative statuses yielded biological advantages. I do acknowledge that this socioecological niche likely selected for improvement in some sociocognitive capacities that we share with nonhuman primates, especially the capacity to adopt the intentional stance.[1] We are better at this than other primates, especially at factoring differences in information access into our judgments of means–ends rationality. The cognitive homogeneity that results from pervasive mindshaping in human populations makes our virtuosity at adopting the intentional stance possible, because it makes it more likely that interpreters and their targets attend to similar information and make similar judgments of means–ends rationality. As I argued in chapters 5 and 6, improved and more powerful versions of the intentional stance can also support more sophisticated mindshaping practices, especially those involving language.

Assuming that this is on the right track, it raises a difficult question. If pervasive, sophisticated mindshaping together with sophisticated versions of the intentional stance are sufficient to explain human cooperation, coordination, and language, what explains the phylogeny of sophisticated mindreading as I have characterized it? If dispositions toward conformity, imitation, pedagogy, and the tracking and enforcement of normative statuses, together with the capacity to parse behavioral sequences into goals and rationally and informationally constrained means of achieving them, are all that is required to maintain the human sociocognitive syndrome, then why do we need to attribute full-blown propositional attitudes, with tenuous, holistically constrained causal influence on behavior? Answering this question is the main burden of this final chapter. I argue that such sophisticated mindreading derives from the practice of undertaking and attributing discursive commitments (Sellars, 1997; Brandom, 1994; Frankish, 2004). Chapters 5 and 6 neutralized some obvious problems with making sophisticated mindreading parasitic on language in this way. With such worries out of the way, I can now turn to a more detailed exploration of this suggestion.

In section 2, I consider two alternative views that make sophisticated mindreading parasitic on discursive competence: Hutto's (2008) and Bermúdez's (2003a, 2009). I argue that their reasons for seeing propositional attitude attribution as parasitic on language are not compelling, and introduce my own reasons for this. In section 3, I explain the increasingly important role that the capacity to track and undertake discursive commitments likely played in human prehistory, given the phylogenetic story defended in chapters 4 and 5. I then argue that, rather than enabling accurate mindreading, the primary raison d'être of full-blown propositional attitude attribution has always been what Malle et al. (2007) call "impression management": the maintenance, diminution, and rehabilitation of status in the wake of apparently counternormative behavior, like apparent reneging on discursive commitments. In section 4, I provide more detail about how the capacity for discursive commitment is implemented, focusing on the sorts of mindshaping mechanisms that enable us to conform to our discursive commitments. I argue that self-constitution in terms of publicly available narrative plays a central role in this and also explains how our capacity to shape ourselves can play both private, cognitive roles and public, coordinative roles. Section 5 wraps up the entire project, relating it to some prominent traditions in philosophy and psychology.

2 Why Propositional Attitude Attribution Depends on Language

A number of theorists maintain that propositional attitude attribution presupposes competence in a public language (Davidson, 1975, 1985, 1997, 1999; Clark, 1998; Bermúdez, 2003a, 2009; Hutto, 2008). However, most of the reasons that have been offered for this claim are not compelling. Hutto (2008), following Davidson (1975), argues that both the capacity to *token* propositional attitudes and the capacity to *attribute* them presuppose competence in a public language. Davidson's reasons for this are largely epistemological. If one has no principled way of determining the precise content of an agent's propositional attitudes, then there is no fact of the matter regarding which propositional attitudes the agent tokens. The only principled way of determining the precise content of an agent's propositional attitudes is by interpreting the agent's utterances of public language sentences. Hence only speakers of public languages token and attribute propositional attitudes.[2,3]

Hutto provides supplementary arguments in support of Davidson's position. His key contention is that the intensionality of propositional attitude attributions that I discussed in chapter 6 requires that targets of such attributions represent their contents under linguistic modes of presentation. For example, consider a dog barking up a tree into which it has just chased a squirrel. It is tempting to attribute to the dog the belief that the squirrel is up the tree. But in what sense does the dog think of the squirrel *as a* squirrel? Clearly the dog does not conceptualize the squirrel as language users do: it does not think of it as a member of a species of mammal that semihibernates in the winter, spends the nonwinter months stocking up on nuts, and so on. So how does the dog think of the squirrel? It seems impossible to say, since we can specify the dog's mode of presentation only using words drawn from a public language, all of which have connotations of which the dog is unaware. This is problematic because specifying the mode of presentation under which believers represent the contents of their beliefs is key to linking their beliefs to their behavior; this is why propositional attitude attributions are intensional. We predict that Lois Lane will not kiss Clark Kent because she represents him as a dorky reporter rather than as the superhero she loves.

This argument, considered on its own, is not persuasive. Just because it is difficult to express in language the mode of presentation under which a nonlinguistic agent represents the contents of her beliefs does *not* mean that she does *not* represent the contents of her beliefs under, presumably, nonlinguistic modes of presentation. This is the problem with Davidson's general approach: epistemological constraints related to our typical evidence for, and means of, attributing propositional attitudes, that is, public language utterances, have no direct implications for metaphysical questions related to the nature of nonlinguistic cognition. Furthermore, several philosophers have proposed rigorous methods for identifying the modes of presentation under which nonlinguistic agents represent the contents of their beliefs (Bermúdez, 2003a; Allen & Bekoff, 1997). However, there is more to Hutto's point. Not only must there be modes of presentation under which a believer represents the contents of her beliefs, but these modes of presentation must have certain formal properties, of a kind that characterize only linguistic vehicles. The reason is that the central role of propositional attitudes consists in the rational guidance of behavior. For a propositional attitude to rationally guide behavior, it must combine with other propositional attitudes in rational, practical inference. The desire to catch the squirrel must combine with the belief that the squirrel is in the tree and the belief that barking at it will help flush it out to yield the intention to bark at the tree. But such practical inference is possible only if it involves syntactically articulated modes of presentation. They must consist of components that can recur in different propositional attitudes. For example, in the bout of practical reasoning I have just sketched, the "squirrel" component of the belief must recur in the desire for the practical inference to work. This suggests that modes of presentation of propositional attitude content must be syntactically constituted; that is, they must be linguistic.

This still does not suffice to show that tokening and attributing propositional attitudes presuppose competence in a *public* language, for two reasons. First, as Hutto grants, it is possible that the medium of thought is a kind of language: the "language of thought" (Fodor, 1975). According to this hypothesis, both human and nonhuman cognition consists in computation over mental representations with the syntactic properties of public languages. If this is true, then competence in a public language is not necessary for a cognizer to represent contents under syntactically articulated modes of presentation. So competence in public language is not required for a cognizer to token full-blown propositional attitudes. However, I agree with Hutto (2008) and others (Bermúdez 2003a) that the language of thought hypothesis is problematic in a variety of ways. Unfortunately Hutto's argument has a second, deeper problem. It is not clear that the concept of belief requires that the modes of presentation under which believers represent contents must be syntactically articulated. It is true that the forms of practical inference studied by philosophers since Aristotle require linguistic vehicles. However, the commonsense concept of belief, like most commonsense concepts, has many dimensions, not all of which are consistent with each other. To many, it seems obvious that individuals incapable of using a language can nonetheless be capable of belief. Such intuitions must be weighed against the philosophical motivations for restricting the class of believers to the class of sentence users. Hutto himself grants that nonlinguistic organisms are capable of iconic or imagistic takes on situations that they can imaginatively manipulate to facilitate the planning of rational action (2008, pp. 79–85). Perhaps this does not technically count as practical inference in the sense in which philosophers have understood this term. However, I see no reason to deny that it comes close enough to qualify as cognition involving beliefs and other propositional attitudes. And, in fact, some influential philosophical analyses of belief deny that its instantiations need be sentential in form (Lewis, 1994; Stalnaker, 1999). Thus Hutto's argument for the claim that only cognizers competent in public language can token propositional attitudes comes up short.

This still does not suffice to show that the capacity to *attribute* propositional attitudes is independent of competence in public language. Since I have been discussing Davidson and Hutto, I have followed them in not distinguishing strongly between the alleged dependence on public language of (1) the capacity to *token* propositional attitudes and (2) the capacity to *attribute* them. However, Bermúdez (2003a, 2009), addressing this issue from an entirely different perspective, does distinguish between these two capacities. He argues that some nonlinguistic agents are capable of tokening propositional attitudes but not attributing them. His argument for the former claim depends on a well worked-out method for attributing determinate propositional contents to the mental states of nonlinguistic agents, based on providing adequate explanations of behavior. According to Bermúdez (2003a), nonhuman animals and prelinguistic infants engage in behavior that can be explained only by positing mental states with determinate propositional contents that combine in "protological" inferences capable of guiding behavior (pp. 140–149). This is sufficient to show that they can token beliefs and desires, without competence in a public language, or even in a language of thought. However, Bermúdez argues, such cognitive resources are insufficient to allow for propositional attitude *attribution* (2003a, 2009).

His reasons are the following. Propositional attitude attribution must take place at the "personal" or conscious level, rather than at the "subpersonal" level. The reason is that reasoning about the propositional attitudes of others often plays an important role in a person's practical reasoning, and practical reasoning takes place at the personal/conscious level, not at the subpersonal level (Bermúdez 2009, p. 159). Given that propositional attitude attribution takes place at the personal/conscious level, it cannot involve sentences in the language of thought, which is supposed to be the medium of subpersonal cognition (p. 163).[4] Bermúdez follows consensus in assuming that we are conscious of only two kinds of representational vehicles at the personal level: public language sentences and iconic representations like images or maps. So these are the only two candidates for the medium in which propositional attitudes can be attributed. But iconic representations are inadequate to this task because they lack the formal structure necessary to model the practical inferences that lead from beliefs and desires to action (pp. 161–162). In contrast, linguistic representations necessarily possess this formal structure. It follows that public language is the only medium capable of supporting propositional attitude attribution (pp. 162–163).

I think this argument fails for a number of reasons. First, there is no reason why practical reasoning, and hence, in Bermúdez's view, propositional attitude attribution, need take place at the conscious/personal level. It is true that the conclusions of bouts of practical reasoning are often conscious; that is, we tend to be aware of the decisions at which we arrive. However, it does not follow from this that the processes that lead to these decisions need take place at the conscious/personal level. In fact, Carruthers (2006) argues that practical reasoning is typically unconscious and involves multiple practical reasoning processes competing for control of behavior. Since Bermúdez's argument for the claim that propositional attitude attribution must take place at the personal/conscious level depends entirely on his claim that practical reasoning must be conscious, the fact that the latter claim is unwarranted undermines the former claim. Minimally, Bermúdez owes an argument that practical reasoning must be conscious, and critiques of theories like Carruthers's, according to which it is not.

Furthermore, others have proposed well worked-out models of subpersonal mechanisms of propositional attitude attribution. For example, Nichols and Stich (2003) argue that subpersonal belief attribution might co-opt a mechanism dedicated to representing counterfactual states of affairs. Representing another agent's discrepant beliefs is a lot like representing states of affairs that are contrary to how the belief attributor takes the world to be. None of this need involve a public language. Bermúdez himself grants that nonhuman animals and prelinguistic infants have beliefs and are capable of representing both how the world is and how it could be (2003a). Once this capacity is integrated with other mindreading capacities in the way that Nichols and Stich (2003, pp. 93–94) envision, attribution of beliefs independently of competence in public language *could* be possible.[5]

There is also something strange about Bermúdez's claim that the "canonical structure of a proposition is only revealed when propositions are represented in a linguistic format" (2009, p. 162). Recall the reason that Bermúdez thinks this matters to propositional attitude attribution: the medium of propositional attitude attribution must have the formal structure necessary to model the inferences that lead from beliefs and desires to actions. As Bermúdez puts it, this "is a matter of reasoning about the logical and inferential relations between propositional attitudes. Accurate predictions depend upon the predictor being able in some sense to track the reasoning that the agent might themselves engage in" (p. 160). This is strange because, in other work, Bermúdez (2003a, pp. 140–149) defends the view that agents incapable of public language engage in a kind of propositional-attitude-involving inference, called "protologic," that differs substantially from the kind of inference made possible by language. It follows that were language used to model such protologic, it would be systematically misleading. For this reason, the claim that the medium of propositional attitude attribution must have the formal structure necessary to model behavior-guiding inferences does not imply that it must be linguistic. By Bermúdez's own lights, some propositional attitudes, that is, those of agents incapable of public language, guide behavior via protological inferences that differ from language-based inferences. Hence such practical inferences are not aptly modeled in language. The "off-line" application of protologic to representations of counterfactual situations to model another agent's perspective, as suggested by Nichols and Stich's (2003) model of discrepant belief attribution, seems a much better way of modeling another agent's application of protologic to propositional attitudes.

Thus Bermúdez's reasons for holding that propositional attitude attribution presupposes competence in a public language, like Davidson's and Hutto's, are inadequate. Still, I agree with this view: I think that full-blown propositional attitude attribution does presuppose competence in a public language. However, my reasons for this are entirely empirical. There is no deep philosophical connection between language and propositional attitude attribution. Rather, propositional attitude attribution presupposes competence in a public language because there is simply nothing to gain from attributing full-blown propositional attitudes independently of language mastery. As I have argued, human cooperation and other feats of social coordination can be explained in terms of sophisticated mindshaping practices together with applications of the intentional stance, that is, the capacity to parse behavioral sequences into goals and rationally and informationally constrained means of achieving them. Applying the intentional stance to interpretive targets that have been shaped to reason and behave similarly to interpreters should be enough for interpreters to anticipate their behavior. In such circumstances, there is no need for concepts of full-blown propositional attitudes, that is, mental states with tenuous, holistically constrained causal influence on behavior.

Language changes things because it gives us both the means and the need to constantly signal a diverse and open-ended range of commitments, many of which, we might not realize as we signal, conflict with each other. In these circumstances, the need arises for a practice of keeping track of commitments and excusing failures to abide by them when we lose track of them. As I argue in the next section, propositional attitude attribution is a powerful mechanism for maintaining or rehabilitating social status in the wake of apparent reneging on publicly expressed commitments. This, not behavioral prediction based on accurate mindreading, is the central function of full-blown propositional attitude attribution. And it is a function that makes sense only once a complex commitment-signaling system, like natural language, is on the scene.

3   The Rise of Sophisticated Mindreading

Since chapter 1, I have reserved the term "sophisticated mindreading" for the attribution of full-blown propositional attitudes. As I have made clear, full-blown propositional attitudes are, at a minimum, states of a mind— understood as an enduring, unobservable causal nexus hypothesized to explain the behavior of enduring agents—with tenuous, holistically constrained causal influence on behavior. I take this to be an uncontroversial understanding of full-blown propositional attitudes. It is certainly what most philosophers mean by beliefs, desires, and their ilk, and many psychologists have adopted this understanding (Malle et al., 2007, p. 493; Apperly & Butterfill, 2009, p. 957; Apperly, 2011). I have also argued that most components of the human sociocognitive syndrome require less sophisticated capacities: various forms of mindshaping, complex signaling, and the capacity to adopt the intentional stance.

The intentional stance is a remarkably flexible and efficient tool for anticipating the behavior of rational agents. The reason is that it focuses entirely on behavioral appearances, with no concern for the mental reality behind them. Behavioral sequences and contexts are parsed into goals, rational means of achieving them, and available information. As long as everything goes smoothly and predictions are borne out, there is no need to second-guess interpretations by looking for evidence whether an interpretive target *really* believes, or mentally represents, information an interpreter assumes is available to her, or whether an interpretive target *really* desires the goal an interpreter thinks rationalizes her behavior. If a goal and a set of available information rationalize some behavior, and if this leads to a prediction that is borne out, no further evidence is required to justify an interpretation from the intentional stance. This is what I mean by the claim that the intentional stance focuses entirely on behavioral appearances, with no concern for an underlying mental reality, that is, what the target of the interpretation really thinks.[6]

Of course, most interpretive acts that adult humans consciously perform seem to involve more than this. We usually take ourselves to attribute full-blown beliefs and desires, understood as unobservable, causally implicated states of mind. However, just because many adult humans tend to conceptualize our interpretive practice in this way does not mean that it is best characterized in this way. First, if Dennett (1991b) is right, then despite the rhetorical gloss, the beliefs and desires we consciously attribute are nothing but abstract posits that help compress and track observable patterns of behavior. Second, even if Dennett is wrong about this, in previous chapters, I have defended the intentional stance as the best characterization of our low-level, unconscious, automatic interpretive capacities. As chapter 5 argued, this best explains how quickly we arrive at interpretations in dynamic communicative contexts. As chapter 6 argued, this best explains the interpretive feats of very young infants who are surely not yet capable of sophisticated, conscious, reflective interpretation. Furthermore, as I have noted, nonhuman animals are capable of rapid interpretation from the intentional stance, though presumably they are incapable of the kind of sophisticated, reflective interpretation of which adult humans are (Wood & Hauser, 2008). So when I speak of interpretation from the intentional stance, I have in mind primarily System 1 social cognition (Carruthers, 2009a; Apperly & Butterfill, 2009; Apperly, 2011; Zawidzki, 2011): our automatic, unconscious, rapid interpretive responses to observed behavior.

I have argued that a System 1 version of the intentional stance is sufficient to explain most components of the human sociocognitive syndrome. The sophisticated mindreading that I claim is the latest-arriving, mindshaping-dependent component of this syndrome, that is, full-blown propositional attitude attribution, is best understood as a System 2 capacity for slow, conscious, and reflective interpretation.[7] The question that concerns me here is why such a capacity evolved. If what matters most for successful mindshaping, cooperation, coordination, and linguistic communication is anticipating the behavior of one's conspecifics, then why would anything beyond an extremely flexible and efficient way of tracking behavioral patterns be required? Parsing an interpretive target's observable behaviors and their contexts into available information, intuitively obvious goals, and rational means of achieving them in light of the available information should suffice to support highly reliable behavioral prediction,[8] especially when this capacity is supplemented by mindshaping practices that homogenize the cognitive profiles of likely interactants. There is no need to limn the mental reality behind the behavioral appearance.

According to influential proposals in comparative and developmental psychology, concern with the unobservable reality behind appearances is one of the most important distinctions between human and nonhuman cognition. For example, Povinelli (2012) explains the failure of chimpanzees to learn both social and physical tasks that human beings find trivial in terms of chimpanzees' lack of a distinctively human capacity to understand observable phenomena as effects of unobservable causes. Over the last three decades, Keil (1992) has marshaled impressive evidence that human children are default essentialists: they identify and categorize objects in terms of their unobservable essences rather than in terms of the way they appear. For example, to human children, a horse painted to look exactly like a zebra remains a horse. Sophisticated mindreading, understood as the attribution of full-blown propositional attitudes, requires the deployment of a similar, essentialistic appearance–reality distinction to the domain of behavior.

Just as an animal's appearance does not fix its kind, or a physical object's behavior does not determine its unobservable causes, so an agent's behavior does not determine the mental causes responsible for it. This explains the key difference between the intentional stance and sophisticated mindreading. If a goal and a set of available information rationalize behavior and enable successful behavioral prediction, then there is no other, deeper fact of the matter of any interest from the intentional stance. But true mindreading must countenance the possibility that the same behavior need not always issue from the same mental causes. Even a counterfactually robust pattern of behavior, that is, the same set of responses to a variety of hypothetical circumstances, may issue from radically different mental states. This is why attributing such mental states encounters the holism problem. The mental reality can be entirely independent of behavioral appearance. Why and how would our prehistoric ancestors have developed such an interpretive framework? If their sociocognitive goals concerned behavioral prediction exclusively, then why would they waste time and energy wondering about mental realities that can be entirely independent of behavioral appearance?

Neither Povinelli nor Keil provides any detailed hypotheses regarding the phylogeny of the distinctively human concern with the reality behind appearances. Of course, once this distinction is appreciated and deployed in reasoning about the world, it can be extremely useful. For example, understanding the true, unobservable causes behind appearances might support creative interventions in the typical course of events to accomplish novel ends. This explains the technological power that science has unleashed.[9] However, this does not explain how or why the distinction first came to be appreciated by our prehistoric ancestors. After all, appreciating that an unobservable reality lies behind appearances does not produce instant practical dividends. One must first develop methods for formulating and verifying accurate models of unobservable reality, and this is a highly difficult task. Our species has mastered it only in the last few hundred years. For most of human history and prehistory, our speculations about the unobservable reality behind appearances have been woefully misguided and supported few practical dividends. Thus it is unlikely that some kind of instant technological boon explains how or why our prehistoric ancestors first developed an appreciation of the appearance–reality distinction.[10]

However, it is possible that applying the appearance–reality distinction to human behavior paid immediate, *nonepistemic, social* dividends in the socioecology that, as I argued in chapters 4 and 5, likely characterized late prehistoric human populations. Explaining how the concept of a mental reality behind behavioral appearance may have emerged in these circumstances requires a short detour through some more detail about the phylogeny of language, as I understand it. Chapter 5 addressed the problem of identifying viable partners for coordination on cooperative projects, given increasing interaction with unfamiliar individuals. I argued that costly signaling of commitment to group endeavors could help solve this problem, especially if individuals who were disposed toward, and competent at, coordination on cooperative projects found these signals less costly to produce than other individuals. This would drive the evolution of ever more costly, complex signaling systems, as a way of filtering reliable and competent cooperation partners from less desirable mimics. Chapter 5 traced the evolution of the human capacity for structurally complex communication, such as recursive language, to such complex signaling systems, which initially probably involved the use of rhythmic display in rituals.

Given such a socioecology, it is plausible that complex signaling could take on a life of its own. Better signalers would be more trusted and hence engage in more cooperative projects, from which they would gain material benefits, but also a good reputation, and hence higher social status, and better or more mates. This would drive the evolution of even more complex signaling capacities as these became means to gain status and sexual access, for which humans, like other primates, compete intensely. Furthermore, as the variety of cooperative projects on which individuals could coordinate grew, commitment-signaling systems would have to become more complex to accommodate the growing variety of commitments, that is, to play different roles in radically different cooperative endeavors. Finally, as I argued in chapter 5, if, as is likely, this commitment signaling coexisted with an earlier, unstructured, lexical protolanguage, devoted to signaling referential and predicative information about salient objects and events, of the kind hypothesized by Bickerton (1990), these two communicative systems would likely become integrated. Thus commitment signaling would gradually evolve into something like contemporary language: a semantically flexible, structurally complex means of signaling intentions related to salient objects and their properties.

In this view, the earliest uses of language were likely something akin to promises, that is, commitments to courses of behavior involving salient objects and properties.[11] An utterance roughly translatable as "I'll set the trap" is a good example: it expresses a commitment to performing a specific role in a cooperative endeavor, using a structurally complex signal consisting of lexical items that refer to relevant objects and actions.[12] But how do we get from such expressions of commitment to courses of behavior to straightforward assertions of facts? Promises, like "I'll set the trap," have what Searle (1979) calls a "world-to-word" direction of fit: they are fulfilled when the world is made to match the promise. But assertions have what Searle calls a "word-to-world" direction of fit: they are true when the assertion is made to match the world. In my view, the earliest uses of complex language involved a world-to-word direction of fit: they regulated behavior such that it conformed to expressions of commitment. How might such promise making have spawned assertive uses of complex language, involving a word-to-world direction of fit?

It is obvious that one of the most important kinds of roles that individuals can play in coordination on cooperative projects is an epistemic one: ascertaining facts to which other team members have no access. For example, one's role in a hunt might be to scout the location and disposition of a herd of prey. This would naturally encourage the evolution of linguistic constructions for reporting facts. Instead of promising just to engage in courses of behavior, such constructions could be used to "promise" that the world is a certain way.[13] In promising that the world is a certain way, a speaker is expressing a specific kind of commitment, what Brandom calls a "*doxastic* or *assertional* commitment" (1994, p. 157). Like the more straightforward kind of commitment expressed in a typical promise, assertional commitments involve commitments to future courses of behavior. Someone who claims that the herd of prey is to the north is thereby committing to act in ways compatible with this fact and opening herself up to sanction if she does not. But an assertional commitment involves more than just a normative constraint on future behavior. It also opens the asserter to potential sanction if the world is not how she says it is (Lance & O'Leary-Hawthorne, 1998). Just as a promise commits the promiser to behave a certain way on pain of sanction, so an assertion commits the asserter to the world's being a certain way on pain of sanction. By committing to the world's being a certain way, for example, to there being a herd of prey to the north, an asserter entitles her audience to verify her claim and sanction her if it is false, just as a promise entitles an audience to sanction the promiser if she fails to fulfill it.

Thus it is relatively straightforward to see how an initially rudimentary practice of signaling commitment to play roles in cooperative endeavors may have gradually evolved into the more complex and sophisticated commitment-signaling practice that constitutes contemporary language. Initially our prehistoric ancestors may have been able to express commitments only to very broad future courses of behavior, associated with specific roles in cooperative endeavors. For example, performance of a mating ritual may have expressed commitment to sexual exclusivity, or performance of a war ritual may have expressed commitment to stand with one's fellows in battle. As cooperative endeavors became more complex and multifarious, driven by group selection for groups capable of more sophisticated cooperation, the commitment-signaling practices supporting them would have to become correspondingly more complex and multifarious. As commitment-signaling systems came to match the expressive power of contemporary language, signalers could express commitments as varied and open-ended as the distinctions encoded in contemporary languages. Signalers could express commitments to more than just some broad role in a war party or sexual exclusivity. They could use the expressive power of language to commit to roles as fine-grained as an "asserter-that-P" where "P" is any proposition encodable in the language.

Despite its complexity, such sophisticated commitment signaling retains the basic properties of earlier commitment signaling. Its point remains the same: signaling commitment to, and reliability at, performing roles in cooperative projects. And it is supported by the same sorts of normative attitudes as more primitive commitment signaling: signalers who violate the norms governing their signals are sanctioned thanks to the normative attitudes of typical interlocutors. Minimally, such reneging on signaled commitments results in costs to status. False assertions jeopardize one's status as a reliable reporter of facts. Unfulfilled promises jeopardize one's status as a reliable promise maker. In human populations—typically highly dependent on smooth coordination on cooperative projects—such costs to status are far from trivial. More active forms of sanctioning, including gossip, mockery, ostracism, and physical punishment, are also employed. The overall point is that even as commitment signaling became more complex and sophisticated, and hence supportive of more complex, sophisticated, and varied forms of cooperation, it continued to rely on the same basic cognitive mechanisms as the earliest forms of commitment signaling, especially the disposition to sanction those who renege on their commitments. Just as an early prehistoric human would have suffered deep reductions in status if she reneged on a commitment to sexual exclusivity expressed in a mating ritual, a contemporary human suffers deep reductions in status if she consistently reneges on assertional commitments, that is, if she is a habitual liar.

Once sophisticated commitment-expressing communication is on the scene, it is possible to understand full-blown propositional attitudes in the way that Brandom does: beliefs that P can be understood as assertional commitments to the claim that P (Brandom, 1994, p. 157). How might this perspective shed light on the puzzle of sophisticated mindreading, or why our ancestors became concerned with the mental reality behind behavioral appearances? As Dennett has long argued, once members of a population are constantly using a complex public signaling system to signal commitments of various kinds, this introduces a new method of interpretation (1978, pp. 19, 303–309). Besides adopting the intentional stance and asking what goals and access to information best rationalize an interpretive target's behavior, interpreters can also attend to the target's explicit expressions of commitment, taking her at her word. But, as Dennett notes, the outputs of these two interpretive strategies are not always compatible: the goals and information access that best rationalize and predict a person's behavior may conflict with the goals and claims to which she explicitly expresses commitment.[14] When interpreters are surrounded by interpretive targets that are constantly making discursive commitments of various kinds and, at the same time, engaging in behavior that may or may not be rationalizable in terms of those commitments, interpreters must inevitably grapple with the question: *what do they really think?* In a population that relies exclusively on applying the intentional stance to bouts of behavior, such a question should never arise. If an initial interpretation leads to a false prediction, then it is withdrawn as incorrect and replaced with a better one.[15] But in a population of individuals constantly signaling discursive commitments of various kinds, anomalies are not so easily resolved. Individuals can persist in their discursive commitments even as their behavior does not live up to them. In such cases, interpreters are faced with the question of what their targets really think: a distinction between behavioral appearance and mental reality is on the scene.

Is either interpretive strategy—the intentional stance or accepting an interpretive target's explicit commitments as definitive—the ultimate guide to what interpretive targets really think? Dennett seems to favor the intentional stance in this regard: an agent's beliefs and desires are whatever states rationalize and predict her behavior; her explicit avowals reveal only her "opinions" (1978, pp. 303–306). However, Dennett's point here is that there is no more fact of the matter regarding what an agent believes and desires than whatever attribution best explains or predicts her *entire* behavioral biography, *including details that are apparent only through scientific investigation* (p. 307). When the choice of canonical interpretation must be made between applications of the intentional stance *that are feasible in quotidian contexts*, and the agent's own explicit commitments, then it is not clear which is a better guide to her true beliefs and desires. Interpreters typically do not have access to as much evidence as their targets, who witness more of their own behavior. An interpretation from the intentional stance that best makes sense of behavior that the interpreter *happens* to have observed might not account for significant behavior that only the target has observed. On the other hand, there is no doubt that people often deceive themselves and make discursive commitments to which they cannot live up.[16]

In my view, neither third-person, *quotidian* interpretation of behavior from the intentional stance nor explicit, first-person discursive commitments count as definitive means of discovering an agent's true beliefs and desires. But, as I suggested earlier, the distinction between behavioral appearance and hidden mental reality can nonetheless serve an important, nonepistemic social function. Once there are two potentially conflicting ways of interpreting people, anomalous behavior is inevitable, and the conceit that someone may really think one thing, despite behavioral evidence to the contrary, can play an important role in rehabilitating status in the wake of behavioral anomalies. As I suggested earlier, when an agent's behavior appears anomalous because, for example, it is at odds with explicit commitments she has made, her status as a reliable cooperation partner is at risk. However, if she can somehow excuse the behavior by appeal to some nonobvious belief or desire that rationalizes the anomaly, she has a tool for rehabilitating status. I think this is the role that the distinction between behavioral appearances and underlying mental reality played initially, before we had reliable methods to put it to epistemic uses, like uncovering "core cognition" (Carey, 2009) and other deep psychological facts about the etiology of behavior. The possibility that a person's behavior might conceal her true thoughts supports the presumption that anomalous behavior can be explained away, for example, that once we know precisely what a person thought, an apparent reneging of a public commitment can be excused. According to Jerome Bruner (1990), this is the primary function of narratives that allude to a person's intentional states, such as beliefs and desires:

> When you encounter an exception to the ordinary, and ask somebody what is happening, the person you ask will virtually always tell a story that contains *reasons* (or some other specification of an intentional state). ... All such stories seem to be designed to give the exceptional behavior meaning in a manner that implicates both an intentional state in the protagonist (a belief or desire) and some canonical element in the culture. ... *The function of the story is to find an intentional state that mitigates or at least makes comprehensible a deviation from a canonical cultural pattern.* (pp. 49–50)

Here, then, is a good candidate for a nonepistemic, social function of distinguishing between behavioral appearances and mental reality that could have paid pragmatic dividends in the socioecology that I have argued characterized late prehistoric human populations.

As an example, consider a scout returning to her hunting party to report that a large herd of prey is to the north. The hunting party proceeds north and finds no trace of the prey. The scout's reliability as a cooperation partner is now in serious jeopardy. However, she can go some way toward rehabilitating it by constructing a Brunerian narrative that appeals to certain nonobvious intentional states. Perhaps she was traveling at night, got lost, and *believed* that she had been heading north, when she had actually been heading east. The conceit that behavioral appearances might mask an exculpatory mental reality can be used to help mitigate the fallout from apparent reneging on discursive commitments. Given the importance of living up to such commitments in the socioecology that I have argued characterized human prehistory, a way of repairing the damage to social status caused by failures to live up to them would have been a highly useful, nonepistemic, social function for the concept of a mental reality behind behavioral appearances.[17]

This social function can also explain why the holism of the propositional attitudes is a feature rather than a "bug." In chapter 3, I argued that holism causes much mischief for propositional attitude attribution considered as a tool for behavioral prediction. The reason is that it jeopardizes the simple links between observable behavior and mental states on which accurate and timely prediction must rely. However, if the original function of full-blown propositional attitude attribution was primarily exculpatory or jus-tificatory, then holism is a feature rather than a bug: if any mental state is compatible with any behavior given adequate adjustments to other mental states, behavior that seems at odds with cooperative intentions or explicit commitments can always be rationalized away by appeal to other mitigat-ing mental factors of which one's interactants may be unaware. Further-more, such exculpatory functions require that these other mental factors be treated as having a *causal* influence on behavior: behavior can be excused only by mitigating mental states that actually caused it. In the socioecology of our late prehistoric ancestors, the idea that the link between interpreta-tions and behavior is not straightforward and requires attention to a whole system of reasons for behaving would already have been in the air, given that individuals sometimes failed to conform to the expectations triggered by their publicly expressed discursive commitments; so appealing to covert commitments to rationalize anomalous behavior would have been an obvi-ous strategy to deflect sanctions. Thus the notion that a mental reality lies behind behavioral appearances, consisting of states with tenuous, holisti-cally constrained, causal influence on behavior, likely played an important social function, even if it was hopeless as a tool for behavioral prediction.[18]

This hypothesis can also explain why the attribution of full-blown prop-ositional attitudes was likely, from the start, a System 2 capacity. Coming up with an excuse for counternormative behavior that is consistent with all potentially relevant evidence and likely to convince a skeptical audience is precisely the sort of context-sensitive, "isotropic" task likely to stymie fast and frugal cognition. In addition, since the task involves establishing consistency with verbally expressed commitments, by verbally express-ing other, previously unacknowledged commitments, language is already involved, and in influential theories of System 2 thinking, the domain inte-gration for which it calls is possible only with the help of a public language (Carruthers, 2006). As Mercier and Sperber (2011) argue, System 2 reasoning was probably selected to support argumentation with interlocutors, rather than individual reasoning. If the evolutionary scenario sketched in chapters 4 and 5 is on the right rack, then such argumentation often involved deter-mining normative statuses, and hence appropriate sanctioning (if any), on the basis of contested, negotiated interpretations of behavior.

It has long been assumed that full-blown propositional attitude attribu-tion can play both predictive and justificatory roles. Knowing an interpre-tive target's beliefs and desires can help both predict her behavior and see why it is rationally justified. This is why the attribution of beliefs and desires plays an important role not just in predictive and explanatory projects like psychology but also in justificatory projects like epistemology and theories of practical rationality. However, philosophers of psychology have tended to stress the former over the latter role (Fodor & Lepore, 1993). Beliefs and desires are posited primarily to causally explain behavior, and it just so happens that because certain contingent regularities relate propositional attitudes to each other and behavior, they can sometimes double as rational justifications of behavior. The scenario sketched in the foregoing reverses this priority. Relative to the socioecology of our late prehistoric ancestors, full-blown propositional attitude attribution was more likely to earn its keep playing a justificatory rather than a predictive role. The distinction between behavioral appearances and hidden mental reality was initially used, in the manner described earlier, to exculpate anomalous behavior, thereby mitigating the threats to status that such behavior triggered.

4   The Role of Propositional Attitude Attribution in Sophisticated Mindshaping

According to the traditional understanding of the relationship between propositional attitude attribution and various forms of mindshaping, propositional attitude attribution makes the following contribution to mindshaping. Before we can shape a mind, through imitation, pedagogy, or normative sanctions, for example, we must first determine the propositional attitudes that animate it. We cannot shape a mind without first knowing the state it is in, and this is the function of propositional attitude attribution. The foregoing has suggested a radically different role for propositional attitude attribution in our mindshaping practices. For example, when it comes to normative sanctions, propositional attitude attribution is part of a negotiated give-and-take aimed at determining the normative status of an interpretive target, and hence whether or which sanctions are appropriate. Apparently anomalous behavior, such as the apparent reneging on an explicit commitment, is assumed to be sanctionable unless the agent can provide an exculpatory narrative, referring to previously unappreciated propositional attitudes. If this interpretation convinces the audience, sanctions can be avoided; however, such interpretations are contestable and hence negotiable (Bruner, 1990, p. 47).[19] The model here is something like plea bargaining in courts of law, rather than inferring mental causes in psychology labs.

This raises the worry that there is no fact of the matter regarding what agents really believe and desire—all that matters is the story that works to justify or rationalize or exculpate some behavior, relative to one's audience. But this does not follow. It is important to stress that the target of my description here is our *quotidian* interpretive practices. Everything I say is compatible with the claim that there are facts of the matter regarding what agents believe and desire that careful scientific study can establish. But, as I stressed earlier, the appearance–reality distinction in general, and the distinction between behavioral appearance and mental reality in particular, are unlikely to play important *epistemic* roles in quotidian contexts because the careful application of the scientific method to the task of uncovering true, unobservable causes is impractical. Hence we must rely on incomplete data, compatible with multiple interpretations, to negotiate an interpretation that settles the normative status of an agent's anomalous behavior in the eyes of the relevant group. Interpreters and their targets must argue over the relevance and importance that ought to be assigned to a variety of available evidence, including observable behavior, recent explicit commitments, and the excuses that targets offer. Due to the impossibility of a rigorous scientific approach to such questions in most quotidian contexts, such arguments are unlikely to identify the true mental causes of an interpretive target's behavior. However, consensus interpretations can be negotiated and determine whether or which sanctions are appropriate, to the satisfaction of a critical mass in the relevant group.[20,21]

A good deal of evidence from social psychology suggests that behavioral interpretation in terms of propositional attitudes plays such a rationalizing role. For example, this hypothesis best explains a number of asymmetries in spontaneous behavioral explanation by adults, depending on whether the explanations concern their own or others' behavior (Malle et al., 2007). The main focus is the distinction between what Malle et al. call "reason explanations" and "causal history explanations" (2007, p. 494). "Reason explanations" refer to propositional attitudes that, in the agent's mind, lead to and *rationalize* the behavior through a process of deliberation. For example, someone might explain why she wore a hat in terms of her desire to shield her face from the sun. "Causal history explanations" refer to situations, character traits, or mental states that lead to behavior but do not figure in the subject's deliberate decision making. For example, one might explain why a subject did not vote in an election by claiming that she is lazy. Or one might explain someone's drug or alcohol abuse by referring to a difficult childhood. Such factors do not figure in the deliberate reasoning by which the subjects arrive at their decisions. One does not choose not to vote on the grounds that one is lazy, or choose to abuse alcohol on the grounds that one had a harsh childhood. Malle et al. (2007) found that subjects are more likely to use reason explanations, appealing to propositional attitudes, to explain their own behavior, and more likely to use causal history explanations to explain others' behavior.

What explains such asymmetries? One possibility is that subjects simply know the reasons for which they act better than the reasons for which others act. It is difficult to accurately gauge the reasons that figure in another person's deliberations, for the sorts of reasons I explored in chapter 3. Perhaps causal history explanations are simply easier to formulate than reason explanations for subjects other than oneself. However, Malle et al. (2007) controlled for this possibility. They ran experiments in which subjects were asked to explain the behavior of (1) persons with whom they were intimately acquainted, like friends or family, (2) strangers whose behavior the subjects personally witnessed, and (3) strangers whose behavior the subjects merely heard about. Obviously, subjects' knowledge of their explanatory targets varied between these three conditions; however, *the likelihood of offering reason rather than causal history explanations did not.* Subjects were just as likely to offer causal history explanations of the behavior of intimates, the behavior of strangers that they had witnessed, and the behavior of strangers about which they had heard. So increasing subjects' access to evidence relevant to determining explanatory targets' reasons did not increase the likelihood of reason explanations, suggesting that something else explains the self–other asymmetry between reason and causal history explanations.

Malle et al. (2007) also consider a different hypothesis: reason explanations play a role in "impression management"; that is, they portray an agent's behavior in a favorable light by showing it to be rational. While subjects are typically motivated to portray their own behavior in a favorable light, they are not typically motivated to portray others' behavior in a favorable light. This hypothesis has obvious affinities with the Brunerian account of the function of propositional attitude attribution sketched earlier. In the view I defend, our ancestors first started attributing full-blown propositional attitudes, understood as the mental reality behind behavioral appearances, to rehabilitate status in the wake of apparently counternormative behavior, especially apparent reneging on explicit commitments. According to Malle et al., behavior explanations serve more than an epistemic function:

They are [also] a social activity to manage ongoing interactions. … Explanations can be used to clarify, justify, defend, attack, or flatter; they serve as tools to guide and influence one's audience's impressions, reactions, and actions. … Such impression management can be used from both the actor perspective and the observer perspective, but actors will more often portray themselves in a positive light. Thus, actors' greater use of impression management may help explain at least some of the actor–observer asymmetries. (Malle et al., 2007, p. 504)

If this is true, then the self–other asymmetry in providing reason versus causal history explanations should disappear if subjects are motivated to portray others' behavior in a positive light. And this is precisely what Malle et al. (2007) found. While manipulating subjects' knowledge of their explanatory targets did not make them more likely to explain their behavior in terms of propositional attitudes, manipulating their motivation to portray even unfamiliar targets' behavior in a favorable light did.

This result favors the mindshaping account of propositional attitude attribution over the mindreading account. If the function of propositional attitude attribution is primarily epistemic, that is, accurately representing the propositional attitudes that lead to an interpretive target's behavior, then one would expect interpreters with more evidence of an interpretive target's propositional attitudes to be more likely to provide reason explanations. But this is not what Malle et al. (2007) found. Instead they found that interpreters are more likely to provide reason explanations, *even of the behavior of complete strangers*, when they are motivated to portray them in a positive light. That the availability of evidence relevant to propositional attitude attribution makes *no difference* to the likelihood of providing reason explanations, while the motivation to portray behavior in a good light does, strongly suggests that the purpose of such explanations is not epistemic but social. In Malle et al.'s (2007) terms, it serves an impression management function; or in my terms, it functions to preserve or rehabilitate status in the wake of apparently counternormative or otherwise puzzling behavior.[22]

Another set of recent experimental results that are entirely unsurprising from the mindshaping perspective suggests that the attribution of intentional states is influenced by normative judgments (Pettit & Knobe, 2009; Knobe, 2003, 2006). In the classic study that first showed the so-called Knobe effect, adult subjects were asked to judge whether or not an interpretive target intentionally allowed a morally significant side effect of a decision she made. For example, subjects read the following two variants of the same vignette and were asked whether or not the protagonist intentionally caused the side effect. In the "help" variant, the vice president of a company proposes a new program to the chairman of the board, saying that it will increase profits and, as a side effect, help the environment. The chairman of the board endorses the program, saying that she cares only about increased profits, and not about helping the environment.

In the "harm" variant, the scenario is exactly the same, except the side effect involves harming the environment. Again, the chairman of the board endorses the program, due to the increased profits, and expresses indifference about the harmful effects on the environment. Although, intuitively, the chairman of the board in the two scenarios is in exactly the same type of mental state, subjects differed in their assessments of whether or not the chairman intentionally helped or harmed the environment. Subjects were significantly more likely to judge that the chairman intentionally harmed the environment in the second scenario than that she intentionally helped the environment in the first scenario.

Theorists have debated vigorously about how to interpret this result, especially whether or not it shows a pervasive influence of normative considerations on our interpretive dispositions. Some argue that the effect is idiosyncratic to judgments of whether or not actions *are intentional* (Nichols & Ulatowski, 2007; Machery, 2008). However, drawing on evidence pertaining to other folk psychological judgments, including *having the intention* to help or harm, *intending* to help or harm, *having the desire* to help or harm, *advocating* help or harm, and *being in favor of* help or harm, Pettit and Knobe (2009) argue persuasively that the influence of normative considerations on folk psychological interpretation is pervasive. They also tentatively propose an explanation of this effect in terms of the structure of our representations of what they call "pro-attitudes," that is, attitudes involving support for some outcome. Pettit and Knobe (2009) are beyond modest about their proposal: they hold out little hope that their explanation will survive future experimental evidence. So the broader theoretical significance of the Knobe effect is still extremely controversial. However, one aspect of it is not controversial: it is extremely surprising. I submit that this is an artifact of the received mindreading view of propositional attitude attribution, that is, that its function is primarily epistemic.

In the received view, normative sanctions and other forms of mindshaping depend on prior, independent, and accurate mindreading via the attribution of propositional attitudes. We decide whether or not a behavior violates a norm based on a prior assessment of the propositional attitudes— the beliefs, desires, and intentions—that caused it. Given this assumption, it is indeed surprising that the normative assessment of a behavior should affect our interpretation of it. We are supposed to determine whether or not, for example, the chairman of the board in the foregoing vignettes has violated a norm, partly on the basis of judgments about whether or not she allowed something to happen intentionally, had the desire that it happen, was in favor of it, and so on. However, the evidence suggests that folk interpretation does not work this way. Prior judgments about the normative status of the outcomes of the chairman's decision affect our willingness to attribute certain intentions, desires, and other pro-attitudes to her. If the mindshaping account is correct, and propositional attitude attribution functions mainly to manage impressions, then the Knobe effect is far less surprising. Of course, in the case of the Knobe effect, the attribution of propositional attitudes functions to justify a *negative* normative status, rather than to rehabilitate or maintain status by providing an exculpatory narrative as a justification of apparently counternormative behavior. However, the broader point remains: propositional attitude attribution is not some kind of independent prelude to normative judgment. Rather, normative judgment influences propositional attitude attribution.

This conforms to the picture I have sketched: propositional attitude attributions are in the service of justifying prior determinations of normative status. If I am defending myself against an assault on my status triggered by some apparently counternormative behavior, I will self-attribute propositional attitudes that support an exculpatory narrative. If I am enforcing a norm against negligent attitudes toward the environment, I will attribute propositional attitudes that justify my indignation. This contrasts the traditional picture, in which, before any normative judgment, I use behavioral evidence to determine the facts about the propositional attitudes of relevant persons.[23]

Again, as I have noted, we have no reason to infer from the picture I advocate that there is no fact of the matter about what people really believe or desire. The point is that the evidence available to *quotidian* interpreters often underdetermines such facts. So there is space for prior normative judgments to nudge interpretations one way or another. Furthermore, nothing that I say implies that we can just make up interpretations to suit our normative prejudices out of whole cloth. Available evidence, for example, the chairman of the board telling the vice president that she doesn't care about the effects on the environment, helps constrain which interpretations are viable, that is, which interpretations are likely to convince an audience. However, such evidence still leaves open a choice of interpretations. And as the Knobe effect demonstrates, prior normative judgments can nudge interpreters toward one of these at the expense of others. The "help" and "harm" variants of the vignette provide exactly the same behavioral evidence of intention; however, given that different propositional attitude attributions are favored in these different circumstances, to the folk, this evidence underdetermines interpretation, and the options can be narrowed further by exclusively normative considerations.

The suggestion here is not that we have the capacity to learn the truth about each other's thoughts, or perhaps already know it on some level, and then cynically suppress this in favor of more self-serving interpretations. Rather, I claim only that the inevitably imperfect evidence to which we have access in quotidian contexts leaves interpretation massively underdetermined. When an interpreter looks at all the observable behavioral evidence to which she has access regarding another's behavior or her own,[24] this does not rule out incompatible interpretations. Instead the interpreter is faced with something like a Necker cube phenomenon or Wittgenstein's duck-rabbit. When the evidence is looked at in one way, and some components are foregrounded at the expense of others, one interpretation in terms of propositional attitudes "pops out." But the same evidence can be looked at differently, with different components foregrounded, and a different interpretation will pop out. Such underdetermination of interpretations by evidence is inevitable even under ideal conditions. As Kuhn (1977, pp. 320–339) notes, it pervades theory selection in natural science. Two equally rational scientists can look at all the same data and arrive at radically different theoretical interpretations because of the different values that they put on different aspects of the evidence and on various scientific virtues, like simplicity, coherence with the rest of science, breadth of scope, accuracy, and suggestiveness of future research. Given that behavioral data available in quotidian interpretive contexts are far less thorough or carefully gathered than data available in scientific contexts, such problems of indeterminacy are bound to be worse in quotidian interpretive contexts. Hence it is entirely unsurprising and not even objectionable that, in quotidian contexts where determinate interpretations are required, "impression management" or status preservation will have a role in eliminating the interpretive indeterminacy of inevitably incomplete and imperfect data.

Besides the difference in data quality, scientific and quotidian contexts differ in another important respect. Kuhn (1977) notes that scientists wedded to a certain paradigm may unconsciously and in good faith engage in selective interpretations of the data to support their preconceptions. However, although scientists inevitably emphasize some data at the expense of other data to promote their favored theories, they do not and cannot typically make data disappear or manufacture data. When it comes to the quotidian interpretation of behavior, on the other hand, such data manipulation is likely to be routine. The reason is the intimate connection between human interpreters and the objects they interpret, for example, themselves. If I am wedded to a particular theory of myself, then I can do more than just emphasize behavioral data that confirm it over behavioral data that confute it. I can directly alter my behavior, such that the confuting data are systematically extinguished and the confirming data systematically promoted. In other words, I can treat self-interpretations as *regulative* (McGeer, 2007) rather than epistemic frameworks, thereby turning them into self-fulfilling prophecies.

Although interpreters' control of *others'* behavior is much less direct than this, it is still far more direct than the control that scientists typically have over their domains. Thus the sorts of automatic mindshaping dispositions discussed in chapter 2 can easily give interpretations a role in the regulation of others' behavior. For example, as Mameli (2001) notes in his discussion of mindshaping, gender-biased interpretations of infant behavior can become self-fulfilling prophecies because children conform to social expectancies: if, for example, their cries are routinely interpreted as expressions of anger rather than sadness, then they will act in ways that conform to these expectations. The process of norm internalization described by Sripada and Stich (2006) is similar. Lower-status individuals, like children, can internalize normative construals supplied by higher-status members of their culture and use these construals to regulate their own behavior. Such phenomena suggest that, in addition to the kind of selective interpretation of data that we find in science, quotidian interpretation allows for the routine, automatic, and unconscious *manufacturing* of data that confirm interpretive preconceptions, as well as the routine, automatic, and unconscious *extinguishing* of data that violate them.

Although the practice of concocting self-regulating justifications in terms of propositional attitudes probably started out as a cognitively demanding System 2 activity in prehistory, given the importance of status to human biological success, it likely became routinized. As status became increasingly dependent on avoiding unjustified reneging on explicit discursive commitments, formulated in terms of increasingly complex signaling systems in which the implications of such commitments were increasingly harder to track, pressure arose to always have at the ready appropriate justificatory narratives to deflect any assaults on status prompted by alleged norm flouting. As a result, it is plausible that, in contemporary self-interpretation, when we find ourselves engaged in some behavior, there are neural mechanisms that continually and automatically generate different construals of the imperfect behavioral data to which we have access, searching for interpretations capable of justifying the behavior in the eyes of our community. Such mechanisms also automatically and continually try out different construals of others' observed behavior to determine status. This process draws on a relatively limited palette of stereotypic justificatory narratives afforded by the ambient culture, which encode the propositional attitudes that are appropriate relative to certain behavioral patterns. The stereotypes encoded in these narratives can then serve a regulative function. This, I claim, is the central role of narrative understanding in human social life.[25]

For example, a person might observe that she has become disposed to blush or otherwise become agitated when someone's name is mentioned. Such behavioral evidence underdetermines interpretation in terms of propositional attitudes. But public narratives involving stereotyped characters afforded by her culture are immediately salient: maybe she interprets the behavior as indicating that she has a crush. This interpretation carries with it a whole set of regulative expectations about how the "crush narrative" might unfold. These then feed back into the person's motivational economy, amplifying an initially vague and indeterminate set of behavioral dispositions into an elaborate set of propositional attitudes that a "crush haver" is *supposed* to token, according to her culture. If the object of the crush is familiar with such narratives and has complementary initial dispositions, interaction is facilitated: both know roughly how such narratives are supposed to play out, the kinds of propositional attitudes that are appropriate, and the roles that each is supposed to play. Attributions of propositional attitudes to self and other, in such circumstances, have more to do with what culturally available narratives indicate characters are *supposed to* believe and desire than with arriving at true representations of individuals' actual mental states on the basis of careful interpretation of behavioral evidence. As David Velleman puts it, reasons for acting are best thought of as "the *elements* of a possible storyline" (2000, p. 28). Since interactants typically share such normative expectations because they share the same culture and hence similar histories of mindshaping, such collaborative stereotype confirmation can facilitate coordination.

In chapter 2, I referred to such sophisticated, language-involving mindshaping as the employment of a "self-constituting narrative." As Ross (2007) argues, such self-constituting narratives shrink the space of games or interactions possible for agents familiar with the same narratives. Culturally sanctioned patterns of thought and behavior constitute socially constructed roles like "parent," "teacher," "priest," "politician," "businessman," "adolescent," and so on. These culturally sanctioned patterns of thought and behavior constitute an extremely small selection from the space of possible patterns of thought and behavior of which human beings are capable. When we interpret each other's behavior or our own, the input is meager behavioral evidence that is compatible with this larger space of possible interpretations. However, those made salient by mindshaping practices prevalent in our culture are primed and automatically triggered by behavioral data. They then exert a regulative pressure: initially indeterminate behavioral data are shaped such that they develop into a culturally acceptable pattern. If most of one's potential interactants self-regulate in complementary directions, coordination is dramatically facilitated. In fact, as Apperly (2011, pp. 29, 160) notes, this explains the ease with which propositional attitude attribution can be used to *predict* behavior, despite the holism problem. Because most interactants are shaped to interpret indeterminate behavioral evidence as implicating the same, or complementary, culturally salient, stereotypic narratives, and then use these narratives to regulate further thought and behavior, the attribution of propositional attitudes expected of characters in such narratives can support reliable behavioral prediction. Thus even if quotidian propositional attitude attribution started off performing a nonepistemic impression management function in prehistory, this does not rule out the possibility that it eventually came to perform an epistemic function: since most interpretive targets actively try to conform to propositional attitude attributions encoded in public, self-constituting narratives, interpreters can *learn* about their targets' psychologies and future behavior by attempting to determine their propositional attitudes.

As I also noted in chapter 2, strong behavioral and neural evidence supports this picture. Gazzaniga's work with split-brain patients shows that, in most people, the left hemisphere functions as a kind of self-interpreter: meager data are rationalized in terms of some culturally acceptable narrative. In one experiment, a split-brain patient induced to stand by a command to which only her language-impoverished right hemisphere had access supplied an on-the-spot false rationalization when her left hemisphere was asked about her motive: she said that she wanted to retrieve a soda from a nearby house (Gazzaniga, 1995a, p. 1393). Furthermore, she then proceeded to act on this confabulated desire: she left the room to retrieve the soda. This illustrates the role that, in my view, sophisticated mindreading plays in sophisticated mindshaping. Whether or not our public self-interpretations are justified or true, we actively work to confirm them (Carruthers, 2009a, p. 127). For the most part, such regulative interpretation is most effective when it is self-directed. In fact, as McGeer (1996) argues, we can understand the apparent *epistemic* authority of self-interpretation in terms of its direct implications for action regulation, rather than in terms of some kind of privileged Cartesian access to our own motivations. However, as I have argued, third-person regulative interpretation is also possible: this is arguably what happens when children accept and conform to the implications of their caretakers' interpretations of their behavior (Mameli, 2001).

Finally, it is relatively straightforward to see how such self-constituting narratives might come to support epistemic or cognitive self-regulation. Among the narratives afforded by cultures are epistemic narratives, constituting such roles as a "good scientist" or "cogent reasoner." Given the salience of such narratives in a culture's mindshaping practices, individual members will interpret their own behavior and circumstances in ways that enable epistemic self-regulation. For example, finding oneself disposed to endorse some claim, one can then interpret oneself in terms of a culturally afforded "cogent reasoner" stereotype and make sure that one also endorses all claims that are logically implied by it, and only claims that are logically compatible with it. Or finding oneself disposed to explain some phenomenon in a certain way, one can then interpret oneself in terms of a culturally afforded "good scientist" stereotype and devise ways of testing one's hypothesis. In other words, the same mechanisms that facilitate interaction among individuals familiar with complementary self-regulating narratives can implement System 2 reasoning. As Frankish (2004) argues, such reasoning is a product of training in culturally and linguistically transmitted epistemic practices—like logic, probability theory, and the scientific method—that avoid the biases of fast, automatic, unconscious System 1 reasoning inherited from our prehistoric ancestors.

In Frankish's view, System 2 reasoning takes place in a "supermind" implemented on the "basic mind" that is a part of our innate biological endowment. The supermind traffics in "superbeliefs" (Frankish, 2004, chap. 5), understood roughly as natural-language sentences that we consciously, explicitly accept for use as premises in further reasoning. Frankish's superbeliefs are close kin of Brandom's doxastic commitments: they involve attitudes of commitment to claims formulated in natural language. Clearly most belief attributions explicitly formulated in natural language are either undertakings (in the case of self-attributions) or attributions of doxastic commitments. If such belief attributions play the role in System 2 reasoning suggested by Frankish, then their mindshaping function is obvious: they function to regulate human minds such that they conform to rational and epistemic norms, formulated and transmitted through cultural and linguistic mechanisms.

5   Final Words

The foregoing has been an examination of two competing stories of the phylogeny of human social cognition. According to the story assumed, I think, by most researchers in the field, human beings came by their distinctive sociocognitive capacities in the following way. In general, evolution by natural selection rewards cognitive sophistication: individuals of any species who know more about how central features of their ecology work do better than individuals who know less. The most important features of most primate ecologies are social. Hence, in the human lineage, individuals who knew more about how their conspecifics worked did better. In particular, individuals who understood that the behavior of their fellows was caused by unobservable states of mind, and especially propositional attitudes, outcompeted those who did not. Such knowledge enabled them to outmanipulate their dimmer conspecifics. It also enabled better cooperation and coordination, thanks to sophisticated policing against free riders, and sophisticated language designed to reveal independently constituted propositional attitudes.

I have argued against this story and in favor of the following alternative. Our ancestors' sociocognitive capacities did not differ significantly from those of other primates; at their best, these capacities amount to highly intelligent behavior tracking, that is, sophisticated versions of the intentional stance. However, ecological circumstances idiosyncratic to our lineage favored groups with cooperative members, more so than in any other primate species. At first, these groups were small and sparse and focused on hunting megafauna. In such circumstances, cooperation was not the challenge that many take it to be; most behavior was public, and public sharing of information was rewarded. As megafaunal populations dwindled and demographics and lifeways changed, cooperation and behavioral anticipation became more challenging, because individuals interacted with a greater variety of other individuals, and a division of labor balkanized the earlier information commons. Cooperation was maintained in such circumstances due to group selection: mindshaping mechanisms like conformism, imitation, pedagogy, and norm enforcement maintained the intragroup homogeneity and intergroup variation necessary for group selection. Groups with mindshaping practices that best promoted coordination on cooperative projects outcompeted other groups. Norms-supporting plural subject formation evolved, allowing for smoother coordination. None of this resulted from better mindreading: groups with better mindshaping simply did better and produced more individual members. Through time, however, the presence of mindshaping practices in such groups may have selected for improved sociocognitive capacities, like more sophisticated versions of the intentional stance. However, there was no need for full-blown propositional attitude attribution or for an understanding of the distinction between behavioral appearance and mental reality on which it depends.

As interaction with relative strangers increased due to increasing population density and diversity, complex, ritualistic communication systems evolved as means of signaling commitment to, and competence in coordination on, cooperative projects. Our capacity for structurally complex language descends from such ritualistic precursors. When integrated with a structureless, purely lexical protolanguage that probably evolved for other reasons, these ritualistic precursors gave rise to contemporary language and, in particular, the capacity to make assertional or doxastic commitments. This introduced two sometimes competing means of interpreting the behavior of our fellows: rationalizing overall behavior from the intentional stance versus accepting public expressions of doxastic commitment. The conflicting interpretations that ensued first triggered an appreciation of the appearance–reality distinction applied to human behavior: suddenly it made sense to ask what interpretive targets really thought. This question was answered with explanations that appealed to full-blown propositional attitudes, but the function of such explanations was not to reveal the true causes of behavior; the only reliable method known for discovering true, unobservable causes—science—arrives very late in the history of the species and is not easily applied in quotidian contexts. Rather, the function of propositional attitude explanations was impression management: the maintenance, diminution, or rehabilitation of status, in the wake of apparent reneging on explicit commitments and other kinds of counternormative behavior.

Obviously, one advantage of the received story over the alternative I defend is simplicity. I can express the received story in a single short paragraph, but to express my alternative account takes more than a page. But I think simplicity in matters of human cognition is often deceptive. The reason is that we have concocted simple self-conceptions that serve a mind-shaping function. The received view is an example of this: we think of ourselves as perceptive natural psychologists who can somehow ascertain each other's mental states quickly and reliably. But this is more of a regulative ideal that puts pressure on human beings to make themselves more interpretable to each other. The true reality hidden behind such comforting illusions is far more complex. Yet it can better explain a variety of recent empirical results in the cognitive sciences.

Here is a list of empirical facts about human social cognition that I think are puzzling in the first story yet entirely unsurprising in the second:

• Of all highly social, highly intelligent primates, only human beings attribute full-blown propositional attitudes (chapter 1, section 3; chapter 3, sections 2 and 5, this volume).

• All and only normal human offspring compulsively overimitate (chapter 1, section 4; chapter 2, section 2; chapter 6, section 6, this volume).

• All and only normal human offspring interpret stereotyped adult communicative behavior as pedagogical (chapter 2, section 3, this volume).

• All and only normal human offspring display an early capacity to acquire norms and enforce them with the help of normative attitudes like resentment, indignation, shame, and guilt (chapter 2, section 4(ii); chapter 6, section 6, this volume).

• Human beings tend to find the reliable attribution of higher-than-first-order propositional attitudes extremely difficult (chapter 4, section 2, this volume).

• Human beings in all societies are willing to pay material costs to punish counternormative behavior (chapter 2, section 4(ii); chapter 4, sections 3 and 5, this volume).

• Human beings are more likely to provide reason explanations when motivated to manage impressions, yet not when provided with more evidence of interpretive targets' reasons (chapter 7, section 4, this volume).

• The Knobe effect, according to which human beings use independent normative judgments to resolve interpretive indeterminacies (chapter 7, section 4, this volume).

• The chameleon effect (chapter 2, section 4(i), this volume).

• Both human adults and human children are more likely to trust and cooperate with partners with whom they have engaged in varieties of rhythmic synchrony, including singing and marching (chapter 4, section 4, this volume).

• Human interpreters employ different brain areas to interpret targets perceived as in-group (including themselves) versus targets perceived as out-group (chapter 4, section 5, this volume).

• Brain mechanisms that generate error signals responsible for individual trial-and-error learning in response to failed predictions are also triggered by failures to conform to majority opinion (chapter 4, section 3, this volume).

This list simply highlights some of the more striking empirical evidence discussed throughout the book. It is the tip of the iceberg: as the foregoing discussions suggest, an impressive variety of evidence is naturally explained by the mindshaping hypothesis but is surprising in the received mindreading hypothesis. In particular, for reasons reviewed in chapters 3 and 4, it is difficult to explain the phylogeny of the human sociocognitive syndrome according to the hypothesis that an ancestral hominid population, with sociocognitive capacities roughly comparable to those of contemporary nonhuman apes, was invaded by mutants that were capable of full-blown propositional attitude attribution, before invasion by mutants capable of humanlike mindshaping. As chapter 3 argued, full-blown propositional attitude attribution is unlikely to be reliable and timely enough to make a difference to behavioral anticipation in the absence of prior mindshaping. As chapter 4 argued, it is difficult to see how full-blown propositional attitude attribution could help solve the sorts of coordination problems success at which explains our species' distinctive evolutionary trajectory; yet it is easy to see how humanlike mindshaping could help solve these sorts of problems.

Although such empirical evidence and arguments support the mindshaping hypothesis, they are, of course, not decisive. As I have stressed in this chapter, empirical evidence can always be reinterpreted in ways that confirm incompatible explanatory hypotheses. I am sure that proponents of the mindreading-first model of the phylogeny of the human sociocognitive syndrome can interpret the evidence I have reviewed in ways that are compatible with their perspective. In light of this inevitable dynamic, it is perhaps best to treat the foregoing as an initial formulation and defense of a heterodox view, aimed at showing that the received view is not the only game in town. Science flourishes when there are competing explanatory frameworks, and my principal goal here has been to suggest that there is a viable and underexplored framework for explaining the phylogeny of the human sociocognitive syndrome that is worth developing.

In closing, let me highlight a nonempirical virtue of the mindshaping view. Besides explaining a variety of otherwise puzzling empirical facts, the mindshaping hypothesis promises to bring extremely diverse and seemingly unconnected traditions of human inquiry under a single framework. It is not easy to see what recent prominent results in comparative psychology, developmental psychology, social psychology, experimental economics, evolutionary game theory, plural subjects theory, hominid paleobiology, evolutionary linguistics, and the neuroscience of social cognition have in common. However, from the mindshaping perspective, it is possible to discern a common theme: human social cognition relies centrally on our capacities and dispositions to shape each other and ourselves to conform to normative expectations that prevail in groups of likely interactants. The explanatory unification suggested by mindshaping does not end there. According to an influential model of human cognition, our most impressive cognitive feats often involve altering the environments in which we act, to make them easier to negotiate using our limited internal cognitive resources. Mindshaping is clearly an example of such "epistemic action" (Kirsh & Maglio, 1994; Kirsh, 1996; Clark, 1997) applied to the social domain. The intensity of so-called tribal instincts (Richerson & Boyd, 2005, pp. 229–230) in driving religiously and ethnically motivated conflict in the contemporary world is also easily explained by the mindshaping hypothesis: we care that our own normative frameworks prevail against others because our ability to understand and flourish in the social world depend on the integrity of the normative frameworks that shaped us and continue to structure our social worlds. Furthermore, the growing evidence that language and culture have profound effects on cognitive style (Gumperz & Levinson, 1996; Nisbett et al., 2001; Gentner & Goldin-Meadow, 2003; Levinson, 2003; Thierry et al., 2009) is also clearly congenial to the mindshaping hypothesis.

Finally, the notion of mindshaping promises to reveal the mutual relevance of philosophical traditions that sometimes seem antithetical. In this chapter, I have noted how well Brandom's (1994) philosophical theory of discursive practice fits with the empirically motivated phylogenetic story defended in chapters 4 chapter 5, as well as with recent empirical results in social psychology. But Brandom's views are often seen as antithetical to the assumptions of mainstream analytic philosophy and, in particular, its focus on a scientifically supported understanding of human cognition. Brandom himself is a critic of certain "naturalistic" projects in the philosophy of mind. From the perspective of the mindshaping hypothesis, this antagonism rests on a fundamental conflation: naturalism, broadly understood as an approach to philosophy constrained by empirical results from science, is conflated with specific philosophical theories about the place of mind in nature. In particular, one prominent assumption of contemporary naturalism about the mind is that our quotidian interpretive practices are in the same business as the sciences of the mind, that is, identifying the unobservable causes of behavior. However, it is possible to reject this assumption and remain a naturalist; the mindshaping hypothesis shows how. The best scientific explanation of the phylogeny and persistence of our interpretive practices might require that we understand their roles as primarily justificatory rather than causal/explanatory, and that we appreciate that they presuppose group-relative normative regimes maintained by the normative attitudes of group members. In short, the mindshaping hypothesis shows how it is possible to be a naturalist about the mind while endorsing the kind of understanding of our quotidian interpretive practices suggested by Brandom's theory of discursive practice.

Indeed, the ecumenical potential of the mindshaping hypothesis is even more dramatic than this. Arguably, one of the central differences between the so-called analytic and continental traditions of Western philosophy concerns the status of explanatory frameworks applied to human behavior. Whereas the goals of such frameworks tend to be taken at face value in the analytic tradition (e.g., as aiming to represent mental reality), the continental tradition treats them in a more circumspect way, wary of the normative regimes that they can sometimes unconsciously enforce. For example, Foucault (1966, 1975) is often read as arguing that allegedly universal scientific truths about human nature "discovered" by science "are, in fact, often mere expressions of ethical and political commitments of a particular society ... the outcome of historically contingent forces" (Gutting, 2011). Such claims are obviously in tension with the naturalistic commitments of contemporary analytic philosophy. For example, Foucault would certainly reject the claim that contemporary concepts of the propositional attitudes constitute an innate biological endowment, as many naturalistic analytic philosophers assume. The mindshaping hypothesis offers the promise of reconciling these seemingly antithetical perspectives. With analytical philosophical naturalism, it accepts that there can be a science of human nature that determines truths about the human mind, like the phylogenetic roots of the human sociocognitive syndrome and the neural bases of human social cognition. However, in the mindshaping hypothesis, Foucault's understanding of the socionormative functions of explanatory frameworks applied to human behavior is on the right track. Our quotidian interpretive practices aim to shape our social environments through a variety of mindshaping mechanisms, including normative attitudes and social institutions based on them, rather than represent them accurately. For this reason, Foucault is right that we must be constantly vigilant against normative assumptions snuck in as scientifically established, universal truths of human nature.

It is possible to dispute that such ecumenical potential is a virtue. Nevertheless any concept with the potential to uncover an underlying unity among apparently antithetical intellectual traditions, persuasive to thousands of intellectually honest and accomplished scholars, deserves exploration. The notion that our sociocognitive feats depend on a variety of sophisticated and pervasive mindshaping practices holds such promise.

Notes

Preface

1. Theorists have hypothesized different forms of group selection to explain the evolution of prosocial traits in humans and other species (West, El Mouden, & Gardner, 2011, pp. 246–249). The most extreme form of group selection explains how individuals willing to sacrifice their genetic contribution to the next generation can nevertheless flourish in a population. This form of group selection explains the social traits of eusocial insects; for example, worker bees sacrifice themselves for their queen because she carries and transmits copies of their genes. It is unlikely that this form of group selection played an important role in human evolution (ibid.). However, some forms of group selection complement standard genetic selection operating on individuals. For example, individuals in successful groups tend to have more offspring, so genes necessary for flourishing in such groups are favored by selection operating on individuals. However, successful groups are products of selection operating at the level of groups: groups that are better organized and better able to exploit scarce resources outcompete other groups. Thus selection at one level, between groups, can affect selection at another level, favoring the kinds of genes that enable individuals to flourish and reproduce in the most successful groups. This is the kind of group selection that, as we will see, was extremely important in human prehistory.

2. David DeGrazia and José Luis Bermúdez have both made this suggestion to me.

3. Sterelny (2012, p. 73) employs similar language, explaining the evolution of human social cognition as the emergence of "the human co-operation syndrome." This book owes a great intellectual debt to Sterelny's work. However, my emphasis is different from his. Sterelny takes for granted that reliable behavior prediction made possible by sophisticated mindreading is an important component of the human cooperation syndrome. He also stresses the importance of what I call mindshaping, focusing on the transgenerational pooling of useful information, for example, about tool construction and use, prey behavior, and so on, made possible by imitation and pedagogy. In my view, information pooling is not the most important function of

sophisticated mindshaping. Far more important is its role in facilitating behavior prediction and sophisticated mindreading by making people easier to interpret in cooperative interactions. My central claim is that reliable behavior prediction and mindreading are made possible by sophisticated mindshaping: rather than two independent capacities contributing to the human cooperation syndrome, they are deeply intertwined, with mindshaping making possible reliable mindreading, which, for this reason, constitutes one of mindshaping's central raisons d'être. It is here that my view goes beyond Sterelny's. Much more on this in chapter 4.

4. Dennett's notion of adopting the intentional stance is often treated as equivalent to mindreading (Baron-Cohen, 1999, p. 261). However, as I argue in chapter 1 and chapter 5, this is a misinterpretation. The intentional stance requires only the capacity to parse observable bouts of behavior and their contexts into goals and means of achieving them that are rational relative to available information. It is not necessary to attribute mental states or even to conceptualize bouts of behavior as products of an unobservable mind animating an enduring agent.

1   The Human Sociocognitive Syndrome

1. Unlike the other three components, "mindshaping" is not commonly recognized, at least not using that term. Indeed, it is part of the goal of this book to raise the profile of this important human capacity. I have much more to say about what I mean by "mindshaping" later in this chapter, and in chapter 2. For now, think of the many human practices that aim to shape behavioral dispositions and hence minds: imitation, pedagogy, norm enforcement, and various forms of propaganda.

2. Siegal (2008) expresses this view with particular force and clarity: "It is impossible to overemphasize the centrality of ToM [Theory of Mind] in human civilization because ToM is necessary for the appreciation and transmission of culture in the form of novels, theatre, and song, and more generally for the maintenance of family and social life" (p. 22).

3. This is admittedly vague. As will emerge in chapters 2 and 5 through 7, I do not deny that sophisticated, distinctively human mindshaping presupposes more sophisticated *social cognition* than what is available to our closest nonhuman cousins. However, these advantages can be understood in terms of more intelligent *behavior* reading, rather than in terms of sophisticated mindreading. In particular, we appear better at parsing behavioral sequences into goals and means for achieving them, and at tracking access to information based on behavioral cues. Although this amounts to a superior capacity to adopt what Dennett calls the "intentional stance" (1987), I argue later that, pace Baron-Cohen (1999), this is not equivalent to mindreading: it does not require positing an unobservable, causal nexus governing some agent's behavior. Rather, it requires the tracking of abstract, yet still observable, behavioral patterns (Dennett, 1991b). Much more on this in section 3, where I discuss the varieties of mindreading in greater detail.

4. How precisely do I intend such modal claims? In the same way that many evolutionary psychologists and anthropologists intend the sorts of claims I criticize later, e.g., that distinctively human social cognition depends on sophisticated mindreading. I think there are two kinds of dependency to which such claims refer. First is the claim of historical dependency: e.g., if our ancestors had not first developed sophisticated mindshaping practices, they would not have later developed capacities for sophisticated mindreading. This sort of claim is common in evolutionary biology; e.g., consider the theory that animals with lungs would not have evolved had there not been fish species that used air sacs for buoyancy. Second is the claim of synchronic dependency: e.g., even today, if human beings lost their capacities for sophisticated mindshaping, sophisticated mindreading would no longer be viable. This sort of claim is common in functional descriptions of evolved structures and capacities; e.g., consider the theory that, without binocular vision, our capacity to see in three dimensions would be impaired. Because such claims concern complex, evolved biological structures, they can be only probabilistic, not categorical. The possibility always exists that some capacity may have evolved in some other way or may currently be maintained even in the absence of certain enabling conditions. But some evolutionary trajectories, and some ways of maintaining capacities, are more likely than others. Dennett (1995, chap. 6) proposes a useful metaphor for conceptualizing such probabilistic modal dependencies in evolutionary biology: the notion of "design space." This is the space of all possible phenomena displaying apparent design, from the lowliest single-celled creatures to the most exalted products of human intelligence. Dennett argues, plausibly, that this space has a certain topology: e.g., some parts of the space are inaccessible from other parts, and alternative trajectories between different parts are more or less likely. The dependency claims I make can be interpreted in terms of this metaphor. The historical dependency claim amounts to the following: the part of design space representing distinctively human mindreading is much more easily accessible via trajectories that pass through the part of design space representing distinctively human mindshaping than vice versa. The synchronic dependency claim amounts to the following: the part of design space representing distinctively human mindreading is likely contained within the part of design space representing distinctively human mindshaping, so one cannot exit the latter without also exiting the former. More concretely, if humans lost their capacities for mindshaping, they would also likely lose their capacities for sophisticated mindreading. As I make clear in later chapters, these sorts of claims are supported by facts about the adaptive utility of sophisticated mindreading and sophisticated mindshaping with and without each other, given plausible conjectures about the social and ecological circumstances of both historical and contemporary human populations. I thank an anonymous reviewer for pushing me to clarify the status of the various modal claims I make.

5. Maynard-Smith originally proposed this notion to explain only social behaviors, like cooperation. The evolution of such traits is likewise the primary focus of this book. However, if we follow Dawkins (1976) and treat genes as strategic agents, the

notion of an evolutionarily stable strategy can help elucidate the evolution of any adaptive trait. The reason is that the stability of a trait in a population depends on its ability to outreproduce variants. The white color of the polar bear's pelt is stable because variants, e.g., brown pelts, cannot outreproduce this trait relative to the polar bear's environment. Hence, in this environment, constructing white pelts is an evolutionarily stable strategy; i.e., it is not susceptible to invasion by variants. In an editorial introduction to a special issue of the journal *Theoretical Population Biology* devoted to ESS theory, Lessard (2006, p. 231; italics mine) notes:

Even today the main idea, and the more general one, remains to look for a population equilibrium, often a fixation state, that can resist the invasion of *any* rare mutant. Such population states are the only ones that can be maintained, and therefore observed, in the long run as new mutants are introduced into the population. The approach can be applied to *any* selection model with *any* population structure, which explains its durable success. From a practical point of view, however, the question of interest is often to identify the factors that can explain the evolution and the maintenance of behavioral traits, for example, cooperation, or genetic mechanisms (e.g., recombination) that may incur individual costs.

6. The use of evolutionary analysis to help determine cognitive function was first proposed by Tooby and Cosmides (1992). For criticism, see Grantham and Nichols (1999).

7. As Dennett puts it, "I have insisted that far from being most perspicuously treated as (1) discrete, (2) semantically interpretable states, (3) playing a causal role, the beliefs and desires of the folk psychological craft are best viewed as abstracta—more like centers of gravity or vectors than as individualizable concrete states of a mechanism" (1991c, p. 139).

8. This interpretation of Dennett is bolstered by his frequent claims that the intentional stance is routinely applied to objects that nobody assumes have minds or mental states, including microorganisms, plants, the process of natural selection, thermostats, and even lightning.

9. Recent evidence suggests that chimpanzees in the wild take such information access into account when warning group mates about the presence of snakes (Crockford et al., 2011).

10. Maibom (2007) presents a clear and thorough exploration of the idea that even highly sophisticated infant and nonhuman social cognition can be understood in terms of a theory of goal-directed behavior, instead of a theory of mind.

11. See also Sterelny (2003, 2007).

12. Sterelny (2012, p. 145) makes a similar point.

13. A prisoner's dilemma (PD) consists of two players who must individually choose between two actions to secure some payoff. As with other games used to model economic interactions, whether or not a choice succeeds in securing the desired payoff depends on what the other agent chooses. However, neither agent knows what the

other will choose. In a PD, the two choices facing each agent are "cooperate" (C) or "defect" (D). The relative values of the payoffs for each agent are the following: DC > CC > DD > CD (the first letter in each pair represents the choice of the agent in question, and the second represents the other agent's choice). Since each agent knows this payoff structure and knows that the other agent knows it, the rational choice for each agent is D. If the other agent chooses C, then choosing D earns the highest payoff. If the other agent chooses D, then choosing D avoids the lowest payoff. Therefore, in a onetime interaction, both agents, if they are rational, will choose D. Cooperation is never chosen because it is never rewarded.

2 The Varieties of Mindshaping

1. However, as I made clear in chapter 1, the view I defend is compatible with the possibility that sophisticated, distinctively human mindshaping presupposes a capacity to adopt the intentional stance. Indeed, in chapters 5 and 6, I argue that varieties of mindshaping involving public language do presuppose this capacity.

2. In this chapter, I do not have the space to address all the worries of this sort that I raise. For example, some important, distinctively human varieties of mindshaping are mediated by language, like the acquisition of norms or group- and self-constituting narratives. And there is relatively strong consensus that language use presupposes attribution of sophisticated propositional attitudes (Sperber, 2000; Sperber and Wilson, 1995, 2002; Bloom, 2000, 2002). Nevertheless many theorists argue that language mastery makes possible rather than presupposes sophisticated propositional attitude attribution (Clark, 1998; de Villiers & de Villiers, 2000; Astington & Jenkins, 1999; Nelson, 2007; Hutto, 2008). I address this dispute in greater detail in chapter 6, where I focus on the role of mindshaping and mindreading in human ontogeny.

3. I use the terms "aim," "goal," "purpose," "function," and their cognates interchangeably.

4. Another problem is that many examples of mindshaping clearly do not involve deliberate guidance by a mind. For example, Mameli's (2001) examples of mindshaping through gender stereotyping likely involve no conscious processing; adults who treat infants differently solely on the basis of perceived gender are typically unaware of their behavior.

5. It is possible, in Millikan's minimalist notion of representation, i.e., what she calls the "intentional icon" (1984, pp. 96–113), that even in such cases the shaping mechanism represents the respects in which target comes to match model. Since a rat pup's perception of the odor on its mother's breath varies systematically with the mother's food preferences, it is arguable that it represents, in a minimal sense, those preferences. The rat pup then ends up matching these preferences. So, by my definition, this would then count as mindshaping. However, even if this turns out to be a

plausible analysis, it poses no threat to my project. My notion of mindshaping will apply to a greater variety of animal capacities if the notion of representation it invokes is more widely applicable in the animal kingdom. But this is compatible with my project, since later in the chapter I identify a number of respects in which human mindshaping is unique. I thank Michael Wilby and Josh Shepherd for pushing me on this point.

6. As Michael Wilby has pointed out to me, it is possible to conceive of genomes as representing respects in which offspring come to match parents. Does this make biological reproduction a mindshaping mechanism? This would certainly trivialize the notion. However, my definition makes clear that mindshaping is supposed to involve *cognitive* mechanisms, and I do not think that biological reproduction counts as cognitive, even in Millikan's understanding of representational icons. Even if it does, the worry is easily defused if I specify that mindshaping mechanisms must involve minds. I deliberately formulate my definition as broadly as possible so as not to rule out the possibility that extramental components, e.g., socially distributed factors, like pedagogical practices and institutions, can be parts of mindshaping mechanisms. However, this is compatible with the stipulation that at least one component of a mindshaping mechanism must be intramental. This would rule out biological reproduction as a mindshaping mechanism.

7. I am overstating this a little. Chimpanzees and other nonhuman great ape species have been found to occasionally engage in such fine-grained imitation when no other alternative is available for securing an important goal, like food. However, no species approaches the extent of fine-grained imitation in human beings. Only humans are default "overimitators" (Nielsen & Tomaselli, 2010), copying the detailed behavioral means by which models secure goals whether or not such imitation is necessary.

8. Whether the mindshaping mechanism involves deliberate, conscious processes or automatic, unconscious ones and the persistence of mindshaping's effects are other possible dimensions of variation. However, these variables are hard to measure and not important enough to the question of the phylogenesis of the human sociocognitive syndrome to discuss here.

9. This part of the argument will require issuing some promissory notes regarding the possibility that language mastery does not require the attribution of propositional attitudes. These promissory notes will be cashed in chapter 5's discussion of the phylogeny of human language, and in chapter 6's discussion of the roles of mindreading and mindshaping in human ontogeny.

10. This is in obvious tension with the thesis of this book. However, Tomasello et al. (1993) do not consider the kind of mindreading that makes human imitation possible a matter of tracking full-blown propositional attitudes, so their perspective is not as antithetical to the mindshaping-as-linchpin view as it seems. Moreover, Toma-

sello has recently changed his view in the light of experimental evidence that chimpanzees can track the goals and perceptual states of their conspecifics (Call & Tomasello, 2008).

11. The authors of this study do not highlight this result because their goal is to show that chimpanzees and orangutans are much more humanlike in physical than in social cognition. Thus they tend to lump results pertaining to social cognition together, failing to note significant distinctions within social cognition. However, the raw data show that chimpanzees were above chance at intention reading (59 percent), but far below chance at social learning (10 percent). Two-and-a-half-year-old human children were 86 percent correct on the social learning task and 85 percent correct on the intention reading task.

12. This is supported by the fact that chimpanzees show sensitivity to intended behaviors in competitive but not cooperative contexts. Herrmann and Tomasello (2006) compared what they call a "informing condition," where the experimenter points at a container with a reward, to a "prohibiting condition," where the experimenter "held her arm out toward the correct container (palm out) and told the subject firmly 'Don't take this one'" (p. 518). Apes are at chance in the informing condition. However, they are above chance in the prohibiting condition. This suggests that apes can understand the intentions of the experimenter in competitive but not in cooperative contexts: seeing that the experimenter is trying to prevent them from looking in a container makes them more likely to look in that container. The pattern of results for the human subjects was interesting: whereas eighteen-month-old children showed the same pattern of results as the apes, two-year-olds showed the opposite pattern, doing better in the informing than in the prohibiting condition.

13. Mirror neurons were first identified in area F5 of the rhesus macaque cortex (Rizzolatti et al., 1996). They are defined by a distinctive response profile: mirror neurons fire both when the subject observes an action and when the subject executes that very same action. Although the evidence is less direct, mirror areas have been identified in the human cortex as well (Rizzolatti & Craighero, 2004). For a great overview of the literature on mirror neurons and its philosophical implications, see Hurley and Chater (2005).

14. This view is also supported by the fact that even autistic children, known to be impoverished in sophisticated mindreading, selectively imitate intended over accidental behaviors (Carpenter, Pennington et al., 2002).

15. Byrne (2003) also argues that gorillas in the wild are capable of acquiring such fine-grained, hierarchically organized behavioral sequences from each other to process food sources. He argues that such imitation is completely independent of sophisticated mindreading and requires only the capacity to parse behavior into significant segments using observed statistical correlations among components of behavioral sequences.

16. This distinction between human and nonhuman imitation is reflected in neurophysiological evidence. So-called mirror systems in nonhuman primates appear to be tuned exclusively to "transitive" behaviors, i.e., behaviors that aim at some goal, like manipulating an object (Rizzolatti & Craighero, 2004). Mirror neurons in such species fire both when the subject observes a transitive behavior and when the subject performs the same transitive behavior. But there is no evidence among nonhuman primates of comparable mirroring of "intransitive" behaviors, i.e., behaviors that do not aim at manipulating some object, like miming. In contrast, human mirror systems appear sensitive to both transitive and intransitive behaviors (Rizzolatti & Craighero, 2004).

17. See Caro and Hauser (1992) for an opposing view. They provide much anecdotal evidence, and some experimental evidence, that adults in many mammalian species modify their behavior in ways that enable their offspring to acquire it more easily. For example, predatory cat species modify typical hunting behavior in ways that, arguably, help their offspring become proficient hunters more quickly. Recently scientists have discovered increasing evidence of this kind of pedagogy, e.g., wild meerkats teaching their young to handle scorpion prey (Thornton & McAuliffe, 2006). However, as Csibra and Gergely (2011) argue, there are important differences between such socially scaffolded learning and the kinds of "natural pedagogy" in which all human populations engage.

18. We have little evidence of pedagogy employing verbal instructions in nonindustrialized cultures (Csibra & Gergely, 2009).

19. See also Bruner (1983) and McGeer (2001).

20. Indeed, Tomasello, Kruger, and Ratner (1993) seem to defend this claim (p. 503). However, it is important to note that, in their view, prelinguistic infants can imitate by virtue of only a low-level type of intention reading. In their view, verbally mediated mindshaping, like pedagogy and collaborative learning, requires sophisticated propositional attitude attribution but is possible only after children have mastered language (ibid.).

21. The claim that norm cognition and enforcement aim only at conformity seems highly controversial. For example, a moral realist might balk at this, claiming that norm cognition aims at discovering normative truths. I do not mean anything I say here to be metaethically controversial, however. Whether or not we intend normative judgments to represent normative truths, the question on which I focus is what norm cognition was selected for in evolution and how it continues to earn its keep. It is an anthropological fact that, throughout human history, mutually inconsistent normative systems have been maintained in different populations through norm cognition and enforcement. Hence their evolutionary raisons d'être cannot concern normative truth, since, given their mutual inconsistency, most if not all normative systems maintained by norm cognition and enforcement have been false. Thus they must have different evolutionary raisons d'être, among which, I think, intragroup

conformity is a prominent one. This does not preclude the possibility that norm cognition can now be used for new, more exalted purposes, like limning the nature of normative reality, just as language can be used to describe the fundamental nature of the physical universe, something for which, presumably, it was not selected in evolution.

22. Such stereotype priming might be what is at work in Mameli's (2001) original example of mindshaping: social expectancies regarding gender. The same infant engaged in the same behavior is interpreted and, presumably, treated differently by adults, depending on perceived gender. This effect is subtler than the chameleon effect, however. Adults appear not to conform to gender stereotypes in their own behavior but to interact with the infant in ways that are consistent with the stereotypes.

23. The chameleon effect is typically relatively short-lived: it does not persist long after the interaction that induces it. In this way, the chameleon effect is significantly different from imitation and pedagogy, which often result in long-term alteration of behavioral dispositions. For this reason, one might resist classifying the chameleon effect as a form of mindshaping. However, it satisfies the definition: what is altered is not a single, onetime behavior but a disposition to a pattern of behavior, albeit a short-lived one. Furthermore, frequent interaction with models, whether concrete individuals or stereotypes, could turn such short-lived dispositions into more long-lasting behavioral patterns; so the chameleon effect can play an important role in more clear cases of long-term mindshaping. I thank Shannon Spaulding for drawing my attention to this difference between the chameleon effect and other forms of mindshaping.

24. Chartrand and Bargh (1999) include an experiment in which confederates either deliberately matched subjects' behavioral mannerisms or engaged in neutral, nondescript ones while engaged in some other task. After the experiment, subjects were asked how much they liked their collaborators and to rate how smoothly the collaboration had gone. Subjects liked their collaborators more and were more likely to rate their collaborations as smooth when mimicked than when not, although they were not aware of the mimicry. This suggests that the chameleon effect does play a role in facilitating interpersonal coordination.

25. Comparable behavior has been shown in other games, including public goods games in which players choose whether to contribute to a common pool from private funds they are allotted at the start of the game (Fehr & Fischbacher, 2004). After the contribution stage, the common pool is distributed evenly among players, and if everyone contributes, the result is a modest financial gain. Despite this outcome, an incentive exists to "free ride": those who do not contribute still get their share of the distribution and so can potentially finish with more money. However, players are also given an opportunity to punish free riders at a cost to themselves; i.e., they pay a small sum of money to have a larger sum of money confiscated from a free rider.

Most players engage in such costly punishment. In other experiments, even third parties who do not participate in the game and hence are not affected by free riding are willing to pay a monetary cost to punish free riders (Fehr & Fischbacher, 2004).

26. Tomasello (2009, pp. 28–47) provides a thorough and concise summary of the comparative and developmental evidence regarding sensitivity to norms.

27. As Frankish (2004) argues, the explicit norms of rationality that govern System 2 reasoning constitute a new level of mentality, involving discursive commitments, the properties of which are very different from the propositional attitudes involved in System 1 reasoning. For example, System 1 beliefs come in degrees, but their System 2 counterparts are discrete: one is either committed to a claim or not. Frankish thinks that System 2 cognition is distinctively human and involves the culturally and linguistically mediated implementation of a new level of mentality, what he calls the "supermind," using the System 1 resources we share with nonhuman species. The supermind is a product of distinctively human mindshaping, especially training in epistemic and rational norms. I have more to say about Frankish's theory in chapter 7, where I discuss the function of sophisticated propositional attitude attribution in distinctively human mindshaping.

28. See also Sterelny (2010, p. 289), for a similar suggestion.

29. It is true that much norm acquisition appears to rely on explicit verbal instruction, and in some views, language cannot be understood independently of sophisticated mindreading. However, as I suggested earlier when discussing sophisticated pedagogy, it is not obvious whether attribution of full-blown propositional attitudes is presupposed by or presupposes linguistic competence. I return to this issue in greater depth in chapter 6, where I consider mindreading and mindshaping in human ontogeny.

30. And hence assumes the psychological facts that narratives make salient are *constituted independently* of such narratives.

31. An anonymous reviewer wonders why such culturally mediated linguistic self-regulation need take a narrative form. Can't nonnarrative public symbols suffice? E.g., a tattoo might indicate a person's status in, and commitments to, a group (Sterelny, 2012, p. 111). But the claim here is not that culturally mediated linguistic self-regulation *needs* to take a narrative form but that, as a matter of fact, it *does*. For this idea, we seem to have a wealth of evidence (Flanagan, 1991; Dennett, 1992; Fivush, 1994; Tekin, 2011). In addition, it is worth pointing out that self-constituting narratives need not be particularly sophisticated; they might correspond to the sorts of low-level "scripts" and "frames" in terms of which individuals understand typical social interactions, e.g., what is supposed to happen and in what order when eating at a restaurant (Bermúdez, 2003b). Finally, it is not difficult to explain why much culturally mediated linguistic self-regulation takes a narrative form. One of the main goals of mindshaping is to enable coordination on cooperative projects.

This requires making interactants competent at temporally extended sequences of interactions, involving complementary expectations about events, e.g., what happens when, when to begin and when to end, and so on, that constitute elaborate bouts of cooperation. Culturally mediated narrative self-constitution appears well suited to such a function.

32. See also Tomasello (2009, pp. 31, 45) and Dweck (2000) for the closely related notion of a "public self."

33. Such cognitive self-discipline is inevitably imperfect. Consider the example of a doting parent who nonetheless forgets her child in the car on a hot day (Dennett, 2003, p. 6). The brain has a hard-to-fathom agenda of its own that does not always conform to socially acceptable narratives. Multiple agencies within the brain are vying for control of attention, and sometimes the wrong ones (from the perspective of a self-constituting narrative) take control, leading to distraction, with often tragic results.

34. As with other language-based varieties of mindshaping, like some forms of pedagogy and norm acquisition, the standard way of explaining the role of propositional attitude attribution in the internalization of narratives conflicts with the agenda of this book: such sophisticated mindreading is seen as making possible such language-based mindshaping. However, chapter 7 defends a very different conception of the role of propositional attitude attribution in language-based mindshaping: propositional attitude attribution is used to express and track public linguistic commitments to courses of behavior that conform to group- and self-constituting narratives. Focusing on human cognitive development, chapter 6 argues that language understanding does not presuppose full-blown propositional attitude attribution.

3 Mindreading and the Challenge of Computational Tractability

1. If the relations between mental states and stimuli or behavior were merely a matter of brute causation, with no inferential or justificatory import, then there would be no point to attributing propositional contents to mental states. The only reason psychological explanations posit mental states with propositional contents is to make sense of the inferential/rational relations between stimuli, mental states and behavior.

2. There are well-known criticisms of holism about propositional attitude *content* (Fodor & Lepore, 1992). However, this is not the sort of holism at issue here. Everything I say here is compatible with the possibility that propositional attitude content is not determined holistically, i.e., that the content of a specific propositional attitude is independent of the content of any other propositional attitude. The holism at issue here is related to confirmation holism, which has been uncontroversial since the demise of logical positivism. In fact, Fodor (1983) often appeals to confirmation holism in defense of his views. One of the reasons he thinks that "cen-

tral cognition," trafficking in full-blown propositional attitudes like beliefs, cannot be modularized is because, in nondemonstrative inference, any belief can be relevant to any other belief. As a consequence, any observable evidence can confirm any belief against the right background beliefs. Confirmation holism concerns input to central cognition; an entirely analogous holism concerns output from central cognition: actions are appropriate relative only to whole systems of propositional attitudes, a phenomenon that might be called "pragmatic holism." Confirmation holism and pragmatic holism raise serious challenges to the tractability of reliable propositional attitude attribution because they concern the relationship between unobservable propositional attitudes and observable evidence, that is, an interpretive target's behavior and circumstances.

3. There are, of course, exceptions. Some people are stoical enough to inhibit typical pain responses. And some "higher-level" emotions are arguably hybrids composed of emotions and propositional attitudes, which are therefore under rational control. For example, while the feeling of anger might not be under rational control, anger with a specific propositional content, like anger that one's goals have not been met, can be defeated by other propositional attitudes, like the realization that one's goals actually have been met. But such sophisticated emotions are not likely to be available to nonhumans or young human infants, and neither is stoical control of pain responses.

4. I defend this claim in greater detail in section 2.

5. This consensus is rapidly eroding. Proponents of "embodied cognition" approaches to social cognition, like Gallagher (2001) and Hutto (2008), argue that even most adult human social cognition does not involve attributing propositional attitudes. Instead it involves perceptual attunement to subtle patterns of behavior relating whole persons to objects and situations in the world. More on this later.

6. As I noted in chapter 1, complex communication presupposes cooperation: speakers must tell the truth, and hearers must trust them, despite the potential costs. And, as I suggest in chapter 1 and argue at length in chapter 4, it is hard to see how cooperation can evolve without sophisticated mindshaping.

7. According to Evans, a system of representation meets the generality constraint if it allows for the general recombination of the elements that compose well-formed representations. For example, in a language-like system, any subject and predicate that the user understands must be combinable. So it should be impossible to represent a cat eating a mouse without also being able to represent a mouse eating a cat, for example. Meeting the generality constraint is clearly relevant to the holism of the propositional attitudes because it allows for any propositional attitude to be potentially relevant to any other. My beliefs about the behavior of fluids are potentially relevant to my beliefs about the behavior of light because it is possible for me to combine representations of light with representations of fluid behavior into single, unified representations like "light is a wave." In fact, Carruthers (2009b)

grants that bee cognitive maps do not meet the generality constraint on the grounds that they cannot be used in the service of all the bees' potential goals, e.g., locating the brood chamber. However, he denies that such generality should be a constraint on belief possession.

8. Some proponents of the received, mindreading-first view suggest that social complexity drove the evolution of sophisticated thinking and thus the need for more sophisticated mindreading (Dunbar, 1996, 1998, 2000, 2003). But they are insufficiently clear about what "social complexity" means. In what ways were the lives of protohumans more socially complex than those of contemporary chimpanzees? Suppose the groups were larger and involved more complex social relations, like instituted social roles, division of labor, and practices like pair bonding (Dunbar, 2003). Such social complexity cannot be maintained in the absence of sophisticated cooperation, coordination, and the mindshaping that makes it possible (see chap. 4). So, in this understanding, sophisticated mindreading presupposes social complexity, which itself presupposes the other components of the human sociocognitive syndrome. Mindreading is no longer the linchpin. If this is not what proponents of the mindreading-first view mean by "social complexity," then they need to be clearer about what they do mean. Clearly they mean more than just larger group size, as it is unclear whether group size alone predicts primate cognitive sophistication, or even whether group sizes large enough to require increasing cognitive sophistication could be maintained for significant periods of time without sophisticated cooperation and coordination, and the mindshaping that makes them possible.

9. Not everyone is so sanguine about the reliability of propositional attitude tracking. For example, Nichols and Stich (2003) provide evidence that we are far less reliable mindreaders than we typically take ourselves to be. However, even they admit that it is hard to see how human mindreading can have evolved if it were not, on the whole, reliable (p. 66). The phenomenology of mindreading may be misleading in its presumption of reliability; however, it is clear that sophisticated mindreading occupies a lot of our time and neural resources. It is hard to see how such a capacity could remain stable in a population without positively affecting fitness. And it is hard to see how it could positively affect fitness without being reliable.

10. I thank Shannon Spaulding for pointing this possibility out to me.

11. I thank J. Robert Thompson for expressing this point in this way in personal correspondence.

12. I do not think that it is obvious that Davidson is right about this. While it is easy to overstate human cognitive heterogeneity, it is also easy to understate it. Many human beings do not have the concept of a meter. This seems to preclude any beliefs about how far the moon is from the earth in meters. It is not implausible that human beings of different genders, ages, socioeconomic classes and cultures fail to share large numbers of significant dispositional beliefs. However, I think the case for

behaviorally relevant cognitive heterogeneity can be made without questioning Davidson's basic assumption. So in what follows, I grant it: human beings are overwhelmingly homogeneous in dispositional beliefs. As I will show, this is still not enough to explain the reliability of fast and frugal theory of mind heuristics.

13. Oddly, Nichols and Stich (2003) draw the opposite conclusion, arguing that the inaccuracy of desire attribution supports the view that it is not the result of simulation (p. 136). Their reasons for this are somewhat obscure. They refer to an earlier passage where they argue that our accuracy at predicting others' *inferences*, even in situations that we have not encountered before, shows that inference prediction must be simulation based. But their only evidence of our accuracy at predicting inferences is that "the so-called 'heuristics and biases' tradition in cognitive social psychology chronicling the ways in which people make what appear to be very bad inferences … [offers no evidence] that people are bad at *predicting* inferences" (p. 105). I suggest an easier explanation: that question did not interest investigators. In fact, they admit that the question has not been studied systematically (p. 105). Furthermore, they give no reason for thinking that simulation would be any more accurate than theory. Prima facie this seems implausible. The reason is that idiosyncratic biases affect what we are prepared to infer. This is how fast and frugal heuristics like "Take the Best" work: what we infer depends on the previous inferences that happen to have worked for us; I may infer German city size based on the presence of a professional soccer team, while you fail to make this inference, focusing instead on crime rates. Even more dramatically, think of the difference between what a fundamentalist Christian and a secular atheist infer from the establishment of the modern state of Israel. The point is that what we are disposed to infer from a belief depends on indefinitely many idiosyncratic and difficult-to-detect background beliefs. So simulation does not guarantee accuracy in the attribution of inferential dispositions. Therefore we have no reason to suppose that desire attribution cannot be a product of simulation because it is typically inaccurate. In fact, citing the same evidence concerning the endowment effect, Goldman (2006) argues that simulation does underlie desire attribution (pp. 166–167).

14. Similarly, if how one remembers a high-profile event depends on the idiosyncratic experiential contexts in which one has recalled the event in intervening years, as Neisser and Harsh (2000) argue, reliable memory attribution and behavior prediction by someone who also witnessed the event would require somehow learning of these intervening experiential contexts, of which even the interpretive target may not be aware. It is implausible that any mindreading process could accomplish such a feat, let alone a fast and computationally frugal one.

15. As I suggested in chapter 1 and argue for at length in chapters 4 and 5.

16. I thank Eric Saidel for raising this problem after reading an earlier version of the argument I present here.

17. This is particularly puzzling given the fact, increasingly appreciated in the literature, that most nonhuman and early human infant social cognition, and much human adult social cognition, can succeed with the kind of subtle behavior tracking made possible by primary and secondary intersubjectivity (Gallagher, 2001, 2008; Gallagher & Hutto, 2008; Hutto, 2008). If such reliable and efficient sociocognitive capacities are already present in a population, then it is hard to see how a mutant with the largely redundant and far less efficient capacity to attribute propositional attitudes could outcompete her conspecifics.

18. This problem is compounded by the fact that many forms of human coordination important both today and among our precursors require anticipating the behavior of relatively large numbers of individuals. If this requires sophisticated mindreading, then interpreters need to track the propositional attitudes of numerous interpretive targets simultaneously. As Bermúdez (2003b) points out, this makes the efficacy of propositional attitude tracking in facilitating the coordinative feats typical of human populations even more mysterious.

19. I say "appear" because I think much of this evidence can be reinterpreted as showing that infants and nonhuman primates adopt versions of the intentional stance, with no commitment to the existence of mental states as such. More on this in chapter 6, devoted to the ontogeny of human social cognition.

20. Carruthers (2006, pp. 355–356) acknowledges that System 2 cognition is acquired from one's culture via various mindshaping mechanisms, like pedagogy, imitation, and norm enforcement. Consequently System 2 mindreading presupposes rather than makes possible sophisticated mindshaping, in line with the thesis of this book.

21. As well as many other kinds of mental states that likely dominate the mental lives of nonhuman animals in the wild, e.g., fear, wariness, aggression, sexual interest.

22. I discuss the view that nonlinguistic social cognition involves adopting a version of the intentional stance in far greater depth in chapter 6, in the context of a discussion of the ontogeny of human mindreading. There I argue that this view is superior to the more common view that nonlinguistic social cognition involves mindreading that employs either theory-like mechanisms or simulation.

23. Gergely (2011, p. 96) makes a similar point:

[Perhaps] non-human primates apply a *naïve "theory of food"* instead of a naïve "theory of mind" as an adaptive mechanism to deal with the contingencies of a social environment that is highly competitive over food resources. This could result from the selection of an adaptive strategy to monitor and represent the relevant properties of items (or sources) of food, such as their location, quantity, elapsed time of presence … and relevant environmental constraints. … If the primate observer detects that the monitored food item has become "attentionally contaminated" by the perceptual regard of a conspecific appearing from the East, this significant contingent fact will become represented as a kind of dispositional property of the monitored food item (and *not* of the mind of the conspecific). Such an object representation would imply that if the same environmental conditions are re-instated in the future by the conspecific's reappearance, the primate observer could correctly anticipate that the "attentionally contaminated" food item will be approached and consumed by the conspecific.

24. But can't a similar argument rescue propositional attitude tracking from the charge of computational intractability? One problem with this is that propositional attitudes are not observable completions of behavioral patterns, so it is hard to see how a statistical, pattern-completing learning algorithm could learn to pair propositional attitudes with observed behaviors. Tracking unobservable states requires something like abductive inference: proposing hypotheses about the unobservable causes of observed behavior and then deciding between them based on evidence and other nonempirical epistemic virtues like simplicity and coherence with other information. Also, as I have pointed out, a priori, it seems as though any finite set of propositional attitudes is compatible with any finite sequence of behavior. It is not clear how the statistics of past interpretive efforts can shrink this hypothesis space, since those statistics concern only correlations between observable behaviors occurring in finite patterns, all of which are compatible with an indefinite variety of finite sets of propositional attitudes.

25. Recently, Apperly and Butterfill (2009) have made congenial points about System 1 mindreading. They argue that a cognitively efficient yet limited and inflexible belief reasoning system, characteristic of nonhuman animal and human infant theory of mind, need not represent beliefs as such. However, contrary to what I have argued, they claim that it does represent states that guide action similarly to the way beliefs do, though these states are unlike beliefs in several respects, including lacking propositional content. So it seems that they think System 1 mindreading tracks what I have been calling attenuated propositional attitudes. In fact, they argue that the states tracked by System 1 mindreading must be attenuated in precisely the way I have suggested: their connection to behavior is not tenuous and holistically mediated (p. 957). It is not clear to me why such a system needs to track states of any kind, rather than patterns of behavior, for the reasons I have given. In either case, however, Apperly and Butterfill's framework is compatible with the thesis of this book, since the System 1 mindreading they describe is available to nonhuman species and so does not distinguish human from nonhuman mindreading. Hence it cannot be used to explain the phylogeny of the human sociocognitive syndrome. I thank Shannon Spaulding for drawing my attention to Apperly and Butterfill's paper.

26. One alternative I will not consider at length is the suggestion that propositional attitudes are nothing but dispositions to engage in distinctive patterns of behavior (Ryle, 1949; Schwitzgebel, 2002). This is certainly not what proponents of the received view of mindreading have in mind when they talk of propositional attitudes. Although sophisticated versions of this proposal, like Schwitzgebel's (2002), are attractive in many respects, they also face many challenges. For example, if the belief that P is just the disposition to behave in certain ways, it is unclear how it can

count as a premise in a practical inference. In any case, the kinds of dispositions that Schwitzgebel claims one must be able to track to attribute belief are arguably unavailable to nonhuman animals: they include an understanding of exceptions to typical behaviors associated with belief and practices of excusing such exceptions. So even if we accept Schwitzgebel's sophisticated dispositionalist account of belief, it will turn out that tracking the behavioral dispositions constitutive of beliefs is impossible without the sophisticated cooperative, communicative, and mindshaping practices of which only humans are capable.

4   Mindshaping and the Phylogeny of Human Cooperation

1. I do not think this jeopardizes any assumptions about our biological continuity with the rest of nature. Such idiosyncratic evolutionary trajectories abound in nature, e.g., the peacock's tail. They are typically the effects of internal dynamics involving positive feedback loops, in the case of the peacock's tail, runaway sexual selection (Cronin, 1991). Although the human sociocognitive syndrome has had significantly more dramatic effects on our own species, other species, and indeed the whole planet than have other internally driven, idiosyncratic evolutionary trajectories, such by-products do not change the fact that the trajectory of our lineage is no more mysterious than other internally driven trajectories. Ross (2007) argues that human biological uniqueness is even more pronounced: that human beings evolve at cultural as well as biological scales introduces new parameters into the dynamics required to model human evolution. If Ross is right, then we are even more unique than what I have suggested here. However, even in this view, our uniqueness is not mysterious. Such "phase shifts" in evolutionary dynamics have occurred before, e.g., perhaps with the evolution of sexually reproducing species.

2. Similar temptations to free ride are obvious in other biologically central domains: if mate access depends on the cooperative self-exclusion of potential competitors, a free-riding individual could take advantage of this while not excluding herself from others' mates; if nutrition depends on cooperative hunts from which meat is evenly distributed, a free rider could eat the meat without contributing to the hunt; if successful reproduction depends on cooperative nurturing and protection of offspring, a free rider could take advantage of other caretakers caring for her offspring while not helping with their offspring; and so on.

3. This has long been recognized as one of the principal boons of distinctively human cultural learning: Boyd and Richerson (1996) call this "cumulative cultural evolution," and Tomasello (1999) calls it the "ratchet" effect.

4. Sterelny identifies a number of reasons for this. First, since the audience is likely to vary in its level of ignorance, what might deceive one member will not deceive another. It becomes extraordinarily difficult for an individual inclined toward deceptive free riding to craft a deceptive message that will work on everyone. Second, participants in such public information pooling are in symmetrical infor-

mational positions: each is ignorant about some things and knowledgeable about others. This makes possible direct reciprocity as a mechanism for ensuring cooperation and honesty. I contribute all I know because I can learn what you know in exchange. Third, if information pooling takes place independently and in advance of using the information in deliberation and planning, then, as Sterelny puts it, this "impose[s] a veil of ignorance between a potentially Machiavellian agent and potential targets. That veil undermines the planning connection between false signal and Machiavellian consequences" (2012, p. 139). Potential deceivers cannot tell how the information they contribute will be used, and so cannot predict whether it will have the consequences they desire.

5. Sterelny (2012, pp. 74–75) argues that the ancestors of human and protohuman megafaunal hunters were already probably more cooperatively disposed than contemporary chimps, due to the requirements of collective defense against predators on the savanna and the need for cooperative child rearing due to prolonged childhood. Thus cooperative predator defense and child care must be added to the other cooperative activities that Sterelny hypothesizes. Together, this cooperative suite likely required substantially larger groupings than seen in contemporary chimpanzees. This would naturally increase the likelihood of interactions among small numbers of participants out of sight of the whole group, in which free riding would not have the disincentives that Sterelny highlights.

6. Sterelny tends to downplay such possibilities, arguing that gossip and other forms of information "leakage" could help dissuade such "ecological parasites" (2012, pp. 127, 183). This is not obvious. For one thing, it presumes that such gossip is trustworthy, which requires solving another cooperation problem, i.e., honest communication. Although Sterelny addresses this problem (2012, p. 183), I am not persuaded by his response. He assumes that the reliability of gossip could be maintained in the same way as the reliability of other forms of public communication: multisourcing and multitargeting could reduce incentives for deception. But all it takes to introduce false information into a gossip network is the deceiver's "seeding" the network via a private exchange with a particularly influential member. Hume (1748/1993) describes precisely this dynamic when discussing the unreliability of testimony to the miraculous. Also, since gossip often concerns anecdotes of unrepeated events, multisourcing is far less feasible than in, e.g., the communication of ecological or technological information. Furthermore, as Sterelny himself acknowledges (p. 140), gossip requires complex language, and it is not clear that this was available at the relevant point in prehistory. Sterelny pays more attention to the problem of controlling free riders than to the problem of detecting them. He argues that the former problem could be solved through punishment coalitions united by bonds of trust made possible through commitment signaling (pp. 103–113). I defend a broadly similar picture of mindshaping's role in enabling cooperation in this chapter and the next.

7. The evidence provided by Csibra and Gergely in favor of their natural pedagogy hypothesis, which I noted in chapter 2 and will discuss further in chapter 6, is also well explained in Sterelny's theory, as he himself recognizes (2012, p. 144).

8. Why should imitators find matching model behavior intrinsically rewarding? They should be motivated to match models only to the extent that doing so helps them achieve some further instrumental goal, like being a better hunter. Why should imitators be maximally flexible in the aspects of model behavior that they can match? All that should matter is matching the goals or abstract structure of the behavior—as in the "cognitive imitation" of which rhesus macaques are capable. Copying the precise behavioral means by which a model accomplishes a goal, e.g., wields a tool or weapon, might even be a hindrance to skill acquisition, since individuals of different sizes, with different body dynamics, often need to engage in different fine-grained bodily motions to accomplish similar goals. The materials that early humans fashioned into tools also require a sensitivity to idiosyncratic constraints: as Carruthers (2006) notes, the stone cores from which symmetrical hand axes and blades were fashioned "are always to some degree unique in shape, size, and the details of their material composition; hence each core presents a unique challenge" (p. 147). Given this, imitating a model's goal or finished product would seem much more apposite than imitating her fine-grained behavior. Finally, Sterelny's story does not explain why so much human mindshaping should involve matching the behavior of nonactual individuals, like fictional characters or idealized agents.

9. If information sharing is restricted to small subgroups of specialists, it is easier for free riders to gauge others' knowledge and engage in effective deception. Also, the steepened "information gradient" (Sterelny, 2012, p. 148; Dennett, 1983, 1988) makes deception of nonspecialists easier: with more division of labor and specialization, most group members with whom a specialist must interact know little of the specialist's domain of expertise and so are vulnerable to deception. For example, with little knowledge of the effort required for some type of specialized foraging, it is difficult for "customers" to gauge whether or not trades proposed by specialists are fair. Given that specialist foragers extract resources alone or in small teams, few of their groups' other members could have firsthand knowledge of their reliability; this contrasts with the extremely public displays of reliability available in large-scale group hunts of megafauna.

10. Bermúdez (2003b) makes this point about contemporary human social cognition as part of an argument against the viability of simulation as a mechanism for accurate mindreading.

11. Kinderman et al. (1998) drew lessons for the causes of paranoid symptoms in some forms of schizophrenia from the study. Prominent among such symptoms is the tendency to explain failed social interactions in terms of external *personal* factors, like the character of one's interactants, instead of external *situational* factors,

like circumstances in which one's interactants find themselves—the normal explanatory strategy. Kinderman et al. hypothesized that explanations in terms of external situational factors require an ability to appreciate others' points of view, hence theory of mind competence. That paranoid schizophrenics tend to focus on enduring negative character traits rather than on transient situational factors suggests that paranoid schizophrenics' ability to appreciate others' points of view, and hence their theory of mind, are impaired. To test this, Kinderman et al. evaluated theory of mind ability, i.e., the ability to attribute intentional states of increasingly higher orders, in a population of normals, dividing the population into high- and low-functioning mindreaders. They then identified a correlation between low-functioning mindreading and a more paranoid causal-explanatory style: normals who were poorer at attributing higher-order intentional states had a stronger tendency to explain failed interactions in terms of others' enduring negative character traits instead of transient situational factors.

12. I anticipate an obvious response to this line of argument: just because attributing mental states of higher orders *seems* difficult, rare, and unreliable based on its phenomenology does not mean that some unconscious subpersonal cognitive module does not frequently excel at this. This objection is not persuasive. Deception and deception detection are precisely the sorts of capacities for which modularized, or fast and frugal, subpersonal cognitive mechanisms are unsuited. Deception depends on undermining reliable links between observable behavior and its typical cognitive etiology. But these are precisely the sorts of links on which the reliability of modularized or fast and frugal social cognition depends. Some argue that we have unconscious subpersonal capacities to recognize second- or even third-order mental states, e.g., Gricean communicative intentions (Sperber, 2000). But such capacities, even if this is an appropriate way to characterize them (about which I defend doubts in chapter 6), depend for their reliability precisely on distinctive, stereotyped behavioral signatures, like eye contact followed by shifts in gaze (Csibra, 2010). Deception seeks to undermine such strong links between behavior and mental states, so it is unlikely to be detectable by subpersonal, modularized, or fast and frugal social cognition.

13. *Pace* Hurley (2005b). I say more about Hurley's argument that solving such coordination problems is the raison d'être of human mindreading in section 4.

14. Kelly (1985) documents what appears to be a historical case of such intergroup competition: the case of the Nuer and the Dinka, two ethnic groups occupying adjacent regions in southern Sudan in the eighteenth and nineteenth centuries. Over about a hundred years, starting in 1820, the Nuer expanded their territory at the expense of the Dinka, driving them off, killing them, or assimilating them. The two groups were similar in technological sophistication and shared the same environment. However, they differed substantially in socioeconomic organization: the Nuer's patrilineal kin system allowed them to organize in much larger numbers across much wider geographic areas than the small-group Dinka. The group with better social organization won out in this competition. If such dynamics occurred

frequently in human prehistory, there would have been strong selection pressures for individuals capable of participating in sophisticated, large-scale social organizations, i.e., individuals with prosocial dispositions.

15. Indeed, Henrich (2004, p. 29) notes that if human beings tend to preferentially imitate successful models (the prestige bias), and if different groups frequently come into contact, then members of less cooperative and hence less successful groups will tend to imitate the behavior of members of more cooperative and hence more successful groups. In this way, prosocial practices can rapidly spread between groups (see also Henrich & Gil-White, 2001).

16. Note the confluence between the requirements on fast and frugal social cognition discussed in chapter 3 and the requirements on group selection for prosocial dispositions. Both require homogeneity within populations. Homogeneity makes other group members easier to predict using fast and frugal sociocognitive resources and also enables group selection for prosocial dispositions.

17. In fact, Henrich (2004) argues that prestige bias is at the root of one of the principal mechanisms of group selection: members of less successful groups should adopt the norms of more successful groups if they are biased to imitate the behavior of more successful individuals.

18. The clearest illustrations of this involve experiments testing behavior on the so-called ultimatum game. Recall from chapter 2 that the ultimatum game characterizes a kind of interaction between two individuals: the proposer has all the money and must propose a distribution of it to the recipient. If the recipient accepts the proposed distribution, the money is distributed accordingly. If the recipient rejects the proposed distribution, neither participant gets any money. Rejection is always costly, since no matter how little the proposer proposes to share with the recipient, it is better than nothing. However, across all human cultures that have been studied, recipients always reject minimal offers. So human beings have a disposition to incur a cost to punish counternormative resource distributions.

19. See also Sterelny (2003, pp. 126–127). Such recursive hierarchies of punishment are familiar from everyday life. For example, employees charged with policing customers to ensure that they pay their fair share are themselves subject to sanction if they fail to do so.

20. This reflects the familiar attitude of an employee deflecting responsibility for sanctioning a client by "kicking it up a level," e.g., by saying, "Sorry, it's against the rules," or "Sorry, just doing my job."

21. Here and throughout, it is important to keep in mind that I mean "punishment" in the broadest possible sense. What counts as punishment depends on what human beings find unpleasant enough to act as a deterrent of some type of behavior. So, for example, if human beings value the attention of other human beings, or compete for the attention of other human beings, then behavior that leads others to

attend less to one person than to others is, in effect, being punished. Similarly for other indicators of status: since human beings, like other primates, value status, the subtlest indication that one is losing status, or someone else is gaining it at one's expense, can function as punishment. Thus, if it is the case, as Michael Wilby has suggested to me, that we tend more to praise those who stand up to norm flouters (think of the high esteem in which Gandhi or Mandela are held) than punish those who do not, such praise can function as an indirect form of punishment for those who want praise and the status that comes with it. Boehm (1999) documents the various subtle forms of sanctioning that many contemporary hunter-gatherer tribes, like the !Kung, use to enforce egalitarian distribution norms, among which mockery or ridicule are prominent. These clearly punish counternormative behavior via verbal assaults on status. Punishment need not involve beating with sticks or physical coercion of any kind. Recent evidence indicates that social rejection can activate the same neural, somatosensory representations as physical pain (Kross et al., 2011). Given the intense value that human beings put on status, as indicated by attention and regard from our fellows, it is relatively easy to imagine sanctioning regimes that take advantage of this.

22. Doesn't such conformism make costly punishment otiose, however? Recall that Henrich introduces costly punishment into his model because he argues that conformism in human populations is not strong enough to counteract the effects of prestige bias, which should ultimately encourage countersocial dispositions in all groups. Perhaps this puzzle can be resolved if conformist dispositions are stronger for punishment than for other forms of prosocial behavior. Henrich (personal communication) suggests that if punishment is relatively rare, then the status differences between those who punish and those who do not should be too small to trigger the prestige bias, and punishment should be driven almost exclusively by the conformist bias. This should especially be the case with higher-order punishment, i.e., the sanctioning of failures to punish at lower levels. According to Henrich, the frequency of such behavior decreases geometrically as one ascends the punishment hierarchy. If he is right, then the effects of failure to engage in higher-order punishment on prestige should be minimal, and hence the conformist bias should not be diluted by the prestige bias in this domain.

23. "Norm internalization," described by Sripada and Stich (2006) and noted in chapter 2, plays an obviously important role in such emotion-driven, automatic conformity to prosocial norms. There is also recent evidence concerning the neural basis for guilt aversion as a motivation for cooperative behavior (Chang et al., 2011).

24. Tomasello et al. (2005) argue that distinctively human cooperation is possible due to an innate, distinctively human capacity for *sharing* mental states, especially intentions. But such sharing can be understood in at least two ways. If it involves first uncovering another's propositional attitudes, and then trying to replicate them in oneself, then it runs into all the difficulties with reliable yet timely sophisticated mindreading discussed previously. If it involves no such mindreading and instead

relies on the kinds of mindshaping phenomena discussed previously, in which attempts to conform to patterns of behavior happen to induce shared mental states, then sharing mental states is often a result of mindshaping, and Tomasello et al.'s notion of sharing fits nicely with the notion of mindshaping. The notion of sharing mental states raises other questions as well. Does it require that parties to such sharing end up in *type-identical* mental states, e.g., both intending the same action? Such sharing would have limited use in facilitating cooperation, since this often requires collaborators to be in different, though complementary, mental states. Perhaps the idea is that, in sharing a mental state, collaborators form a plural subject that realizes a collective intentional state (Gilbert, 1996, 2009). This is, indeed, an important component of human cooperation; section 4 is devoted to discussing it. However, as I argue there, it is not clear that implementing such collective intentional states requires parties to them to engage in sophisticated mindreading. Nor does it always require being in type-identical individual mental states.

25. Of course, in the contemporary world, punishment often requires establishing that the transgressor had the appropriate intentions, etc. But as long as punishing counternormative behavior alone, irrespective of its cognitive etiology, had cooperation-enhancing effects in prehistory, there is no need to attribute such sophisticated, mindreading-dependent practices to our prehistorical ancestors. Later, as practices of punishment became more complex, transgressors could perhaps cite ignorance or good intentions to avoid punishment for counternormative behavior, and this gave rise to contemporary practices in which punishment requires establishing that transgressors are motivated in the right way. I say more about this in chapter 7.

26. That is, each agent prefers that both pick "Hi" over both picking "Lo," and prefers that both pick "Lo" over the two unmatched alternatives, and is indifferent between the unmatched alternatives.

27. This, argues Gilbert, is the main advantage of her account of joint commitment over what she calls the "summative account" (1996, p. 2)—the view that joint commitments are mere sums of individual commitments (as in, e.g., Bratman, 1993). The summative account cannot explain why parties to a joint commitment are *entitled* to sanction parties who unilaterally shirk the commitments: on what grounds could parties complain if the shirker was merely changing her individual desires or intentions? Gilbert (2009) has recently updated this argument. According to what she calls the "concurrence criterion," parties to a shared intention cannot be released from, rescind, or change it without the concurrence of all parties (p. 173).

28. It is not clear why such low-level mindshaping can have such dramatic effects on social bonding and cooperation. Perhaps behavioral synchrony acts as a signal of like-mindedness, and, as I have stressed, interacting with the like-minded is key to coordinative and cooperative success.

29. I thank Richard Moore for drawing my attention to the study reported in Kirschner and Tomasello (2010).

30. The word "expectation" can be understood in a purely descriptive sense, i.e., as a prediction about the future, as in, "we expect it to rain tonight," or in a normative sense, i.e., as a prescription governing behavior, as in, "we expect you to wear a tie to the office."

31. Indeed, Wiltermuth and Heath's (2009) demonstration that behavioral mimicry is sufficient to induce the kind of trust required for coordination on cooperative projects to succeed seems to refute Hurley's claim that sophisticated mindreading is necessary to distinguish trustworthy coordination partners from free riders who fake signals of trustworthiness (Hurley, 2005b, pp. 600–601). It seems that, in the circumstances in which human coordinative and cooperative capacities likely evolved, behavioral synchrony was a sufficient signal of trustworthiness. This makes sense if such capacities are products of group selection, and default, complementary cooperative and coordinative dispositions dominate groups due to mechanisms of mindshaping. It does not make sense if successful cooperation and coordination rely on sophisticated mindreading selected for via a coevolutionary arms race between deception and deception detection.

32. Sterelny (2012, p. 145) makes a similar point.

33. The data supporting the existence of a "cheater detection module"—one of the foundational hypotheses of evolutionary psychology—are also consistent with mindshaping-centered models of cooperation. I briefly described these data in chapter 1: human subjects appear to show a domain-specific capacity to evaluate the truth of conditional statements of the form "If A, then B." In nondeontic contexts, they fail to verify whether cases in which B is false are cases in which A is true. However, this oversight disappears in deontic contexts: given the rule "If a person is drinking alcohol, then she must be at least twenty-one years old," subjects not only check the age of those drinking but also check whether those younger than twenty-one are drinking. Such dispositions are arguably involved in norm enforcing, and hence mindshaping, behavior. Note that no mindreading appears necessary here: norm violations can be detected entirely on the basis of nonmental properties, like behavior (e.g., drinking alcohol) and status (e.g., having reached drinking age).

34. In fact, given individual variation in bodily dynamics and materials used for, e.g., tool construction, imitating goals or finished products seems better suited to the functions that Sterelny attributes to mindshaping than imitating precise behavioral means.

35. For example, the disposition of human children from a variety of cultures to "overimitate" (Nielsen & Tomaselli, 2010).

36. As I noted earlier, we have at least one historically documented case of an ethnic group (the Nuer) outcompeting a rival ethnic group (the Dinka) due to social organization that permitted coordination among larger numbers of more geographically dispersed members.

5   Sophisticated Mindreading and the Phylogeny of Language

1. Ultimately this requires regulation of the causes of behavior, i.e., states of mind, so behavior regulation requires mindshaping of some kind.

2. As I suggested in chapter 2, there is no reason to conceive of infant intention detection as involving the attribution of full-blown propositional attitudes. In chapter 6, I provide further grounds for doubting that prelinguistic infants attribute full-blown propositional attitudes in the course of behavior tracking that appears sensitive to their targets' false beliefs.

3. In fact, as Sperber and Wilson (1995) argue, inferring communicative intentions relies on assumptions of cooperative dispositions, so this model of the evolution of language presupposes the kinds of mindshaping necessary to give rise to cooperative dispositions via group selection.

4. Assumptions are like facts but not necessarily true. They are propositions the communicator takes to be true.

5. As Bermúdez (2003b, 2009) argues, certain behaviors, including productive and receptive communicative acts, constitute parts of familiar scripts, frames, or scenarios, like birthday parties or restaurant outings, for example. Without doing any mindreading, we can expect others to behave in ways that conform to such stereotypical interactive contexts. Mindshaping practices and mechanisms can ensure that members of the same pool of likely interlocutors have similar expectations about such contexts.

6. I say "culturally specific" because communication norms can vary dramatically between cultures. For example, Kato (2000, pp. 35–36) notes that in Japanese culture, language is often used to hide one's true intentions. For example, a child who wants a piece of cake at a dinner party might repeatedly deny this when asked by the host. The host takes such denials as conventional expressions of reserve, masking the child's true desires. The appropriate response, on the part of the host, is to almost force the cake on the child, knowing that the child really wants it but must overtly deny wanting it to abide by reserve-enforcing interaction norms. In such cases, we need not interpret the host as reading the child's mind. Rather, she may simply realize that the most rational explanation of the child's overt refusals is that the child is concealing her desire for the cake to abide by Japanese interaction norms. This is the sense in which I claim the human capacity for communication might deploy a culturally specific, communication-dedicated version of the intentional stance.

7. For example, if I see someone with a paper plate and plastic fork in hand, scanning the room with a puzzled look on her face, I need only ask what makes that pattern of behavior rational in context to produce a relevant utterance like "The cake is in the other room." Given the context, the best rationalization of the behavior, relative to tacit, culturally specific assumptions that products of similar mind-

shaping practices are likely to share, is that the agent is looking for the birthday cake. Of course, this interpretation is not forced by the behavior; deeper mindreading would require ruling out indefinitely many interpretations equally compatible with it. But this would jeopardize rapid communication.

8. This perspective applies as much to the interpretive task facing the audience as the communicative task facing the speaker. Consider an analogy borrowed from Susan Haack's (1993) exposition of her "foundherentist" epistemology: the crossword puzzle. Deciphering crossword puzzles is like interpreting extremely cryptic, linguistically encoded messages. But no mindreading is involved. Typically one does not even know the puzzler and so has no evidence of the psychological states implicated in constructing the puzzle. To solve a crossword puzzle, one simply adopts something like the intentional stance to narrow the space of possible words compatible with the clues. Typically this requires an extremely parochial version of the intentional stance—one that works only for members of one's subculture: the population of individuals who read the same books, see the same movies, follow the same sports, and so on, as the puzzler. Knowledge of spelling and other formal properties of words provides further constraints. But no mindreading is involved. It is true that, in being guided by culturally specific, rational norms and orthography, one ends up reading the puzzler's mind. But that is more like a side effect of deciphering the normatively most plausible message based on clues and other constraints. Because puzzlers and puzzle solvers are products of similar mindshaping, interpretation is possible without mindreading.

9. In this section, I focus on recent prominent philosophical critiques of Dennett's claim that quotidian interpretation involves adopting the intentional stance. I provide further empirical support for Dennett's approach in chapter 6, where I focus on the ontogeny of human mindreading.

10. Although I claim earlier that many find such authorial modesty "natural," this is not the same as claiming that we do not consider it irrational or attribute propositional attitudes underlying it independently of a rationality assumption. People say many things that we find natural, perhaps because they are statistically prevalent idioms, although they are irrational and, because of this, compromise easy interpretability, for example, atheists thanking God.

11. As Shannon Spaulding has pointed out to me, it is possible for the theory-theorist to accommodate the fact that interpreters often react to anomalous behavior with criticism. Perhaps a two-stage process is involved: first mental states are attributed independently of any assumption of rationality, and then the behavior is evaluated for rationality, prompting criticism if it is found to be wanting in this respect. Although this process is possible, I think the often extremely rapid triggering of critical responses to behavior perceived as irrational favors the intentional stance over the theory-theory. It often seems almost as though the act of interpretation includes automatic monitoring for counternormative behavior. However, I acknowl-

edge that this line of argument is highly impressionistic, and a definitive verdict must await empirical research on whether it is possible to dissociate interpretation from sensitivity to normative status.

12. This is more than merely a desperate ploy to make Dennett's proposal palatable. As I argue in chapter 6, good evidence indicates that behavioral interpretation by very young infants involves attributing, to short bouts of behavior, goals and means of achieving them that are rational in the light of immediately available information. This suggests that the earliest and hence "default" objects of human interpretation are short bouts of behavior. It is likely that interpretations are attributed to enduring persons only later, on the basis of prior interpretations of bouts of behavior.

13. It is true that early versions of Dennett's proposal focused exclusively on rationality; however, later, in response to criticism by Stich (1981), he acknowledges that interpretation will sometimes involve supplementation by nonrational principles (Dennett, 1987, pp. 53–54).

14. I consider other advantages of the intentional stance over competing theories of behavior interpretation and prediction in chapter 6. There I focus on mindreading and mindshaping in contemporary human ontogeny. I argue that the alleged mindreading skills of which preverbal infants appear capable and seem to require to acquire language are better conceived of as capacities to apply the intentional stance, that is, to parse observable behavior into goals and rationally and informationally constrained means of achieving them.

15. For example, the syntax of English enables me to generate an arbitrarily long noun phrase composed of nested lower-order noun phrases, as in "The house behind the hill, by the river, in the valley, beyond the meadow. ..." The reason is that there is a syntactic rule according to which a noun phrase can be composed of a determiner ("the"), a noun ("house") and a qualifier that can be a prepositional phrase ("behind the hill"), which itself can be composed of a preposition ("behind") and another noun phrase ("the hill"), to which the general noun phrase rule once again applies.

16. Bickerton (1990) sees the language of two-year-olds and pidgin languages as linguistic fossils from which we can infer the properties of the protolanguage. Classic pidgins are communication systems improvised by slaves with no common language in colonized lands. They use the lexicon of the colonial power to produce short, unsystematic strings sufficient for most quotidian purposes. Interestingly, offspring of pidgin users automatically impose a grammatical structure on the unsystematic communication they hear from their parents, thereby producing creoles. Two-year-olds likewise employ unsystematic two- or three-word strings in their communicative acts.

17. The same logic explains the evolution of the peacock's tail.

18. According to one theory, energy-intensive display is a reliable signal of mate quality because it correlates with an effective immune system (Cronin, 1991, pp. 198–200): fighting off bacteria and other parasites is not a significant drain for an individual capable of lengthy, complex, and predator-attracting birdsong.

19. Sterelny (2012, pp. 109–113) argues that commitment signaling, though costly and hard to fake, is not akin to phenomena like birdsong. I agree that there are important distinctions, many of which Sterelny identifies. However, birdsong and commitment signaling share many properties relevant to my purpose here: explaining how human communication became structurally complex without assuming that it evolved to express analogously structured, preexisting thought. Both birdsong and commitment signaling were subject to selection pressures for increasing complexity, and for similar reasons: just as more complex birdsong is an honest signal of underlying genetic quality, I argue hereafter that more complex, ritualistic communication in human prehistory was an honest signal of cooperative skills and motivations. Sterelny is probably right that group rituals had, in addition, more complex bonding functions and effects on socioecological niche (pp. 110–111). But all that matters to my story is that there existed, in human prehistory, selection for ever more complex commitment signaling. Nothing in Sterelny's account of commitment signaling contradicts this.

20. Scott Atran (2002) likewise defends this view as part of his theory of the evolution of religion and religious ritual.

21. Mustering tribal war parties likely constituted a less regular form of interaction at this level.

22. Although the fossil and archaeological records are not detailed enough to date the emergence of this socioecology with any precision, there is no doubt that it emerged at some point in the last 100,000 years. This nested hierarchy of group affiliations characterizes not just contemporary hunter-gatherer populations but, arguably, all human populations. Consider the typical academic who must regularly manage interactions at the level of her family, department, college, university, and various professional organizations, not to mention merchants and service providers of various kinds. All such interactions are extremely important to survival and flourishing, yet only a small fraction of them depend on intimate personal knowledge of interactants. In fact, as Paul Seabright (2010) argues, our capacity to coordinate with complete strangers is the key sociocognitive innovation distinctive of our species.

23. Gintis et al. (2006) provide further reasons to expect such biologically central cooperative interactions with relative strangers. First, prehistoric foraging groups were likely maintained for relatively short periods of about thirty years due to population contractions and even crashes caused by social and environmental crises (p. 26; see also Boone & Kessler, 1999; Keckler, 1997). Furthermore, if contemporary nonhuman primate and hunter-gatherer societies are appropriate models for prehistoric human populations, we have even greater reason to expect frequent interac-

tions with strangers: these contemporary populations experience a constant turnover of members. One of the primary reasons is exogamy: mating with out-group members, which protects against inbreeding. Contemporary foragers, for example, are far more outbred than even the simplest farming societies (Fix, 1999). Finally, Gintis et al. (2006) note that if interaction with strangers were rare, it would be unlikely that our cognitive and motivational systems would be finely tuned to degrees of familiarity; we would treat all persons in the same way, given that our sociocognitive capacities were selected for in environments dominated only by kin and other familiar individuals. But this is manifestly not the case. The evidence of sensitivity to familiarity in contemporary humans is overwhelming, from the "stranger anxiety" reliably displayed at developmental milestones (Greenberg et al., 1973) to the evidence cited in chapter 4 that neural areas activated during interpretive tasks vary depending on the degree to which the interpreter identifies with her interpretive target (Mitchell et al., 2006).

24. Hagen and Bryant (2003) argue that music and dance evolved to signal coalition quality in the context of intergroup warfare. Groups capable of elaborate coordination in rhythmic rituals were likely capable of elaborate coordination in martial endeavors and hence were likely seen as formidable enemies not worth engaging except as a last resort.

25. I thank an anonymous reviewer for drawing my attention to this issue.

26. The evidence of a direct link between rhythmic synchrony and cooperative behavior that I mentioned in chapter 4 provides a dramatic confirmation of this hypothesis. Recall that both adults (Wiltermuth & Heath, 2009) and four-year-old children (Kirschner & Tomasello, 2010) behave more cooperatively after engaging in bouts of rhythmic synchrony with each other.

27. Presumably this Bickertonian protolanguage could have been selected for transmitting information relevant to the kinds of free-rider-proof interactions that typified pre-BSM communal megafaunal hunting populations highlighted by Sterelny (2012). Recall that some kind of communication would have been required to support such lifeways, given their reliance on the reliable intergenerational transmission of cultural knowledge and coordination during difficult hunts.

28. This is arguably what happens in poetry and song: lexical units with semantic significance are arranged in complex ways based on their structural properties, e.g., phonology, rhythm, and rhyme, to yield performances with complex structure and often very creative and cognitively useful semantic juxtapositions.

29. This account constitutes an example of the unprincipled, opportunistic operation of natural selection. The evolution of an extremely useful and complex capacity—a form of communication capable of encoding propositions of arbitrary generality and complexity—is explained in terms of the integration of two far more limited capacities that happened to be present in early human populations for entirely unrelated reasons: an unstructured, lexical, Bickertonian protolanguage of

limited power used to transmit referential and predicative information relevant only to endeavors typical of pre-BSR hominins, and a largely meaningless though structurally complex ritualistic communication system used to honestly signal cooperative motivations and capacities. Out of these raw materials, selection gradually cobbled together language as we know it: an extremely powerful and flexible means of explicitly representing propositions of arbitrary complexity and scope.

30. This is essentially Frankish's (2004) notion of the "supermind." He argues that human cognition comes in two varieties: System 1 cognition is fast, automatic, unconscious, and largely innate, while System 2 cognition is slow, deliberate, conscious, and acquired from one's culture. For Frankish, System 2 cognition is made possible by discursive commitments expressed through linguistic self-attribution of beliefs. More on this in chapter 7.

31. Imagine a mutant human who does not waste valuable resources on indulgence in auditory cheesecake, devoting her savings to adaptive ends like becoming a better mindreader or using language to express her thoughts more effectively. In Pinker's view, such a mutant would outcompete the rest of us, have more offspring, and soon such "amusics" would dominate human populations. That is how natural selection works. But as soon as this proposal is so baldly stated, it is obvious how absurd it is. Such an individual would be a pariah and lose all the benefits of social intercourse that music and rhythmic performance in general make possible. Music is extremely important to our social identities. An amusic would find it exceedingly difficult to bond with, and earn the trust of, normal humans.

6   Mindreading and Mindshaping in Human Ontogeny

1. In many ways, these philosophers are strange bedfellows. However, they all argue that there is a special kind of propositional attitude attribution that requires relating speakers to claims made in a public language. This is the key idea defended in chapter 7.

2. Especially the kinds of normative attitudes that chapter 4 argued are key to explaining the phylogeny of distinctively human cooperation and coordination.

3. In chapter 7, I also discuss the importance of self-constituting narratives to sophisticated mindreading: because we can commit to behavior modeled on well-known characters in public narratives, we can make each other's behavior easier to predict.

4. Interestingly, when children younger than four years are asked what *they* thought was in the candy box before looking inside it, they make the same mistake: they attribute to their past selves the belief that the box contained crayons, though they actually claimed it contained candy.

5. The meta-analysis by Wellman et al. (2001) reviews a wide range of studies that support this timeline in the development of SFBT mastery. For critiques of this meta-analysis, see Yazdi et al. (2006).

6. In fact, supplementary evidence suggests that mastering a syntactically complex language is actually necessary for passing the SFBT. Deaf children of nonsigning parents are often massively delayed in acquiring syntactically complex language and show corresponding delays in passing the SFBT (de Villiers & de Villiers, 2000). This sort of evidence seems to support views like the one I defend: sophisticated mind-reading, i.e., the capacity to attribute full-blown propositional attitudes, presupposes discursive competence (see also Hutto, 2008).

7. The scenario with which Onishi and Baillargeon (2005) presented the infants was not precisely the same as in the original Sally-Anne task; I describe it this way only for ease of exposition. The fundamental structure of the scenario was the same, and nothing turns on the differences in details.

8. Onishi and Baillargeon also ran a true belief version of the task to make sure that infants do not just look longer, by default, at scenarios where Sally goes to the new toy/candy location. If Sally *sees* the toy/candy moved, the pattern of results is reversed: they look longer if she subsequently goes to where she left the toy/candy than if she goes to the new location, suggesting that infants understand that Sally has a true belief about the new location in this condition.

9. Of course, when it is put this baldly, most researchers impressed with the NVFBT results would adamantly deny such an interpretation. However, when one looks at their published discussions of such results, one encounters phrases like "The infants … had to reason that … the agent['s] … inference would lead the agent to form … [a] false belief that … would in turn lead the agent to falsely believe that. … Success in the false-belief conditions thus required the attribution of a complex, interlocking set of motivational states, reality-congruent informational states, and reality-incongruent informational states" (Scott & Baillargeon, 2009, p. 1192). Furthermore, all these researchers claim parity between what the SFBTs and the NVFBTs show about understanding belief. So if one thinks passing SFBTs is the most important milestone in the acquisition of the belief concept, then either one should reject this assumption (as I urge), or one must accept that passing NVFBTs is the most important milestone in the acquisition of the belief concept.

10. Apperly notes that "in a variety of studies using stories or real objects and using verbal or behavioural judgments, including scenarios where false belief and dual identity problems are very closely matched … the consistent pattern is that children who pass false belief tasks do not necessarily pass such Oedipus problems" (2011, p. 17).

11. Hutto (2008) makes closely related points very clearly and forcefully. For Hutto, to *fully* understand belief, i.e., as a potential reason for action, one must understand

how it conspires with other propositional attitudes and various noncognitive factors to lead to behavior. He argues that such understanding is not available until children have been exposed to folk psychological narratives, which illustrate how propositional attitudes and noncognitive factors typically interrelate to yield behavior.

12. Eighteen-month-old infants appear to consider only information that is perceptually available at the time when or immediately before the decision is taken. They do not seem capable of taking into account information to which their interpretive target had access much earlier, i.e., during the familiarization phase. As I noted earlier, this gives us reason to doubt that the infants are engaged in sophisticated mindreading. If they treated their interpretive target as having an enduring mind—a nexus of standing mental states with potential causal influence over behavior—then they would not expect her to reach for the opaque cover in the false belief condition of the test phase, given that she had herself assembled the two-piece penguin to look like the one-piece penguin in the familiarization phase.

13. Of course, such behavioral expectations are constantly, dynamically updated on the fly as teammates constantly monitor each other's behavior. So at one moment a player may expect a teammate to not be "pass-worthy," while the next moment a change in her demeanor (e.g., a quick glance in the direction of the ball) can induce a real-time revision of this expectation. Given the constant behavioral monitoring, and context-appropriate behavioral expectations, there appears to be no need for sophisticated mindreading, i.e., full-blown propositional attitude attribution.

14. Most infants are so spontaneously helpful that they do not need encouragement; they can't wait to get the key to help the adult unlock the box.

15. Here I am deliberately ignoring an important distinction within the theory-theory camp. Some theory-theorists see the process by which human infants acquire mature interpretive competence as exactly analogous to the process of theory formulation and confirmation in science. For example, three-year-olds are seen as working within a simple perception/desire paradigm that is increasingly unable to accommodate data. This leads to a Kuhnian revolution around age four, when children acquire the full concept of a belief, i.e., a mental state that can be false (Gopnik, 1996). Other theory-theorists see interpretive competence as embedded in a module that is fully formed at birth. Applying the information in this module to complex social stimuli is initially extremely difficult, given domain-general limitations on memory, attention, and executive function (Fodor, 1995). The developmental time course is explained in terms of the gradual easing of such performance limitations. This distinction within the theory-theory literature is irrelevant here. Both sides distinguish their view from the intentional stance hypothesis on the same basis: they claim that the principles of interpretation are nonnormative, make no appeal to rationality, and involve the attribution of unobservable mental states bearing nomic/causal relationships to stimuli, behavior, and each other.

16. The rudimentary sense of rationality at work here is slowly being elucidated through empirical evidence in Csibra and Gergely's paradigm, which I describe hereafter. It in no way implies that infants have a *concept* of rationality, at least not in the rich philosophical sense. The idea is merely that they display a differential sensitivity to behavioral patterns in which a goal is pursued by the most efficient means available in the context. More on this later, including discussion of concrete examples.

17. As Dennett (1995) often notes, people infer invisible, supernatural agency as an explanation of patterns of rational means/ends relations among natural phenomena, which means they can recognize such patterns in the absence of visible agents.

18. Why preferentially to paradigmatic agents like humans and animals? Well, if infants are indeed deploying a theory of *mind*, then it should apply primarily to agents with minds. At a minimum, a mind is an enduring causal nexus, states of which causally explain the behavior of the enduring agent to which it belongs. Therefore, if infants are deploying a theory of mind, it should be restricted to enduring agents, and humans and animals are the best examples of enduring agents with which infants are likely familiar. Most inanimate objects, though they are enduring, do not typically display patterns of behavior that require explanation by appeal to mental states. Occasional patterns of behavior that appear intelligent but do not seem to involve an observable, enduring agent, e.g., fortuitously apt natural events, like rain on a hot day or the wind closing a door at the right moment, should not trigger attributions of mind, since there is no enduring agent. As will become clear in what follows, infants automatically attribute agency, goals, and plans to patterns of behavior involving no visible agent. The intentional stance predicts this. The theory-theory seems at a loss to explain it: in such cases there is no enduring agent to which causally potent mental states can be attributed. I thank Shannon Spaulding for forcing me to be clearer on this.

19. Note that many of these infants are at ages at which they can barely control their own limbs; yet, according to simulation theory, they are somehow supposed to simulate actions like jumping over obstacles, when these actions are performed by objects as unlike them as computer-animated circles. This is highly implausible. Of course, the simulation theorist might claim that behavioral patterns involving selection of efficient means to salient goals are automatically treated as "like me." But this makes adopting the intentional stance a necessary condition on simulation. It also makes simulation gratuitous: once behavior has been parsed into goals and means, why should an interpreter waste time determining how she would represent such goals and means if she were engaged in the behavior?

20. In fact, Dennett (1995) explicitly invokes the intentional stance in explaining the intuitions that drive arguments for intelligent design: we can't help but interpret nature as fulfilling the goals of invisible agents because of the appearance of design. However, this is possible only if we can attribute rationally constrained means of

accomplishing goals to agentless phenomena. We must be able to see rain as aiming to water crops, for example, in the absence of a visible agent creating rain for this reason, before we can posit invisible agents as explanations of such apparently intentional phenomena.

21. As Shannon Spaulding has pointed out to me, there appears to be a tension between these two results. In one case, infants refuse to treat nonrational behavioral patterns as agentive, while in the other case they reinterpret an apparently nonrational behavioral pattern in a way that makes it turn out rational. I think this discrepancy is easily explained by the ages of the subjects in the different studies: the subjects in the nonrational object-grasping study were significantly younger than the subjects in the imitation study. As I suggest hereafter, the ontogeny of human social cognition can be understood as the gradual development of an ever more sophisticated capacity to adopt the intentional stance, based on increasing sensitivity to contextual factors relevant to judgments of rationality. Very young infants do not realize all the factors that might bear on the rationality of some behavior; e.g., they do not know that what an interpretive target has recently witnessed might affect what counts as a rational response, or that an interpretive target might have a nonobvious goal with similar consequences. As infants grow older, they gradually learn to appreciate the diversity of factors that bear on the rationality of behavior, including nonobvious goals like touching a light box with one's head.

22. As I argue in section 6, once infants have sufficient discursive competence, they make such normative attitudes explicit by correcting behavior that is counternormative relative to interpretations for which interpretive targets provide good grounds.

23. It is important to keep in mind here that these discoveries were completely unanticipated. The light box imitation experiment was, prima facie, definitive evidence against the operation of a rationality assumption. If infants imitate nonrational means to goals that they could accomplish in more efficient ways, it seems that what matters are arbitrary, nonrational choices of adult models, not rationally constrained behavioral patterns. But Gergely et al.'s (2002) manipulation—introducing a condition where the adult's hands were otherwise occupied—showed that this phenomenon was the exception that proved the rule: infants were interpreting forehead touching as the whole point of the demonstration, and hence assimilating it to their default assumption of rationality.

24. Or, indeed, to whether or not there even *is* a visible agent.

25. In fact, it is hard to imagine empirical results more congenial to Dennett's program.

26. I have carefully avoided following him in this regard. I think attribution of fullblown propositional attitudes requires an appreciation of their tenuous, holistically mediated connection to observable circumstances and behavior. But one can successfully apply the intentional stance without appreciating this, as the infant data

show. In chapter 7, I argue that an appreciation of full-blown propositional attitudes is equivalent to the capacity to track discursive commitments, which are useful precisely because of their tenuous, holistically constrained connection to observable circumstances and behavior. So, in my view, full-blown propositional attitudes are more like what Dennett calls "opinions" (1978, pp. 304–309; 1998, pp. 89–90): attitudes of acceptance or rejection directed at claims expressed in public language. I think this is a largely terminological difference. We both hold that there is a kind of propositional attitude attribution that essentially involves claims in public language, and another kind of interpretation that involves merely adopting the intentional stance.

27. Gopnik and Meltzoff (1997) provide the following description of how the human perceptual system categorizes a typical dinner party:

Around me bags of skin are draped over chairs, and stuffed into pieces of cloth; they shift and protrude in unexpected ways. ... Two dark spots near the top of them swivel restlessly back and forth. A hole beneath the spots fills with food and from it comes a stream of noises. (p. 31)

In this view, minds and mental states are not seen. They must be inferred from purely physical/behavioral evidence. See Gallagher (2008) and Gallagher & Hutto (2008) for persuasive critiques of this view.

28. The computer-generated scenario used in the experiments described by Gergely & Csibra (2003) that I discussed previously.

29. For a clear, precise, and thorough development of this idea, see Maibom (2007, pp. 558–563).

30. As I noted in chapter 1, evidence suggests that even nonhuman primates expect behavior to be the most efficient means to achieving a goal (Wood & Hauser, 2008).

31. They looked at populations from a large industrialized city and from remote Bushmen communities in southern Africa.

32. This distinction between human and nonhuman primate social learning is hard to explain on the hypothesis that human overimitation is an adaptation to learning how to construct and use tools. The reason is that, as I noted in chapter 4, successful tool use is sensitive to idiosyncratic bodily properties and dynamics, and successful tool manufacture is sensitive to idiosyncratic properties of raw materials. For these reasons, tool manufacture is better learned through the imitation of goals, i.e., figuring out one's own idiosyncratic means to match the generic end result of some model's bout of tool construction or use. The capacity to acquire precise, arbitrary sequences of bodily motions is important only in communicative behaviors, such as song and dance deployed in ritual, aimed at costly and hence honest advertising of cooperative and coordinative potential.

33. See Lyons (2009) for a proposal along these lines.

34. As I noted there, recent evidence demonstrates such normative attitudes in children as young as eight and one-half months (Hamlin et al., 2011).

35. Maibom (2007, pp. 568–571) provides a philosophical framework for understanding such behavioral prediction based on "social models."

36. This evidence also suggests an understanding of folk psychology proposed by Bruner (1990) that I explore in more detail in chapter 7. Bruner argues that the attribution of propositional attitudes in the context of exculpatory narratives constitutes a mechanism of normalizing apparently counternormative behavior. The experiments performed by Kalish and colleagues seem to confirm this: they show a developmental arc beginning with preschool-aged children assuming that people do what they are supposed to do, and ending with an adult understanding of psychological factors that might excuse behavior that contradicts this assumption.

7 The Role of Sophisticated Mindreading in Human Mindshaping

1. As the account I defend makes clear, other distinctively human sociocognitive capacities are selected for because of the changes to human socioecology wrought by pervasive mindshaping. As I noted in chapter 2, from a very young age, human infants interpret certain stereotyped adult gestures as preludes to pedagogical interactions. In chapter 5, I argued that our capacity to produce and process structurally complex communicative performances evolved due to the importance in human prehistory of reliable signals of commitment to, and capacity for, coordination on cooperative projects.

2. If only speakers of public languages token propositional attitudes, then, a fortiori, only speakers of public languages attribute them, since to attribute a propositional attitude, one must token a higher-order one, i.e., the belief that one's interpretive target has the attributed propositional attitude. Also, in a Davidsonian approach, one cannot determine which propositional attitude to attribute to a target without first interpreting her public-language utterances.

3. Davidson fleshes out this argument in various ways. For example, he argues that (1) tokening a specific propositional attitude is possible only against the background of whole systems of propositional attitudes available only to language users (1985, p. 475); (2) possession of concepts—the components of propositional attitudes—requires appreciating what it is to misapply them, something of which only language users are capable (1997, pp. 24–25); and, most famously, (3) tokening beliefs presupposes possession of the concept of belief, which requires an appreciation of the distinction between true and false beliefs, something of which only members of a community of language users, subject to public standards of correct sentence use, are capable (1975). I do not address these arguments because their deficits have been thoroughly explored by others. See especially Glock (2000), Lurz (2011, sec. 4.1), and the various contributions to the *Erkenntnis* special issue on nonlinguistic thought (1999, vol. 51).

4. Bermúdez (2003a) also has reasons for general skepticism about the language of thought hypothesis.

5. Of course, I actually think it is not possible, but for reasons other than Bermúdez's. In my view, it simply does not pay to attribute full-blown propositional attitudes to predict behavior. There are far less computationally intensive and time-consuming ways of succeeding at behavioral prediction, especially if one is part of a community shaped by robust and reliable mindshaping practices. Nichols and Stich's model of belief attribution is not necessarily at odds with this perspective, since it can be used to explain how language users do it; and in my view, once language is on the scene, full-blown propositional attitude attribution can be useful (more on this later). The key point here is that Bermúdez fails to show why propositional attitude attribution *requires a linguistic medium*: Nichols and Stich's model shows that it doesn't. In contrast, in my view, propositional attitude attribution *requires a linguistic motivation* (roughly, the tracking and undertaking of discursive commitments). This is compatible with the possibility that much of the machinery of propositional attitude attribution functions the way Nichols and Stich's model proposes, without necessarily employing a linguistic medium. The products of such machinery can be attributions of discursive commitment, even if the medium employed in generating them does not involve a public language.

6. One needn't even have a concept of mind—understood as an enduring, unobservable causal nexus that explains behavioral appearances—to adopt the intentional stance. In fact, to adopt the intentional stance, an interpreter needn't even distinguish between herself and her interpretive targets or even treat behaviors as products of enduring agents. An interpreter adopting the intentional stance can be restricted to an ontology of disjoint bouts of behavior, with no concern for the enduring agents that produce them. This is not to say that the more sophisticated versions of the intentional stance on which most human beings rely for their quotidian interpretations have such minimal presuppositions. It is likely that adult human applications of the intentional stance presume that the behavior they are used to interpret issues from an enduring agent that is distinct from the interpreter. However, this is likely an ontogenetic development; it is plausible that the earliest applications of the intentional stance, by infants as young as six and one-half months (Csibra, 2008), rely on no such presuppositions.

7. This categorization of sophisticated mindreading as a reflective, conscious, slow System 2 capacity is consistent with influential characterizations of System 2 reasoning. For example, Carruthers (2006, pp. 354–356) claims that System 2 capacities form the basis for scientific reasoning, i.e., speculation about the unobservable causes of observed phenomena; and in my view, full-blown propositional attitude attribution involves precisely such speculation. On the other hand, I do not want to rule out the possibility that some full-blown propositional attitude attribution might be the product of fast, automatic, unconscious System 1 capacities. The reason is that human beings can often learn to apply sophisticated concepts in an almost

"perception-like" way. For example, scientists can just visually recognize instantiations of abstract concepts: a physicist might see a "hooked vapor trail" as the presence of a subatomic particle. Similarly, with suitable training in culturally specific signs of mental states, adult human interpreters may learn to perceptually recognize the presence of even full-blown propositional attitudes. Still, such entrained, reflex-like applications of sophisticated concepts presuppose prior System 2 capacities, both in science and in quotidian sophisticated mindreading. In addition, applying the intentional stance need not always be restricted to System 1 inference. For example, someone who accepts Dennett's understanding of beliefs and desires might reflectively interpret behavior using the intentional stance.

8. Such interpretative heuristics can easily be adapted to accommodate predictive failure. An interpreter need only revise her parsing, treating some other behavioral component as the goal, or looking for some difference in information access between her and her target.

9. E.g., diseases with similar symptoms must often be treated very differently, and such differences can be appreciated only once differences in their unobservable causes are.

10. Nor is there any reason to expect that an appearance–reality distinction, applied to the social domain, is immune to the general epistemological challenges of accurately modeling unobservable causes. This is the whole point of the holism problem: it is extraordinarily difficult to quickly and frugally formulate accurate representations of unobservable causes that do not make obvious differences to typical behavioral patterns, whether in the social domain or any other.

11. See Brandom (1994, pp. 163–165) for a characterization of promising that fits with the commitment-signaling story I have proposed.

12. Of course, short sentences like this do not *seem* structurally complex, but as Chomsky has taught us, such surface simplicity conceals deep structural complexity. The structure of any sentence requires complex hierarchical representations, unlike, say, lists of lexical items.

13. Even in contemporary English, it is possible to emphasize one's commitment to an assertion by saying "I promise, it's the truth!"

14. Dennett uses the distinction between interpretation based on adopting the intentional stance toward a target's behavior and interpretation based on taking her explicit avowals seriously to address a variety of thorny issues in the philosophy of mind and action, including changing one's mind and weakness of the will (1978, pp. 303–309), and consciousness (1991a). More recently, Frankish (2004) has applied this distinction to explaining how System 1 reasoning can come to implement System 2 reasoning via discursive commitment.

15. Many nonhuman primates form expectations about each other's behavior, which are sometimes disappointed. However, if Povinelli (2012) is right, this has not led to the evolution of an appreciation for the appearance–reality distinction in nonhuman primate species. Hence mistaken expectations alone are not sufficient for inducing an appreciation of the appearance–reality distinction. This makes sense. When behavioral expectations derived from adopting the intentional stance are disappointed, it is natural to conclude that one has simply made an error in applying the intentional stance: perhaps one has assumed an inaccurate parsing of a bout of behavior, mistaking a goal for a means, for example. But this is not the same as appreciating the appearance–reality distinction presupposed by full-blown propositional attitude attribution. This involves more than the realization that one can be mistaken about behavioral appearances; it requires appreciating the possibility that there are multiple, mutually incompatible, unobservable mental realities that are equally compatible with observed behavior.

16. It seems that the choice between trusting third-personal versus first-personal interpretations as revealing a person's true thoughts is relevant to a deep fault line in the philosophical tradition. Some philosophers are inclined toward skepticism about first-person expressions of doxastic commitment, preferring third-person interpretive frameworks like the intentional stance, due perhaps to worries about self-deception. Other philosophers put more credence in first-person expressions of doxastic commitment, perhaps on the grounds that behavior interpretable from the third person often masks a person's true thoughts.

17. An anonymous reviewer worries about the adaptive advantages of understanding such exculpatory narratives. Obviously, producing such narratives might help salvage status, and this would have advantages. But what advantages accrue to consumers of such narratives? However, this worry assumes, contrary to the evidence (Rizzolatti & Arbib, 1998), that our productive and receptive linguistic competences are entirely disjoint. It is unclear how someone could produce an exculpatory narrative without also understanding it.

18. Obviously, this is a version of Sellars's "myth of Jones" (1997). Discursive practice is used as a model of the unobservable causes of behavior. The difference is that, as David Beisecker once put it to me, Jones was not a scientist. That is, the goal of using discursive practice to model the unobservable causes of behavior is not to produce a true theory of human behavior but as Bruner (1990) suggests, to provide exculpatory justifications of apparently counternormative behavior.

19. See Andrews (2009) for a persuasive defense of a similar conception of the relationship between norms and propositional attitude attribution.

20. The distinction between the ontological question of whether or not there are facts of the matter regarding what agents believe or desire, and the pragmatic question regarding the raison d'être of *quotidian* interpretation, helps deflect another potential objection: how can nonhuman animals have beliefs and desires if they do

not participate in the negotiation of interpretations aimed at determining normative status? I have assumed throughout the foregoing that nonhuman animals have
beliefs and desires, whether or not they can attribute them. But my claim here is *not*
that only participants in our discursive practices *have* beliefs and desires. Rather, the
claim is that only participants in our discursive practices *attribute* beliefs and desires,
primarily in quotidian contexts, to help maintain status via justificatory narratives.
This does not mean that the attribution of beliefs and desires cannot have other
uses, e.g., the epistemic function of accurately representing the psychological causes
of human and nonhuman behavior in scientific explanations. It is entirely possible
(and, I claim, actually true) that the practice of attributing beliefs and desires started
as a means of justifying behavior and was later co-opted by scientific psychology as
a means of causally explaining both human and nonhuman behavior in terms of
accurate representations of mental states causally responsible for it.

21. See Matthew and Boyd (2011) for a compelling account of how such communal
determinations of normative status and punishment are conducted among the Tur-
kana, a contemporary nomadic culture in East Africa.

22. Malle et al. (2007) provide an extremely rich discussion of a very interesting set
of experimental results, and I have touched only the tip of the iceberg here. They
also identify two other strong self–other asymmetries in behavior explanation: the
tendency to refer to beliefs versus desires in reason explanations, and the tendency
to leave appeals to beliefs unmarked versus explicitly marked in belief explanations.
Their discussions of these asymmetries are also very interesting, and congenial to
my project. For example, they explain the self–other asymmetry in explanations of
belief versus desire by reference to the difficulty of determining others' beliefs given
the idiosyncratic means people have of forming them (p. 495). This fits nicely with
the arguments of chapter 3. They explain the self–other asymmetry in unmarked
versus marked belief attributions in terms of subjects' desire to distance themselves
from the beliefs of others: marking a belief reason *as a belief* functions to highlight
that the attributor does not necessarily endorse it (p. 496). This has clear affinities
with Brandom's theory of belief attribution, according to which self-attribution of
belief or, equivalently, doxastic/assertional commitment amounts to *undertaking* or
endorsing a claim, while attribution to others does not (Brandom, 1994, pp. 161–
163). In addition, Malle et al. (2007) make a persuasive case against the traditional
characterization of self–other attributional asymmetries in social psychology,
according to which subjects explain their own behavior in terms of situational
causes and others' behavior in terms of dispositional/person causes. Malle et al.'s
(2007) arguments and the experiments on which they draw are a convincing refuta-
tion of this traditional framework, and a vindication of their own alternative: "the
folk-conceptual theory of behavior explanations."

23. I acknowledge that the story I defend is counterintuitive. The attribution of
propositional attitudes does not *seem* like an exercise in "on the fly" grasping at
exculpatory justifications or condemnatory interpretations. It seems like an entirely

epistemic activity: ascertaining the true reasons for an agent's behavior, i.e., the mental states that actually caused it. However, it is by now a commonplace that we are often very mistaken about the true functions of our practices and behaviors. The nineteenth-century theories of Marx, Darwin, and Freud all imply that the ideological glosses with which we comfort ourselves often conceal unpleasant truths about the raisons d'être of our belief systems. For example, persons may sincerely defend theories of the differences between races or genders on the grounds that their aims are purely epistemic, i.e., that they aim only to uncover the truth behind some phenomenon. Yet the persistence and persuasiveness of such theories may have nothing to do with truth and everything to do with maintaining some normative regime, like slavery or sexist political institutions. Twentieth-century social psychology provides an array of empirical results showing that we are masters at rationalizing self-deception (Kahneman, 2011). I think that the intuitive plausibility of the traditional view that the attribution of propositional attitudes aims to accurately represent mental causes of behavior is a similar self-deception. We like to think of ourselves as engaged in dispassionate inquiry into the truth about what we think. This is more comforting than the view that we are actually desperately fishing for interpretations that justify our normative intuitions.

24. Here I deliberately eschew theories of interpretation according to which interpreters have a kind of privileged and *direct* access to their own propositional attitudes that they lack to those of others (Goldman, 2006). I agree with Carruthers (2009a) that interpreters' access to their own *propositional attitudes* is just like their access to those of others: inferred from evidence. It is compatible with this idea that the kind of evidence on which interpreters draw to infer their own propositional attitudes is of a much higher quality and sometimes of an entirely different kind than the evidence on which they draw to infer the propositional attitudes of others. For example, interpreters might have privileged, direct access to their own non-propositional sensory states, which constitute a kind of evidence for their own propositional attitudes that is unavailable when interpreting others.

25. As I noted in chapter 2, Dennett (1991a) argues that the conscious self is constituted by a narrative that the brain "weaves" to organize the tumult of parallel processes in which it engages into coherent, linear sequences of thought. This allows for a kind of cognitive self-control that yields adaptive advantages. Dennett often likens this use of narrative to examples of "extended phenotypes" in other species, like the spider's web or the nests that male bowerbirds construct, as a form of sexual advertising, out of random, attention-drawing components they happen to find. Like narratives, such external factors play an indispensable role in the biological success of the species that rely on them: though they are not coded for in genes, they are so reliably present in species-typical environments that mechanisms devoted to incorporating them into survival and reproductive strategies are genetically encoded. This understanding of the role of narrative in self-regulation is even more apt given the social role I identify for it. When we cobble together justificatory

narratives from the palette of alternatives afforded by the ambient culture, we are quite literally using reliably available external factors to arm ourselves for one of the biologically most important tasks that humans and other primates face: acquiring and maintaining status. It is plausible that our brains are wired to expect such culturally afforded resources and to automatically incorporate them into self-regulating narratives capable of justifying behavior and hence maintaining status relative to the expectations of our fellows.

References

Aiello, L. C. (1996). Terrestriality, bipedalism, and the origin of language. *Proceedings of the British Academy, 88,* 269–289.

Aiello, L. C., & Wheeler, P. (1995). The expensive tissue hypothesis: The brain and the digestive system in human and primate evolution. *Current Anthropology, 36,* 199–221.

Aldridge, M. A., Stone, K. R., Sweeney, M. H., & Bower, T. G. R. (2000). Preverbal children with autism understand the intentions of others. *Developmental Science, 3*(3), 294–301.

Alechina, N., & Logan, B. (2010). Belief ascription under bounded resources. *Synthese, 173,* 179–197.

Allen, C., & Bekoff, M. (1997). *Species of mind.* Cambridge, MA: MIT Press.

Andrews, K. (2007). Critter psychology: On the possibility of nonhuman animal folk psychology. In D. D. Hutto & M. Ratcliffe (Eds.), *Folk psychology re-assessed.* Dordrecht: Springer.

Andrews, K. (2008). It's in your nature: A pluralistic folk psychology. *Synthese, 165*(1), 13–29.

Andrews, K. (2009). Understanding norms without a theory of mind. *Inquiry, 52*(5), 433–448.

Apperly, I. A. (2011). *Mindreaders.* Hove: Psychology Press.

Apperly, I. A., & Butterfill, S. A. (2009). Do humans have two systems to track beliefs and belief-like states? *Psychological Review, 116*(4), 953–970.

Astington, J. W. (1990). Narrative and the child's theory of mind. In B. K. Britton & A. D. Pellegrini (Eds.), *Narrative thought and narrative language.* Hillsdale, NJ: Lawrence Erlbaum.

Astington, J. W., & Jenkins, J. M. (1999). A longitudinal study of the relation between language and theory-of-mind development. *Developmental Psychology, 35*(5), 1311–1320.

Atran, S. (2002). *In gods we trust*. New York: Oxford University Press.

Avramides, A. (1989). *Meaning and mind: An examination of a Gricean account of language*. Cambridge, MA: MIT Press.

Axelrod, R. (1984). *The evolution of cooperation*. New York: Basic Books.

Bacharach, M. (2006). *Beyond individual choice*. Princeton: Princeton University Press.

Bacharach, M., & Gambetta, D. (2001). Trust in signs. In K. Cook (Ed.), *Trust in society*. New York: Russell Sage Foundation.

Baldwin, D. A. (1993). Infants' ability to consult the speaker for clues to word reference. *Journal of Child Language, 20*, 395–418.

Baldwin, D. A., Markman, E. M., Bill, B., Desjardins, R. N., Irwin, J. M., & Tidball, G. (1996). Infants' reliance on a social criterion for establishing word-object relations. *Child Development, 67*, 3135–3153.

Bargh, J. M., Chen, M., & Burrows, L. (1996). The automaticity of social behavior: Direct effects of trait concept and stereotype activation on action. *Journal of Personality and Social Psychology, 71*(2), 230–244.

Baron-Cohen, S. (1995). *Mindblindness*. Cambridge, MA: MIT Press.

Baron-Cohen, S. (1999). The evolution of a theory of mind. In M. C. Corballis & S. E. G. Lea (Eds.), *The descent of mind*. New York: Oxford University Press.

Bermúdez, J. L. (2003a). *Thinking without words*. New York: Oxford University Press.

Bermúdez, J. L. (2003b). The domain of folk psychology. In A. O'Hear (Ed.), *Minds and persons*. Cambridge: Cambridge University Press.

Bermúdez, J. L. (2009). Mindreading in the animal kingdom. In R. Lurz (Ed.), *The philosophy of animal minds*. Cambridge: Cambridge University Press.

Bickerton, D. (1990). *Language and species*. Chicago: University of Chicago Press.

Bickerton, D. (1995). *Language and human behavior*. Seattle: University of Washington Press.

Bickerton, D. (1998). Catastrophic evolution: The case for a single step from protolanguage to full human language. In J. R. Hurford, M. Studdert-Kennedy, & C. Knight (Eds.), *Approaches to the evolution of language: Social and cognitive bases*. Cambridge: Cambridge University Press.

Bickerton, D. (2000). How protolanguage became language. In C. Knight, M. Studdert-Kennedy, & J. R. Hurford (Eds.), *The evolutionary emergence of language: Social function and the origins of linguistic form*. Cambridge: Cambridge University Press.

Bickerton, D. (2002). Foraging versus social intelligence in the evolution of protolanguage. In A. Wray (Ed.), *The transition to language*. Oxford: Oxford University Press.

Birch, S. A. J., & Bloom, P. (2007). The curse of knowledge in reasoning about false beliefs. *Psychological Science, 18*(5), 382–386.

Bloom, P. (2000). *How children learn the meaning of words.* Cambridge, MA: MIT Press.

Bloom, P. (2002). Mindreading, communication, and the learning of names for things. *Mind and Language, 17*(1), 37–54.

Boehm, C. H. (1993). Egalitarian behavior and reverse dominance hierarchy. *Current Anthropology, 34*(3), 227–254.

Boehm, C. H. (1996). Emergency decisions, cultural selection mechanics, and group selection. *Current Anthropology, 37,* 763–793.

Boehm, C. H. (1999). *Hierarchy in the forest: The evolution of egalitarian behavior.* Cambridge, MA: Harvard University Press.

Boehm, C. (2004). What makes humans economically distinctive? A three-species evolutionary comparison and historical analysis. *Journal of Bioeconomics, 6,* 109–135.

Boesch, C. (1994). Hunting strategies of Gombe and Taï chimpanzees. In R. Wrangham, W. McGrew, F. de Waal, & P. Heltne (Eds.), *Chimpanzee cultures* (pp. 77–91). Cambridge, MA: Harvard University Press.

Bolender, J. (2007). Prehistoric cognition by description: A Russellian approach to the Upper Paleolithic. *Biology and Philosophy, 22,* 383–399.

Boone, J. L., & Kessler, K. L. (1999). More status or more children? Social status, fertility reduction, and long-term fitness. *Evolution and Human Behavior, 20*(4), 257–277.

Boyd, R., & Richerson, P. J. (1985). *Culture and the evolutionary process.* Chicago: University of Chicago Press.

Boyd, R., & Richerson, P. J. (1992). Punishment allows the evolution of cooperation (or anything else) in sizable groups. *Ethology and Sociobiology, 13,* 171–195.

Boyd, R., & Richerson, P. J. (1996). Why culture is common but cultural evolution is rare. *Proceedings of the British Academy, 88,* 73–93.

Brandom, R. B. (1994). *Making it explicit.* Cambridge, MA: Harvard University Press.

Bratman, M. E. (1993). Shared intention. *Ethics, 104*(1), 97–113.

Bruner, J. (1983). *Child's talk: Learning to use language.* New York: W. W. Norton.

Bruner, J. (1990). *Acts of meaning.* Cambridge, MA: Harvard University Press.

Burney, D. A., & Flannery, T. F. (2005). Fifty millennia of catastrophic extinctions after human contact. *Trends in Ecology and Evolution, 20,* 395–401.

Buttelmann, D., Carpenter, M., & Tomasello, M. (2009). Eighteen-month-old infants show false belief understanding in an active helping paradigm. *Cognition, 112,* 337–342.

Byrne, R. W. (2003). Imitation and behaviour parsing. *Philosophical Transactions of the Royal Society of London: Series B, 358,* 529–536.

Call, J., Hare, B. H., Carpenter, M., & Tomasello, M. (2004). "Unwilling" versus "unable": Chimpanzees' understanding of intentional action. *Developmental Science, 7*(4), 488–498.

Call, J., & Tomasello, M. (2008). Does the chimpanzee have a theory of mind? 30 years later. *Trends in Cognitive Sciences, 12,* 187–192.

Camp, E. (2004). The generality constraints and categorical restrictions. *Philosophical Quarterly, 54,* 209–231.

Camus, A. (1958). *Discours de Suède.* French and European Pubns.

Caporael, L. R. (2001). Evolutionary psychology: Toward a unifying theory and a hybrid science. *Annual Review of Psychology, 52,* 607–628.

Carey, S. (2009). *The origin of concepts.* New York: Oxford University Press.

Caro, T. M., & Hauser, M. D. (1992). Is there teaching in nonhuman animals? *Quarterly Review of Biology, 67*(2), 151–174.

Carpenter, M., Akhtar, N., & Tomasello, M. (1998). Fourteen- through 18-month-old infants differentially imitate intentional and accidental actions. *Infant Behavior and Development, 21*(2), 315–330.

Carpenter, M., Call, J., & Tomasello, M. (2002). Understanding 'prior intentions' enables two-year-olds to imitatively learn a complex task. *Child Development, 73*(5), 1431–1441.

Carpenter, M., Pennington, B., & Rogers, S. J. (2001). Understanding of others' intentions in children with autism and developmental delays. *Journal of Autism and Developmental Disorders, 31*(6), 589–599.

Carpenter, M., Pennington, B., & Rogers, S. J. (2002). Interactions among social-cognitive skills in young children with autism. *Journal of Autism and Developmental Disorders, 32*(2), 91–106.

Carruthers, P. (1996). Simulation and self-knowledge: A defence of theory-theory. In P. Carruthers & P. K. Smith (Eds.), *Theories of theories of mind.* Cambridge: Cambridge University Press.

Carruthers, P. (2002). The cognitive functions of language. *Behavioral and Brain Sciences, 25,* 657–726.

Carruthers, P. (2006). *The architecture of the mind.* New York: Oxford University Press.

Carruthers, P. (2009a). How we know our own minds: The relationship between mindreading and metacognition. *Behavioral and Brain Sciences, 32*, 121–182.

Carruthers, P. (2009b). Invertebrate concepts confront the generality constraint (and win). In R. Lurz (Ed.), *The philosophy of animal minds* (pp. 89–107). Cambridge: Cambridge University Press.

Chang, L. J., Smith, A., Dufwenberg, M., & Sanfey, A. G. (2011). Triangulating the neural, psychological, and economic bases of guilt aversion. *Neuron, 70*, 560–572.

Chartrand, T., & Bargh, J. (1999). The chameleon effect: The perception-behavior link and social interaction. *Journal of Personality and Social Psychology, 76*(6), 893–910.

Chisholm, R. (1957). *Perceiving*. Ithaca: Cornell University Press.

Chomsky, N. (2005). Three factors in the language design. *Linguistic Inquiry, 36*, 1–22.

Churchland, P. S., Ramachandran, V. S., & Sejnowski, T. J. (1994). A critique of pure vision. In C. Koch & J. L. Davis (Eds.), *Large-scale neuronal theories of the brain* (pp. 23–60). Cambridge, MA: MIT Press.

Cialdini, R. B., & Goldstein, N. J. (2004). Social influence: Compliance and conformity. *Annual Review of Psychology, 55*, 591–621.

Clark, A. (1997). *Being there: Putting brain, body and world together again*. Cambridge, MA: MIT Press.

Clark, A. (1998). Magic words: How language augments human computation. In P. Carruthers (Ed.), *Language and thought*. Cambridge: Cambridge University Press.

Clayton, N. S., Dally, J. M., & Emery, N. J. (2007). Social cognition by food-caching corvids: The western jay as a natural psychologist. *Philosophical Transactions of the Royal Society of London: Series B, 362*, 507–522.

Cooper, J. C., Kreps, T. A., Wiebe, T., Pirkl, T., & Knutson, B. (2010). When giving is good: Ventromedial prefrontal cortex activation for others' intentions. *Neuron, 67*(3), 511–521.

Cosmides, L. (1989). The logic of social exchange: Has natural selection shaped how humans reason? Studies with the Wason selection task. *Cognition, 31*(3), 187–276.

Cosmides, L., & Tooby, J. (1992). Cognitive adaptations for social exchange. In J. H. Barkow et al. (Eds.), *The adapted mind: Evolutionary psychology and the generation of culture* (pp. 163–228). New York: Oxford University Press.

Crockford, C., Wittig, R. M., Mundry, R., & Zuberbühler, K. (2011). Wild chimpanzees inform ignorant group members of danger. *Current Biology, 22*(2), 142–146.

Cronin, H. (1991). *The ant and the peacocke*. Cambridge: Cambridge University Press.

Csibra, G. (2008). Goal attribution to inanimate agents by 6.5-month-old infants. *Cognition, 107*(70), 705–717.

Csibra, G. (2010). Recognizing communicative intentions in infancy. *Mind and Language, 25*, 141–168.

Csibra, G., & Gergely, G. (2006). Social learning and social cognition: The case for pedagogy. In Y. Munakata & M. H. Johnson (Eds.), *Processes of change in brain and cognitive development*. London: Oxford University Press.

Csibra, G., & Gergely, G. (2009). Natural pedagogy. *Trends in Cognitive Sciences, 13*(4), 148–153.

Csibra, G., & Gergely, G. (2011). Natural pedagogy as evolutionary adaptation. *Philosophical Transactions of the Royal Society of London: Series B, 366*, 1149–1157.

Currie, G., & Sterelny, K. (2000). How to think about the modularity of mind-reading. *Philosophical Quarterly, 50*(199), 145–160.

Damasio, A. R. (1994). *Descartes' error: Emotion, reason, and the human brain*. New York: Grosset & Putnam.

Danielson, P. (1992). *Artificial morality: Virtuous robots for virtual games*. London: Routledge.

Darwin, C. (1871/1981). *The descent of man and selection in relation to sex*. Princeton: Princeton University Press.

Davidson, D. (1973). On the very idea of a conceptual scheme. *Proceedings and Addresses of the American Philosophical Association, 47*, 5–20.

Davidson, D. (1975). Thought and talk. In S. Guttenplan (Ed.), *Mind and language*. Oxford: Oxford University Press.

Davidson, D. (1985). Rational animals. In E. LePore & B. McLaughlin (Eds.), *Actions and events*. Oxford: Blackwell.

Davidson, D. (1997). Seeing through language. In J. Preston (Ed.), *Thought and language*. Cambridge: Cambridge University Press.

Davidson, D. (1999). The emergence of thought. *Erkenntnis, 51*, 7–17.

Dawkins, R. (1976). *The selfish gene*. Oxford: Oxford University Press.

de Villiers, J. G., & de Villiers, P. A. (2000). Linguistic determinism and the understanding of false beliefs. In P. Mitchell & K. John (Eds.), *Children's reasoning and the mind* (pp. 191–228). Hove: Psychology Press.

de Waal, F. B. M. (2000). *Chimpanzee politics*. Baltimore: Johns Hopkins University Press.

Dennett, D. C. (1978). *Brainstorms: Philosophical essays on mind and psychology*. Montgomery, VT: Bradford Books.

Dennett, D. C. (1983). Intentional systems in cognitive ethology: The "Panglossian Paradigm" defended. *Behavioral and Brain Sciences, 6,* 343–390.

Dennett, D. C. (1987). *The intentional stance.* Cambridge, MA: MIT Press.

Dennett, D. C. (1988). Out of the armchair and into the field. *Poetics Today, 9,* 205–221.

Dennett, D. C. (1991a). *Consciousness explained.* Boston: Little, Brown.

Dennett, D. C. (1991b). Real patterns. *Journal of Philosophy, 88*(1), 27–51.

Dennett, D. C. (1991c). Two contrasts: Folk craft versus folk science and belief versus opinion. In J. D. Greenwood (Ed.), *The future of folk psychology* (pp. 135–148). Cambridge: Cambridge University Press.

Dennett, D. C. (1992). The self as a center of narrative gravity. In F. Kessel, P. Cole, & D. Johnson (Eds.), *Self and consciousness: Multiple perspectives.* Hillsdale, NJ: Erlbaum.

Dennett, D. C. (1995). *Darwin's dangerous idea: Evolution and the meanings of life.* New York: Simon & Schuster.

Dennett, D. C. (1998). *Brainchildren.* Cambridge, MA: MIT Press.

Dennett, D. C. (2003). *Freedom evolves.* New York: Viking Press.

DeSilva, J. M., & Lesnik, J. (2008). Brain size at birth throughout human evolution: A new method for estimating neonatal brain size in hominins. *Journal of Human Evolution, 55*(6), 1064–1074.

Diaz, R., & Berk, L. (Eds.). (1992). *Private speech: From social interaction to self-regulation.* Hillsdale, NJ: Lawrence Erlbaum.

Dijksterhuis, A., & van Knippenberg, A. (1998). The relation between perception and behavior, or how to win a game of Trivial Pursuit. *Journal of Personality and Social Psychology, 74*(4), 865–877.

Dissanayake, E. (1992). *Homo aestheticus: Where art comes from and why.* New York: Free Press.

Donald, M. (1991). *Origins of the modern mind: Three stages in the evolution of culture and cognition.* Cambridge, MA: Harvard University Press.

Dugatkin, L. A. (1997). *Cooperation among animals: An evolutionary perspective.* New York: Oxford University Press.

Dunbar, R. (1996). *Grooming, gossip, and the evolution of language.* Cambridge, MA: Harvard University Press.

Dunbar, R. (1998). The social brain hypothesis. *Evolutionary Anthropology, 6,* 178–190.

Dunbar, R. (2000). On the origin of the human mind. In P. Carruthers & A. Chamberlain (Eds.), *Evolution and the human mind: Modularity, language, and meta-cognition* (pp. 238–253). Cambridge: Cambridge University Press.

Dunbar, R. (2003). The social brain: Mind, language, and society in evolutionary perspective. *Annual Review of Anthropology, 32,* 163–181.

Dunbar, R. (2009). Why only humans have language. In R. Botha & C. Knight (Eds.), *The prehistory of language* (pp. 12–35). Oxford: Oxford University Press.

Dweck, C. (2000). *Self-theories: Their role in motivation, personality and development.* Philadelphia: Psychology Press.

Edwards, C. P. (1987). Culture and the construction of moral values: A comparative ethnography of moral encounters in two cultural settings. In J. Kagan & S. Lamb (Eds.), *The emergence of morality in young children.* Chicago: University of Chicago Press.

Enard, W., Przeworski, M., Fisher, S. E., Lai, C. S. L., Wiebe, V., Kitano, T., ..., Pääbo, S. (2002). Molecular evolution of FOXP2, a gene involved in speech and language. *Nature, 418,* 869–872.

Evans, G. (1982). *The varieties of reference.* Oxford: Oxford University Press.

Fehr, E., & Fischbacher, U. (2004). Social norms and human cooperation. *Trends in Cognitive Sciences, 8*(4), 185–190.

Fitch, W. T. (2004). Kin selection and "mother tongues": A neglected component in language evolution. In D. Oller & U. Griebel (Eds.), *Evolution of communication systems* (pp. 275–296). Cambridge, MA: MIT Press.

Fitch, W. T. (2010). *The evolution of language.* Cambridge: Cambridge University Press.

Fitch, W. T., & Hauser, M. D. (2004). Computational constraints on syntactic processing in a nonhuman primate. *Science, 303,* 377–380.

Fivush, R. (1994). Constructing narrative, emotion, and self in parent-child conversations about the past. In U. Neisser & R. Fivush (Eds.), *The remembering self: Construction and accuracy in self-narrative* (pp. 136–158). New York: Cambridge University Press.

Fix, A. G. (1999). *Migration and colonization in human microevolution.* Cambridge: Cambridge University Press.

Flanagan, O. (1991). *Varieties of moral personality.* Cambridge, MA: Harvard University Press.

Fodor, J. A. (1975). *The language of thought.* Cambridge, MA: Harvard University Press.

Fodor, J. A. (1983). *The modularity of mind.* Cambridge, MA: MIT Press.

Fodor, J. A. (1995). A theory of the child's theory of mind. In M. Davies & T. Stone (Eds.), *Mental simulation.* Oxford: Blackwell.

Fodor, J. A., & Lepore, E. (1992). *Holism: A shopper's guide.* Cambridge, MA: Blackwell.

Fodor, J. A., & Lepore, E. (1993). Is intentional ascription intrinsically normative? In B. Dahlbom (Ed.), *Dennett and his critics.* Cambridge, MA: Blackwell.

Ford, K. M., & Pylyshyn, Z. W. (1996). *The robot's dilemma revisited: The frame problem in artificial intelligence.* Norwood: Ablex.

Foucault, M. (1966). *Folie et déraison.* Paris: Gallimard.

Foucault, M. (1975). *Surveiller et punir.* Paris: Gallimard.

Frank, R. H. (1988). *Passions within reason.* New York: W. W. Norton.

Frankish, K. (2004). *Mind and supermind.* Cambridge: Cambridge University Press.

Galef, B. G., Wigmore, S. W., & Kennett, D. J. (1983). A failure to find socially mediated taste aversion learning in Norway rats (*R. norvegicus*). *Journal of Comparative Psychology, 97*(4), 358–363.

Gallagher, H. L., & Frith, C. D. (2003). Functional imaging of "theory of mind." *Trends in Cognitive Sciences, 7,* 77–83.

Gallagher, S. (2001). Emotion and intersubjective perception: A speculative account. In A. Kaszniac (Ed.), *Emotions, qualia, and consciousness* (pp. 95–100). London: World Scientific.

Gallagher, S. (2008). Direct perception in the intersubjective context. *Consciousness and Cognition, 17,* 535–543.

Gallagher, S., & Hutto, D. (2008). Understanding others through primary interaction and narrative practice. In J. Zlatev et al. (Eds.), *The shared mind.* Amsterdam: John Benjamins.

Gallese, V. (2005). "Being like me": Self-other identity, mirror neurons, and empathy. In S. Hurley & N. Chater (Eds.), *Perspectives on imitation* (Vol. 1, pp. 101–118). Cambridge, MA: MIT Press.

Gallese, V., Keysers, C., & Rizzolatti, G. (2004). A unifying view of the basis of social cognition. *Trends in Cognitive Sciences, 8*(9), 396–403.

Gallistel, C. R. (1990). *The organization of learning.* Cambridge, MA: MIT Press.

Gallistel, C. R., & Cramer, A. E. (1996). Computations on metric maps in mammals: Getting oriented and choosing a multidestination route. *Journal of Experimental Biology, 199,* 211–217.

Garcia, J. (1990). Learning without memory. *Journal of Cognitive Neuroscience, 2*(4), 287–305.

Gazzaniga, M. S. (1995a). Consciousness and the cerebral hemispheres. In M. S. Gazzaniga (Ed.), *The cognitive neurosciences* (1st ed., pp. 1391–1400). Cambridge, MA: MIT Press.

Gazzaniga, M. S. (1995b). Principles of human brain organization derived from split-brain studies. *Neuron, 14,* 217–228.

Gentner, D., & Goldin-Meadow, S. (2003). *Language in mind.* Cambridge, MA: MIT Press.

Gergely, G. (2011). Kinds of agents: The origins of understanding instrumental and communicative agency. In U. Goshwami (Ed.), *Blackwell handbook of childhood cognitive development* (2nd ed., pp. 76–105). Oxford: Blackwell.

Gergely, G., Bekkering, H., & Király, I. (2002). Rational imitation in preverbal infants. *Nature, 415,* 755–756.

Gergely, G., & Csibra, G. (2003). Teleological reasoning in infancy: The naive theory of rational action. *Trends in Cognitive Sciences, 7*(7), 287–292.

Gigerenzer, G., Todd, P., & the ABC Research Group. (1999). *Simple heuristics that make us smart.* New York: Oxford University Press.

Gilbert, M. (1996). *Living together: Rationality, sociality, and obligation.* Lanham, MD: Rowman & Littlefield.

Gilbert, M. (2009). Shared intention and personal intentions. *Philosophical Studies, 144,* 167–187.

Gintis, H., Bowles, S., Boyd, R., & Fehr, E. (2006). Moral sentiments and material interests: Origins, evidence, and consequences. In H. Gintis, S. Bowles, R. Boyd, & E. Fehr (Eds.), *Moral sentiments and material interests.* Cambridge, MA: MIT Press.

Glimcher, P. W. (2004). *Decisions, uncertainty, and the brain: The science of neuroeconomics.* Cambridge, MA: MIT Press.

Glock, H.-J. (2000). Animals, thoughts, and concepts. *Synthese, 123*(1), 35–64.

Godfrey-Smith, P. (2002). On the evolution of representational and interpretive capacities. *Monist, 85*(1), 50–69.

Goldman, A. I. (1989). Interpretation psychologized. *Mind and Language, 4*(3), 161–185.

Goldman, A. I. (1992). In defense of the simulation theory. *Mind and Language, 7*(1–2), 104–119.

Goldman, A. I. (2006). *Simulating minds: The philosophy, psychology, and neuroscience of mindreading.* Oxford: Oxford University Press.

Gomez, J. C. (1998). Some thoughts about the evolution of LADs, with special reference to TOM and SAM. In P. Carruthers & J. Boucher (Eds.), *Language and thought*. Cambridge: Cambridge University Press.

Gopnik, A. (1996). Theories and modules: Creation myths, developmental realities, and Neurath's boat. In P. Carruthers & P. K. Smith (Eds.), *Theories of theories of mind*. Cambridge: Cambridge University Press.

Gopnik, A. (2003). The theory theory as an alternative to the innateness hypothesis. In L. Antony & N. Hornstein (Eds.), *Chomsky and his critics*. Oxford: Wiley-Blackwell.

Gopnik, A. (2004). Finding our inner scientist. *Daedalus, 133*(1), 21–28.

Gopnik, A., & Meltzoff, A. N. (1997). *Words, thoughts, and theories*. Cambridge, MA: MIT Press.

Gordon, R. M. (1996). "Radical" simulationism. In P. Carruthers & P. K. Smith (Eds.), *Theories of theories of mind* (pp. 11–21). Cambridge: Cambridge University Press.

Gordon, R. M. (2005). Intentional agents like myself. In S. Hurley & N. Chater (Eds.), *Perspectives on imitation* (Vol. 2, pp. 95–106). Cambridge, MA: MIT Press.

Gould, J. L., & Gould, C. G. (1988). *The honey bee*. New York: Scientific American Library.

Grantham, T., & Nichols, S. (1999). Evolutionary psychology: Ultimate explanations and Panglossian predictions. In V. G. Hardcastle (Ed.), *Where biology meets psychology: Philosophical essays*. Cambridge, MA: MIT Press.

Greenberg, D. J., Hillman, D., & Grice, D. (1973). Infant and stranger variables related to stranger anxiety in the first year of life. *Developmental Psychology, 9*, 207–212.

Grice, H. P. (1989). *Studies in the way of words*. Cambridge, MA: Harvard University Press.

Gumperz, J. J., & Levinson, S. C. (1996). *Rethinking linguistic relativity*. Cambridge: Cambridge University Press.

Gutting, G. 2011. Michel Foucault. *The Stanford Encyclopedia of Philosophy* (fall 2011 edition), ed. E.N. Zalta. http://plato.stanford.edu/archives/fall2011/entries/foucault/.

Haack, S. (1993). Double-aspect foundherentism: A new theory of empirical justification. *Philosophy and Phenomenological Research, 53*(1), 113–128.

Hagen, E., & Bryant, G. (2003). Music and dance as a coalition signaling system. *Human Nature, 14*(1), 21–51.

Hamilton, W. D. (1964). The genetical evolution of social behaviour I and II. *Journal of Theoretical Biology, 7*, 1–52.

Hamlin, J. K., Wynn, K., Bloom, P., & Mahajan, N. (2011). How infants and toddlers react to antisocial others. *Proceedings of the National Academy of Sciences of the United States of America, 108*(50), 19931–19936.

Hare, B., Call, J., Agnetta, B., & Tomasello, M. (2000). Chimpanzees know what conspecifics do and do not see. *Animal Behaviour, 59,* 771–785.

Hare, B., Call, J., & Tomasello, M. (2001). Do chimpanzees know what conspecifics know? *Animal Behaviour, 61,* 139–151.

Hatfield, E., Cacioppo, J., & Rapson, R. L. (1994). *Emotional contagion.* Cambridge: Cambridge University Press.

Hauser, M. D., Chomsky, N., & Fitch, W. T. (2002). The faculty of language: What is it, who has it, and how did it evolve? *Science, 298,* 1569–1579.

Henrich, J. (2004). Cultural group selection, coevolutionary processes, and large-scale cooperation. *Journal of Economic Behavior and Organization, 53,* 3–35.

Henrich, J. (2009). The evolution of costly displays, cooperation, and religion: Credibility enhancing displays and their implications for cultural evolution. *Evolution and Human Behavior, 30*(4), 244–260.

Henrich, J., & Gil-White, F. J. (2001). The evolution of prestige: Freely conferred deference as a mechanism for enhancing the benefits of cultural transmission. *Evolution and Human Behavior, 22,* 165–196.

Henrich, J., Boyd, R., Bowles, S., Camerer, C., Fehr, E., Gintis, H., ..., Tracer, D. (2005). "Economic Man" in cross-cultural perspective: Behavioral experiments in 15 small-scale societies. *Behavioral and Brain Sciences, 28,* 795–855.

Henrich, J., McElreath, R., Barr, A., Ensminger, J., Barrett, C., Bolyanatz, A., ..., Ziker, J. (2006). Costly punishment across human societies. *Science, 312,* 1767–1769.

Henrich, J., Ensminger, J., McElreath, R., Barr, A., Barrett, C., Bolyanatz, A., ..., Ziker, J. (2010). Markets, religion, community size, and the evolution of fairness and punishment. *Science, 327,* 1480–1484.

Henrich, N. S., & Henrich, J. (2007). *Why humans cooperate: A cultural and evolutionary explanation.* Oxford: Oxford University Press.

Herrmann, E., Call, J., Hernàndez-Lloreda, M. V., Hare, B., & Tomasello, M. (2007). Humans have evolved specialized skills of social cognition: The cultural intelligence hypothesis. *Science, 317,* 1360–1366.

Herrmann, E., & Tomasello, M. (2006). Apes' and children's understanding of cooperative and competitive motives in a communicative situation. *Developmental Science, 9*(5), 518–529.

Hill, K. R., Walker, R. S., Božičević, M., Eder, J., Headland, T., Hewlett, B., et al. (2011). Co-residence patterns in hunter-gatherer societies show unique human social structure. *Science, 331*, 1286–1289.

Hirst, W., & Manier, D. (2008). Towards a psychology of collective memory. *Memory, 16*(3), 183–200.

Holloway, R. L., Broadfield, D. C., & Yuan, M. S. (2004). *The human fossil record* (Vol. 3): *Brain endocasts: The paleoneurological evidence*. New York: John Wiley & Sons.

Horner, V., & Whiten, A. (2005). Causal knowledge and imitation/emulation switching in chimpanzees (*Pan troglodytes*) and children (*Homo sapiens*). *Animal Cognition, 8*, 164–181.

Howard, J. (1988). Cooperation in the prisoner's dilemma. *Theory and Decision, 24*, 203–213.

Huang, C. T., & Charman, T. (2005). Gradations of emulation learning in infants' imitation of actions on objects. *Experimental Child Psychology, 92*, 276–302.

Hume, D. [1748] (1993). *An enquiry concerning human understanding*. Indianapolis: Hackett.

Humphrey, N. (1980). Nature's psychologists. In B. D. Josephson & V. S. Ramachandran (Eds.), *Consciousness and the physical world* (pp. 57–80). Oxford: Pergamon Press.

Hurley, S. (2005a). The shared circuits hypothesis: A unified functional architecture for control, imitation, and simulation. In S. Hurley & N. Chater (Eds.), *Perspectives on imitation* (Vol. 1, pp. 177–193). Cambridge, MA: MIT Press.

Hurley, S. (2005b). Social heuristics that make us smarter. *Philosophical Psychology, 18*(5), 585–612.

Hurley, S., & Chater, N. (Eds.). (2005). *Perspectives on imitation*. Cambridge, MA: MIT Press.

Hutto, D. D. (2008). *Folk psychological narratives: The sociocultural basis of understanding reasons*. Cambridge, MA: MIT Press.

Jackendoff, R. S. (2002). *Foundations of language: Brain, meaning, grammar, evolution*. Oxford: Oxford University Press.

James, W. (1890). *The principles of psychology*. New York: Dover.

Kahneman, D. (2011). *Thinking fast and slow*. New York: Farrar, Straus & Giroux.

Kalish, C. W., & Lawson, C. A. (2008). Development of social category representations: Early appreciation of roles and deontic relations. *Child Development, 79*(3), 577–593.

Kalish, C. W., & Shiverick, S. M. (2004). Children's reasoning about norms and traits as motives for behavior. *Cognitive Development, 19*(3), 401–416.

Kato, K. 2000. *Necktie-Alcoholics: Cultural Forces and Japanese Alcoholism.* MA thesis, Washington State University.

Keckler, C. N. W. (1997). Catastrophic mortality in simulations of forager age-of-death: Where did all the humans go? In R. Paine (Ed.), *Integrating archaeological demography: Multidisciplinary approaches to prehistoric populations.* Center for Archaeological Investigations, Occasional Papers No. 24. Carbondale: Southern Illinois University Press.

Keil, F. C. (1992). *Concepts, kinds, and cognitive development.* Cambridge, MA: MIT Press.

Kelly, R. C. (1985). *The Nuer conquest.* Ann Arbor: University of Michigan Press.

Kinderman, P., Dunbar, R., & Bentall, R. P. (1998). Theory-of-mind deficits and causal attributions. *British Journal of Psychology, 89,* 191–204.

Kirschner, S., & Tomasello, M. (2008). Joint drumming: Social context facilitates synchronization in preschool children. *Journal of Experimental Child Psychology, 102*(3), 299–314.

Kirschner, S., & Tomasello, M. (2010). Joint music making promotes prosocial behavior in 4-year-old children. *Evolution and Human Behavior, 31*(5), 354–364.

Kirsh, D. (1996). Adapting the environment instead of oneself. *Adaptive Behavior, 4*(3–4), 415–452.

Kirsh, D., & Maglio, P. (1994). On distinguishing epistemic from pragmatic action. *Cognitive Science, 18,* 513–549.

Klein, W., & Perdue, C. (1997). The basic variety (or: Couldn't natural languages be much simpler?). *Second Language Research, 13,* 301–347.

Klucharev, V., Hytönen, K., Rijpkema, M., Smidts, A., & Fernández, G. (2009). Reinforcement learning signal predicts social conformity. *Neuron, 61,* 140–151.

Knobe, J. (2003). Intentional action and side effects in ordinary language. *Analysis, 63,* 190–193.

Knobe, J. (2006). The concept of intentional action: A case study in the uses of folk psychology. *Philosophical Studies, 130,* 203–231.

Kovács, Á. M., Téglás, E., & Endress, A. D. (2010). The social sense: Susceptibility to others' beliefs in human infants and adults. *Science, 330,* 1830–1834.

Krachun, C., & Call, J. (2009). Chimpanzees (*Pan troglodytes*) know what can be seen from where. *Animal Cognition, 12*(2), 317–331.

Kross, E., Berman, M. G., Mischel, W., Smith, E. E., & Wager, T. D. (2011). Social rejection shares somatosensory representations with physical pain. *Proceedings of the National Academy of Sciences of the United States of America, 108*(15), 6270–6275.

Kuhn, T. S. (1977). *The essential tension: Selected studies in scientific tradition and change.* Chicago: University of Chicago Press.

Lai, C. S. L., Fisher, S. E., Hurst, J. A., Vargha-Khadem, F., & Monaco, A. P. (2001). A forkhead-domain gene is mutated in a severe speech and language disorder. *Nature, 413,* 519–523.

Laland, K. N., Odling-Smee, F. J., & Feldman, M. W. (2001). Niche construction, ecological inheritance, and cycles of contingency in evolution. In S. Oyama, P. E. Griffiths, & R. D. Gray (Eds.), *Cycles of contingency* (pp. 117–126). Cambridge, MA: MIT Press.

Lance, M., & O'Leary-Hawthorne, J. (1998). *The grammar of meaning.* Cambridge: Cambridge University Press.

Lashley, K. S. (1951). The problem of serial order in behavior. In L. A. Jeffress (Ed.), *Cerebral mechanisms in behavior* (pp. 112–146). New York: Wiley.

Lerdahl, F., & Jackendoff, R. S. (1996). *A generative theory of tonal music.* Cambridge, MA: MIT Press.

Leslie, A. M. (1994). Pretending and believing: Issues in the theory of ToMM. *Cognition, 50,* 211–238.

Leslie, A. M. (2000). How to acquire a "representational theory of mind." In D. Sperber (Ed.), *Metarepresentations: A multidisciplinary perspective* (pp. 197–223). Oxford: Oxford University Press.

Lessard, S. (2006). ESS theory now. *Theoretical Population Biology, 69,* 231–233.

Levinson, S. C. (2003). *Space in language and cognition.* Cambridge: Cambridge University Press.

Lewis, D. (1969). *Convention: A philosophical study.* Cambridge, MA: Harvard University Press.

Lewis, D. (1994). Lewis, David: Reduction of mind. In S. Guttenplan (Ed.), *A companion to the philosophy of mind* (pp. 412–431). Oxford: Blackwell.

Loewenstein, G. (2005). Hot-cold empathy gaps and medical decision making. *Health Psychology, 24*(4), S49–S56.

Loftus, E. F. (1996). *Eyewitness testimony.* Cambridge, MA: Harvard University Press.

Lovejoy, C. O., Suwa, G., Simpson, S. W., Matternes, J. H., & White, T. D. (2009). The great divides: *Ardipithecus ramidus* reveals the postcrania of our last common ancestors with African apes. *Science, 326*(5949), 73, 100–106.

Lurz, R. (2009). If chimpanzees are mindreaders, could behavioral science tell? Toward a solution of the logical problem. *Philosophical Psychology, 22*(3), 305–328.

Lurz, R. (2011). *Mindreading animals.* Cambridge, MA: MIT Press.

Lyons, D. E. (2009). The rational continuum of human imitation. In J. A. Pineda (Ed.), *Mirror neuron systems: The role of mirroring processes in social cognition* (pp. 77–106). New York: Human Press.

Machery, E. (2008). Understanding the folk concept of intentional action: Philosophical and experimental issues. *Mind and Language, 23,* 165–189.

Maibom, H. (2007). Social systems. *Philosophical Psychology, 20*(5), 557–578.

Malle, B. F., Knobe, J., & Nelson, S. E. (2007). Actor-observer asymmetries in behavior explanations: New answers to an old question. *Journal of Personality and Social Psychology, 93,* 491–514.

Mameli, M. (2001). Mindreading, mindshaping, and evolution. *Biology and Philosophy, 16,* 597–628.

Marr, D. (1982). *Vision.* San Francisco: W. H. Freeman.

Matthew, S., & Boyd, R. (2011). Punishment sustains large-scale cooperation in prestate warfare. *Proceedings of the National Academy of Sciences of the United States of America, 108*(28), 11375–11380.

Maynard-Smith, J. M. (1982). *Evolution and the theory of games.* Oxford: Cambridge University Press.

McBrearty, S., & Brooks, A. S. (2000). The revolution that wasn't: A new interpretation of the origin of modern human behavior. *Journal of Human Evolution, 39,* 453–563.

McGeer, V. (1996). Is "self-knowledge" an empirical problem? Renegotiating the space of philosophical explanation. *Journal of Philosophy, 93*(10), 483–515.

McGeer, V. (2001). Psycho-practice, psycho-theory and the contrastive case of autism. *Journal of Consciousness Studies, 8*(5–7), 109–132.

McGeer, V. (2007). The regulative dimension of folk psychology. In D. D. Hutto & M. Ratcliffe (Eds.), *Folk psychology re-assessed* (pp. 137–156). Dordrecht: Springer.

Mellars, P. (2005). The impossible coincidence. A single-species model for the origins of modern human behavior in Europe. *Evolutionary Anthropology, 14,* 12–27.

Meltzoff, A. N. (1988). Infant imitation after a 1-week delay: Long-term memory for novel acts and multiple stimuli. *Developmental Psychology, 24,* 470–476.

Meltzoff, A. N. (1995). Understanding the intentions of others: Re-enactment of intended acts by 18-month-old children. *Developmental Psychology, 31,* 838–850.

Meltzoff, A. N. (2005). Imitation and other minds: The "like me" hypothesis. In S. Hurley & N. Chater (Eds.), *Perspectives on imitation: From neuroscience to social science* (Vol. 2, pp. 55–77). Cambridge, MA: MIT Press.

Menzel, E. (1974). A group of young chimpanzees in a one-acre field: Leadership and communication. In A. Schrier & F. Stollnitz (Eds.), *Behavior of non-human primates*. New York: Academic Press.

Mercier, H., & Sperber, D. (2011). Why do humans reason? Arguments for an argumentative theory. *Behavioral and Brain Sciences, 34*, 57–111.

Milgram, S. (1963). Behavioural study of obedience. *Journal of Abnormal and Social Psychology, 67*, 371–378.

Miller, G. (2001). *The mating mind*. New York: Anchor Books.

Millikan, R. G. (1984). *Language, thought, and other biological categories: New foundations for realism*. Cambridge, MA: MIT Press.

Millikan, R. G. (1993). *White Queen psychology and other essays for Alice*. Cambridge, MA: MIT Press.

Millikan, R. G. (2005). *Language: A biological model*. Oxford: Oxford University Press.

Milner, A. D., & Goodale, M. A. (2006). *The visual brain in action*. New York: Oxford University Press.

Milosz, C. (1994). *A year of the hunter*. New York: Farrar, Straus & Giroux.

Mitchell, J. P., Macrae, C. N., & Banaji, M. R. (2006). Dissociable medial prefrontal contributions to judgments of similar and dissimilar others. *Neuron, 50*, 655–663.

Mithen, S. (1996). *The prehistory of the mind*. New York: Thames & Hudson.

Mithen, S. (2000). Palaeoanthropological perspectives on the theory of mind. In S. Baron-Cohen, H. Tager-Flusberg, & D. J. Cohen (Eds.), *Understanding other minds*. Oxford: Oxford University Press.

Mithen, S. (2006). *The singing Neanderthals*. Cambridge, MA: Harvard University Press.

Morton, A. (1996). Folk psychology is not a predictive device. *Mind, 105*(417), 119–137.

Morton, A. (2003). *The importance of being understood: Folk psychology as ethics*. London: Routledge.

Müsseler, J., & Hommel, B. (1997). Detecting and identifying response-compatible stimuli. *Psychonomic Bulletin and Review, 4*, 125–129.

Nairne, J. S., & Pandeirada, J. N. S. (2008). Adaptive memory: Is survival processing special? *Journal of Memory and Language, 59*, 377–385.

Neisser, U., & Harsh, N. (2000). Phantom flashbulbs: False recollections of hearing the news about *Challenger*. In U. Neisser & I. E. Hyman Jr. (Eds.), *Memory observed.* New York: Worth Publishers.

Nelson, K. (2007). *Young minds in social worlds.* Cambridge, MA: Harvard University Press.

Neumann, R., & Strack, F. (2000). "Mood contagion": The automatic transfer of mood between persons. *Journal of Personality and Social Psychology, 79*(2), 211–223.

Nichols, S., & Stich, S. (2003). *Mindreading: An integrated account of pretense, self-awareness and understanding other minds.* Oxford: Oxford University Press.

Nichols, S., & Ulatowski, J. (2007). Intuitions and individual differences: The Knobe effect revisited. *Mind and Language, 22,* 346–365.

Nielsen, M., & Tomaselli, K. (2010). Overimitation in Kalahari Bushman children and the origins of human cultural cognition. *Psychological Science, 21*(5), 729–736.

Nisbett, R. E., Peng, K., Choi, I., & Norenzayan, A. (2001). Culture and systems of thought: Holistic versus analytic cognition. *Psychological Review, 108*(2), 291–310.

Nowak, M. A., & Sigmund, K. (2005). Evolution of indirect reciprocity. *Nature, 437,* 1291–1298.

Okanoya, K. (2002). Sexual display as a syntactical vehicle: The evolution of syntax in birdsong and human language through sexual selection. In A. Wray (Ed.), *The transition to language* (pp. 46–63). Oxford: Oxford University Press.

Onishi, K. H., & Baillargeon, R. (2005). Do 15-month-old infants understand false beliefs? *Science, 308*(5719), 255–258.

Origgi, G., & Sperber, D. (2000). Evolution, communication, and the proper function of language. In P. Carruthers & A. Chamberlain (Eds.), *Evolution and the human mind: Language, modularity, and social cognition* (pp. 140–169). Cambridge: Cambridge University Press.

Papousek, M. (1996). Musicality in infancy research: Biological and cultural origins of early musicality. In I. Deliege & J. Sloboda (Eds.), *Musical beginnings.* Oxford: Oxford University Press.

Parr, L. (2001). Cognitive and physiological markers of emotional awareness in chimpanzees (*Pan troglodytes*). *Animal Cognition, 4*(3), 223–229.

Patel, A. D. (2008). *Music, language, and the brain.* New York: Oxford University Press.

Penn, D. C., & Povinelli, D. J. (2007). On the lack of evidence that non-human animals possess anything remotely resembling a "theory of mind." *Philosophical Transactions of the Royal Society of London: Series B, 362,* 731–744.

Perner, J., & Ruffman, D. (2005). Infants' insight into the mind: How deep. *Science, 308,* 214–216.

Pettit, D., & Knobe, J. (2009). The pervasive impact of moral judgment. *Mind and Language, 24*(5), 586–604.

Pinker, S. (1997). *How the mind works.* New York: W. W. Norton.

Pinker, S. (2003). Language as an adaptation to the cognitive niche. In M. Christiansen & S. Kirby (Eds.), *Language evolution: States of the art.* New York: Oxford University Press.

Pinker, S., & Bloom, P. (1990). Natural language and natural selection. *Behavioral and Brain Sciences, 13*(4), 707–784.

Pinker, S., & Jackendoff, R. (2005). The faculty of language: What's special about it? *Cognition, 95*(2), 201–236.

Povinelli, D. J. (2012). *World without weight.* New York: Oxford University Press.

Povinelli, D. J., & Vonk, J. (2003). Chimpanzee minds: Suspiciously human? *Trends in Cognitive Sciences, 7*(4), 157–160.

Povinelli, D. J., & Vonk, J. (2004). We don't need a microscope to explore the chimpanzee's mind. *Mind and Language, 19*(1), 1–28.

Powell, A., Shennan, S., & Thomas, M. G. (2009). Late Pleistocene demography and the appearance of modern human behavior. *Science, 324,* 1298–1301.

Premack, D., & Premack, A. J. (1996). Why animals lack pedagogy and some cultures have more of it than others. In D. R. Olson (Ed.), *The handbook of education and human development: New models of learning, teaching and schooling.* Malden, MA: Blackwell.

Premack, D., & Woodruff, G. (1978). Does the chimpanzee have a "theory of mind"? *Behavioral and Brain Sciences, 4,* 515–526.

Price, M. E., Cosmides, L., & Tooby, J. (2002). Punitive sentiment as an anti–free rider psychological device. *Evolution and Human Behavior, 23,* 203–231.

Prinz, W. (1990). A common coding approach to perception and action. In O. Neumann & W. Prinz (Eds.), *Relations between perception and action.* New York: Springer.

Putnam, H. (1965). Brains and behavior. In R. J. Butler (Ed.), *Analytical philosophy* (Vol. 2). Oxford: Blackwell.

Quine, W. V. (1960). *Word and object.* Cambridge, MA: MIT Press.

Rakoczy, H., & Tomasello, M. (2009). Done wrong or said wrong? Young children understand the normative directions of fit of different speech acts. *Cognition, 113*(2), 205–212.

Rakoczy, H., Warneken, F., & Tomasello, M. (2008a). The sources of normativity: Young children's awareness of the normative structure of games. *Developmental Psychology, 44*(3), 875–881.

Rakoczy, H., Warneken, F., & Tomasello, M. (2008b). Young children's selective learning of rule games from reliable and unreliable models. *Cognitive Development, 24*(1), 61–69.

Regan, D. (1980). *Utilitarianism and co-operation.* Oxford: Clarendon Press.

Richerson, P. J., & Boyd, R. (2005). *Not by genes alone.* Chicago: University of Chicago Press.

Rizzolatti, G., & Arbib, M. A. (1998). Language within our grasp. *Trends in Neurosciences, 21*(5), 188–194.

Rizzolatti, G., & Craighero, L. (2004). The mirror-neuron system. *Annual Review of Neuroscience, 27*, 169–192.

Rizzolatti, G., Fadiga, L., Gallese, V., & Fogassi, L. (1996). Premotor cortex and the recognition of motor actions. *Brain Research: Cognitive Brain Research, 3*, 131–141.

Ross, D. (2007). *H. sapiens* as ecologically special: What does language contribute? *Language Sciences, 29*(5), 710–731.

Ruffle, B. J., & Sosis, R. (2007). Does it pay to pray? Costly ritual and cooperation. *B.E. Journal of Economic Analysis and Policy, 7*(1). DOI: 10.2202/1935-1682.1629.

Ryle, G. (1949). *The concept of mind.* Chicago: University of Chicago Press.

Schiffer, S. R. (1972). *Meaning.* Oxford: Clarendon Press.

Schoenemann, P. T. (2006). Evolution of the size and functional areas of the human brain. *Annual Review of Anthropology, 35*, 379–406.

Schull, J. (1990). Are species intelligent? *Behavioral and Brain Sciences, 13*, 68–113.

Schwitzgebel, E. (2002). A phenomenal, dispositional account of belief. *Noûs, 36*(2), 249–275.

Scott, R. M., & Baillargeon, R. (2009). Which penguin is this? Attributing false beliefs about object identity at 18 months. *Child Development, 80*(4), 1172–1196.

Seabright, P. (2010). *The company of strangers.* Princeton: Princeton University Press.

Searle, J. R. (1969). *Speech acts.* Cambridge: Cambridge University Press.

Searle, J. R. (1979). *Expression and meaning.* Cambridge: Cambridge University Press.

Sellars, W. (1997). *Empiricism and the philosophy of mind.* Cambridge, MA: Harvard University Press.

Senft, G., & Basso, E. B. (2009). *Ritual communication.* New York: Berg Publishers.

Sherwood, C. C., Subiaul, F., & Zawidzki, T. W. (2008). A natural history of the human mind: Tracing evolutionary changes in brain and cognition. *Journal of Anatomy, 212*(4), 426–454.

Siegal, M. (2008). *Marvelous minds: The discovery of what children know.* Oxford: Oxford University Press.

Sigmund, K. (2007). Punish or perish? Retaliation and collaboration among humans. *Trends in Ecology and Evolution, 22*(11), 593–600.

Skyrms, B. (1996). *Evolution of the social contract.* Cambridge: Cambridge University Press.

Skyrms, B. (2003). *The stag hunt and the evolution of social structure.* Cambridge: Cambridge University Press.

Skyrms, B. (2009). Forum. In M. Tomasello (Ed.), *Why we cooperate* (pp. 137–148). Cambridge, MA: MIT Press.

Sober, E., & Wilson, D. S. (1998). *Unto others.* Cambridge, MA: Harvard University Press.

Song, H., & Baillargeon, R. (2008). Infants' reasoning about others' false perceptions. *Developmental Psychology, 44,* 1789–1795.

Sosis, R. (2003). Why aren't we all Hutterites? Costly signaling theory and religious behavior. *Human Nature, 14,* 91–127.

Sosis, R., & Alcorta, C. (2003). Signaling, solidarity, and the sacred: The evolution of religious behavior. *Evolutionary Anthropology, 12,* 264–274.

Sosis, R., & Bressler, E. (2003). Cooperation and commune longevity: A test of the costly signaling theory of religion. *Cross-Cultural Research, 37,* 211–239.

Sosis, R., & Ruffle, B. (2003). Religious ritual and cooperation: Testing for a relationship on Israeli religious and secular Kibbutzim. *Current Anthropology, 44,* 713–722.

Spaulding, S. (2010). Embodied cognition and mindreading. *Mind and Language, 25*(1), 119–140.

Sperber, D. (Ed.). (2000). *Metarepresentations.* New York: Oxford University Press.

Sperber, D., & Wilson, D. (1995). *Relevance.* Malden, MA: Blackwell.

Sperber, D., & Wilson, D. (2002). Pragmatics, modularity, and mind-reading. *Mind and Language, 17*(1 & 2), 3–23.

Sripada, C., & Stich, S. (2006). A framework for the psychology of norms. In P. Carruthers, S. Laurence, & S. Stich (Eds.), *The innate mind: Culture and cognition* (pp. 280–301). New York: Oxford University Press.

Stalnaker, R. (1999). *Context and content.* Oxford: Oxford University Press.

Stanovich, K. (1999). *Who is rational?* Mahwah, NJ: Lawrence Erlbaum.

Sterelny, K. (2003). *Thought in a hostile world.* Oxford: Blackwell.

Sterelny, K. (2007). Social intelligence, human intelligence, and niche construction. *Philosophical Transactions of the Royal Society of London: Series B, 362,* 719–730.

Sterelny, K. (2010). Moral nativism: A sceptical response. *Mind and Language, 25*(3), 279–297.

Sterelny, K. (2012). *The evolved apprentice.* Cambridge, MA: MIT Press.

Stevens, J. R., Cushman, F. A., & Hauser, M. D. (2005). Evolving the psychological mechanisms for cooperation. *Annual Review of Ecology Evolution and Systematics, 36,* 499–518.

Stevens, J. R., & Hauser, M. D. (2004). Why be nice? Psychological constraints on the evolution of cooperation. *Trends in Cognitive Sciences, 8*(2), 60–65.

Stich, S. P. (1981). Dennett on intentional systems. *Philosophical Topics, 12,* 38–62.

Stich, S. P. (1993). Moral philosophy and mental representation. In M. Hechter, L. Nadel, & R. Michod (Eds.), *The origin of values* (pp. 215–228). New York: Aldine de Gruyter.

Stich, S. P., & Nichols, S. (1998). Theory-theory to the max. *Mind and Language, 13*(3), 421–449.

Subiaul, F. (2007). The imitation faculty in monkeys: Evaluating its features, distribution, and evolution. *Journal of Anthropological Sciences, 85,* 35–62.

Subiaul, F., Cantlon, J. F., Holloway, R. L., & Terrace, H. S. (2004). Cognitive imitation in rhesus macaques. *Science, 305,* 407–410.

Surian, L., Caldi, S., & Sperber, D. (2007). Attribution of beliefs by 13-month-old infants. *Psychological Science, 18,* 580–586.

Tekin, Ş. (2011). Self-concept through the diagnostic looking glass: Narratives and mental disorder. *Philosophical Psychology, 24*(3), 357–380.

Thierry, G., Athanasopoulos, P., Wiggett, A., Dering, B., & Kuipers, J.-R. (2009). Unconscious effects of language-specific terminology on preattentive color perception. *Proceedings of the National Academy of Sciences of the United States of America, 106*(11), 4567–4570.

Thompson, D. E., & Russell, J. (2004). The ghost condition: Imitation versus emulation in young children's observational learning. *Developmental Psychology, 40,* 882–889.

Thornton, A., & McAuliffe, K. (2006). Teaching in wild meerkats. *Science, 313,* 227–229.

Thorndike, E. L. (1898). Animal intelligence: An experimental study of the associative processes in animals. *Psychological Review, Monograph Supplements* 8.

Tomasello, M. (1996). Do apes ape? In C. M. Heyes & B. G. Galef Jr. (Eds.), *Social learning in animals: The roots of culture* (pp. 319–346). San Diego: Academic Press.

Tomasello, M. (1999). *The cultural origins of human cognition.* Cambridge, MA: Harvard University Press.

Tomasello, M. (2009). *Why we cooperate.* Cambridge, MA: MIT Press.

Tomasello, M., & Call, J. (1997a). Distinguishing intentional from accidental actions in orangutans (*Pongo pygmaeus*), chimpanzees (*Pan troglodytes*), and human children (*Homo sapiens*). *Journal of Comparative Psychology, 112*(2), 192–206.

Tomasello, M., & Call, J. (1997b). *Primate cognition.* Oxford: Oxford University Press.

Tomasello, M., Carpenter, M., Call, J., Behne, T., & Moll, H. (2005). Understanding and sharing intentions: The origins of cultural cognition. *Behavioral and Brain Sciences, 28,* 675–735.

Tomasello, M., Kruger, A., & Ratner, H. H. (1993). Cultural learning. *Behavioral and Brain Sciences, 16,* 495–552.

Tooby, J., & Cosmides, L. (1990). The past explains the present: Emotional adaptations and the structure of ancestral environments. *Ethology and Sociobiology, 11*(4–5), 375–424.

Tooby, J., & Cosmides, L. (1992). The psychological foundations of culture. In J. H. Barkow, L. Cosmides, & J. Tooby (Eds.), *The adapted mind.* Oxford: Oxford University Press.

Tooby, J., & Cosmides, L. (1995). The language of the eyes as an evolved language of mind. In S. Baron-Cohen (Ed.), *Mindblindness: An essay on autism and theory of mind.* Cambridge, MA: MIT Press.

Topál, J., Gergely, G., Miklósi, A., Erdőhegyi, Á., & Csibra, G. (2008). Infants' perseverative search errors are induced by pragmatic misinterpretation. *Science, 321,* 1831–1834.

Trevarthen, C. (1998). The concept and foundations of infant intersubjectivity. In S. Braten (Ed.), *Intersubjective communication and emotion in early ontogeny* (pp. 15–46). Cambridge: Cambridge University Press.

Trevarthen, C., & Hubley, P. (1978). Secondary intersubjectivity: Confidence, confiding, and acts of meaning in the first year. In A. Lock (Ed.), *Action, gesture, and symbol: The emergence of language* (pp. 183–229). London: Academic Press.

Tversky, A., & Kahneman, D. (1983). Extension versus intuitive reasoning: The conjunction fallacy in probability judgment. *Psychological Review, 90*(4), 293–315.

Van Boven, L., & Loewenstein, G. (2003). Social projection of transient drive states. *Personality and Social Psychology Bulletin, 29*(9), 1159–1168.

Velleman, J. D. (2000). *The possibility of practical reason.* Oxford: Clarendon.

Visalberghi, E., & Fragaszy, D. (2002). Do monkeys ape? Ten years after. In K. Dautenhahn & C. Nehaniv (Eds.), *Imitation in animals and artifacts* (pp. 473–499). Cambridge, MA: MIT Press.

Vygotsky, L. S. (1962). *Thought and language.* Cambridge, MA: MIT Press.

Warneken, F., Chen, F., & Tomasello, M. (2006). Cooperative activities in young children and chimpanzees. *Child Development, 77*(3), 640–663.

Wellman, H., Cross, D., &Watson, J. (2001). Meta-analysis of theory-of-mind development: The truth about false belief. *Child Development, 72*, 655–684.

West, S. A., El Mouden, C., & Gardner, A. (2011). Sixteen common misconceptions about the evolution of cooperation in humans. *Evolution and Human Behavior, 32*, 231–262.

White, S. A., Fisher, S. E., Geschwind, D. H., Scharff, C., & Holy, T. E. (2006). Singing mice, songbirds, and more: Models for FOXP2 function and dysfunction in human speech and language. *Journal of Neuroscience, 26*(41), 10376–10379.

Whiten, A. (1996). When does smart behaviour-reading become mind-reading? In P. Carruthers & P. K. Smith (Eds.), *Theories of theories of mind* (pp. 277–292). Cambridge: Cambridge University Press.

Wilby, M. (2010). The simplicity of mutual knowledge. *Philosophical Explorations, 13*(2), 83–100.

Wiltermuth, S. S., & Heath, C. (2009). Synchrony and cooperation. *Psychological Science, 20*(1), 1–5.

Wood, J. N., & Hauser, M. D. (2008). Action comprehension in nonhuman primates: Motor simulation or inferential reasoning? *Trends in Cognitive Sciences, 12*(12), 461–465.

Wrangham, R. (2009). *Catching fire.* New York: Basic Books.

Yazdi, A. A., German, T. P., Defeyter, M. A., & Siegal, M. (2006). Competence and performance in belief-desire reasoning across two cultures: The truth, the whole truth, and nothing but the truth about false belief? *Cognition, 100*, 343–368.

Zahavi, A., & Zahavi, A. (1997). *The handicap principle.* New York: Oxford University Press.

Zangwill, N. (2005). The normativity of the mental. *Philosophical Explorations, 8*, 1–19.

Zawidzki, T. W. (2003). Mythological content: A problem for Millikan's teleosemantics. *Philosophical Psychology*, *16*(4), 535–547.

Zawidzki, T. W. (2006). Sexual selection for syntax and kin selection for semantics: Problems and prospects. *Biology and Philosophy*, *21*(4), 453–470.

Zawidzki, T. W. (2008). The function of folk psychology: Mind reading or mind shaping? *Philosophical Explorations*, *11*(3), 193–210.

Zawidzki, T. W. (2011). How to interpret infant socio-cognitive competence. *Review of Philosophy and Psychology*, *2*, 483–497.

Zawidzki, T. W. (2012). Unlikely allies: Embodied social cognition and the intentional stance. *Phenomenology and the Cognitive Sciences*, *11*, 487–506.

Zentall, T. R. (2006). Imitation: Definitions, evidence, and mechanisms. *Animal Cognition*, *9*, 335–353.

Index